Without plants there is no orisha
Sin hoja no hay orisha
Sem folha não há orixá.

I would like to thank so many people that have made this work possible.

My Iyátobbí (mother) and Babátobbí (father); both being extremely educated and simple, with a great emphasis of knowledge no matter what it was. My Babárósa Robert D. Abreu "Oba Ikuro", my Iyáré Michele Abreu "Eshu Alatilegua", and my Iyáwónna Mercedes Abreu "Odu Aremu" who have instilled a great respect and knowledge in this religion.

My brother Ed and sisters Becky and Ruth; La China Juana, and Ofe; Samantha, Karina, Gabriela, Mei-Lin, Eddy, Marcos, Casey, Caleb, and Cacha (our next generation); Titi and Jorge (my putative parents); and my many friends, Mauricio, Bert, Mabel, Domingo; who gave me the necessary impetus to make this work possible.

> De Nada Sirve el Conocimiento si no se Divulga
> Knowledge is Useless unless it is Disclosed
> MÁA FÈRÈ FÚN YEMOJÁ
> MÁA FÈRÈ FÚN ÒSANYÌN

ÀWÀ NÍ ÌBÍ TÍ ÀWÀ LÒNÌ, NÍTÒRÍPÈ À DÚRÒ LÉJÌKÀ, AWÒ N TÍ WÒN WA SÍWÀJÚ WÀ
We are where we are because we are standing on the shoulders of those who came before us.
Estamos hoy donde estamos porque estamos parados en los hombros de los que vinieron antes de nosotros
Estamos aonde estamos hoje porque estamos sobre os ombros daqueles que vieram antes de nós.

OLÓGBÓN Á D'ÒMÙGÒ L'ÀÍ L'OGBÓN-INÚ.
The person that stops using his wisdom becomes mute/an idiot.
La persona que deja de usar su sabiduría se vuelve tonta.
A pessoa que não consegue usar sua sabedoria torna-se mudo.

Yoruba Proverbs: Ìbà'sè Òrìsà; Fa'Lokun Fatunmbi

The purpose of this book is to bring into context and greater accessibility the knowledge of the plants used in the Santeria Religion. Many books have been written about said plants, but there seems to be no standardized version where the plant in question can be narrowed down to a more common name and proper scientific taxonomy.

When I say that this book is "Ewe for the New Diaspora" it is because we are now in a "New Diaspora". The first great diaspora that occurred was when the natives from Africa were brought to the "New World" as slaves of the Spanish, Portuguese, English, etc. These natives brought with them a very ample religious macrocosm and an intimate knowledge of the plants that surrounded them. This knowledge was used in the "New World" by their ability to find equal or similar plants that had been used in Africa.

Although people have moved between the United States and countries of Central and South America for centuries; the coming of Fidel Castro in Cuba caused a massive outflow of people and their religious beliefs. Since then, other nationalities have emigrated to the United States causing what can be called a "New Diaspora". With this "New Diaspora", unknown religious beliefs have been brought to the shores of the United States. Now, it is not unusual to find "Botanicas" (stores that cater to the Afro-Caribbean and Afro-Brazilian religious beliefs) in most big cities in the United States (or the world).

Unfortunately, with this massive inflow, very little was brought as to the written vernacular needed for the proper identification of the plants needed for the religious rituals. Of note, there are several writers that have taken said labors. These writers are:

- Lydia Cabrera who wrote "El Monte (1954)" with almost a 95% record for proper plant identification.
- Juan Tomás Roig who wrote "Diccionario Botánico de nombres vulgares cubanos (1928)" and "Plantas Medicinales, Aromáticas y Venenosas de Cuba (1945)"
- Pierre Fatumbi Verger who wrote "Ewé: O uso das plantas na sociedade Iorubá (1995)" who gave the Yoruba name for most plants used in these religions
- Jose Flávio Pessoa de Barros and Eduardo Napoleão who wrote "Ewé òrìsà: Uso litúrgico e terapêutico dos vegetais nas Casas de Candomblé Jêje-Nagô (1998)" who provided almost the same information and background on plants used in the Afro-Brazilian religion of Candomblé as Lydia Cabrera did with her book "El Monte".
- Jose Flávio Pessoa de Barros who wrote "A floresta sagrada de Ossaim: O segredo das folhas (2010)" with the plants arranged by their scientific name.

It should be noted that I have not offered an opinion on the tutelar Orisha or the usage of any of these plants. This is just a compilation of available information (which has been cross-referenced) on each of these plants from available sources. It is the responsibility of the person using this book to get guidance from their elders as to what is the proper use of these plants and the tutelar Orisha it belongs to. You can also access additional information on the names of the plants in "EWE for the New Diaspora: A Quick Guide to the Names". Due to the amount of additional information, it only includes the names of the plants in Cuba and in the English language (with USDA name as preferred name placement). You will also be able to find the names of the plants with their current scientific nomenclature, in Yoruba, Lucumí, Anagó, Congo/Palo, Bantú, Abakuá, Carabalí/Brikamo and Cuban-Haitian-Creole (if applicable).

Table of Contents

NAME-CUBA	Helecho de Rio, Lecho de Rio	(LC)
	Helecho de Rio, Helecho Acuático, Helecho Real	(Roig)
Owner	Eleggua (TDF)	
	Ochún (TDF2, Diaz)	
	Ochún, Osain (Quiros)	
	All Orishas (Madan, Irizarry)	
	Yemayá, Ochún (Menéndez)	
Odun	Osa-odi (Madan, Irizarry, Diaz, Orula.org)	

NAME-SCIENTIFIC	*Osmunda regalis* L.	(Roig)

NAME-BRAZIL	Feto-real, Afentos, Fento-real, Fento-de-flor	(Jb.Utad.pt)

NAME-Lucumí	Imoshún, Imo, Ití ibú	(LC)
	Himo	(TDF2)
	Imo	(TDF)
YORUBA		

NAME-CONGO	Vititi lángo, Nfita massa	(LC)
	Yerua, Bititi lango	(TDF)
PALO	Alúmamba	(LC)
	Nfita Masa	
	OWNER Mamá Chola	

NAME-OTHER	Royal Fern	(USDA)
	Royal Fern, Flowering Fern	(CRC)

USES	Goes to Osain (Omiero)	
	Goes to the Omiero of Ochún	(TDF2)
	One of the MOST important Ewé in the Omiero	
	For ritual baths (Ebomisi)	(Irizarry)
PALO	To give clairvoyance	
Hoodoo/Root Magic (USA)	Ferns of various species prevent evil from entering the home and reverse jinxes.	

NAME-CUBA	Helecho Hembra		(Roig)
	Imo de Ochún		(Diaz)
Owner	Eleggua (TDF)		
	Ochún (Diaz)		
Odun	Ejiogbe-irete (Diaz)		

NAME-SCIENTIFIC   *Athyrium filix-femina* (L.) Roth   (Roig)

NAME-BRAZIL   Fentanha-fêmea, Fento-fêmea, Feto-manso

NAME-Lucumí	Imo		(TDF)
ANAGO	Ewe imo	**Helecho Hembra**	(LC)
	Amó omí	**Helecho**	(LC)
YORUBA			

NAME-CONGO   Yerua, Bititi lango (TDF)
PALO

| **NAME-OTHER** | Common ladyfern | (USDA) |
| | Common Lady Fern, Lady Fern | (CRC) |

USES   Goes to Osain (Omiero)
         Used for ritual baths to conquer someone   (Diaz)
Hoodoo/Root Magic (USA)   Ferns of various species prevent evil from entering
         the home and reverse jinxes.

NAME-CUBA	Helecho Macho	(Menéndez, EcuRed)
Owner	Ochosi (TDF2)	
	Eleggua (Menéndez)	
	Yemayá (Diaz)	
Odun	Osa-odi (Diaz, Orula.org)	
NAME-SCIENTIFIC	*Dryopteris filix-mas* (L.) Schott	(EcuRed)
NAME-BRAZIL	Fento-macho, Feto-macho, Fentanha-macha	

NAME-Lucumí	Imó, Imochún, Iti ibú	**Helecho Macho de Rio**	(TDF2)
YORUBA			

NAME-CONGO	Bishembegere	(CRC)
PALO		
NAME-OTHER	Male Fern	(USDA)
	Male Fern, Common Wild Fern	(CRC)
USES	Goes to Osain (Omiero) for Eleggua	(Menéndez)
	Goes to Osain (Omiero)	(Diaz)
	Used for home cleansings to refresh, and Ebomisi	(Diaz)

Hoodoo/Root Magic (USA) Ferns of various species prevent evil from entering the home and reverse jinxes. The Shield Root Fern/Male Fern is said to provide personal protection or "shielding" from Conjure

INDIA	Used in Unani and Siddha	(CRC)

NOTE   This plant is NOT listed by Juan Tomás Roig.

NAME-CUBA	Henequén, Heniquén, Jeniquén		(Roig)
Owner	Babalú-Ayé (TDF2)		
	Obatalá, Babalú-Ayé (Quiros)		
Odun			

NAME-SCIENTIFIC	*Agave fourcroydes* Lem.	(Roig)

NAME-BRAZIL	NOT found in Flora do Brasil

NAME-Lucumí	Kunweko	(LC, TDF2)
YORUBA		

NAME-CONGO
PALO	**OWNER**	Centella

NAME-OTHER	Henequen	(USDA)

USES

Used for the clothing of Babalú-Ayé.

Iyessá	Boku-Bokú -	The fringes on the clothes of devotees/followers
		called "mariwó" as protection of ALL types of Evil **(ECR)**
Abakúa	Iremes -	The masks and clothing partly made of hemp **(ECR)**

NOTE   ECR   ECR is "The Encyclopedia of Caribbean Religions"

NOTE   Henequén is **different** from **Magüey**

NAME-CUBA	Hicaco, Hicaco de costa, Hicaco de playa, Hicaco dulce	(Roig)
Owner	Ibeyis (LC, Quiros, Diaz)	
Odun	Oyekun-ejiogbe (Quiros, Diaz, Orula.org)	
NAME-SCIENTIFIC	*Chrysobalanus icaco* L.	(Roig)
NAME-BRAZIL	Abajerú, Guajerú, Guajiru, Ajuru, Ajuru-branco	
NAME-Lucumí	KInseke	(LC)
YORUBA	Ìkatè	(PV, CRC)
	Awonrinwan, Ikatee	(Elsevier)
NAME-CONGO	Mungaoka	(LC, TDF)
PALO	Mungaoka	
NAME-OTHER	Coco plum	(USDA)
	Cocoplum, Pigeon plum	
	Hicaco (PR, Venezuela); Jicaco (DR);	
	Hikuku, Ikak (Creole Haiti)	(Elsevier)
USES	Goes to Osain (Omiero)	
	For cleansings of home/personal of dark spirits/bad energy.	(Diaz)
	Medicinal	

NAME-CUBA	Higuera, Higo	(Roig)
Owner	Osain (Quiros, Madan)	
	Changó, **Orishanlá** (Irizarry)	
Odun	Owonrin-irete, Irete-owonrin (Madan, Quiros, Irizarry, Orula.org)	
NAME-SCIENTIFIC	*Ficus carica* L.	(Roig)
NAME-BRAZIL	Figo, Figueira comum, Figueira-da-Europa, Figueira-mansa	
Candomblé	Iansã, Ibeji	
Umbanda	Oxum, Obaluaiè, Omolu, Pomba-Gira	

NAME-Lucumí	Potó, Popó, Opopó		(LC, TDF2)
YORUBA	ÈSO ÒPÒTÓ	**Fig**	
	ÒPÒTÓ	**Common fig**	(jairoinglat)

NAME-CONGO	
PALO	Niasa

NAME-OTHER	Edible fig	(USDA)
	Common Fig, Edible Fig, Fig tree	(CRC)

USES	Goes to Osain (Omiero)	(Madan)
	Used for ritual baths (Ebomisi)	
	As food offerings (Adimú)	
	Medicinal	
Candomblé	As ritual food offerings (Addimú)	
Umbanda	As ritual food offerings (Addimú)	
Hoodoo/Root Magic (USA)	Used for Luck, Protection and to gain friends	
INDIA	Used in Ayurveda, Unani and Siddha	(CRC)

NOTE	**Orishanlá**	**Orishanlá/Ochanlá** is an avatar of Obatalá. It is a very old, frail female Obatalá.	(NBA)

NAME-CUBA	Higuereta, Ricino, Palma Christi		(Roig)
Owner	Obatalá (LC, Madan)		
	Obatalá (TDF2, Menéndez)	**Higuereta Blanca**	
	Changó (TDF2)	**Higuereta Morada**	
	Obatalá, Odudúa (Quiros)		
	Obatalá, Changó (Irizarry)		
	Obatalá, Oyá, Babalú-Ayé (Diaz)		
	Oyá (Menéndez)	**Higuereta Morada**	
Odun	Iwori-ogunda (Quiros, Diaz, Madan, Irizarry)		
	Obara-odi (Irizarry, Orula.org)		

NAME-SCIENTIFIC	*Ricinus communis* L.	(Roig, Barros)
	Ricinus communis L.; *Ricinus sanguineus* Groenl.	(Barros)

NAME-BRAZIL	Mamona, Mamona-branca, Palma-de-cristo		**Èwé Lárà funfun**
Candomblé Jêje-Nagô	Oxalá	Ar/Feminino	(Barros)
CANDOMBLÉ Bantu-Angola	Inkisis		
CANDOMBLÉ Ketú	Ossaim, Omolu		
CULTO DE NAÇÃO IORUBÁS	Omolu, Oyá, Nanã, Exú, Egúngún, Ìyàmi Agbás		See NOTE
CULTO DE NAÇÃO JEJE	VÒDÚN SÁKPÁTÁ E LÉGBÀ		See NOTE
Umbanda	Oxossi, Exú		

NAME-BRAZIL	Mamona-vermelha, Mamona-roxa		**Èwé Lárà pupa**
Candomblé Jêje-Nagô	Ossaim, Egum Fogo/Feminino		(Barros)
CANDOMBLÉ Bantu-Angola	**Pambu Njila, Nzazi, Matamba**	**See NOTE**	
CANDOMBLÉ Ketú	Exú, Ossaim		
CULTO DE NAÇÃO IORUBÁS	Omolu, Oyá, Nanã, Exú, Egúngún, Ìyàmi Agbás		
CULTO DE NAÇÃO JEJE	VÒDÚN SÁKPÁTÁ E LÉGBÀ		
Umbanda	Oxossi, Exú		

NAME-Lucumí		
YORUBA	Lárà, Lárà pupa, Ilárà, Ilárùn, Làpálàpá adétè, Arà pupa	(PV, CRC)

NAME-CONGO

NAME-OTHER	Castorbean	(USDA)
	Castor Bean, Castor bean tree, Castor oil tree, Palma Christi	(CRC)

USES   Goes to Osain (Omiero)
Used for Ritual baths (Ebomisi)
Medicinal

Candomblé Jêje-Nagô Èwé Lárà funfun   the leaves are used as serving recipients for the food offerings (Addimú) to Obaluaê
Èwé Lárà pupa used in the Ritual of **Axexê**. It is said that if someone, as a prank, should hit an initiated member with a leaf/branch of this plant, the Orixá will depart; demonstrating the incompatibility between the Orixá and Egun.

CANDOMBLÉ Bantu-Angola   Mamona-branca   the leaves are used as a serving recipient for ALL food offerings (Addimú) to ALL Inkisis
Mamona-vermelha and **Mamona-roxa** the leaves are used as a serving recipient for food offerings (Addimú) for Pambu Njila, Nzazi and Matamba

INDIA   Used in Ayurveda, Unani and Siddha. Sacred plant, used in religion and magico-religious belief: very effective against evil magic.   (CRC)

NOTE Ìyàmi Agbás   The dead females receive the title of **Ìyàmi Agbás** (my ancient/old mother) within the cult of Egúngún and Ìyàmi-Ajé
See: **https://pt.wikipedia.org/wiki/Iyami-Ajé**

VÒDÚN   Is an Ewe-Fon religion from Benin. It is practiced in Brazil, Haiti and Cuba among some of the countries of the diaspora.
See: **https://pt.wikipedia.org/wiki/Vodum**

SÁKPÁTÁ   Is an Ewe-Fon/Vodun deity. The equivalent is Asojuano/Babalú-Ayé
See: **https://pt.wikipedia.org/wiki/Sakpata**

LÉGBÀ   Is an Ewe-Fon/Vodun deity. The equivalent is Eleggua
See: **https://pt.wikipedia.org/wiki/Legba**

Pambu Njila   Is a Nkisi in the Bantu-Angola religions. The Equivalent to Eleggua
See: **https://pt.wikipedia.org/wiki/Pambu_Njila**

Nzazi   Is a Nkisi in the Bantu-Angola religions. The Equivalent to Changó
See: **https://pt.wikipedia.org/wiki/Nzazi**

Matamba   Is a Nkisi in the Bantu-Angola religions. The Equivalent to Oyá
See: **https://pt.wikipedia.org/wiki/Matamba_(Nkisi)**

Axexê   The funeral rites performed for the initiated members of the religion. It much like the ones performed in Cuba for initiated members in the religion and which is called **ITUTO**.
See: **https://pt.wikipedia.org/wiki/Axexê**
      https://religionysanteria.blogspot.com/2009/11/ituto.html

NAME-CUBA   Higuerón   (Roig)
    Owner
    Odun

NAME-SCIENTIFIC   *Ficus gomelleira* Kunth & C.D.Bouché;
                Ficus doliaria (Miq.) Mart.   **See NOTE**   (Roig)

NAME-BRAZIL   Gameleira, Gameleira-branca, Figueira-brava, Figueira-grande
   Candomblé Jêje-Nagô Oxalá, **Ìrókò**, Exú   Fogo/Masculino   (Barros)
   Candomblé Nagô   **Ìrókò**, Oxalá, Exú   **See NOTE**
   Candomblé Jêje   **Vodum Loko**   **See NOTE**
   Candomblé Bantu   **Kindembu/Tempo**   **See NOTE**
   Candomblé Angola   **Kavungo, Zaze**   **See NOTE**

NAME-Lucumí
   YORUBA   Èrò ìrókò, Ìrókò, Ìrókò aládé oko, Ìràwé igbó, Ìrókò èwò **See NOTE**   (PV)

NAME-CONGO

NAME-OTHER   Gomelleira Fig   (Elsevier)

USES
   Candomblé Jêje-Nagô   The leaves are used in initiation rituals and in baths for people with serious health problems; but, they must be used for the rituals and nothing else because the leaves are "Very Hot" and if used after mid-day, they belong to Exú, and will not cure.
   Candomblé Nagô/Jêje-Nagô   This tree is very sacred since is the personification of the Orixá **Ìrókò**
   Candomblé Angola   Kavungo – The fallen leaves used for ritual baths and Abô
                      Zaze – The fallen leaves used for ritual baths

NOTE   Juan Tomás Roig also names another tree as Higuerón; i.e.:
              Ficus aurea **Nutt.;** *Ficus sapotifolia* **Kunth & C.D.Bouché**
         AKA   Higerón-Jagüey, Higón, **Jagüey Hembra**

NOTE   **Ìrókò**   **Ìrókò** is an Orixá that inhabits the ***Milicia excelsa*** in Africa, the
                    Gameleira (***Ficus gomelleira***) in Brazil and the Ceiba (***Ceiba pentandra***)
                    in Cuba. He is associated with **Vodum Loko** in Candomblé Jêje; inkice
                    Kindembu/Tempo in Candomblé Bantu.
                    See: **https://pt.wikipedia.org/wiki/Iroko_(orixá)**
        Kavungo   Is a Bantu deity, equivalent to Obaluaiè
                    See: **https://pt.wikipedia.org/wiki/Kaviungo**
        Zaze   **Zaze/Nzazi** is a Bantu deity, equivalente to Xangô
                    See: **https://pt.wikipedia.org/wiki/Nzazi**

NOTE The Yoruba names are for the real Iroko (***Chlorophora excelsa*** **(Welw.) Benth**.); BUT,
they have substituted the names of this tree for the one that they found in Brazil.
The correct nomenclature is:
              Milicia excelsa **(Welw.) C.C.Berg;** *Chlorophora excelsa* **(Welw.) Benth.**

NAME-CUBA	Hinojo, Hinojo de Florencia		(Roig)
Owner	Obatalá (LC, Quiros)		
	Obatalá, Osain (TDF2)		

| **NAME-SCIENTIFIC** | *Foeniculum vulgare* Mill. | | (Roig) |

NAME-BRAZIL	Funcho, Erva-doce, Erva-doce-de-cabeça, Funcho-comum		
Candomblé Jêje-Nagô	Oxalá, Oxum	Água/Masculino	(Barros)
Candomblé Angola	Lembá		
CULTO DE NAÇÃO	Oxalá, Oxossi		
Umbanda	Oxalá, Oxossi		

NAME-Lucumí	Korico	(LC)
YORUBA		
NAME-CONGO		
PALO	Korico	

NAME-OTHER	Sweet fennel	(USDA)
	Fennel, Common fennel, Sweet fennel	(CRC)
USES		
	Used to destroy the actions of hexes and witchcraft	
	To banish witchcraft (bilongo)	
	Medicinal	
PALO	Used in the funeral rites for Mayomberos Judíos.	
Candomblé Jêje-Nagô	Purification baths	
Candomblé Angola	Baths and for **Tirar Mão de Vumbi**	**See NOTE**
Umbanda	Baths, incense and head cleansings (obrigações de cabeça)	
INDIA	Used in Ayurveda	

NOTE **Tirar Mão de Vumbi** **Mão de Vumbe** are funerary rites (Same as Ituto)
See: **https://pt.wikipedia.org/wiki/Mão_de_Vumbe**

NAME-CUBA	Huevo de Gallo, Huevo de perro, Pegojo, Pitiminí	(Roig)
Owner	Eleggua, Osain (LC, Quiros)	
	Ochosi (TDF2)	
	Eleggua, Obatalá, Osain (Diaz)	
	Eleggua (Madan)	
	Oggún, Ochosi, Yemayá, Ochún (Menéndez)	
Odun	Okanran-irosun (Madan, Diaz)	
NAME-SCIENTIFIC	*Tabernaemontana citrifolia* L.	(Roig))
NAME-BRAZIL	NOT found in Flora do Brasil	
NAME-Lucumí	Chotón	(LC)
YORUBA		
NAME-CONGO		
NAME-OTHER	Milkwood	(USDA)
	Milkwood, Milky tree, Milky bush	
	Palo de Leche, Palo Lechoso (PR);	
	Bwa lèt, Bwa lèt mal, Lète (Creole Haiti)	(Elsevier)
USES	**DOES NOT** go to Osain (Omiero)	
	Medicinal	
PALO	Very good to sicken and kill	(LC)
	Powder (afoche) to separate couples	(Diaz)

NAME-CUBA	Huevo de Gallo-2	(Menéndez)
	Huevo de Gallo, Alelí, Lirio	(Roig)
Owner	Ochosi (TDF2)	
	Oggún, Ochosi (Menéndez)	
Odun		
NAME-SCIENTIFIC	*Rauvolfia nitida* Jacq.	(Roig)
NAME-BRAZIL	NOT found in Flora do Brasil	
NAME-Lucumí		
YORUBA		
NAME-CONGO		
PALO		
NAME-OTHER	Palo Amargo	(USDA)
	Bitter-ash, Smooth Devil Pepper, Bitterbush	
	Palo Amargo, Palo de Muñeco (PR); Palo de Leche (DR);	
	Bwa lèt, Bwa lèt femèl (Creole Haiti)	(Elsevier)
USES	Goes to Osain (Omiero) for Oggún, Ochosi	(Menéndez)
NOTE	This is an alternative "Huevo de Gallo" per Juan Tomás Roig	
	This plant chosen as an alternative since "Pegojo" and "Huevo de Gallo" are the same plant	

NAME-CUBA	Humo, Cenizo, Abey Blanco, Encinillo	(Roig)
Owner	Obatalá, Oddúa (LC, TDF2, Quiros)	
Odun		
NAME-SCIENTIFIC	*Abarema obovalis* (A.Rich.) Barneby & J.W.Grimes;	
	Pithecellobium obovale (A.Rich.) C.Wright	(Roig)
NAME-BRAZIL	NOT listed in Flora do Brasil	

NAME-Lucumí	Eyereyó		(LC, TDF2)
ANAGO	Igbelefín	**Palo Cenizo**	(LC)
YORUBA			

NAME-CONGO	Choná		(LC)
	Shona		(TDF)
PALO	**PALO CENIZO/**HUMO DE SABANA	**See NOTE**	
	Nchúngo, Chúngora Mofototo		(Nfinda)

NAME-OTHER	NO common name. Native to Cuba and Hispaniola	
	Obovate abarema (English)	
	Encinillo (PR)	(Elsevier)

USES		
	For a marriage to occur without any problems	(LC)
PALO	It can be used for good or bad	(LC)
	It is used to balance the powers of all the other "palos" in	
	the Nganga and talismans.	(Nfinda)

NOTE	*Pithecellobium obovale* **(A.Rich.) C.Wright** is a synonym of *Abarema obovalis* **(A.Rich.) Barneby & J.W.Grimes.** Information found at powo.science.kew.org and Elsevier's.
NOTE	Lydia Cabrera **LISTS Palo Cenizo** in a separate entry

NAME-CUBA	Humo con Espinas		(LC)
	Humo, Humo Espinoso, Humo de Sabana,		
	Humo de Costa, Guayabillo		(Roig)

Owner
Odun

NAME-SCIENTIFIC *Chloroleucon mangense* var. *lentiscifolium* (C.Wright) Barneby & J.W.Grimes;
Pithecellobium lentiscifolium C. Wright (Roig)

NAME-BRAZIL NOT listed in Flora do Brasil

NAME-Lucumí	Amloi		(LC)
ANAGO	Igbelefín	**Humo de Sabana**	(LC)
YORUBA			

NAME-CONGO
PALO   **PALO CENIZO, HUMO DE SABANA**
Nchúngo, Chúngora Mofototo (Nfinda)

NAME-OTHER No common name found. Native to Cuba, Haiti and Belize
Lentiscusleaf Manga chloroleucon (Elsevier)

USES

Used as a defense against the evil eye.
It is also used to do bad. (LC)

NAME-CUBA	Incienso, Abrótamo, Abrótamo Macho	(Roig)
Owner	Babalú-Ayé, Obatalá (LC, TDF)	
	Babalú-Ayé (TDF2)	
	Babalú-Ayé, Oggún, Orishaoko (Diaz)	
Odun	Odi-ogunda, Ose-meji (Diaz)	
NAME-SCIENTIFIC	*Artemisia abrotanum* L.	(Roig)
NAME-BRAZIL	Abrótega, Abrótica, Abrótono, Alfacinha-do-rio, Artemísia, Erva-lombrigueira	
NAME-Lucumí YORUBA	Turare, Minselo	(LC, TDF2)
NAME-CONGO	Minselo, Turare	(TDF)
NAME-OTHER	Southernwood	(USDA)
	Southern wormwood, Southernwood, Old man, Lady's love	(CRC)
USES	Goes to Osain (Omiero) for Babalú-Ayé	
	Cleansings (Sarayéyé) and ritual baths (Ebomisi)	
	Cleansing baths, cleansings for the home	
	Medicinal	
Hoodoo/Root Magic (USA)	Protective herb. Burned as incense will keep trouble away from you and/or home.	

NAME-CUBA	Incienso de Guinea	(LC)
	Incienso de Guinea, Copal	(Quiros)
	Incienso	(Roig)
Owner	Ochosi (LC, Quiros, Madan)	
Odun	Iwori-ose (Quiros, Madan)	

| **NAME-SCIENTIFIC** | *Protium fragrans* (Rose) Urb.; | |
| | *Icica fragrans* Rose | (Roig) |

| **NAME-BRAZIL** | NOT listed in Flora do Brasil | |

| **NAME-Lucumí YORUBA** | Ewe Turere | (LC) |

NAME-CONGO

| **NAME-OTHER** | No common name found. Native to Cuba. | |
| | Fragrant resin-tree | (Elsevier) |

USES

| | Ewé MUST be picked at 3:00am | (LC) |
| | It will enable someone to become invisible in order to get out of jail. For the innocent as well as the guilty. | (LC) |

NOTE   Lydia Cabrera names this tree/Ewé; but gives no scientific name
Juan Tomás Roig does list this tree (*Icica fragrans* **Rose**) as Incienso.

NOTE   This tree (*Protium fragrans* **(Rose) Urb**) is **NATIVE** to Cuba

NAME-CUBA	Incienso de Playa, Incienso de Costa, Balsamillo	(Roig)
Owner	Yemayá (LC, TDF2, Quiros)	
Odun		
NAME-SCIENTIFIC	*Tournefortia gnaphalodes* (L.) R.Br. ex Roem. & Schult.	(Roig)
NAME-BRAZIL	NOT listed in Flora do Brasil	
NAME-Lucumí	Eggbado **Incienso de Playa**	(LC, TDF2)
	Lakode **Incienso de Costa**	(LC)
YORUBA		
NAME-CONGO		
NAME-OTHER	Sea Rosemary	(USDA)
	Sea Lavender, Sea Rosemary	
USES		
	Cleansings with sea water	
	Medicinal	
Abakuá	for the purification of sacred objects in the "Batamú"	
	(Inside the temple)	(LC)

NAME-CUBA	Ítamo Real, Ítamo, Díctamo Real, Díctamo	(Roig)
Owner	Eleggua (TDF2, Diaz)	
	Eleggua, Oggún, Ochosi (Menéndez)	
	Eleggua, Yemayá (Madan)	
	Eleggua, Ochún (Quiros)	
	Eleggua, Ochún, Changó (Concordia)	
	Oggún, Yemayá (Irizarry)	
Odun	Oyeku-okanran (Diaz, Irizarry, Concordia, Quiros, Madan, Orula.org)	
	Irete-ogunda (Diaz, Irizarry, Madan, Quiros, Orula.org)	

NAME-SCIENTIFIC	*Euphorbia tithymaloides* L.	(Roig)

NAME-BRAZIL	Sapatinho-do-Diabo, Dois-irmãos, Sapatinho-de-Judeu	
Candomblé de Angola	Aluvaiá	
Umbanda		

NAME-Lucumí	Ewe Itauko	(Irizarry)
YORUBA	Aperejó	(CRC)

NAME-CONGO

NAME-OTHER	Bird cactus, Devil's backbone, Jew-bush, Ribbon cactus	(CRC)
	Devil's backbone, Jacob's ladder, Redbird cactus	(Wiki)

USES	Goes to Osain (Omiero)	
	Ritual bath (Ebomisi) to open paths	
	Medicinal	
Candomblé de Angola	with the dry leaves, a powder (afoche) is made for increased/good business (é feito pó benfazejo, para obtenção de bons negócios)	
INDIA	Used in Siddha. Magic, ritual: crushed leaves used against illness or pains caused by black magic.	(CRC)

NAME-CUBA	Jaboncillo		(Roig)
Owner	Ochún (LC, TDF2, Madan)		
	Yemayá (TDF)		
	Eleggua, Ochún (Irizarry)		
	Obatalá, Ochún (Diaz)		
	Ochún, Oggún (Quiros)		
	Ochún, Yemayá (Menéndez)		
Odun	Owonrin-meji (Madan, Irizarry, Diaz, Quiros)		
NAME-SCIENTIFIC	*Sapindus saponaria* L.	**See NOTE**	(Roig)
NAME-BRAZIL	Ibaró, Jequitiguaçu, Salta-martim		
NAME-Lucumí YORUBA	Obueno, Kekeriongo		(LC, TDF2)
NAME-CONGO	Lángui		(LC)
	Languí		(TDF)
PALO	**Palo Jabon**	Langui	
NAME-OTHER	Wingleaf soapberry		(USDA)
	Soapberry, Florida Soapberry, Mexican soapberry		
	Jaboncillo (DR, PR);		
	Bwa savon, Bwa savonèt peyi (Creole Haiti)		(Elsevier)
USES	Goes to Osain (Omiero)		
	Omiero for Obatalá and Ochún		(Diaz)
	Used for ritual baths (Ebomisi) and Inche Osain		
PALO	Used for cleansings and protection		
INDIA	Used in Ayurveda. Ritual: rosaries made of seeds.		(CRC)

NOTE   Per Juan Tomás Roig, there are other plants known as Jaboncillo:
- *Gouania polygama* (Jacq.) Urb.   AKA Bejuco de Cuba
- *Cordia alba* (Jacq.) Roem. & Schult.   The one MOST similar to real Jaboncillo but AKA Uva Gomosa

NAME-CUBA	Jagua, Jagua Blanca, Jagua Común		(Roig)
Owner	Yemayá (LC, TDF2, Madan, Quiros)		
	Obatalá (Menéndez)	**Jagua Blanca**	
	Oddúa (Menéndez)	**Jagua Macho**	
Odun	Iwori-ika (Madan, Quiros)		
	Irete-okanran (Madan, Orula.org)		

NAME-SCIENTIFIC	*Genipa americana* L.		(Roig)

NAME-BRAZIL	Jenipapeiro, Jenipapo, Conheça, Assacou, Arrieiro, Caçaú		
Candomblé Jêje-Nagô	Omolú/Obaluaiyé, Nanã	Terra/Masculino	(Barros)
Candomblé de Angola	**Katendê, Kavungo**	**See NOTE**	
Candomblé	Obaluaiyé, Iansã, Obá, Yewá	Terra/Masculino/Gùn	(Carvalho)
Umbanda	Jemanjá		
CULTO DE NAÇÃO	Omolú		
Odun	Ejiogbe-meji		(PV)

NAME-Lucumí	Góontongo, Diambula	(TDF2)
YORUBA	Bùjé dúdú, Dàndòjé, Osàngodó, àsógbódùn,	
	àsógbódò, Onípowòjé	(PV)

NAME- CONGO	Góontongo, Diambula	(LC)
	Bootongo, Diambula	(TDF)
PALO	Diámbula	

NAME-OTHER	Jagua	(USDA)
	Marmalade box, Jagua;	
	Carcarutoto, Caruto, Caruto Montañero (Venezuela)	
	Genipayer, Jinpa (Creole Haiti)	(Elsevier)

USES		Goes to Osain (Omiero)	(Madan)
		Used for ritual baths (Ebomisi) and Inche Osain (Talisman)	
	PALO	With the smoke of this "palo", the sight of a Mayombero is clouded; it also blinds the **Nganga "Judía"** so that the **Nfume** (spirit) cannot see and work their witchcraft.	**See NOTE**
	Candomblé	Leaves considered indispensable as considered a fundamental Ewé of this Orixá. Great prestige due to Odun Ejiogbe-meji- Was used to save a man from death	
	Candomblé Jêje-Nagô	This Ewé is essential in the initiation of initiates of Obaluaiè.	
	Candomblé de Angola	**Katendê** – Baths and head cleansings (obrigações no Orí)	
	Umbanda	Ritual baths, cleansings, etc. Also used for "Head" cleansing (obrigações no Orí)	
	CULTO DE NAÇÃO	Used in funerary rites of initiated religious member **(Mão de Vumbe)**	**See NOTE**

NOTE	**Katendê**	Is a Bantu deity, equivalent to Ossaim
		See: **https://pt.wikipedia.org/wiki/Katendê**
	Kavungo	Is a Bantu deity, equivalent to Obaluaiè
		See: **https://pt.wikipedia.org/wiki/Kaviungo**
	Mão de Vumbe	Are the funerary rites performed for initiated religious members (same as **Ituto**)
		See: **https://pt.wikipedia.org/wiki/Mão_de_Vumbe**

NOTE **Nganga "Judía"** it refers to a **Nganga** in Regla Conga where initial practitioners either baptized them with Christian symbolisms (Nganga Cristiana) or not (Nganga Judía) as a traditional Nganga from their homeland. As a general rule when one refers to a Nganga Judía is when they are made to work with **Lukankazi** (the devil).
  See: **https://es.wikipedia.org/wiki/Palo_(religión)**

Nganga it refers to the vessel that Regla Conga uses as a representation of their religious entities. This vessel is a microcosm where the "palos" of different trees are places along with other things that give it "Life". Within this are Ngangas which include the ritualized bones from ancestors (as in the past), or other dead people which becomes the **Nfume** (spirit) of the vessel and through which the Mayombero/Palero can communicate with and have it do his/her bidding. The Nganga which DO NOT include the ritualized bones are called **Spiritual Nganga**.

NAME-CUBA	Jagüey, Jagüey común, Jagüey de vaca	(Roig)
Owner	Oggún "Musi Nganga" (LC)	
	Oggún, Changó (TDF2, Quiros)	
	Changó, Oggún, Oyá (Diaz)	
	Oggún, Ochosi (Menéndez)	
Odun	Idi-ejiogbe, Ika-oturupon, Irosun-osa, Osa-okanran	
	(Diaz, Madan, Quiros, Orula.org)	

NAME-SCIENTIFIC	*Ficus membranacea* C.Wright.	**See NOTE**	(Roig)

NAME-BRAZIL	NOT found in Flora do Brasil

NAME-Lucumí	Fiapabba, Afomá, Uendo	(LC)
	Fiapabba, Afomá, Uendo, Vendo	(TDF2)
YORUBA	Àba, Odán, Òpòtó, Iréré, Odán ilé, Odán oko, Odán wéwé	
	Àfòmó àpé, Òpòtó wéré, Oláfòmógi, Alábe wéré (***Ficus Sp.***)	(PV)

NAME-CONGO	Nkunia Bracanone/Baracanone, Nkunia Sanda sanda, Otakóndo	(LC)
PALO	**Jagüey, Yo Puedo Más Que Tú**　　　Barakanone Otakondo	
	OWNER　　Siete Rayos (But ALL use it)	(Nfinda)

NAME-OTHER	Membranous Fig	(Elsevier)

USES	Goes to Osain (Omiero)	
	Used for ritual baths (Ebomisi) and Inche Osain	
PALO	Its almost the strongest "palo". It will "swallow" almost any tree,	
	with the exception of the "Palma Real" and "Guamá"	(LC)
	It can be used for good or bad.	

NOTE　Per Juan Tomás Roig, there are several other trees that are commonly called Jagüey in Cuba; i.e.
- *Ficus maxima* Mill.; *Ficus subscabrida* Warb.
- *Ficus citrifolia* Mill.; *Ficus brevifolia* Nutt. & *Ficus populoides* Warb.
- *Ficus crocata* (Miq.) Mart. ex Miq.; *Ficus havanensis* Rossberg

NAME-CUBA	Jagüey - Árbol Ficus Pendurata		(LC)
	Jagüey		(Roig)
Owner			
Odun			
NAME-SCIENTIFIC	*Ficus lyrata Warb.;*		
	Ficus pandurata Hance		(Roig)
NAME-BRAZIL	NOT listed in Flora do Brasil		
NAME- ANAGO	Oké	**Jagüey**	(LC)
	Igui oké	**Jagüey-the tree**	(LC)
YORUBA			

NAME-CONGO

PALO	**Jagüey, Yo Puedo Más Que Tú**	Barakanone Otakondo	
	OWNER Siete Rayos (But ALL use it)		(Nfinda)
BANTU	Musenda	**Árbol Ficus Pendurata**	(LC)

NAME-OTHER	Fiddle leaf fig	(USDA)

USES

Since it is a type of Jagüey, it should have the same uses

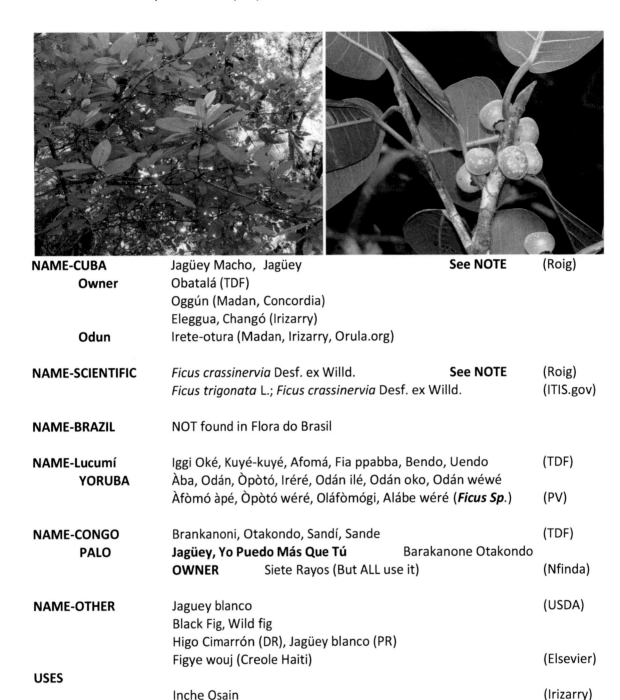

NAME-CUBA	Jagüey Macho, Jagüey	**See NOTE**	(Roig)
Owner	Obatalá (TDF)		
	Oggún (Madan, Concordia)		
	Eleggua, Changó (Irizarry)		
Odun	Irete-otura (Madan, Irizarry, Orula.org)		

NAME-SCIENTIFIC	*Ficus crassinervia* Desf. ex Willd.	**See NOTE**	(Roig)
	Ficus trigonata L.; *Ficus crassinervia* Desf. ex Willd.		(ITIS.gov)

NAME-BRAZIL	NOT found in Flora do Brasil

NAME-Lucumí	Iggi Oké, Kuyé-kuyé, Afomá, Fia ppabba, Bendo, Uendo	(TDF)
YORUBA	Àba, Odán, Òpòtó, Iréré, Odán ilé, Odán oko, Odán wéwé	
	Àfòmó àpé, Òpòtó wéré, Oláfòmógi, Alábe wéré (***Ficus Sp.***)	(PV)

NAME-CONGO	Brankanoni, Otakondo, Sandí, Sande	(TDF)
PALO	**Jagüey, Yo Puedo Más Que Tú** Barakanone Otakondo	
	OWNER Siete Rayos (But ALL use it)	(Nfinda)

NAME-OTHER	Jaguey blanco	(USDA)
	Black Fig, Wild fig	
	Higo Cimarrón (DR), Jagüey blanco (PR)	
	Figye wouj (Creole Haiti)	(Elsevier)
USES		
	Inche Osain	(Irizarry)

NOTE   Per Lydia Cabrera there is Jagüey Macho (**Iyákara**) and a Jagüey Hembra (**Kalayánga**)
Juan Tomás Roig lists a **Jagüey Hembra** as:
- *Ficus aurea* Nutt.; *Ficus sapotifolia* Kunth & C.D.Bouché **AKA**-Higuerón-Jagüey, Higón
- *Ficus citrifolia* Mill.; Ficus *laevigata* Vahl   **AKA**-Pinipiní
- *Ficus americana* Aubl.; *Ficus jacquinifolia* A.Rich.   **AKA**- Jagüeicillo

NOTE   Per Juan Tomás Roig, there are several other trees that are called **Jagüey Macho** in Cuba; i.e.
- *Ficus maxima* Mill.; *Ficus subscabrida* Warb.
- *Ficus trigonata* L.; *Ficus wrightii* Warb.
- *Ficus crocata* (Miq.) Mart. ex Miq.; *Ficus combsii* Warb.

NAME-CUBA	Jía Amarilla, Jía Yana	(Roig)
Owner	Ochún (LC, TDF, TDF2, Quiros)	
Odun	Osa-ika (Quiros, Orula.org)	
NAME-SCIENTIFIC	*Casearia guianensis* (Aubl.) Urb.;	
	Casearia ramiflora Vahl	(Roig)
NAME-BRAZIL	Café-do-diabo, Fruta-de-saíra	
NAME-Lucumí	Erere, Yasé	(LC, TDF, TDF2)
YORUBA		
NAME-CONGO	Mosúmbila, Tótókongo	(LC)
	Mosombila, Totokomgo	(TDF)
PALO	Mosumbila	
NAME-OTHER	Guyanese Wild Coffee	(USDA)
	Café marrón (DR); Palo amarillo (Venezuela)	
	Cafetillo (PR), Kafe mawon (Creole Haiti)	(Elsevier)
USES	Used for the Omiero of Ochún	(TDF2)
PALO	For the "Omiero" used to wash animal bones that	
	are to be used in amulets	(LC)

NAME-CUBA	Jía Blanca	(Roig)
Owner	Ochosi (LC, Quiros, Diaz)	
Odun	Obara-ose (Diaz, Quiros, Orula.org)	
NAME-SCIENTIFIC	*Casearia aculeata* Jacq.;	
	Casearia alba A.Rich.	(Roig)
NAME-BRAZIL	NOT found in Flora do Brasil	
NAME-Lucumí	Erefunfún, Unkua	(LC)
YORUBA		
NAME-CONGO	Mosúmbila	(LC)
	Ntuenke, Botta	(TDF)
NAME-OTHER	Rabo de Raton **See NOTE**	(USDA)
	Thom pickle, Wild coffee	(CRC)

USES

	To combat bad influences-spiritual and physical	(LC)
	Purification of the home.	
PALO	Used to pack **Npaka** (a protective talisman)	(LC)

NOTE   This tree/shrub shares the same common name as Jía Brava since the scientific name (*Casearia alba* **A.Rich**) is considered a synonym for *Casearia aculeata* **Jacq.**

NAME-CUBA	Jía Brava, Jía Morada, Jía Prieta, Jía Peluda	(Roig)
Owner	Babalú-Ayé (LC, TDF2)	
Odun		
NAME-SCIENTIFIC	*Casearia aculeata* Jacq.;	
	Casearia hirta Sw.	(Roig)
NAME-BRAZIL	Cruzeiro, Espinheiro	(Elsevier)
NAME-Lucumí		
YORUBA		
NAME-CONGO	Mosúmbila	(LC)
PALO	Totokongo	
	OWNER Tata Pansúa	
NAME-OTHER	Rabo de Raton	(USDA)
	Thom pickle, Wild coffee	(CRC)
	Palo de Avispas (DR), Pikan arada (Creole Haiti)	(Elsevier)

USES

                To cover Babalú-Ayé

PALO   The shadow of this tree is maleficent.

                All dark shadows/spirits go there to congregate and that is
where the Mayombero will make a pact with them.   (LC)

                With the spines, terrible hexes/witchcraft (Malifecios)
are made.   (LC)

                It is said that wasps are born/created in this tree   (LC)

NAME-CUBA	Jibá, Jibá común, Jibá colorado, Arabo	(Roig)
Owner	Orishaoko (LC, Madan)	
	Orishaoko, Ochún (Diaz)	
	Orishaoko, Inle (Quiros)	
	Changó, Agayú (Menéndez)	
Odun	Iwori-odi (Madan, Diaz)	

NAME-SCIENTIFIC   *Erythroxylum havanense* Jacq.   (Roig)

NAME-BRAZIL   NOT found in Flora do Brasil

NAME-Lucumí
   YORUBA

NAME-CONGO
   PALO   **OWNER**   Sarabanda   **Espiritu Cruzado**

NAME-OTHER   Ovate cocaine-tree
   Quiebra Hacha (DR)   (Elsevier)

USES

	To ward off witches (espanta brujos)	(LC)
	Crosses made of the wood to keep dark forces away	
	The root is VERY medicinal. ALL "curanderos" should have it	(LC)
PALO	To harvest root, the person must speak to it and state what	
	they are doing and pay (pagar el derecho); or the root will	
	break and be no good.	(LC)
ESPIRITU CRUZADO	For the Spiritual Nganga of Sarabanda	
	Used for Spiritual work and charms (resguardos)	

NAME-CUBA   Jícama, Jícama cimarrona, Jíquima, Bejuco Peludo   (Roig)
    Owner   Obatalá (LC, TDF2, Quiros)
    Odun

NAME-SCIENTIFIC   *Calopogonium caeruleum* (Benth.) Sauvalle;
                    Calopogonium coeruleum (Benth.) Sauvalle   (Roig)

NAME-BRAZIL   Feijao-de-macaco, Feijãozinho-da-mata, Cipó-araquan

NAME-Lucumí   Jicama   (LC)
               Jikama   (TDF2)
    YORUBA

NAME-CONGO   Túakao   (LC)

NAME-OTHER   Wild Jicama, Jicama   (USDA)

USES
        Medicinal

NOTE   This is NOT the Jicama (*Pachyrhizus erosus* (L.) Urb.) that you see at the supermarket which Juan Tomás Roig names **Jícama de Agua** or **Jícama Dulce**.

NAME-CUBA	Jiquí, Jiquí común, Jiquí de ley	(Roig)
Owner	Oggún (LC, Quiros)	
Odun	Okanran-obara; Osa-okanran (Quiros, Orula.org)	
NAME-SCIENTIFIC	*Pera bumeliifolia* Griseb.	(Roig)
NAME-BRAZIL	NOT found in Flora do Brasil	
NAME-Lucumí	Iggisóro	(LC)
YORUBA		

NAME-CONGO	Ntuenke, Bótta		(LC)
PALO	**Palo Jiquí**	Monsongo, Nkomblo	
	OWNER	Lucero, Centella, Mamá Chola	(Nfinda)

NAME-OTHER	Jiqui	(USDA)
	Black Ebony	(Fairchild)
	Jaiquí (DR); Kase rach, Kase raj (Creole Haiti)	(Elsevier)

USES

	To make Oggún mad.	
	This Ewé kills witchcraft (mata brujeria)	(LC)
	Medicinal	
PALO	For cleansings with the leaves	
	The root and the "palo" to give vigor to the Nganga	(LC)

NAME-CUBA	Jobo, Jobo Negro, Jobito		(Roig)
Owner	Changó, Eleggua (LC)		
	Changó (TDF2)		
	Changó, Eleggua, Obatalá (Irizarry)		
	Changó, Eleggua, Oddua (Quiros)		
	Changó, Agayú (Madan, Menéndez)		
	Changó (Diaz)		
Odun	Odi-ogunda; Irosun-meji; Irete-ogunda		
	(Madan, Diaz, Irizarry, Quiros, Orula.org)		

NAME-SCIENTIFIC	*Spondias mombin* L.	(Roig)

NAME-BRAZIL	Cajazeira, Cajá-mirim, Taperebá, Cajazeiro-miúdo		
Candomblé Jêje-Nagô	Ogum	Terra/Masculino	(Barros)
Candomblé de Angola	Inkosse, Katendê, Dandalunda, Lembá		
Vodum	**Fá**, **Gú**, Azanadó (**Bessén**)	See NOTE	
Umbanda			

NAME-Lucumí	Abbá, Okinkán, Wakika, Kinkao	(LC)
	Abbá, Okinkán, Wakika, Kinkao, Menguéngué, Guengué	(TDF2)
YORUBA	Èkikà, Òkikà, Ìyeyè, Olósàn, Iléwò olósán	(PV, CRC)

NAME-CONGO	Grengerengué kunansieto, Guengué, Menguéngué	(LC)
	Grenguerenge, Kunansieto, Guengue, Maguengue	(TDF)
PALO	**Palo Jobo**	Nkunia guenguere kunansieto
	OWNER	Siete Rayos

NAME-OTHER	Yellow mombin	(USDA)
	Hog-plum, Spanish plum, Yellow mombin	(CRC)
	Ciruela (DR); Guama zapatero (Venezuela);	
	Jobillo (PR); Gran monben, Gwo monben (Creole Haiti)	(Elsevier)

USES		Goes to Osain (Omiero)	
		Inche Osain. Addimú for Changó (the fruit)	
		With the leaves the "Piedra de Rayo" and the wooden doll	
		that represents Changó are baptized	(LC)
		With a preference over "Alamo", the leaves of Jobo are given	
		to the "ram/sheep" offered to Changó before immolation.	(LC)
	PALO	With the leaves, it helps to place the bones (Kangome)	
		in the Nganga	(LC)
	ESPIRITU CRUZADO	To baptize the "Matari-Nsasi" (Piedra de Rayo)	(LC)
	Candomblé	It is a very sacred tree with great prestige for members	
		of Casa das Minas, Candomblé Ketu, Candomblé da Bahia,	
		Candomblé do Rio de Janeiro and Xangô de Pernambuco.	
		It is considered to be the home (assentamento) of Ogum.	(Barros)
		The leaves of this tree are fed to animals (four legged) prior	
		to the immolation/sacrifice. (see Guava/Goiabeira)	(Barros)

Candomblé de Angola Inkosse   Leaves used for offerings to animals (folhas
usadas nos oferecimentos do **Erankó**), baths, **Abô** (Omiero)

          Katendê   Used for the initiation of **Tempo**, leaves
offered to animals, head cleansings (obrigações no Orí), and for the
confirmation of **Babalosayin**

          Dandalunda   Head cleansings (obrigações no Orí)
          Lembá   Head cleansings (obrigações no Orí)

NOTE	**Vodum**	Fá, Gú, Azanadó (**Bessén**) are deities in the Vodum pantheon.
		Fá is a Vodum deity, equivalent to Orunmila
		Gú is a Vodum deity, equivalent to Oxossi
		Azanadó (**Bessén**) Is a Vodum deity, equivalente to Oxumarê
		See: **https://pt.wikipedia.org/wiki/Vodum**
	Erankó	Yoruba word meaning animal, four legged animals
	Abô	Sacred water, Omiero
		See: **https://pt.wikipedia.org/wiki/Águas_sagradas**
	Tempo	Is an Nkissi, deity in the Bantu/Candomblé Bantu religion
		See: **https://pt.wikipedia.org/wiki/Kindembu**
	Babalosayin	Is the person in charge of finding and choosing the necessary plants
		needed in the rituals.
		See: **https://pt.wikipedia.org/wiki/Babalosaim**
	LEGEND	The tree is called "Igí Ìyeyè" or "Árvore de Mãe". It is one of
		the trees picked by the Ìyàmi to rest. They then decided to give
		happiness or grief (felicidade ou infelicidade) depending on
		the wish of the people. Its leaves have the power to ward off
		evil and bring luck (suas folhas tem o poder de afastar as coisas
		ruins e atrair sorte)

NAME-CUBA	Jocuma, Jocuma prieta, Jocuma amarilla, Caguaní	(Roig)
Owner	Changó, Oggún (LC, TDF2, Quiros, Diaz)	
	Changó, Oggún, Mayombe (Madan)	
Odun	Owonrin-ika; Oturupon-ika (Madan, Quiros, Orula.org)	
NAME-SCIENTIFIC	*Sideroxylon foetidissimum* Jacq.	(Roig)
NAME-BRAZIL	Acoma	
NAME-Lucumí	Okuma	(TDF2)
YORUBA		
NAME-CONGO		
NAME-OTHER	False mastic	(USDA)
	Wild Mastic, False Mastic	(CRC)
	Caya Amarilla (DR); Tortugo Colorado (PR)	
	Akoma, Coma, Koma (Creole Haiti)	(Elsevier)
USES	**DOES NOT** go to Osain (Omiero)	
	Medicinal	
	Cleansings for people who have an obsessive spirit;	
	but person who does the cleansing must do a self-cleansing	
	(Ibora Omitutu)	(Diaz)

NAME-CUBA	Júcaro Bravo, Júcaro de Uña	(LC)
	Júcaro Bravo, Júcaro espinoso, Júcaro prieto, Jucarillo	(Roig)
Owner	Changó, Oyá (LC, Diaz, Quiros)	
	Changó (TDF2)	
	Eleggua (Irizarry)	
Odun	Irete-ogunda (Diaz, Quiros, Irizarry, Madan, Orula.org)	
NAME-SCIENTIFIC	*Terminalia molinetii* M.Gómez;	
	Bucida spinosa Jenn. **See NOTE**	(Roig)
	Bucida buceras L.	(LC)
NAME-BRAZIL	NOT found in Flora do Brasil	
NAME-Lucumí YORUBA	Oddé	(LC, TDF2)
NAME-CONGO	Tontoine	(LC)
	Toleme, Kalunga maddiada	(TDF)
NAME-OTHER	Spiny Black Olive (florida.plantatlas.usf.edu)	
	Spiny bucida, Brier tree, Prickly tree, Spiny black olive (Bahamas);	
	Guara Guao (DR)	(Elsevier)
USES	Goes to Osain (Omiero)	
	CANNOT go to Osain since it has spines.	
	When lighting strikes a person is because Oyá is mad; so, smoke	
	from this tree will appease Oyá and bring the person around (LC)	
NOTE	*Bucida spinosa* Jenn. is a synonym of ***Bucida molinetii* (M.Gómez) Alwan & Stace**	
	at theplantlist.org and Elsevier's.	
	Lydia Cabrera lists ***Bucida buceras* L.** as Júcaro Bravo when in reality it is	
	Arará, Júcaro, Júcaro Común	

NAME-CUBA	Junco Marino, Espinillo, Palo de rayo		(Roig)
Owner	Yemayá (LC, TDF2, Quiros)		
Odun	Owonrin-ejiogbe (Quiros, Orula.org)		

NAME-SCIENTIFIC	*Parkinsonia aculeata* L.		(Roig)

NAME-BRAZIL	Espinho-do-Jerusalém, Rosa-da-Turquia, Sensitivo		(CRC)

NAME-Lucumí	Júneo, Atékun-Iféfé		(LC, TDF2)
ANAGO	Ikán olokún, Ité kún	**Junco Marino**	(LC)
	Iféfé, Itákún	**Junco**	(LC)
YORUBA	Ogbe-okuye		(Elsevier, CRC)

NAME-CONGO	Kalúnga maddiada		(LC)
PALO	Kalunga Madiada		
BANTU	Kalunga madiada	**Junco Marino**	(LC)

NAME-OTHER	Jerusalem Thorn	(USDA)
	Jerusalem thorn, Horse bean	
	Espinillo (Venezuela), Acacia de los Masones (DR)	
	Madam nayiz, Madam yas (Creole Haiti)	(Elsevier)

USES		
	Medicinal	(LC)
INDIA	Used in Siddha	(CRC)

NAME-CUBA	Jurabaina, Frijolillo, Guamá Piñón, Frijolillo Baría		(Roig)
	Jurabaina, Jurubana		(LC)
Owner	Eleggua, Changó, Oggún (LC, Quiros)		
	Changó (TDF2)		
Odun			
NAME-SCIENTIFIC	*Hebestigma cubense* (Kunth) Urb.	**See NOTE**	(Roig)
NAME-BRAZIL	NOT found in Flora do Brasil		
NAME-Lucumí			
YORUBA			
NAME-CONGO	Ngrúbá		(LC)
PALO	**Palo Jurubana/Jurubaina**	Mabambo	
	OWNER	Lucero, Sarabanda, Siete rayos	
NAME-OTHER	False Locust		(USDA)
	Cuban Hebestigma		(CRC)

USES

	It is anti-hex (diambo or bilongo)
	It will expel any hex ingested
PALO	It will kill (destroy) a Nganga if placed in it.

NOTE   *Hebestigma* is a monotypic genus with *Hebestigma cubense* **(Kunth) Urb** being it's ONLY member. **It is NATIVE to Cuba.**

NAME-CUBA	Lagaña de Aura, Malacara		(Roig)
	Legaña de Aura, Lagaña de Aura	**See NOTE**	(LC)
Owner	Ochún (LC, TDF2, Quiros)		
Odun			
NAME-SCIENTIFIC	*Plumbago zeylanica* L.;		
	Plumbago scandens L.		(Roig)
NAME-BRAZIL	NOT found in Flora do Brasil		
NAME-Lucumí	Ewe Iwago, Icolékoké		(LC)
	Ewe Ywago, Ycolékoké		(TDF2)
YORUBA	Ìnábìrì, Ìnábìí		(PV, CRC)
NAME-CONGO	Malacara		(TDF)
NAME-OTHER	Wild leadwort		(USDA)
	Ceylon leadwort, White leadwort, White-flowered leadwort		(CRC)

USES

	Used for personal cleansings (Sarayéyé) and home cleansings.	
	With the seed, a very strong spell is made to tie down someone (para amarres).	(LC)
	Medicinal	
INDIA	Used in Ayurveda, Unani and Siddha.	
	Magico-religious beliefs: for general debility in children a piece of root tied on the neck	(CRC)

NOTE   Lydia Cabrera lists Malacara separately

NAME-CUBA	Laurel de España, Laurel, Laurel de especia	(Roig)
Owner	Ochún (TDF)	
	Changó (Madan)	
	Eggun, Eleggua, Obatalá, Orunmila (Irizarry)	
Odun	Okanran-irete; Otura-owonrin (Madan, Irizarry, Orula.org)	
NAME-SCIENTIFIC	*Laurus nobilis* L.	(Roig)
NAME-BRAZIL	Louro, Loureiro, Folha-de-louro	
Candomblé de Angola	Lembá, Matamba	
Candomblé Ketu	Iansã	
CULTO DE NAÇÃO	Oxalá, Ossaim, Iansã	
Umbanda	Oxalá, Xangô, Iansã, Oxossi, Ciganos	
NAME-Lucumí	Ewé Oyaoko	(Irizarry)
YORUBA	EWÉ ASÁ	(jairoinglat)
NAME-CONGO	Osereké	(TDF)
NAME-OTHER	Sweet bay	(USDA)
	Bay Laurel, True laurel, Sweet Bay Tree, Laurel	(CRC)

USES

	Medicinal	
	Aromatic baths, Inche Osain and Paraldo	
PALO	A tea is made with rain-water and honey to increase spiritual sight	
Umbanda	Used as incense to attract prosperity, victory and positive energy	
	Used in baths, head cleansings (obrigações de cabeça)	
Candomblé Ketu	Since this plant symbolizes victory it is assigned to Iansã and used as incense to attract financial success.	
	Used to decorate "Acarajá" (an Addimu) for Iansã	
Candomblé de Angola	**Matamba** – Leaves used as incense against evil eye	
	Lembá - Leaves used as incense	
INDIA	Used in Unani	(CRC)

NAME-CUBA	Laurel, Laurel de la India, Laurel Criollo	(Roig)
Owner	Changó (LC, TDF2, Quiros, Diaz)	
Odun	Okanran-irete; Otura-owonrin (Quiros, Diaz, Orula.org)	
NAME-SCIENTIFIC	*Ficus benjamina* L.; *Ficus nitida* Thunb.	(Roig)

NAME-BRAZIL Figueira-benjamim, Figo-Benjamim
  Candomblé de Angola Aluvaiá, Kavungo
    Candomblé Exú
    Umbanda Obaluaiè, Exú

NAME-Lucumí	Igginile itiri, Iggi gafiofo	(LC)
	Iggi gafiofo	(TDF2)
YORUBA		
NAME-CONGO	Ocereké	(LC)
PALO	Osereke	
OWNER	Siete Rayos/Nsasi-Nsasi	(Nfinda)
OWNER	Cuatro Vientos/Lucero	(LC)
OWNER	Siete Rayos, Sarabanda **Regla Kimbisa**	

NAME-OTHER Ficus, Benjamin fig, Weeping fig (CRC)

USES	Goes to Osain (Omiero)	(Nfinda)
	Used for Ebomisi and cleansings. The branches draw away Ayé	(LC)
	Leaves combat witchcraft (Brujeria)	(LC)
PALO	The tree is "FULL" of spirits, deities; much like the Ceiba	
	The Ewé and "palo" used to prepare the **Vititi-Mensu**	(LC)
PALO MONTE	Fundamental "palo" (Palo de fundamento) of Sarabanda	
	Used for ritual baths for the **Ngueyo** (initiate)	
ESPIRITU CRUZADO	ALL spirits can be invoked in this tree	
Candomblé	Used for the purification of sacred items and fetish of Exú	
Candomblé de Angola	**Aluvaiá** – Assento Eré Exú	
	Kavungo – Assento Okutá	

NOTE	**Vititi-Mensu**	Is the mirror of the Mayombero; where he can see the unseen.
	Ngueyo	An initiate in the Palo Monte religion (**AKA** New Pine)

NAME-Spanish   Lavanda, Alhucema, Espliego, Cantueso   (es.wikipidia)
    Owner
    Odun

NAME-SCIENTIFIC   *Lavandula angustifolia* Mill.   (CRC)

NAME-BRAZIL   Alfazema, Lavanda
    Candomblé de Angola Lembá
    Candomblé Ketu Obaluaiè
    CULTO DE NAÇÃO Iemanjá, Oxum
    Umbanda Iemanjá

NAME-Lucumí
    YORUBA   ÀRÙSÒ   (DeJagun)

NAME-CONGO

NAME-OTHER   English lavander   (USDA)
    Lavender, English lavender, Common lavender, True lavender   (CRC)

USES
    Medicinal
    Candomblé de Angola Used in love magics as a perfume
    Candomblé Ketu Used in all head cleansings (obrigações de cabeça).
        Used as incense and in love magics as a perfume
    Umbanda Ritual baths, incense, ritual oils and head cleansings
        (obrigações de cabeça)

NAME-CUBA   Lechuga, Lechuga arrepollada   (Roig)

      Owner   Ochún, Yemayá (LC, TDF2, Quiros, Menéndez)

      Odun   Odi-meji (Quiros)

NAME-SCIENTIFIC   *Lactuca sativa* L.   (Roig)

NAME-BRAZIL   Alface, Alfaces-repolhudas, Alfaces-romanas

      Candomblé Jêje-Nagô Oxum   Água/Feminino   (Barros)

      Candomblé de Angola Matamba

      Umbanda   Iansã

NAME-Lucumí   Ilénke, Oggó yeyé   (LC)

                      Ylénke, Oggo Yéyé, Ilenke, Oggó Yeyé   (TDF2)

      YORUBA   IRÚ ÈFÓ KAN   (jairoinglat)

NAME-CONGO

NAME-OTHER   Garden lettuce   (USDA)

                      Lettuce, Common lettuce, Garden Lettuce   (CRC)

USES

                      To refresh Ochún and Yemayá   (LC)

                      For home cleansings to drive away bad influences.

      Candomblé   To decorate the food offerings (Addimú) for Oxum, Logun Edé,

                              Oxumaré, etc.

      Umbanda   To decorate food offerings for Iansã

                      For cleansings of Egun (obrigações de Egun)

      Candomblé de Angola   For offerings to Eguns

      INDIA   Used in Unani and Siddha   (CRC)

NAME-CUBA	Lechuguilla, Lechuga Cimarrona	(Roig)
Owner	Yemayá, Eleggua (TDF2)	
	Yemayá, Ochún (Quiros, Menéndez)	
	Yemayá (Madan, Irizarry)	
	Yemayá, Olokun (Concordia)	
Odun	Irete-oturupon (Irizarry, Orula.org)	
	Obara-oturupon (Madan)	
	Odi-irosun (Concordia)	

NAME-SCIENTIFIC	*Pistia stratiotes* L.	(Roig)

NAME-BRAZIL	Alface-d'água, Erva-de-Santa-Luzia, Lentilha-d'água, Golfo	
Candomblé Jêje-Nagô	Oxum Água/Feminino	(Barros)
Umbanda	Iemanjá, Oxum Ervas Frias	

NAME-Lucumí	Ewé Oyouro	(Irizarry)
	Oyoro	(Quiros)
	Oyu-oro	(Concordia)
YORUBA	Ojú oró	(PV, CRC)

NAME-CONGO	Okula	(CRC)
PALO	**OWNER** Madre de Agua	

NAME-OTHER	Water lettuce	(USDA)
	Water Lettuce, Nile Cabbage, Nile Lettuce	(CRC)

USES	Goes to Osain (Omiero); specially for Yemayá	(Irizarry)
	Ritual baths (Ebomisi) and Inche Osain	
Candomblé	Great importance for Babalawo (Babalaôs) since it is one of the Ewé used to wash the divinatory shells	
Candomblé Jêje-Nagô	Used in the initiation rituals of the "filhos" of Oxum; as well as for other water Orixá (orixás das águas) such as Jemanjá, Nanã and Oiá.	
Umbanda	Used for cleansings, baths, Abô and head cleansings.	
INDIA	Used in Ayurveda and Unani	(CRC)

NAME-CUBA	Lengua de Vaca, Piel de majá, Sanseviera	(Roig)
Owner	Eleggua (TDF2, Menéndez)	
	Obatalá, Oggún (Quiros, Irizarry)	
	Changó, Eleggua, Ochosi (Diaz)	
Odun	Obara-meji, Obara-ose, Ose-obara (Diaz)	

NAME-SCIENTIFIC   *Sansevieria hyacinthoides* (L.) Druce; Sansevieria *guineensis* (L.) Willd.   (Roig)

NAME-BRAZIL   Espada-de-São-Jorge, Espada-de-Ogum, Espada-de-Santa-Barbara
- **Candomblé Jêje-Nagô** Ogum   Terra/Masculino   (Barros)
- **Candomblé de Angola** Inkosse, Matamba
- **CULTO DE NAÇÃO**   Ogum – **Verde**   Iansã – **Verde e Amarela**
- **Umbanda**   Ogum, Exú – **Verde**   Iansã – **Verde e Amarela**

NAME-BRAZIL   Lança-de-São-Jorge   *Sansevieria cylindrica* **Bojer ex Hook.**
- **CULTO DE NAÇÃO**   Ogum
- **Umbanda**   Ogum, Exú

NAME-Lucumí	Wé Wé	(TDF2)
	Ewé Wewe	(Irizarry, Madan)
YORUBA	Ojá kòríkò, Ojá ìkòokò, Pàsán kòríkò,	
	Agbomolówóibi *Sansevieria liberica* **Gérôme & Labroy** (PV, CRC)	
NAME-CONGO	Ilanga la ngovi	*Sansevieria liberica* **Gérôme & Labroy** (CRC)

NAME-OTHER	Iguana Tail	(USDA)
	African bowstring hemp	(CRC)

USES   **DOES NOT** go to Osain (Omiero)
Planted for protection and against evil eye. Used to calm indiscrete tongues.
- **Candomblé Jêje-Nagô** although it belongs to Ogum it can be used for Oxossi, Ossaim, Iansã and Jemanjá. To consecrate religious objects
- **Umbanda/Candomblé** Protection for the home and the removal of the evil eye
- **Candomblé de Angola** **Inkosse**   Head cleansings (obrigações no Orí)
- **Matamba**   Leaves funfamental for Initiation cleansings
- **INDIA**   Used in Ayurveda   (CRC)

NAME-CUBA	Limo de Mar, Algas	(LC)
	Alga Sensitiva, Lechuga de Mar	(Roig)
Owner	Yemayá (LC, TDF2, Quiros)	
	Eleggua, Oggún, Osún, Yemayá, Olokun (Irizarry)	
Odun	Oyeku-meji (Quiros, Orula.org)	
	Ogunda-irosun (Irizarry)	

NAME-SCIENTIFIC	*Ulva lactuca* Linnaeus	(Roig)
	Anadyomene stellata (Wulfen) C.Agardh	(Roig)

NAME-BRAZIL	Alface-do-mar, Algas

NAME-Lucumí	Ewé Olokún	(LC, TDF2)
YORUBA	KORÍKO ETÍ ÒKUN	
	(***Macrocystis pyrifera* (Linnaeus) C.Agardh** -Alga Marinha/Giant Kelp)	

NAME-CONGO	
PALO	Nfita Kalunga
OWNER	Madre Agua, Mamá Chola

NAME-OTHER	Sea Lettuce	(USDA)

USES

Used as Ebbó, and Inche Osain	(Irizarry)
To sweeten Yemayá and make her happy	(LC)

Hoodoo/Root Magic (USA) Agar-Agar is the name applied to several mucilaginous seaweeds and their products. In the whole form is called Sea Spirit. It is used for: To protect against unsettled or Evil Spirits; for Semi-Invisibility (being unnoticed) and for Lucky hands for gambling.

NOTE	Taxonomic information from AlgaeBase
	See: **http://www.algaebase.org/search/species/**

NAME-CUBA	Limo de Río	**See NOTE**	(LC)
	Lino de Río		(Roig)
Owner	Ochún (LC, Quiros)		
	Ochún, Ochosi (TDF2)		
	Ochún, Eleggua, Osún (Irizarry)		
	Ochún, Yemayá (Menéndez)		
Odun	Oyeku-iwori (Irizarry, Quiros, Orula.org)		
	Irete-owonrin (Madan, Quiros, Orula.org)		
NAME-SCIENTIFIC	*Potamogeton lucens* L.		(Roig)
NAME-BRAZIL	NOT found in Flora do Brasil		
NAME-Lucumí	Imo, Oshún, Ewe Odo		(LC)
	Ymo Oshún, Ewe Odo, Imó, Imochún, Iti ibú		(TDF2)
YORUBA			
NAME-CONGO			
PALO	Nfita Masa Lango		
	OWNER	Mamá Chola	
NAME-OTHER	Shinning Pondweed		(CRC)
USES	Goes to Osain (Omiero)		(LC)
	To make Ochún happy and garner favors from Ochún		

NOTE   Although Lydia Cabrera and Juan Tomas Roig name the same plant, the description by J. T. Roig **DOES NOT** match the plant named. The plant that has the highest probability is ***Spirogyra porticalis*** **(O.F.Müller) Dumortier** which is commonly called **Water silk** or **Mermaid's tresses (See 2nd photo)** Taxonomic information from AlgaeBase

See: **http://www.algaebase.org/search/species/**

NAME-CUBA	Limón, Limón Persa, Limón agrio, Limonero silvestre	(Roig)
	Limón Criollo, Lima criolla, Lima de Rangpur **See NOTE**	(Roig)
Owner	Ochún (TDF)	
	Oggún, Orishanlá (Irizarry)	
Odun	Oyeku-meji, Ogunda-meji (Irizarry)	

NAME-SCIENTIFIC	*Citrus limon* (L.) Osbeck;	
	Citrus × limonia Osbeck	(Roig, Barros)
	Citrus aurantiifolia (Christm.) Swingle	(Roig, PV)

NAME-BRAZIL	Limão, Limoeiro, Lima-acida, Limão-verde, Limão-verdadeiro	
Candomblé Jêje-Nagô	Orumilá, Ossaim Terra/Feminino	(Barros)
Candomblé de Angola	Inkosse - **Limão Bravo**	
CULTO DE NAÇÃO	Ogum - **Limão Vermelho, Bravo ou Cravo** **See NOTE**	
Umbanda	Xangô Ogum - **Limão Vermelho, Bravo ou Cravo**	

NAME-Lucumí	Oróco, Oromboueré	(LC)
	Oróco, Oromboueué, Olómbo	(TDF2)
	Orombo, Orombó nikan	(TDF)
YORUBA	Òsàn wéwé, Òrombó wéwé, Ìlèmú, Ewé ìlèmú, Ewé órónbó wéwé,	
	Gàn-ín gàn-ín wéwé, Osàn gìngìn	(PV, CRC)

NAME-CONGO	Koronko, Kiángana	(LC)
	Koronko	(TDF)
	Londjimo, Malimbungo, N'ndjimo *Citrus aurantiifolia*	(CRC)
PALO	Kiángana	

NAME-OTHER	*Citrus limon* Lemon	(USDA)
	Lemon, Persian Lime	
	Citrus aurantiifolia Key lime	(USDA)
	Key lime, Common lime, Indian lime, Mexican lime	(CRC)

USES

Used as ritual baths (Ebomisi) and food offerings (Addimu)
Medicinal

PALO   It is used to dominate or hex someone. It can be used for very dark/maleficent hexes/witchcraft (bilongos)

Candomblé   Used as medicinal as well as in dark/maleficent witchcraft (utilizado por feiticeiros para fazer diversos malefícios)

Umbanda   Used in ritual baths, as incense, in ABÔS and in head cleansings (obrigações de cabeça)

Candomblé de Angola   Ritual baths, ABÔS and head cleansings (obrigações no Orí)

Hoodoo/Root Magic (USA)   Used against the evil eye, in cleansing and clearing spells to separate a person from past ties.

INDIA   *Citrus limon*   Used in Ayurveda and Unani   (CRC)

Citrus aurantiifolia   Used in Ayurveda, Unani and Siddha. Magico-religious beliefs: linked with the belief that limes drive evil spirits away; chew the leaf and bespatter the face of the bewitched who sees ghosts in his sleep.   (CRC)

NOTE   Both lemon species are VERY common in Cuba and used interchangeably.

NOTE   **Limão Vermelho, Bravo ou Cravo**   This is a variety of lemon that is called Rangpur in Brazil which is a cross between the lemon and a mandarin, but very acidic. See: **https://en.wikipedia.org/wiki/Rangpur_(fruit)**

NAME-CUBA		Lirio, Frangipani, Alelí, Lirio de Costa, Lirio Dulce,		
		Lirio de Sábana, Lirio de Sierra, Lirio de Montaña		(Roig)
		Lirio	**See NOTE**	(LC)
		Lirio, Lirio Blanco, Alelí Blanco, Súcheli Blanco		(TDF)
	Owner	Obatalá (LC, TDF, TDF2, Quiros)		
	Odun	Okanran-osa (Quiros, Orula.org)		

NAME-SCIENTIFIC   *Plumeria* Sp.; *Plumeria rubra* L.   (Roig)

NAME-BRAZIL		Jasmim-manga, Frangipani, Árvore-pagode, Plumelia		
	Candomblé Jêje-Nagô	Oxossi	Terra/Masculino	(Barros)
	Candomblé de Angola	Lembá		
	CULTO DE NAÇÃO	Oxossi		

NAME-Lucumí		Peregún fún fún, Merefé, Osumare	(LC, TDF2)
		Itana-fun	(TDF)
	YORUBA	ÈWÉ ITÉTÉ	(Barros)

NAME-CONGO		Tunkanso	(LC)
		Tukanso	(TDF)
	PALO	Tunkanso	

NAME-OTHER		Templetree	(USDA)
		Frangipani, Plumeria	(Elsevier)

USES			
		It is good against witchcraft (arranca bilongo)	(LC)
	Candomblé Jêje-Nagô	Initiation rituals, purification baths	
	Candomblé de Angola	Head cleansings (obrigações no Orí)	
	CULTO DE NAÇÃO	Ornamental	
	INDIA	Used in Ayurveda	(CRC)

NOTE   While Lydia Cabrera fails to name a tree species, Teodoro Díaz Fabelo does
name a tree species that matches with possible species called Lirio
in Cuba by Juan Tomás Roig. (as well as in Brazil)

NAME-CUBA	Llantén		(Roig)
Owner	Ochún (LC, Diaz, Madan)		
	Obatalá (TDF2, Irizarry)		
	Odudúa (Quiros, Menéndez)		
Odun	Okanran-meji (Quiros, Diaz, Madan, Orula.org)		

NAME-SCIENTIFIC	*Plantago major* L.		(Roig)

NAME-BRAZIL	Tanchagem, Transagem, Orelha-de-veado, Tachã		
Candomblé Jêje-Nagô	Obaluaiè	Terra/Masculino	(Barros)
Candomblé Ketu	Ogum		
Candomblé de Angola	Inkosse		
Umbanda	Ogum		

NAME-Lucumí

YORUBA	EWÉ ÒPÁ	(Barros)

NAME-CONGO

NORTH AFRICA	Massasah, Mesaisa	(CRC)

NAME-OTHER	Common plantain	(USDA)
	Broad leaf plantain, Common plantain, White man's foot	(CRC)
	Gwo Bannann, Plantain Grann Fèy (Creole Haiti)	(Duke's)

USES	Goes to Osain (Omiero)	
	Used in ritual baths (Ebomisi), Inche Osain and Paraldo	
	Medicinal	
PALO MONTE	Used for the removal of tears (Nyoro – Secar la Lágrima)	
Candomblé Jêje-Nagô	Used in purification baths for "filhos" of Obaluaiè, as well as for those of Nanã and Oxumarê	(Barros)
Candomblé de Angola	Assento Okutá, ritual baths, Abô and head cleansings	
Candomblé Ketu	Ritual baths, Abô and head cleansings (banhos, Abô, obrigações de cabeça)	
Umbanda	Ritual baths, Abô and head cleansings (banhos, Abô, obrigações de cabeça)	
Hoodoo/Root Magic (USA)	Protects against Snakes, Thieves and Fever	
INDIA	Used in Ayurveda, Unani and Siddha	(CRC)

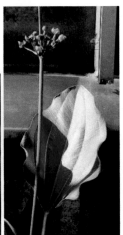

NAME-CUBA	Llantén Cimarrón, Llantén de Agua		(Roig)
Owner	Ochún (LC, TDF2, Quiros)		
Odun			

NAME-SCIENTIFIC	*Echinodorus grisebachii* Small		(Roig)
	Echinodorus grandiflorus (Cham. & Schltdl.) Micheli		(Barros)

NAME-BRAZIL	Chapéu-de-couro, Chá-da-campana, Erva-do-pântano, Erva-de-brejo		
Candomblé Jêje-Nagô	Oxalá	Água/Feminino	(Barros)
Candomblé de Angola	Lembá		
Candomblé	Oxumarê		
Umbanda	Iemanjá, Omolú		

NAME-Lucumí	Checheré	(LC, TDF2)
YORUBA	EWÉ ŞÉ$ÉRÉ	(Barros)

NAME-CONGO

NAME-OTHER	*Echinodorus grisebachii*	Burhead	(forestryimages.org)
	Amazon Sword plant		(Wikipidia)
	Echinodorus grandiflorus	Florida burhead (florida.plantatlas.usf.edu)	

USES		
	Medicinal	
Candomblé	Purification baths	
Candomblé de Angola	Abô (Omiero)	
Umbanda	Baths to ward off the evil eye	

NAME-CUBA	Llerén, Leirén, Lleren, Yerén, Llerenes	(Roig)
Owner	Ochún (LC, TDF2, Quiros)	
Odun	Irete-osa (Quiros, Orula.org)	
NAME-SCIENTIFIC	*Calathea allouia* (Aubl.) Lindl.	(Roig)
NAME-BRAZIL	Ariá, Láirem	(Duke's)
NAME-Lucumí	Yeren	(TDF2)
YORUBA		
NAME-CONGO		
NAME-OTHER	Llerenes	(USDA)
	Guinea arrowroot, Sweet corn-root, Leren	(Duke's)
USES		
	Medicinal	

NAME-CUBA	Maboa, Maboa común, Maboa blanca, Maboa de loma	(Roig)
Owner	Obatalá, Oggún (LC, Quiros)	
	Obatalá (TDF2)	
Odun		
NAME-SCIENTIFIC	*Cameraria latifolia* L.	(Roig)
NAME-BRAZIL	NOT found in Flora do Brasil	
NAME-Lucumí YORUBA	Léchu ibayé	(LC, TDF2)
NAME-CONGO	Melembe	(LC)
NAME-OTHER	Savanna Poison wood, Savanna white poison wood;	
	Palo de Leche (DR); Ayitye, Bwa lèt (Creole Haiti)	(Elsevier)
USES		
	Medicinal	
PALO	To make poisons	(LC)

NAME-CUBA	Madreselva	(Roig, LC)
	Madreselva, Madreselva Criolla, Madreselva Americana	(Roig)
Owner	Oddúa (Quiros)	
Odun		

NAME-SCIENTIFIC	*Lonicera japonica* Thunb.		(Roig, LC)
	Lonicera confusa DC.	**See NOTE**	(Roig)

NAME-BRAZIL	Madressilva
Candomblé	Oxum
Umbanda	Oxum

NAME-Lucumí
   YORUBA

NAME-CONGO

NAME-OTHER	*Lonicera japonica*	Japanese honeysuckle	(USDA)
		Honeysuckle, Japanese Honeysuckle	(CRC)
	Lonicera confusa	Honeysuckle	(USDA)

USES	Goes to Osain (Omiero)	(LC)
	Used for ritual baths (Ebomisi), ritual cleansings (Sarayéyé)	(LC)
Candomblé	Used for ritual baths	
Umbanda	Ritual baths and as incense (defumação)	

NOTE   Juan Tomás Roig notes that the first (***Lonicera japonica***) only has two flowers per axilla; whereas the second (***Lonicera confusa***) has up to six flowers.

NAME-CUBA	Magüey, Magüey de coquí, Magüey de cocuy, Pita	(Roig)
Owner	Yemayá (LC, TDF2, Quiros)	
NAME-SCIENTIFIC	*Furcraea hexapetala* (Jacq.) Urb.;	
	Furcraea cubensis (Jacq.) Vent.	(Roig)
	Agave americana L. **See NOTE**	(Roig, Barros)
NAME-BRAZIL	Pita, Piteira, Babosa-brava, Gravatá-açu, Agave, Caraotá-açu	
Candomblé Jêje-Nagô	Ossaim, Omolu, Tempo Terra/Masculino	(Barros)
Candomblé de Angola	Katendê	
NAME-Lucumí	Ikeri	(LC)
	Ikerí	(TDF2)
YORUBA		
NAME-CONGO		
NAME-OTHER	*Furcraea hexapetala* Cuban Hemp	(USDA)
	Silk grass (Jamaica); Pitre (Haiti)	(Elsevier)
	Agave Americana American century plant	(USDA)
	Agave, American agave, Century plant	(CRC)
USES	Medicinal	
PALO	Very good at doing bad.	
	Fish and turtles will say "kikiribú" (i.e. die) when a Magüey	
	falls into the river.	(LC)
Candomblé Jêje-Nagô	Is common practice to put Addimu in the Ifá sign	
	of Obará at the foot of a VERY large Piteira in a night	
	with a full moon with the purpose to acquire money	
	and prosperity in a business.	(Barros)
Candomblé de Angola	Baths and head cleansings (obrigações no Orí)	
INDIA	*Agave Americana* Used in Ayurveda, Unani and Siddha	(CRC)
NOTE	Both of these plants are listed as Magüey by Juan Tomás Roig	

NAME-CUBA	Maíz, Maíz blanco, Maíz dulce		(Roig)
Owner	All Orisha (LC, TDF2, Diaz, Madan)		
	Orishaoko (Quiros)		
	Eggun, Eleggua, Orishaoko, Oggún, Ochosi, Osun, Yemayá, Orunmila (Irizarry)		
Odun	Oturupon-odi (Quiros, Diaz, Irizarry, Madan, Orula.org)		
	Obara-oturupon, Okanran-owonrin (Quiros, Diaz, Irizarry, Orula.org)		

NAME-SCIENTIFIC	*Zea mays* L.	(Roig)

NAME-BRAZIL	Milho, Milho-branco, Milho-vermelho, Milho-alho		
Candomblé Jêje-Nagô	Ogum, Oxossi, Xangô, Iemanjá, Oxalá Terra/Masculino		(Barros)
Candomblé de Angola	Inkosse, Mutalumbô, Matamba, Vunge		
Candomblé Ketu	Oxossi, Oxalá, Ogum, Iemanjá, Xangô		
Candomblé Jêje	Dandalunda		
Candomblé	Ogum, Oxossi		
Umbanda	Oxossi, Caboclos		

NAME-Lucumí	Agguádo, Abáddo, Oká		(LC, TDF2)
	Ewe Echín	**Maloja**	(LC)
	Echín	**Maloja**	(TDF2)
YORUBA	Àgbàdo, Ìgbàdo, Okà, Yangan, Erinigbado, Erinkà,		
	Eginrin àgbàdo, Elépèè, Ìjèéré		(PV, CRC)
NAME-CONGO	Masango		(LC)
	Sambia futo, Masango		(TDF)
	Lele, Masongo	**Tusa de Maíz**	(TDF)

NAME-OTHER	Corn, American Indian corn, Indian corn	(CRC)

USES	Goes to Osain (Omiero)-the roasted corn kernels	
	Roasted corn kernels **NECESSARY** for all Omiero	
	Medicinal	
	Leaves	Ebomisi, Paraldo, Ebó
	Roots, Leaves, Corn	Inche Osain

	Corn	Inche Osain, Addimu
	Husk	Ebó
Addimu	Roasted corn in cob	Babalú-Ayé
	Roasted corn kernels	Eleggua, Oggún, Ochosi
	Corn cob cut in pieces	Ochún, Yemayá
	Maíz Finado	Yemayá, Olokun
	Popcorn	All orisha, specially Obatalá, and Ibeyis
Candomblé	Àgbàdo funfun – Milho branco	Oxalá and all other Orixá
	Àgbàdo pupa – Milho vermelho	Exú, Ogum, Oxossi, Logun Edé, Obá
	Àgbàdo kékeré – Milho alho	Obaluaiè, Nanã, Oxum
	Corn on the cob w/ leaves	Oxossi, Xangô
	Leaves used for **Omi-Eró** (Omiero) for prosperity and Exú	
Candomblé	Milho Vermelho is **Èwó of Oxossi, Ossaim**	
	Milho derivados (fubá, etc) is **Èwó of Oxossi**	
	Milho pipoca (popcorn) is **Èwó of Obaluaiè, Oxumarê**	
Candomblé Jêje	Milho Vermelho is **Èwó of Odé/Oxossi**	
	Milho derivados (fubá, etc) is **Èwó of Odé/Oxossi**	
	Milho pipoca (popcorn) is **Èwó of Bessém/Oxumarê**	
ODUN (PV)	Iwori-ofun	Leaves to bring good luck
	Ogbe-oturupon	deals with the birth of children
	Ose-meji	Corn cob used to come out victorious in a fight/problem
	Ose-otura	To get protection FROM Exú
	Ejiogbe-otura	Roasted corn kernels to make legal problems go away
Candomblé/Umbanda	Corn used as Addimu in various forms of food that are offered to the Orixá. The leaves, stalks, corn silk used for ritual baths, cleansings, the cleaning/sacramentation of different Orixá. Corn is used to attract prosperity and good luck.	
Candomblé de Angola	**Inkosse**	Corn hung at the entrance of the Axé
	Mutalumbô	the grains for food for the Orixá
	Matamba	the cooked ear offered to the Orixá
	Vunge	**Èwó for filhos of Ogum;** roasted over charcoal
	and used in Apanan Erê	
Umbanda	Corn meal (fubá de milho) is **Èwó of Oxossi**	
	Red and green corn (milho vemelho, milho verde) is **Èwó of Oxossi**	

NOTE   Story of **Changó** being the **first to grind corn** into cornmeal by both Lydia Cabrera and José Flavio Pessoa de Barros
- In one of his many travels, Changó was able to get a bag of corn from some travelers not native to Africa. Being hungry, he opened the bag, took out some corn and ground it into cornmeal, which he ate. Once he arrived to the lands of the **Tákua**, he taught them to eat the ground cornmeal. With this, he converted corn to the gold of the land of the **Tákua**.

Tákua	Tapa or T'kua	(LC)
Xangô -Tápà	He is of Nupê origin (another name for the Tapas); he is the third Aláàfin Oyo (emperor of the medieval empire of Oyo)	(PV)

NAME-CUBA	Majagua, Majagua colorada, Majagua hembra	(Roig)
	Majagua, Majagua Azul, Majagua prieta	(Roig)
Owner	Yemayá, Oggún (LC, Quiros, Madan)	
	Yemayá (TDF2)	
	Yemayá, Changó (Diaz)	
	Eleggua (Irizarry)	
Odun	Oturupon-ika, Otura-irosun, Okanran-ofun	
	(Quiros, Diaz, Irizarry, Madan, Orula.org)	
NAME-SCIENTIFIC	*Hibiscus tilliaceus* L.;	
	Pariti tiliaceum (L.) A. St.-Hil.	(LC, Roig)
	Hibiscus elatus Sw.	(Roig)
NAME-BRAZIL	NOT found in Flora do Brasil	
NAME-Lucumí YORUBA	Musenguené, Gúsinga, Musinga	(TDF2)
NAME-CONGO	Musenguené, Gúsinga, Musinga	(LC)

NAME-OTHER	*Hibiscus tilliaceus*	Sea Hibiscus	(USDA)
	Sea Rose-mallow (US); Najagua (PR); Demajagua (DR);		
	Gran maho, Koton maho (Creole Haiti)		(Elsevier)
	Hibiscus elatus	Mahoe	(USDA)
	Blue Mahoe, Linden Hibiscus (US); Majagua (DR, Vzla);		
	Majó (PR); Maho ble (Creole Haiti)		(Elsevier)

USES	Goes to Osain (Omiero)
	Used for ritual baths (Ebomisi) and Inche Osain
	Medicinal
PALO	Used to silence the tongue of indiscreet people
	The fibers of the tree for binding spells NOT easily broken

NAME-CUBA	Malá		(Roig)
SPANISH	Espinazo del Diablo, Mala Madre, Aranto		
Owner	Oddúa, Obatalá (Diaz)		
Odun	Ejiogbe-meji, Ofun-meji (Diaz)		

NAME-SCIENTIFIC	*Kalanchoe delagoensis* Eckl. & Zeyh.;		
	Kalanchoe tubiflora (Harv.) Raym.-Hamet		(Roig)
	Kalanchoe daigremontiana Raym.-Hamet & H. Perrier		(Diaz, Barros)

NAME-BRAZIL	Mae-de-milhares, Aranto, Fortuna-serralha		
Candomblé	Exú	Água/Feminino	
Umbanda			

NAME-Lucumí			
YORUBA	Òdundún Odò	(***Kalanchoe daigremontiana***)	

NAME-CONGO

NAME-OTHER	***Kalanchoe delagoensis***	Chandelier plant	(USDA)
	Kalanchoe daigremontiana	Devil's backbone	(USDA)

USES	Goes to Osain (Omiero)	(Diaz)
	Ritual baths (Ebomisi) and cleansings	(Diaz)
Candomblé	For cleansings	

NAME-CUBA	Malacara, Jazminillo, Jazminillo de Costa, Lagaña de Aura	(Roig)
Owner	Changó (TDF2)	
	Mayombe (TDF)	
Odun	Irosun-odi (Quiros)	
	Ogunda-odi (Madan)	
NAME-SCIENTIFIC	*Plumbago zeylanica* L.;	
	Plumbago scandens L.	(Roig)
NAME-BRAZIL	NOT found in Flora do Brasil	
NAME-Lucumí	Mubino	(LC, TDF2)
YORUBA	Ìnábìrì, Ìnábìí	(PV, CRC)
NAME-CONGO	Malacara	(TDF)
PALO		
NAME-OTHER	Wild leadwort	(USDA)
	Ceylon leadwort, White leadwort, White-flowered leadwort	(CRC)
USES		
	Much used in matters of divorces	
	Used to cause quarrels and trouble	(LC)
	Medicinal	
INDIA	Used in Ayurveda, Unani and Siddha.	
	Magico-religious beliefs: for general debility in children a piece	
	of root tied on the neck	(CRC)

NAME-CUBA	Malanga, Malanga Amarilla, Malanga Blanca,	
	Malanga Morada, Yautía, Guagüí	(Roig)
Owner	Yemayá (LC)	
	Ochún (LC) **Malanga Amarilla**	
	Yemayá (TDF2, Concordia, Quiros)	
	Yemayá, Ochún (TDF, Menéndez)	
	Yemayá, Orishaoko (Madan)	
	All Orisha (Diaz)	
	Orula, Yemayá, Olokun, Orishaoko (Irizarry)	
Odun	Owonrin-ogbe (Irizarry, Quiros, Orula.org)	
	Ejiogbe-owonrin (Diaz, Madan)	

NAME-SCIENTIFIC	*Xanthosoma sagittifolium* (L.) Schott	(Roig)

NAME-BRAZIL	Taioba, Macabo, Mangará, Mangará-mirim		
Candomblé Jêje-Nagô	Oxossi, Iemanjá, Logun Edé	Água/Feminino	(Barros)
Candomblé de Angola	Inkosse, Zaze		
CULTO DE NAÇÃO	Oxossi, Erinlé, Iemanjá		
Umbanda	Oxossi, Jemanjá		

NAME-Lucumí	Ikoku, Marababo		(LC, TDF2)
	Okoku, Ikoko, Marabado		(TDF)
YORUBA	Kókò àrìrà òjà	**(*Xanthosoma Sp.*)**	(PV)
	Ewé Kókò		(Barros)

NAME-CONGO	Nkumbia, Mbi nkanda, Gánkua	(LC)
	Mbi nkanda, Gankua nti	(TDF)
PALO	Nkumbia	

NAME-OTHER	Arrowleaf elephant's ear	(USDA)
	Black Malanga, Blue Taro, Danchi	(CRC)

USES	**DOES NOT** go to Osain (Omiero)	
	Extensively used in all the religion since it removes problems	**See NOTE**
	With the leaf, the rights are paid, and Ebbó is done	
	It is **taboo (Èwó)** to the followers (hijos/hijas) of Oyá	

PALO   **Regla Kimbisa del Santo Cristo del Buen Viaje**   It is used to do bad; and it is **taboo (Èwó)** for **ALL its followers.**   (LC)

Candomblé de Angola   Inkosse   Honey put at the foot of the Taro plant in order to ease the situation in Ile Axé

                    Zaze   Prepare Ebô for Ibeije

Candomblé   **Èwó of Obá**; also, Candomblé practitioners should avoid it because it is an **Èwó of Nanã Buruquê**

Umbanda   The leaves are used for religious cooking (Addimu) for Xangô, whereas the tubers are only used as Ebô
Èwó of Nanã

OTHER   Magico-religious beliefs: rituals, ceremonial   (CRC)

NOTE   In **the Odun Oddi (7)**, the saying is "This is where the first burial took place" (Donde por primera vez se hizo un entierro)

PATAKI

- Orula had a wife that no longer wanted to be with him, so she went to live with Osain. Osain who is knowledgeable in the matters to do with plants, told her that he would make a "drink" that would mimic death. The reason for this was at that time, the dead were not buried but left at the foot of Iroko so that their spirit could rise and be with the other spirits. She agreed, and when her body was placed under Iroko, Osain cam and gave her the antidote. Together then they moved to another town where she would tend the plant stand in the marketplace. One day Orula needed some okra for and Ebbó, so he sent his oldest child to the next town to get it since Osain was the only one with okra. When he got to the market, he immediately recognized his mother, but she said she did not know him. Once he got home, he told his father, Orula. But Orula did not believe him. The next week Orula needed to do another Ebbó with okra, so he decided to go himself. Once he got to the market, he recognized his wife. She, seeing Orula, fell dead immediately. Osain seeing his wife dead started fighting with Orula. The commotion was so great that Olofi came down to see what was happening. Hearing the story from Orula, Olofi declared that from that moment on, all the dead would be buried in order to make sure they were dead. From this first grave rose a plant; the Malanga, **Ewe Ikoko**. This plant was considered to be the reincarnation of the dead woman and that it was infused with the Aché to remove all negativity and represent rebirth. The three tips of the leaves represent the most difficult and prevalent **Osogbos** (misfortunes) in life; **Eyó** (litigation or acusations), **Arayé** (chaos and arguments) and **Ikú** (death). Hence, in order for the plant to provide its healing Aché, these three tips must be removed.   (Concordia)

NAME-CUBA	Malanga Isleña, Calalú	(Roig)
Owner		
Odun		

NAME-SCIENTIFIC	*Colocasia esculenta* (L.) Schott	(Roig)

NAME-BRAZIL   Inhame, Inhame-branco, Inhame-de-São-Tomé, Taro

Candomblé Jêje-Nagô	Oxum, Nanã	Água/Feminino	(Barros)
Candomblé de Angola	Inkosse, Zaze		
CULTO DE NAÇÃO	Nanã, Oxum, Obá, Oxumarê, Yewá		
Umbanda	Oxalá, Ogum		

NAME-Lucumí

YORUBA	Kókò, Kókò ebo, Kókò funfun, Kókò pupa, Isu kókò, Kókò efúe	(PV, CRC)
	Ewé BÀLÁ	(Barros)

NAME-CONGO	Bifumu, Igitiga, Itiko pele, Madekere gw'elwishi, Ngundu	(CRC)

NAME-OTHER	Cocoyam	(USDA)
	Arrow Leaf, Taro, Black Taro, Dasheen, Cocoyam, Yam	(CRC)

USES

Candomblé Jêje-Nagô   Food offerings for Nanã (Latipá) and Oxum (Efó); but prohibited to the "filhos" of Obá because of the dispute between Obá and Oxum over Xangô.

Candomblé de Angola **Inkosse**   Honey put at the foot of the Taro plant in order to ease the situation in Ile Axé (religious center/congregation)

                    Zaze   leaves used in the initiation (assento **Axé**)

Candomblé   **Èwó of Ogum, Jemanjá**

Umbanda   The leaves are offered as a food offering (Latipá) to Nanã and (Efó) to Oxum; the tubers are used as Ebô and offerings to the Orixá **Èwó of Obá.**

NOTE **Axé**   Means energy, force, power. That which is imparted during any religious work In Spanish is "**Aché**". See: **https://pt.wikipedia.org/wiki/Axé**

NAME-CUBA	Malanguilla, Malanga Cimarrona		(Roig)
	Sacu-Sacu, **Malanguilla**	**See NOTE**	(LC)
Owner	Inlé, Osain (LC)		
	Yemayá (TDF2, Quiros)		
	Inlé, Ochún (Diaz)		
Odun	Oturupon-odi (Diaz)		
NAME-SCIENTIFIC	*Xanthosoma cubense* (Schott) Schott		(Roig, LC)
NAME-BRAZIL	DOES NOT occur in Brazil per Flora do Brasil		
NAME-Lucumí			
ANAGO	Ewe koko	**Malanguilla**	(LC)
YORUBA	Kókò àrìrà òjà	***Xanthosoma spp.***	(PV)
NAME-CONGO			
NAME-OTHER	NO common name found. Native to Cuba		
	Cimarron Taro		(biomedres.us)
USES	**DOES NOT** go to Osain (Omiero)		
PALO	Used by Mayombero since with this "palo"		
	the **Nfumbe** (the spirit that inhibit the ritualized		
	bones in the Nganga) will not leave the Nganga		(LC)
	Used for love matters		(LC)

NOTE   Lydia Cabrera only mentions the name/names of this Ewe. This listing is from her name "Malanguilla" which is listed by Juan Tomás Roig.

NOTE   Although Lydia Cabrera uses the names of these plants interchangeably, they have been separated. Sacu-Sacu and Malanguilla under their own listings

NOTE   Per Kew Science, ***Xanthosoma cubense* (Schott) Schott** native range is Cuba.

NAME-CUBA   Malva Blanca, Malva   (Roig)
    Owner   Obatalá (LC, TDF2, Diaz, Quiros, Madan, Irizarry)
    Odun   Irosun-ejiogbe, Oturupon-ogunda (Diaz, Quiros, Madan, Irizarry, Orula.org)

NAME-SCIENTIFIC   *Waltheria indica* L.; *Waltheria americana* L.   (Roig)
    Sida cordifolia L.   **See NOTE**   (Roig, Barros)

NAME-BRAZIL   Malva-branca, Malva-veludo, Guaxima
    Candomblé Jêje-Nagô   Oxalá   Ar/Feminino   (Barros)
    Batuque de Rio Grande do Sul Xapanã   (Barros)
    Candomblé   Oxalá, Iemanjá, Oxum, Oxossi, Erinlé   Ar/Feminino/èró
    Umbanda   Oxalá, Iemanjá

NAME-Lucumí   Lánlá, Dede fún   (LC, TDF2)
    YORUBA   Erokosunkasi, Ekuru, Olorun kunmi lefun, Wara wara odan,
        Opa emere, Korikodi, Opa abiku, Agamago   (CRC)
    Èkuru oko   (*Sida cordifolia*)   (PV)
NAME-CONGO   Dubue   (LC)
    Malembe   (TDF)

NAME-OTHER   *Waltheria indica*   Uhaloa   (USDA)
    Marshmallow, Velvet leaf   (CRC)
    Sida cordifolia   'Ilima   (USDA)
    Country mallow, White burr   (CRC)

USES   Goes to Osain (Omiero)
    Cleansing baths (Ebomisi)
    Ceremony of Abikú   (Irizarry)
    For Babalú-Ayé rituals and ceremonies   (Quiros)
    Medicinal
    Candomblé   Purification baths for everyone, but mainly to those Orixá
    associated with Oxalá; i.e.: Jemanjá, Oxum and Oxossi

NOTE   Both of these plants are listed by Juan Tomás Roig as Malva Blanca.

NAME-CUBA		Malva de Cochino, Malva de Puerco, Malva	(Roig)
	Owner	Oya (Diaz)	
		Ifá (Madan)	
	Odun	Oyeku-ose (Diaz, Quiros, Madan, Orula.org)	

NAME-SCIENTIFIC	*Sida rhombifolia* L.	(Roig)

NAME-BRAZIL		Vassourinha-de-relógio, Mata-pasto, Malva-preta, Guanxuma	
	Candomblé Jêje-Nagô	Oxum	Água/Feminino/Gùn	(Barros)
	Candomblé Ketu	Exú		
	Candomblé de Angola	Aluvaiá, Inkosse		
	CULTO DE NAÇÃO	Oxum, Ogum, Exú, Oxossi		
	Umbanda	Omolú, Exú		

NAME-Lucumí			
	YORUBA	Ifin, Ewé ifin	(PV, CRC)

NAME-CONGO	Akisingolezi, Ekisingorosi, Kanjunju, Kitoito, Mundundu	(CRC)

NAME-OTHER	Cuban Jute	(USDA)
	Arrow-leaf Sida, Broomstick, Broom-weed	(CRC)

USES		Goes to Osain (Omiero)	(Diaz)
		Used for cleansing of the home	
	Candomblé Jêje-Nagô	Much used for cleansings – personal and home	
	Candomblé Ketu	Cleansings of the home	
	Candomblé de Angola	**Aluvaiá**	Cleansings to increase wealth
		Inkosse	Cleansings, head cleansings
	Umbanda	Ritual baths, cleansings and Abô (Omiero)	
	INDIA	Used in Ayurveda and Siddha. Plant with magical properties, against possession by spirits, and to subside fever due to evil spirits; magico-religious beliefs, people use to pray to the tree with some offerings (CRC)	

NAME-CUBA	Malva Té, Malva, Té de la Tierra	(Roig)
Owner	Ochún (LC)	
	Ochún, Chango (TDF2, Madan)	
	Ochún, Agayú (TDF)	
	Changó (Quiros, Irizarry)	
	Agayú (Diaz)	
	Changó, Agayú (Menéndez)	
Odun	Irosun-owonrin, Odi-ogunda (Diaz, Madan, Quiros, Orula.org)	
NAME-SCIENTIFIC	*Corchorus siliquosus* L.	(Roig)
NAME-BRAZIL	NOT found in Flora do Brasil	
NAME-Lucumí	Dédé	(LC, TDF2)
	Ewe Laibó	(TDF)
YORUBA	Oóyólè, Amúgbà dúdú (*Corchorus Spp.*)	(PV)
NAME-CONGO	Dubue	(LC, TDF)
NAME-OTHER	Slippery Burr	(USDA)
	Slippery Dick, Slippery Burr	(levypreserve.org)
USES	Goes to Osain (Omiero)	
	Used for ritual baths (Ebomisi), Sarayéyé and Inche Osain	
	To wash attributes/Otanes of various Orisha	
	Used for home cleansings	
	Medicinal	

NAME-CUBA	Malvira, Flor de Azufre, Guacamaya Americana	(Roig)
	Bauhinia, Bauhinia Roja	(Roig)
Owner	Ochún (LC, TDF2, Quiros)	
	Osain (Madan)	
Odun	Otura-ogunda (Madan)	

NAME-SCIENTIFIC	*Bauhinia tomentosa* L.	(Roig)
	Bauhinia purpurea L.	(Roig, Barros)
See NOTE	*Bauhinia multinervia DC.*; *Bauhinia megalandra* Griseb.	(Roig, LC)

NAME-BRAZIL	Pata-de-vaca, Pé-de-boi, Mororó, Mão-de-vaca, Bauhinia	
Candomblé Jêje-Nagô	Obaluaiè (**Branca**), Oiá (**Púrpura**) Terra/Feminino	(Barros)
Candomblé de Angola	Inkosse, Kaiá	
Culto de Nação	Omolú (**Branca**); Nanã (**Branca, Rosa, Lila**); Oyá (**Rosa**)	
Umbanda	Iemanjá	

NAME-Lucumí	Kiyo	(LC, TDF2)
YORUBA	ABÀFÈ	(Barros)
NAME-CONGO	Kónlóbanto	(LC)
	Konlóbanto	(TDF)
NAME-OTHER	*Bauhinia tomentosa* St.Thomas tree	(USDA)
	Bell bauhinia, Yellow butterfly tree	(CRC)
	Bauhinia purpurea Butterfly tree	(USDA)
	Orchid tree, Purple butterfly tree	(CRC)
	Bauhinia multinervia Petit flamboyant bauhinia	(USDA)

USES	Goes to Osain (Omiero)	(Madan)
	Medicinal	(LC)
Candomblé Jêje-Nagô	Used for Abô and ritual baths for "filhos de santo"	(Barros)
Candomblé de Angola	Tree called **Ewe oWo Maluu**. Used in Abô and ritual baths.	
Umbanda	Used in Amacis, ritual baths, Cleansings, Abô	
INDIA	Used in Ayurveda and Siddha (*Bauhinia tomentosa*)	(CRC)
	Used in Ayurveda, Unani and Siddha. Magico-religious beliefs:	
	the bark used to keep evil spirits away. (*Bauhinia purpurea*)	(CRC)

NOTE Although Lydia Cabrera chose *Bauhinia megalandra* **Griseb.**, and Juan Tomá Roig also
has the same tree; he provides another name for the tree *Bauhinia tomentosa* **L.** Also;
CRC does not list *Bauhinia megalandra* **Griseb.**; whereas it does for *Bauhinia tomentosa* **L.**

NAME-CUBA	Mamey Colorado, Mamey, Mamey Sapote	(Roig)
Owner	Changó (LC, TDF, Diaz)	
	Changó, Ochún, Oyá (Quiros)	
Odun	Otura-odi (Quiros, Diaz, Orula.org)	
NAME-SCIENTIFIC	*Pouteria sapota* (Jacq.) H.E.Moore & Stearn;	
	Calocarpum sapota (Jacq.) Merr. **See NOTE**	(Roig)
NAME-BRAZIL	Mamey	
NAME-Lucumí	Emí	(LC)
	Ami rú	(TDF)
YORUBA		
NAME-CONGO	Nyúmba, Machafio, Nini yánga	(LC)
	Nyumba, Niniyamba	(TDF)
PALO	Machafio Nini Yanga	
NAME-OTHER	Mammee Sapote	(USDA)
	Mamey Rojo (PR); Mamey (Venezuela); Sapote (DR)	
	Sapotiye jòn dèf, Sapoti (Creole Haiti)	(Elsevier)
USES	Goes to Osain (Omiero)	
	The fruit as Addimu for Changó	
	The seed can be used in various hexes, some being maleficent	(LC)
	Medicinal	

NOTE   Lydia Cabrera names another tree for Mamey Colorado. The one she names is
Manilkara zapota (L.) P.Royen; Achras zapota L which is the Sapote or Níspero

NAME-CUBA	Mamey de Santo Domingo, Mamey Amarillo, Mamey	(Roig)
Owner	Changó (TDF, TDF2, Diaz)	
	Ibeyis, Orula (Quiros)	
	Ibeyis, Oggún, Orunmila (Irizarry)	
	Ibeyis (Madan)	
Odun	Irosun-iwori (Diaz, Irizarry, Madan, Orula.org)	
NAME-SCIENTIFIC	*Mammea americana* L.	(Roig)
NAME-BRAZIL	Abricó-do-pará, Abricó-da-Amazônia, Abricó-de-São-Domingos	
NAME-Lucumí	Emi	(TDF)
	Emí	(TDF2)
YORUBA		
NAME-CONGO	Machafio Bongoló	(LC)
	Bongolo	(TDF)
PALO	Machafio Nini Bongolé	
NAME-OTHER	Mammee Apple	(USDA)
	Mamey (DR, PR, Venezuela); Sabriko (Creole Haiti)	(Elsevier)
USES	Goes to Osain (Omiero)	
	Used in ritual baths (Ebomisi) and as Addimu	
	Home cleansings but NOT where a Nganga is located	(Diaz)

NAME-CUBA	Mamoncillo	(Roig)
Owner	Ibeyis (LC, Quiros, Diaz)	
	Obatalá (TDF)	
	Ibeyis, Eleggua (Irizarry, Madan)	
Odun	Otura-odi (Madan, Diaz, Irizarry, Quiros, Orula.org)	
	Otura-irosun (Irizarry, Diaz, Quiros, Orula.org)	

NAME-SCIENTIFIC	*Melicoccus bijugatus* Jacq.;	
	Melicocca bijuga L.	(Roig)

NAME-BRAZIL	Ginepa, Genip, Mamoncillo, Genipe, Limoncillo ou Lima-espanhola

NAME-Lucumí YORUBA	Omóyla, Omú	(LC)

NAME-CONGO	Dumbuande	(TDF)

NAME-OTHER	Spanish Lime	(USDA)
	Guenepa (DR, PR); Mamón (Venezuela)	
	Kenèp, Kenèp fwi, Kenèp mal (Creole Haiti)	(Elsevier)

USES	Goes to Osain (Omiero)
	Used as Addimu for Ibeyis
	Leaves used for ritual baths (Ebomisi)
	Medicinal

NAME-CUBA	Manajú	(Roig)
Owner	Ibeyis (LC, Quiros)	
	Ochosi (TDF2)	
	Oggún, Ochosi (Menéndez)	
Odun	Irete-osa (Quiros, Madan, Orula.org)	
NAME-SCIENTIFIC	*Garcinia aristata* (Griseb.) Borhidi;	
	Rheedia aristata Griseb.	(Roig)
NAME-BRAZIL	NOT found in Flora do Brasil	
NAME-Lucumí	Neri	(LC)
YORUBA		
NAME-CONGO	Mopúsúa	(LC)
	Mapusua	(TDF)
NAME-OTHER	NO common name found. Native to Cuba and Hispaniola	
	Aristate Garcinia; Garcinia Aristata	
	Palo de Cruz (DR)	(Elsevier)
USES		
	Medicinal	
	Will dislocate bones if someone, however mild,	
	is hit with a branch of this tree	(LC)

NOTE   This tree is **ENDANGERED** by ICUN Red List
This tree is **CRITICAL ENDANGERED** by BISSEA
This tree is NATIVE to Cuba, Hispaniola and Puerto Rico
This tree is of the Mangosteen genus

NAME-CUBA	Mangle, Mangle Rojo, Mangle Colorado, Mangle de Uña	(Roig)
Owner	Inle, Ochún, Yemayá (LC, TDF, Quiros)	
	Inle, Ochún (TDF2)	
	Eggun, Eleggua, Changó, Orunmila (Irizarry)	
	Changó (Diaz, Madan)	
Odun	Otura-osa (Madan, Quiros, Diaz, Irizarry)	
	Ejiogbe-meji (Irizarry, Diaz, Orula.org)	
NAME-SCIENTIFIC	*Rhizophora mangle* L.	(Roig)
NAME-BRAZIL	Mangue-vermelho, Sapateiro	
Candomblé	Omolú	
Umbanda	Obaluaiè	
NAME-Lucumí	Ewe atiodo, Kasioro	(LC)
	Ewe Atíodo, Kasioro	(TDF2)
	Iggi atioko, Kasiero	(TDF)
YORUBA		
NAME-CONGO	Musi kwilo	(LC)
	Nkunia musi kwilo	(TDF)
PALO	Nkunia Kalunga Masa	
MANGLE ROJO	Nsonke	
OWNER	Siete Rayos	(Nfinda)
NAME-OTHER	Red Mangrove	(USDA)
	Mangle Colorado (PR, DR, Vzla); Mang chandèl (Creole Haiti)	(Elsevier)
USES	**DOES NOT** go to Osain (Omiero)	
	Used for ritual baths (Ebomisi) and Inche Osain	
	Used for cleansings and Sarayéyé	
	Medicinal	
	Used for Eggun rituals	(Irizarry)
PALO	Siete Rayos uses this "palo" so that the enemy does not see where the attack is coming from. ONLY used for good and for defense	(Nfinda)
Candomblé	Leaves used for ritual discharge baths	
Umbanda	Leaves used only	

NAME-CUBA	Mangle Prieto		(Roig)
Owner	Oggún (Quiros)		
Odun	Obara-oyeku (Quiros, Orula.org)		

| **NAME-SCIENTIFIC** | *Avicennia germinans* (L.) L.; | | |
| | *Avicennia nitida* Jacq. | | (Roig) |

NAME-BRAZIL   Sereíba, Siriúba, Siriúva, Siribeira, Saraíba

| **NAME-Lucumí** | | | |
| YORUBA | Ògbun | | (PV, CRC) |

NAME-CONGO

| PALO | **MANGLE PRIETO** | Kosondo | |
| | **OWNER** | Madre de Agua, Mamá Chola | (Nfinda) |

NAME-OTHER	Black Mangrove	(USDA)
	Mangle Prieto (DR, Venezuela); Mangle Negro (PR)	
	Mand nwa (Creole Haiti)	(Elsevier)

USES

	Medicinal	
PALO	As opposed to the Mangle/Mangle Rojo; this "palo"	
	is very good for doing bad.	(Nfinda)

NAME-CUBA	Mango, Manga, Manga Amarilla, Manga Blanca		(Roig)
Owner	Ochún (LC, TDF2) -but ALL Orisha like it		
	Ochún, Changó (Diaz)		
	Ochún, Ibeyis, Orishaoko (Madan, Quiros)		
	Ochún, Oggún, Obatalá, Ibeyis, Orishaoko, Yemayá, Orula (Irizarry)		
Odun	Ika-irosun (Diaz, Irizarry, Madan, Orula.org)		
	Owonrin-iwori (Quiros, Irizarry, Orula.org)		

NAME-SCIENTIFIC	*Mangifera indica* L.	(Roig)

NAME-BRAZIL	Mangueira, Manga, Manga-espada, Manga-rosa		
Candomblé Jêje-Nagô	Ogum, Ìrókò	Terra/Masculino	(Barros)
Candomblé Jêje	Vodum Dangbê		(Barros)
Candomblé de Angola	Aluvaiá, Inkosse, Mutalumbô		
Casas-de-Nagô no Pará	Oxossi		(Barros)
NAÇÃO Ketu	Ogum, Exú		(Barros)
Candomblé	Ogum, Oyá, Ìrókò		
CULTO DE NAÇÃO	Ogum (Manga-espada), Ìrókò, Exú		
Umbanda	Xangô, Exú, Ogum		

NAME-Lucumí	Oro, Eléso, Orun béke		(LC)
	Abán, Eléso, Orun Béke	**Mango Macho**	(TDF2)
	Oróo	**Mango – fruto**	(TDF2)
YORUBA	Mángòrò, Séri		(PV, CRC)
	ÒRO ÒYÌNBÓ		(Barros)

NAME-CONGO	Emá bengá, Tuñé macondo	(LC)
	Emabenga, Tupe makondo, Nego	(TDF)
	Iémbe, Loumangou, Maémbe, Manga, Muti-a-nsafu	(CRC)
PALO	Mabenga	

NAME-OTHER	Mango	(USDA)

USES		Goes to Osain (Omiero)
		Ritual baths (Ebomisi), Inche Osain
		Cleansing baths to refresh
		Medicinal
		It is said that if the mango tree has too much fruit, it is
		a portent of misfortune. (LC)
	PALO	Used in the Nganga.
		Used to secure shaky situations

Candomblé	In the days where there are celebrations or feats, the leaves are used to cover the floor since the leaves are attributed to have powers that avoid problems from malicious elements (pois acredita-se que estas tenham poderes para evitar demandas provocadas por elemento mal-intencionado) (Barros)
	Manga-espada **Èwó of Ogum**

Candomblé de Angola	**Aluvaiá**	Leaves used to cover the floors during Xirê (dance)
	Inkosse	Leaves used in **Abô** (Omiero) **See NOTE**
	Mutalumbô	Leaves used to cover the home/temple

NAÇÃO Ketu	The fruit is avoided (**Èwó**) for the **filhos of Ogum**	(Barros)
Umbanda	Manga-espada is **Èwó of Ogum**	
	Manga-rosa is **Èwó of Iansã**	
INDIA	Used in Ayurveda, Unani and Siddha. Used in religion and magico-religious beliefs, ceremonial: leaves in marriage ceremony and festival auspicious, garland hung around gate; ingredient of Patra pooja/puja in different religious pooja ceremonies; prohibited to climb the fruit tree in the fruiting season by any women; the raw fruit is not a taboo, the fruit in any form is a taboo until the ceremony of Marka Uksana has been performed before the Goddess Danteshwari	(CRC)

NOTE	**Abô**	**Abô** or **Água sagrada** is the process of preparing the Ewe and the water for the process of initiation and rituals (i.e.- Omiero)
		See: **https://pt.wikipedia.org/wiki/Águas_sagradas**

NAME-CUBA	Maní, Cacahuete	(Roig)
Owner	Babalú-Ayé (LC, TDF2, Quiros)	
	All Orisha (TDF)	
	Asojuano, Eggun, Eleggua, Ochún (Irizarry)	
	Asojuano (Madan)	
Odun	Okanran-osa, Oturupon-obara (Irizarry, Quiros, Madan, Orula.org)	

NAME-SCIENTIFIC	*Arachis hypogaea* L.	(Roig)

NAME-BRAZIL	Amendoim, Mendoí, Amendoís, Mendubi, Menduí		
Candomblé Jêje-Nagô	Oxumaré, Oxum	Água/Feminino	(Barros)
Candomblé de Angola	Inkosse, Katendê		
Candomblé Ketu	Ossaim		
Umbanda			

NAME-Lucumí	Epá, Efá	(LC)
	Ejá	(TDF2)
	Maní, Ebisón, Epa ubisón, Efá	(TDF)
YORUBA	Èpà (gidi), Òróré èpàda	(PV, CRC)

NAME-CONGO	Mindo, Guba	(LC)
	Ngubi, Nguba	(TDF)
	Kabemba, Kalanga	(CRC)
PALO	Baja, Nkuba, Buanga, Eguanla, Ngulo	(TDF)

NAME-OTHER	Peanut, Groundnut, Goober	(CRC)

USES

	Used in ritual baths (Ebomisi) and Paraldo	(Irizarry)
	During times of epidemics, Santeros are prohibited from consuming/eating peanuts	(LC)
Candomblé Jêje-Nagô	The nuts as offerings for Oxumaré, the ground nuts as offerings for Oxum; BUT the consumption of peanuts is prohibited (**Èwó**) for the **filhos of Oxalá**.	(Barros)
Candomblé de Angola **Inkosse**	Used as parto of Addimu	
Katendê	ritual baths and head cleansings (obrigações no Orí)	
Candomblé Ketu	Ossaim has great predilection for the peeled roasted nuts	

NAME-CUBA	Manopilón	**See NOTE**	(LC)
	Mano-Pilón, Mano de Pilón, Torcido, Lebrero		(Roig)
Owner	Oggún (LC, TDF2, Quiros)		
Odun	Owonrin-oturupon (Quiros, Orula.org)		

| **NAME-SCIENTIFIC** | *Mouriri valenzuelana* A. Rich. | **See NOTE** | (Roig) |

| **NAME-BRAZIL** | NOT found in Flora do Brasil | |

| **NAME-Lucumí** | Móréle, Owodón | (LC, TDF2) |
| **YORUBA** | | |

| **NAME-CONGO** | Alumbende, Dianfinda, Otutua | (TDF) |

| **NAME-OTHER** | No common name found. Endemic to Cuba | |
| | Valenzuela Mouriri | (CRC) |

USES

	Used for making attributes and decorations for	
	the Orishas	(LC)
	A small piece/carving used as an amulet	(LC)

NOTE Lydia Cabrera has a separate entry for **Palo Torcido**, although
it is the same species, it has different attributes

NOTE This species (*Mouriri valenzuelana* A. Rich.) is endemic to Cuba (KewScience)
This species is listed as **Near Threatened** by BISSEA

NAME-CUBA	Manto de la Virgen		(Roig)
Owner	Obatalá (LC, Quiros)		
	Obatalá, Oyá (TDF2)		
	Babalú-Ayé (Diaz)		
	Oyá, Asojuano (Irizarry)		
	All Orisha (Madan)		
Odun	Osa-ika (Diaz, Irizarry, Madan, Orula.org)		

NAME-SCIENTIFIC	*Plectranthus scutellarioides* (L.) R.Br.;		
	Coleus blumei Benth.		(Roig)
	Plectranthus barbatus Andrews;		
	Coleus barbatus (Andrews) Benth. ex G.Don		(Barros)

NAME-BRAZIL	Tapete-de-Oxalá, Falso-boldo, Boldo-brasileiro		
Candomblé Jêje-Nagô	Oxalá	Ar/Feminino	(Barros)
Candomblé de Angola	Lembá		
Umbanda	Oxalá		

NAME-Lucumí	Ocharé		(LC, TDF2)
YORUBA	EWÉ BÀBÁ, EWÙRO BÀBÁ		(Barros)
NAME-CONGO			

NAME-OTHER	*Plectranthus scutellarioides*	Common coleus	(USDA)
	Coleus, Flame nettle, Painted nettle		(CRC)
	Plectranthus barbatus	Forskohlii	(USDA)

USES	Goes to Osain (Omiero)	
	To wash the Otán and religious items of Obatalá	(LC)
	For ritual bath for sick people	(Diaz)
Candomblé Jêje-Nagô	Used for purification baths	(Barros)
Candomblé de Angola	Used for head cleansings (obrigações no Orí), ritual	
	Bath and **Assento Okutá**. **Tirada de Vumbi** (funerary rites)	
	for any "filho de santo"	
Umbanda	Head cleansings, ritual baths, cleansings and Abôs (Omiero)	
OTHER	Hallucinogenic, leaves used in divinatory rites	(CRC)

NAME-CUBA	Manzanilla, Manzanilla del País, Manzanilla de la Tierra	(Roig)
Owner	Ochún (LC, TDF2, Quiros, Diaz, Irizarry)	
Odun	Oturupon-osa (Quiros, Diaz, Irizarry, Madan, Orula.org)	

NAME-SCIENTIFIC	*Chrysanthellum americanum* (L.) Vatke	(Roig)

NAME-BRAZIL	NOT found In Flora do Brasil	

NAME-Lucumí	Nikirio	(LC)
	Nikirío	(TDF2)
YORUBA	Òyígí, Abílèré	(PV, CRC)

NAME-CONGO	Dúnbuande	(LC)

NAME-OTHER	Chrysanthellum americanum	(drugs.ncats.io)
	African wild daisy	(Web)

USES	Goes to Osain (Omiero)	
	For cleansings of the home	
	Ritual baths (Ebomisi)	
	Medicinal	

NOTE	This plant is **NOT** Chamomile	
	Chamomile is ***Chamaemelum nobile*** or ***Matricaria chamomilla***	

NAME-CUBA	Marabú, Aroma	(Roig)
Owner	Oggún (Diaz)	
Odun	Osa-okanran (Diaz)	
NAME-SCIENTIFIC	*Dichrostachys cinerea* (L.) Wight & Arn.;	
	Cailliea glomerata (Forssk.) J.F.Macbr.	(Roig)
NAME-BRAZIL	Brinco-de-princesa-aromático, Lanterna-chinesa	
NAME-Lucumí		
YORUBA	Kará	(PV, CRC)
NIGERIA	Burli, Dun'du, Kara	(CRC)
BENIN	Gbadawèn	(CRC)
NAME-CONGO	Bapenga, Dikekele, Ekanya, Ikie kelele, Loanga, Nkanga	(CRC)
NAME-OTHER	Aroma	(USDA)
	Marabou Thorn, Sickle Bush	(pfaf.org)
USES	**DOES NOT** go to Osain (Omiero)	
	Medicinal	
	To decorate Oggún's throne	(Diaz)
PALO	The thorns used to dominate or destroy an enemy	(Diaz)
INDIA	Used in Ayurveda and Siddha	(CRC)
NOTE	Although this tree has beneficial aspects it is considered to be invasive and included in the Global Invasive Species Database	(Wikipidia)

NAME-CUBA	Marañón	(Roig)
Owner	Ochún, Inlé, Changó (LC, TDF2, Quiros)	
	Eleggua, Changó (Diaz)	
Odun	Obara-irosun (Quiros, Orula.org)	
	Irosun-meji, Irosun-obara (Diaz)	

NAME-SCIENTIFIC   *Anacardium occidentale* L.   (Roig)

NAME-BRAZIL	Cajueiro;	Castanha-de-caju, Caju (**Fruit**)	
Candomblé Jêje-Nagô	Oxum, Xangô, Inlé	Terra/Feminino	(Barros)
Candomblé Ketu	Exú		
Umbanda	Obaluaiè		

NAME-Lucumí
    YORUBA   Èjojú, Èkajú, Kajú   (PV, CRC)
NAME-CONGO

NAME-OTHER	Cashew	(USDA)
	Cashew, Cashew Nut, Cashew Apple	(CRC)
	Cacajuil (DR), Marañón (PR); Merey (Venezuela)	
	Mutua, Nwa kajou (Creole Haiti)	(Elsevier)

USES	Goes to Osain (Omiero)	
	The fruit as Addimu. Medicinal	
	Used to bring couples together	(Diaz)
PALO	With the seeds and "palo" used for talismans	
Candomblé	Leaves used for ritual baths and cleansings	
	Fruit offered as Addimu to Oxum and Jemanjá	(Barros)
Candomblé Ketu	The leaves are used by **Axogun** for the sacrificing	
	of four-legged animals	
Cultos de Umbanda, Omolokô and Angola	Leaves used in ritual baths for	
	discharging negative energy and baths for the initiates of Ogum	(Barros)
Umbanda	Fruit/nut as Addimu	
INDIA	Used in Ayurveda and Siddha	(CRC)

NOTE   Axogun   **Axogun, Axogum, Ogã de faca, Mão de faca**   It is the
Candomblé priest responsible for the animal sacrifices.
See: **https://pt.wikipedia.org/wiki/Axogun**

NAME-CUBA	Maravilla, Jalapa, Clavellina		(Roig)
Owner	Obatalá, Yewá, Oyá (LC, Concordia)		
	Obatalá, Yewá, Ochún, Ochosi (TDF2)		
	Obatalá, Yewá (TDF)		
	Obatalá, Yewá, Oyá, Orula (Quiros)		
	Obatalá, Orunmila (Madan)		
	Eleggua, Obatalá, Changó, Ochún (Diaz)		
	Ochún, Orula, Changó (Irizarry)		
	Obatalá, Ochún, Yemayá (Menéndez)		
Odun	Okanran-oturupon (Madan, Diaz, Irizarry, Quiros, Orula.org)		
	Owonrin-obara (Madan, Irizarry, Quiros, Orula.org)		

NAME-SCIENTIFIC	*Mirabilis jalapa* L.		(Roig)

NAME-BRAZIL	Maravilha, Jalapa, Bela-noite, Batata-de-purga, Boa-noite		
Candomblé Jêje-Nagô	Orumilá, Ewã, Oiá	Ar/Feminino/èró	(Barros)
Candomblé Ketu	Yansã		
Candomblé de Angola	Matamba		
CULTO DE NAÇÃO	Oyá, Yewá		

NAME-Lucumí	Ewe ewa, Inkuallo		(LC)
	Ewe ewa, Inkuayo	**Maravilla, Maravilla Blanca**	(TDF2)
	Ewe Ewa, Inkuayo Pupa	**Maravilla Amarilla**	(TDF2)
	Ewe Ewa Kukua, Inkuayo	**Maravilla Morada**	(TDF2)
	Ewa, Inkauyo		(TDF)
YORUBA	Tannáposó, Òdòdó elédè, Tannápakú, Tannátanná,		
	Tannápowó, Tanná pa osó		(PV, CRC)
	ÈKÈLÈYÍ		(Barros)
NAME-CONGO	Boddulé		(LC, TDF)
	Dila-dila		(Duke's)
PALO	Bóddule		

NAME-OTHER	Marvel of Peru		(USDA)
	Four O'clock, False Jalap; Maravilla (DR);		
	Jalapa Falsa (Vzla); Bel de nuyi (Creole Haiti)		(Duke's)

USES	Goes to Osain (Omiero)	
	Used for ritual baths (Ebomisi), Inche Osain,	
	Used for Paraldo and Eggun rituals	(Irizarry)
	Used for cleansings (Sarayéyé) and to neutralize	
	Ogú (witchcraft)	(Concordia)
	The toasted and ground seeds used to bring luck	(LC)
PALO MONTE	Used for love spells	
ESPIRITU CRUZADO	To clean the house when it needs to be refreshed	
Candomblé Jêje-Nagô	It is attributed to Oiá	(Barros)
Candomblé Ketu	Used for head cleansings (obrigações no Orí),	
	related work for the Orixá (feitura de santo), and **Abô**;	
	but **NOT** that which will be taken orally/drunk.	
Candomblé de Angola	Used for work related to the Orixá (feitura de santo);	
	but **NOT** to be taken orally/drunk	
Umbanda	Used strictly as decoration	
INDIA	Used in Ayurveda, Unani and Siddha	(CRC)

NOTE There are different types/colors of this plant. They are as follows

NAME-CUBA	Maravilla Amarilla (**Yellow**)	
OWNER	Ochún (TDF2)	
	Oggún (Quiros)	
	Ochún, Yemayá (Menéndez)	
USES	Goes to Osain (Omiero)	(TDF2, Quiros)
	To make Oggún mad	(Quiros)

NAME-CUBA	Maravilla Blanca (**White**)	
OWNER	Obatalá (TDF2, Quiros, Menéndez)	
USES	Goes to Osain (Omiero)	(Quiros)

NAME-CUBA	Maravilla Puzo, Maravilla Roja (**Red, Dark Pink**)	
OWNER	Changó (Quiros)	
USES	Goes to Osain (Omiero)	(Quiros)

NAME-CUBA	Maravilla Morada (**Purple, Lilac**)
OWNER	Ochosi (TDF2)

NOTE Although this plant is called in Cuba Jalapa, this is NOT the real Jalapa
The real Jalapa or Jalap are
- *Ipomoea purga* (Wender.) Hayne
- *Ipomoea jalapa* (L.) Pursh

and of which a cathartic drug was made in the State of Veracruz, Mexico (Wikipedia)

Hoodoo/Root Magic (USA) Called High John the Conqueror Root, Bindweed, Jalap, John the Conqueror and King of the Woods. The root of these plants (***Ipomoea purge & Ipomoea jalapa***) are used to enjoy commanding power, gain personal mastery and strengthen nature (virility)

NAME-CUBA	Marilope, Mari-Lope, Marilopez	(Roig)
Owner	Oggún, Yemayá (Quiros)	
	Ochún (Diaz, Irizarry, Madan)	
	Ochún, Yemayá (Menéndez)	
Odun	Obara-ogunda (Quiros, Diaz, Irizarry, Madan, Orula.org)	
NAME-SCIENTIFIC	*Turnera ulmifolia* L.	(Roig)
NAME-BRAZIL	Flor-do-Guarujá; Turnera; Chanana; Albina.	
NAME-Lucumí		
YORUBA		
NAME-CONGO		
NAME-OTHER	Ramgoat Dashalong	(USDA)
	Cuban Buttercup, Buttercup, Yellow Alder	(CRC)
	Marí López (DR, PR); Cumaná (Venezuela)	
	Thym marron (Haiti)	(Duke's)

USES
                 Goes to Osain (Omiero)
                 Used for ritual baths (Ebomisi) and Inche Osain
                 Used for Love baths to attract

PALO MONTE   To make **Ncangues** (trabajos de amarres/joininig spells)
                 for lovers.

ESPIRITU CRUZADO   Spiritual works

NOTE   This plant (***Turnera ulmifolia* L.**) has been found to have a beneficial
           effect when used with an antibiotic in the treatment of MRSA
           MRSA - Methicillin – resistant Staphylococcus aureus
           See: Herbal therapy associated with antibiotic therapy: potentiation
                  of the antibiotic activity against methicillin – resistant Staphylococcus
                  aureus by Turnera ulmifolia L

https://bmccomplementalternmed.biomedcentral.com/articles/10.1186/1472-6882-9-13

NAME-CUBA	Mariposa, Mariposa Blanca	(Roig)
Owner	Yemayá (Quiros)	
Odun		

NAME-SCIENTIFIC	*Hedychium coronarium* J.Koenig	(Roig)

NAME-BRAZIL   Lírio-do-brejo, Gengibre-branco, Lágrima-de-moça, Lágrima-de-vênus

Candomblé Jêje-Nagô	Jemanjá, Ogum	Água/Masculino/èró	(Barros)
Candomblé de Angola	Zaze, Lembá		
Candomblé	Oxum, Oxalá, Logun-Edé		
Umbanda	Xangô, Jemanjá		

NAME-Lucumí	Balabá, Aróao	(LC)
	Balabá, Aroao	(TDF2)
YORUBA	BALABÁ	(Barros)

NAME-CONGO	Kánda, Fititi nkangriso	(LC)
	Kanda, Bititi nkougriso	(TDF)

NAME-OTHER	White Garland Lily	(USDA)
	Butterfly Ginger, White Ginger, Butterfly Lily	(CRC)

USES

    Medicinal

Candomblé Jêje-Nagô	The leaves used for initiation rites and purification baths	(Barros)
Candomblé de Angola	**Zaze, Lembá** Head cleansings (obrigações no Orí)	
Umbanda	Leaves used in cleansing baths (emotional and spiritual), incense, head cleansings (obrigações de cabeça), offerings, Ebós	
Hoodoo/Root Magic (USA)	Ginger gives a "fiery" form of protection and "heats up" love and money spells	
OTHER	Magic: root as charm against evil spirits, and when the Goddess of jungle harms men for their misdeeds	(CRC)

NAME-CUBA	Marpacífico, Borrachona, Amapola, Guasintón, Leche de Venus (Roig)
Owner	Oyá (TDF2)
	Inlé, Odudúa (Quiros)
	Inlé, Eggun (Madan)
	Inlé, Yemayá (Diaz)
Odun	Oyeku-meji, Odi-meji (Quiros, Madan, Diaz, Orula.org)

| **NAME-SCIENTIFIC** | *Hibiscus rosa-sinensis* L. | (Roig) |

NAME-BRAZIL   Mimo-de-Vênus, Hibisco, Graxa-de-estudante
Candomblé Jêje-Nagô   Ossaim, Ogum, Oxum   Terra/Feminino   (Barros)
Candomblé Ketu   Xangô
Candomblé de Angola   Matamba
CULTO DE NAÇÃO   Ossaim, Oxossi, Oxum
Umbanda   Oxossi, Jemanjá

NAME-Lucumí   Ewe Atorí (Madan)
 YORUBA   ÈSÁ PUPA   (Barros)
NAME-CONGO
NAME-OTHER   Shoeblackplant   (USDA)
  Chinese Hibiscus, Hawaiian Hibiscus, Rose Mallow   (Wiki)

USES   Goes to Osain (Omiero)
  Used for ritual baths (Ebomisi), Sarayéyé, and Paraldo
  For cleansing of person and/or home
  Spiritual: for the Seven African Powers (Siete Potencias Africanas)   (Diaz)
  Essential to wash attributes of Eggun   (Madan)
Candomblé Jêje-Nagô   Used in purification baths and cleansings
  Flowers used over Oxum during sacrifices and offerings   (Barros)
Candomblé Ketu   The leaves, branches and flowers used in the purification
  of the "filhos" of Oyá. Much used in Love magics
Candomblé de Angola   Used in Love magics
Umbanda   Used in baths, incense, head cleansings, offerings. Used to help break
  hexes and witchcraft (auxilia na quebra de feitiços e magias)
Hoodoo/Root Magic (USA)   Fresh or dried, the flowers used in Love Spells.
INDIA   Used in Ayurveda, Unani and Siddha. Ceremonial: red flowers
  used for adorning of bow and arrow, petals taken on all religious
  ceremonies to sprinkle divine water   (CRC)

NAME-CUBA	Mastuerzo, Sabelección	(Roig)
Owner	Eleggua, Babalú-Ayé (LC, Quiros, Madan)	
	Eleggua (TDF2, Menéndez)	
	Ochún (TDF)	
	Ochún, Eleggua (Diaz)	
	Eleggua (Irizarry)	
	Eleggua, Asojuano (Concordia)	
Odun	Oturupon-osa (Quiros, Madan, Diaz, Irizarry, Concordia, Orula.org)	

NAME-SCIENTIFIC	*Lepidium virginicum* L.	(Roig)
	Lepidium sativum L.	(Barros)

NAME-BRAZIL	Mastruço, Agrião-de-jardim, Agrião, Agrião-mouro	
Candomblé Jêje-Nagô	Exú, Eggun	(Barros)
Candomblé de Angola	Kavungo, Dandalunda, Lembá	
Candomblé Ketu	Oxalá	
Umbanda	Linha de Oxalá, Linha das Senhoras, Linha das Almas	

NAME-Lucumí	Eribo		(LC, TDF2)
	Ichini-chini, Eribosa	**Sabe Lección**	(LC, TDF2)
	Eribo, Simisini, Brebosa		(TDF)
YORUBA	EWÉ IŞINIŞINI		(Barros)
NAME-CONGO	Sobunoró		(TDF)
	Sobunoro	**Sabe Lección**	(LC)
PALO	Sobunoro		

NAME-OTHER	Virginia Pepperweed	(USDA)
	Boiled-seed, Pepper bush, Pepper weed, Virginia peppercress	(CRC)

USES	Goes to Osain (Omiero)	
	Used in ritual baths (Ebomisi) and Inche Osain	
	Used for LOVE spells, potions	
	Medicinal	
Candomblé Jêje-Nagô	Used in cleansings and baths, but ONLY from the neck down; since it is related to Eggun, never used on the head	(Barros)
Candomblé de Angola	**Kavungo, Lembá** — No specific use	
	Dandalunda — Head cleansings	
Candomblé Ketu	No application in ritualistic ceremonies	

NAME-CUBA	Matanegro, Bejuco Baracoa	(LC)
	Mata Negro, Bejuco Baracoa, Bergajo	(Roig)
Owner	Yemayá (LC, TDF2, Quiros)	
	Oddúa (Menéndez) **Bergajo**	
Odun		
NAME-SCIENTIFIC	*Rourea glabra* Kunth	(Roig)
NAME-BRAZIL	NO common name found	
NAME-Lucumí	Konri, Kukenkeleyo	(LC, TDF2)
YORUBA		
NAME-CONGO		
NAME-OTHER	Bejuco de garrote, Canjuro, Juan caliente, Mata negro,	
	Tietie (Vernacular names)	(CRC)
USES		
	Yemayá uses this Ewe to do battle	(LC)
PALO	Used so that Chíchérikú can move more easily	(LC)
NOTE	Called Mata-Negro because in colonial times, slaves were	
	whipped with this plant.	(LC)

NAME-CUBA	Mazorquilla	(Roig)
Owner	Ochosi (TDF2)	
	Eleggua, Yemayá, Changó (Quiros)	
	Changó (Irizarry)	
	Olokun, Yemayá, Changó (Diaz)	
	Ochún, Yemayá, Oyá (Menéndez)	
Odun	Oturupon-meji (Diaz)	
NAME-SCIENTIFIC	*Blechum pyramidatum* (Lam.) Urb.;	
	Blechum brownei Juss.	(Roig)
NAME-BRAZIL	NOT found in Flora do Brasil	
NAME-Lucumí		
YORUBA		
NAME-CONGO		
PALO		
NAME-OTHER	Browne's Blechum	(USDA)
	Green Shrimp Plant	(florida.plantatlas.usf.edu)
USES	Goes to Osain (Omiero) for Ochún, Yemayá	(Menéndez)
	Goes to Osain (Omiero)	(Diaz)
	Used in ritual baths (Ebomisi) and Inche Osain	
	Used to refresh the home	

NAME-CUBA	Mejorana		(Roig)
Owner	Eleggua, Obatalá, Yemayá (Quiros)		
	Eleggua, Obatalá, Ochún (Irizarry, Madan)		
	Ochún (Diaz)		
Odun	Osa-odi, Oturupon-otura (Quiros, Diaz, Irizarry, Madan, Orula.org)		
	Okanran-meji (Irizarry, Quiros, Madan, Orula.org)		

NAME-SCIENTIFIC	*Origanum majorana* L.		(Roig)

NAME-BRAZIL	Manjerona		
Candomblé Jêje-Nagô	Xangô	Terra/Feminino	(Barros)
Candomblé Ketu	Oxalá		
Candomblé de Angola	Zaze, Lembá		
Umbanda	Oxalá, Oxumaré, Iemanjá	Ervas Mornas	

NAME-Lucumí
    YORUBA

NAME-CONGO

	OWNER	Mamá Chola	**Regla Kimbisa**

NAME-OTHER	Sweet Marjoram	(USDA)

USES	Goes to Osain (Omiero)	
	A branch will serve as **Iggidé** (amulet)	(LC)
	Used in ritual baths (Ebomisi), Inche Osain and Paraldo	
	Used in baths for luck, prosperity and love	(Diaz)
	This is a VERY jealous Ewe, and should not be mixed with other Ewe	(LC)
	Medicinal	
PALO MONTE	Part of the fundament of Mamá Chola in Regla Kimbisa. Used in ritual baths of Mamá Chola and for the preparation of lamps with the purpose of Love Magics	
ESPIRITU CRUZADO	For cleansing that clear negative energies. Spiritual works.	

PALO	Used by Mayomberos/Paleros in accordance with the Book of St. Cyprian	(LC)
	See: **https://en.wikipedia.org/wiki/Book_of_Saint_Cyprian**	
	Can be used with other Ewe for works with Mamá Chola	(Nfinda)
Candomblé Jêje-Nagô	Used in purification baths and as incense to attract good luck	(Barros)
Candomblé Ketu	Used in ALL head cleansings (obrigações no Orí), cleansing/discharge baths and Abôs (Omiero)	
Candomblé de Angola	Zaze Head cleansings (obrigações no Orí)	
	Lembá Head cleansings (obrigações no Orí) for ANY	
Omorixá (filho de Orixá/hijo de Santo)		
Hoodoo/Root Magic (USA)	It confers protection from harm, enhances love in marriages and assuages grief and sorrow	
INDIA	Ceremonial, ritual: ingredient of Patra pooja in different religious pooja ceremonies, in Ganesh-pooja	(CRC)

NOTE   **Story of Marjoram and Mint (Yerba Buena y Mejorana)** per Lydia Cabrera

- One day the Virgin Mary and St. Ana (Santa Ana) went into the woods looking for herbs. St. Ana picked one, smelled it, tasted it and said "this is a good herb" (esta es Yerba Buena). But the Virgin Mary had found another and said to St. Ana "this is better, Ana" (esta es major, Ana). Since then, the one that the Virgin Mary found is called Mejorana while the one that St. Ana found is called Yerba Buena.

NAME-CUBA	Melón de Agua, Sandía			(Roig)
Owner	Yemayá (LC, TDF, TDF2, Quiros, Madan)			
Odun	Ofun-iwori (Quiros, Orula.org)			
	Ofun-obara (Madan, Orula.org)			

NAME-SCIENTIFIC	*Citrullus lanatus* (Thunb.) Matsum. & Nakai;			
	Citrullus vulgaris Schrad.			(Roig)
	Citrullus citrullus H.Karst.			(LC, Barros)

| **NAME-BRAZIL** | Melão-de-água | ***Citrullus citrullus* H.Karst** | **Agbéye** | |
| **Candomblé Jêje-Nagô** | Iemanjá, Oxum | Água/Feminino | | (Barros) |

NAME-BRAZIL	Melancia	***Citrullus vulgaris* Schrad**	**Bàrà**	
Candomblé Jêje-Nagô	Iemanjá	Água/Feminino		(Barros)
Candomblé de Angola	Vunge			
Umbanda	Iemanjá			

NAME-Lucumí	Agbéye, Agüe tútú, Itakún, Oyé, Oggure		(LC)
	Agbéye, Egüe Tútú, Itakún, Oyé, Oggure		(TDF2)
	Meme, Itakún, Eguri, Abara, Abeye, Ogurián, Omoiki, Oso itakun		(TDF)
YORUBA	Bàrà, Ègúsí, Ègúnsí, Egusi, Ògìrì, Sòfín		(PV, CRC)

NAME-CONGO	Machafio suri mámba	(LC)
	Mashafio surimamba	(TDF)
PALO	Machafio Suri Mamba	

| **NAME-OTHER** | Watermelon, Tsamma melon, Egusi Melon, Wild watermelon | (CRC) |

USES

	Medicinal	
	Fruit as Addimu for Yemayá	
	Ritual baths (Ebomisi) to ward-off accidents, calamity, hostility	(Quiros)
Candomblé Jêje-Nagô	Used as offerings to **Iabás** (female Orixá), specially to	
	Jemanjá to attract good fortune	(Barros)
Candomblé de Angola	**Vunge** Fruit is **Èwó of Jemanjá**. Fruit used in Apana Erê	
Candomblé	**Èwó of Obaluaiè**	
Umbanda	Fruit as offering to Jemanjá, but to be avoided-it is **Èwó of Oxum**	
INDIA	Used in Ayurveda	(CRC)

NAME-CUBA	Melón de Castilla, Melón de Valencia, Melón Moscatel		(Roig)
Owner	Ochún (LC, TDF2, Quiros)		
	Ochún, Ibeyis (Madan)		
	Ochún, Orunmila (Irizarry)		
Odun	Otura-obara (Quiros, Irizarry, Madan, Orula.org)		

NAME-SCIENTIFIC *Cucumis melo* L. (Roig)

NAME-BRAZIL	Melão, Meloeiro, Melão-amarelo, Melão-Gália, Melão-cantalope		
Candomblé Jêje-Nagô	Oxum	Água/Feminino	(Barros)
Candomblé de Angola	Vunge		
CULTO DE NAÇÃO	Iemanjá, Oxum (some others Oxossi, Logun Edé)		
Umbanda	Oxalá, Iemanjá, Oxum, Xangô (some others Oxumarê)		

NAME-Lucumí	Eggure, Léseitaku	(LC)
	Eggure, Léscitaku, Ibára	(TDF2)
YORUBA	Ègúsí	(Barros)

NAME-CONGO	Machafio suri yánga	(LC)
	Mashafio suriyamba	(TDF)
PALO	Mashafio Suriyamba	

NAME-OTHER Cantaloupe, Musk Melon, Rock Melon (CRC)

USES

	Fruit used as Addimu for Ochún	
	Fruit given out to children as gifts because Ibeyis are children	(LC)
	Fruit used as Ebó and leaves for ritual baths (Ebomisi)	(Irizarry)
Candomblé Jêje-Nagô	Fruit as Addimu for **Iabás** (female Orixá)	
Candomblé de Angola	**Vunge** Fruit is **Èwó of Òsányìn**. Fruit used in Apanan (Initiation ritual) Erê	
UMBANDA	The fruit is used for magics since it is associated with fertility, fecundity and prosperity. Used in ritual baths, Amassi, Abôs, offerings and Ebôs	
INDIA	Used in Ayurveda, Unani and Siddha.	
	Sacred plant, garland of fruits	(CRC)

NAME-CUBA	Meloncillo, Pepino Cimarrón	(Roig)
Owner	Eleggua, Oyá (TDF2)	
	Eleggua (Quiros)	
	Yemayá (Diaz)	
	Oggún (Irizarry, Madan)	
	Eleggua, Yemayá, Ochún (Menéndez)	
Odun	Irosun-otura (Quiros, Irizarry, Diaz, Madan, Orula.org)	
	Irosun-ogunda, Otura-obara (Quiros, Diaz, Irizarry, Orula.org)	
NAME-SCIENTIFIC	*Melothria pendula* L.;	
	Melothria guadalupensis (Spreng.) Cogn.	(Roig)
NAME-BRAZIL	Pepino-do-mato, Abóbora-do-mato, Pepino-silvestre, Abobrinha-do-mato	
NAME- ANAGO YORUBA	Ewé bara, Omi bara	**Meloncillo**	(LC)
NAME-CONGO		
NAME-OTHER	Guadalupe Cucumber	(USDA, CRC)
	Guadalupe Cucumber, Creeping cucumber, Meloncito	(wildflower.org)
USES	Goes to Osain (Omiero)	(Madan)
	Used for ritual baths (Ebomisi) and Inche Osain	(Irizarry)
	A beverage prepared with the fruit will relieve a person of ingested witchcraft	(Diaz)
	Medicinal	

NAME-CUBA	Mierda de Gallina, Abrán de Costa	**See NOTE**	(Roig)
Owner	Ibeyis (LC, Quiros)		
Odun			
NAME-SCIENTIFIC	*Bunchosia nitida* (Jacq.) A.Rich.		(Roig)
NAME-BRAZIL	NOT found in Flora do Brasil		
NAME-Lucumí	Addié igbemí		(LC)
YORUBA			
NAME-CONGO			
NAME-OTHER	Glossy Bunchasia, Chink wood		
	Cabra, Cabra Hedionda (DR)		
	Merde rouge de la montagne (Haiti)		
	Bwa ami, Kayman (Creole Haiti)		(Elsevier)
USES			
	Used for cleansings (Sarayéyé) of children against		
	bad influences or dark spirits in children that are		
	born sickly		(LC)
	Medicinal		

NOTE Juan Tomás Roig lists both trees (Mierda de Gallina, Abrán de Costa) as being the same family name, although both Lydia Cabrera and Juan Tomás Roig list **Abrán de Costa** as a different sub-species.
Lydia Cabrera has both trees listed with basically the same usage but with attribution to different Orisha

NAME-CUBA	Mil Flores, Mil Rosas, Juan Grande, Hortensia	(Roig)
Owner	Oyá, Yewá (LC, Quiros, Irizarry, Diaz)	
	Yewá (TDF2)	
Odun	Oturupon-ofun (Quiros, Diaz, Madan, Orula.og)	
NAME-SCIENTIFIC	*Clerodendrum chinense* (Osbeck) Mabb.;	
	Clerodendrum fragrans (Vent.) R.Br.	(Roig)
NAME-BRAZIL	Clerodendro (no other common name found)	
NAME-Lucumí		
YORUBA		
NAME-CONGO		
NAME-OTHER	Stickbush	(USDA)
	Fragrant Clerodendrum, Glory Bower, Honolulu Rose	(CRC)
	Glory Bower, Cashmere Bouquet, Chinese Glory Flower	
	(florafaunaweb.nparks.gov.sg)	
USES	Goes to Osain (Omiero)	
	Baths for good luck and prosperity	(LC)
	Baths to cleanse the mind when one dreams of death and/or	
	death related dreams	(LC)
	Ritual baths (Ebomisi)	
	Medicinal	

NAME-CUBA	Millo, Millo Blanco, Millo Morado, Millo Negro	(Roig)
Owner	Babalú-Ayé (LC, TDF2)	
	Babalú-Ayé, Odudúa (Quiros)	
Odun		
NAME-SCIENTIFIC	*Sorghum bicolor* (L.) Moench;	
	Sorghum vulgare Pers.	(Roig)
	Sorghum bicolor (L.) Moench	
	Holcus sorghum L.	(LC)
NAME-BRAZIL	Sorgo, Milho-zaburro, Milho-da-guiné, Sorgo-negro-da-áfrica	
NAME-Lucumí	Okáblebba, Okuaré	(LC)
	Okáblebba	(TDF2)
YORUBA	Okà pupa, Bàbà, Okà bàbà	(PV, CRC)
NAME-CONGO		
ANGOLA	Massa-mbala, Massambala	(CRC)
DAHOMEY	Abokun, Obo, Vo	(CRC)
NAME-OTHER	Grain sorghum	(USDA)
	Broom Corn, Guinea Corn, Broom Millet, Cultivated Sorghum	(CRC)

USES

To prevent epidemics and sickness to enter the home, a
sheaf is placed behind the door.   (LC)

NOTE   Although sorghum was used in the old world (Africa), when the slaves came to
the New World, they were faced with corn instead of sorghum. Hence, although
sorghum was the grain used in Africa in Ebó and offerings, it was replaced by corn.

NOTE   How Changó changed his beads from red to red and white by Lydia Cabrera
- Changó's mother, Obatalá, was having great financial difficulty. She went to Ifá to ask for advice. She was told to go see her son Changó, who was a king; but first she must do Ebó with a sheaf of sorghum. She was also advised that she would have three encounters that would make her mad, but that she should not say anything. So Obatalá did the Ebó and in her white dress went to see her son with the sheaf of sorghum. On her way she met Eshú dressed as a seller of charcoal asking for her help. He then put his hands on her white dress and got it dirty. Obatalá was about to say something, but remembered Ifá's advice. She went on her way, and again met Eshú dressed as a fruit seller asking for her help. She tried to help him but ended up having her dressed get dirty with "corojo". Again, she held her anger and went on. As she travelled through a field that was really dry due to the long dry-spell, a horse saw the sheaf of sorghum. The horse happened to be Changó's favorite horse that had been lost for 12 years. The horse being hungry kept following her no matter what she did. When they got to the palace of Changó, the soldiers recognize the horse and took Obatalá prisoner. When Changó came to see his horse, he saw his mother and in great happiness tumbled to her feet. He then built her a new home and changed his beads from just red to white and red due to his happiness at seeing his mother.

NOTE   The Odu Ogbe-otura and Ogbe-ogunda refer to "no process in judicial justice" (não tem processo na justicia) where grains of corn, sorghum and beans are taken, roasted and placed in a little pot and shaken before going to court, after repeating the following incantation:
- The power of disappearance said that my lawsuits will disappear
- That the case in court does not appear anymore
- Toasted corn does not grow
- Toasted beans do not grow
- Toasted sorghum does not grow
- Let me sit down, said that it will settle.
- They will not remember him anymore. That is, the process in justice will not progress in the same way as the grains cannot germinate after being toasted

NAME-CUBA	Miraguano, Miraguano de Lana, Guano de Campeche,		
	Guano de Costa, Palma Blanca		(Roig)
Owner	Changó, Agayú (LC, Quiros)		
	Changó (TDF2)		
Odun			

NAME-SCIENTIFIC	*Thrinax radiata* Lodd. ex Schult. & Schult.f.;		
	Thrinax wendlandiana Becc.		(Roig)
	Elaeis guineensis Jacq.;		(Roig, PV)

NAME-BRAZIL	Dendezeiro	(***Elaeis guineensis* Jacq.**)	
Candomblé Jêje-Nagô	Ogum	Ar/Masculino	(Barros)
Candomblé de Angola	Inkosse, Katendê		
CULTO DE NAÇÃO	Ogum		

NAME-Lucumí	Mariwó	(LC, TDF2)
YORUBA	**LEAVES/ Màrìwò** (***Elaeis guineensis* Jacq.**)	
	Òpè, Igi òpè, Imò òpè, Eyìn, Bánga, Eésan, Èètán, Èkùró,	
	Idi eyìn, Odi eyìn, Àko, Màrìwò, Òpè olówá,	
	Ògómò òpè, Soso eyìn	(PV)

NAME-CONGO

NAME-OTHER	Florida thatch palm	(USDA)
	Florida Thachpalm, Silktop palmetto, Silktop thachpalm	
	Guanillo (DR), Latanier de mer (Haiti)	(Elsevier)

USES		
	With the leaves, fringes are made (**Malipó**) to decorate the	
	Igbodú (sacred room) when Yewá is being crowned/assented	(LC)
	Same said fringes are placed in the inside of doorways in	
	honor of Agayú	(LC)

Candomblé Jêje-Nagô   It is a sacred tree called **Igi òpè.** The leaves (**Màrìwò**) are used in the Cult of Ogum.

The new-born plants of the Igi òpè are called Màrìwò and constitute the greatest representation of Ogum; just as important as his iron machete, with which he opens pathways.   (Barros)

Ogum was naked at one time and Oxalá (being his father and owner of the **Igi òpè**; gave him the new born leaves of the Dendezeiro in order to dress him and calm him down.

There is a song that states "**Ogún ko l'aso; Màrìwò l'aso Ogún o!**"
i.e.: "**Ogum now has clothes, Màrìwò is the clothe of Ogum**"   (Barros)

Màrìwò is placed on the doorways to serve as protection against all types of noxious/disastrous entities   (Barros)

Ossaim also uses Màrìwò as part of his principal Ewe   (Barros)

Candomblé de Angola   **Inkosse**   the leaves are used in the different obligations/cleansings (obrigações)

Katendê   The leaves are used in the initiation of the neophytes (Feitura de Iyawo)

CULTO DE NAÇÃO   Màrìwò used in the vestments, clothing and ritual objects for Ogum and Oiá/Yansã.

Màrìwò has the power to draw away negative energies and dark spirits

Placed at the entrance of the home/temple will protect/keep away Eggun.

NAME-CUBA	Mirra			
Owner	Babalú-Ayé (TDF2, Quiros)			
	Ochún (Madan)			
Odun	Otura-ogunda (Quiros, Madan, Orula.org)			

NAME-SCIENTIFIC   *Commiphora myrrha* (Nees) Engl.   (theplantlist.org)

NAME-BRAZIL	Mirra			
Candomblé Jêje-Nagô		Oxalá	Ar/Masculino	(Barros)
Umbanda		Ogum, Oxalá, Xangô		

NAME-Lucumí
    YORUBA   Ojia   (Google translate)

NAME-CONGO

NAME-OTHER	Common Myrrh, True Myrrh	(CRC)
	Myrrh (Arabic)	(CRC)

USES

	Used as incense to purify and protect	(Quiros)
Candomblé	Used as incense	(Barros)
Umbanda	Used as incense	(Barros)
Hoodoo/Root Magic (USA)	Usually burned blended with at least one more resin (i.e.- Copal, Benzoin, Frankincense, Dragon's Blood or Sandalwood). The effects change depending on the blend, but its tendency overall is said to be peaceful, healing relaxing, protective and to stimulate sensual love.	
INDIA	Used in Ayurveda, Unani and Siddha.	(CRC)

NOTE   Myrrh is mentioned in the Bible. In Exodus, chapter 30; God tells Moses that Myrrh blended with cinnamon is to be burned inside the Tabernacle. When Jesus was born, one of the gifts given by the Maggi was Myrrh (and Frankincense and Gold). When Jesus died, he was covered in aromatic oils (Myrrh being one of them).

NAME-CUBA	Moco de Pavo, Amaranto, Acediana	(Roig)
Owner	Changó, Agayú (Menéndez)	
Odun		
NAME-SCIENTIFIC	*Amaranthus cruentus L.*	(Roig)
NAME-BRAZIL	Bredo-vermelho, Caruru-vermelho, Caruru-roxo	
NAME-Lucumí		
YORUBA		
NAME-CONGO		
PALO		
NAME-OTHER	Red Amaranth	(USDA)
	Blood amaranth, Red amaranth, Mexican grain amaranth	(Wiki)
USES	Goes to Osain (Omiero) for Changó, Agayú	(Menéndez)

NAME-CUBA	Moruro, Moruro Rojo, Moruro Prieto, Sabicú Moruro	(Roig)
Owner	Mayombe (LC)	
	Changó (Diaz)	
	Osún (Madan)	
	Eggun, Eleggua, Osún (Irizarry)	
Odun	Ose-otura (Quiros, Diaz, Madan)	
NAME-SCIENTIFIC	*Cojoba arborea* (L.) Britton & Rose;	
	Pithecellobium arboreum (L.) Urb.	(Roig)
NAME-BRAZIL	NOT found in Flora do Brasil	
NAME-Lucumí	Orudán, Efúnkoko	(LC, TDF2)
	Alorí	(TDF)
YORUBA		
NAME-CONGO	Kasaoasa, Kinpase	(LC)
	Kasauasa, Kampase, Ngrefo, Nkela, Nguefá,	
	Kasawuasa-mpase, Atorí	(TDF)
NAME-OTHER	Wild Tamarind	(USDA)
	Abey, Abey Hembra (DR); Cojoba, Cojóbana (PR);	
	Cojoba collier, Bois collier (Haiti)	(Elsevier)
USES	**DOES NOT** go to Osain (Omiero)	
	Used for ritual baths (Ebomisi) and Eggun Rituals	(Irizarry)
	This tree is can be used for both good and bad	(LC)
	Medicinal	
	With the wood of this tree, puppets are made which are	
	imbued with spirits (i.e.-Chíchérikú)	(LC)
PALO	Only when this tree is without leaves can it be used for bad	(LC)

NAME-CUBA	Muralla, Muraya, Murallera, Murraya, Boj de Persia, Mirto	(Roig)
	Mirto, Muralla	(LC)
Owner	Ochún (LC, TDF2)	
	Changó, Obatalá (Diaz)	
	Eggun (Madan)	
Odun	Owonrin-iwori (Quiros, Diaz, Madan, Orula.org)	
NAME-SCIENTIFIC	*Murraya paniculata* (L.) Jack;	(Roig)
	Murraya exotica L.	(LC)
NAME-BRAZIL	Falsa-murta, Jasmim-laranjeira, Jasmim-laranja, Murta-de-cheiro	
NAME-Lucumí	Urari	(LC)
	Urarí	(TDF2)
YORUBA		
NAME-CONGO		
NAME-OTHER	Chinese Box	(USDA)
	Orange Jessamine, Common Jessamine Orange, Chinese Myrtle	(CRC)
USES	**DOES NOT** go to Osain (Omiero)	
	Cleansings (Sarayéyé) for dark spirits/influence	(Diaz)
	Planted in front of home to keep dark forces/spirits away	(Quiros)
	Medicinal	
Hoodoo/Root Magic (USA)	Jasmin will aid in the reception of psychic dreams, and to enhance the power of love herb mixtures	
OTHER	Sacred plant, magic: the wood, stick of plant kept in house to prevent the entry of snakes; a pole fixed near the door of the huts to keep away evil spirits.	(CRC)

NAME-CUBA	Naranja, Naranja de China, Naranja de ombligo,	
	Naranja de Valencia, Naranja dulce	(Roig)
Owner	Ochún (LC, TDF, TDF2, Madan)	
	Ochún, Ibeyis (Quiros)	
	Ochún, Ibeyis, Oggún (Irizarry)	
Odun	Oyeku-odi (Quiros, Madan, Irizarry)	

| **NAME-SCIENTIFIC** | *Citrus sinensis* (L.) Osbeck | (Roig) |

NAME-BRAZIL	Laranja, L.-da-china, L.-de-umbigo, L.-doce, Laranjeira		
Candomblé Jêje-Nagô	Xangô, **Iabás**	Terra/Feminino	(Barros)
Candomblé Angola	Lembá, Vunge		
Umbanda	Xangô, **Egunitá**, **Exú Mirim**		

NAME-Lucumí	Orolocun, Orómbo, Olómbo, Osán, Obburuku, Osaeyimbo, Esá	(LC)
	Osán Kimú, Osán, Esá, Olómbo, Orómbo, Orolokun,	
	Obburuku, Osaeyímbo	(TDF2)
	Orombo, Osán, Oburaiko	(TDF)
YORUBA	Osàn, Òrónbó (*Citrus sp.*)	(PV)
	Osàn **Laranja** Òrónbó **Laranjeira**	

NAME-CONGO	Bolo mámba, Máamba, Mbelia kala, Mbefo malala, Nkiánkián	(LC)
	Bolo mambá, Maaba, Mbelia kala, Mbefo malala,	
	Nkianka, Malata	(TDF)
	Ilala, Malala	(CRC)
PALO	Bolo Mamba **Naranja**	
	Mbellika Laémbefo **Naranjo**	

| **NAME-OTHER** | Sweet Orange | (USDA) |
| | Orange, Sweet Orange, Blood Orange | (CRC) |

USES

Leaves and/or dried peel used for Ebomisi, Cleansings
Fruit used as Addimu and Ebbó
This is thee fruit that Ochún wants when she comes
Oranges are the Addimu and/or Ebbó par-excellence for Ochún

Candomblé Jêje-Nagô   Fruit used as Addimú for Iabás and Xangô. The leaves are attributed to Oxalá and used for cleansings of the head (lavagem de cabeça) and baths to unite lovers.

Candomblé Angola   **Lembá**   Flowers used for head cleansings (obrigações no Orí) and for baths to unite lovers

                Vunge   Fruit used for Apanan Erê

INDIA   Used in Ayurveda and Siddha   (CRC)

Hoodoo/Root Magic (USA)   Flowers are a symbol of married life.

NOTE   **Iabás**   **Iabás** are the female Orixá (Jemanjá, Oxum, Iansã, Obá, Yewà, etc)

    See: **https://pt.wikipedia.org/wiki/Yabas**

    Egunitá   **Egunitá** is considered a feminine Orixá associated with the mystery of Fire

    See: **https://pt.wikipedia.org/wiki/Egunitá**

    Exú Mirim   According to Umbanda, these are spirits that are like teenagers, not quite grown up, and like to do mischievous things.

    See: **https://pt.wikipedia.org/wiki/Exu-Mirim**

NOTE   **Pataki for Irete-owonrin**: Why are some oranges sweet and others sour?

- Ochún once lived in a very prosperous land where everything grew thanks to her. For her pleasure she had orange trees along the shore of her river and it was taboo for the town's people to touch them, under penalty of death. One morning she woke up and found the trees all broken up, with the fruit on the ground. It had been the town's people who wanted to taste the sweet oranges that Ochún so much enjoyed. She got so upset that her trees had seen so much mistreatment that she decided to go away and went to live in a cave whose entrance was covered by "Dormidera" (Sensitive plant). Everything dried up and the town's people went to see Orunmila. Orunmila told them that they had to do Ebbó and have Eleggua take it to Ochún. Eleggua went to see how Ochún was, and got near the river. Seeing that everything was calm, he got closer. Ochún came out and offered him some "Bollitos". When he went to take them, Ochún grabbed him and entrapped him in the "Dormidera". The town's people went to see Orunmila again but since Eleggua was not around, the Ebbó could not be delivered. Orunmila checked with the oracle and found out that he must go to the river since it was Ochún's fault that Eleggua was not around. Orunmila then went to the river with some "Bollitos" and honey and started to sing to Ochún. As she was eating, Orunmila liberated Eleggua and took him to his hut. There he did Ebbó for Eleggua and told the town's people that it was now fine to take the Ebbó to Ochún. Ochún soon lost her anger at the sight of the Ebbó and said that everything would return to normal, except the orange trees. From then on, the oranges would be sour so that the town's people would remember her bitterness as to what had happened to her orange trees.

NAME-CUBA	Naranja Agria	(Roig)
Owner	Yemayá, Ochún (TDF2)	
	Oggún (Quiros, Irizarry)	
Odun	Oyeku-irete (Irizarry)	
NAME-SCIENTIFIC	*Citrus × aurantium* L.	(Roig)
NAME-BRAZIL	Laranja-azeda, Laranja-de-Sevilha	
BATUQUE	Bará/Elegbara	
UMBANDA	Exú	
NAME-Lucumí	Korosán	(LC)
	Korosán, Osan Tiu Yiyé	(TDF2)
YORUBA	Jàganyìn, Osàn nlá, Òròmbó, Òròmbó igún, Òsàn òyìnbó,	
	Òrombó-dídùn, Osàn múmu, Òro òyìbó, Gàn-ín gàn-ín,	
	Òrombó làkúègbé, Jàgbure, Òrombó efin, Òrombó jagànyin	(PV, CRC)
NAME-CONGO		
PALO	Machafio Nkián-Nkián	
NAME-OTHER	Sour orange	(USDA)
	Bitter Orange, Sour Orange, Bergamot Orange, Seville Orange	(CRC)
USES		
	Cleansing baths with leaves and/or fruit	(Irizarry)
	It is used to make **Shekete** (a drink Addimu), preferred	
	drink for Yemayá; but all Orixá partake in it. It is sometimes	
	offered to the Orishas in order to bring luck and win over enemies.	
NOTE Shekete	It is a drink which is made with ground corn, sour orange juice	
	and honey or cane honey (a type of molasses). The corn and the	
	sour orange with some water is put in a jar/bottle and buried or put	
	in a dark corner until it ferments somewhat. The taste is then made	
	sweeter with the addition of honey/molasses.	
NOTE	It is with the rind of the sour orange that Orange Marmalade is made.	

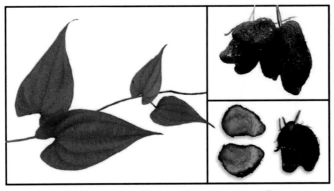 

NAME-CUBA Ñame, Ñame Blanco, Ñame Morado, Ñame Negro, Ñame Bobo (Roig)
Ñame, Ñame de Cuba (Roig)

Owner Eleggua; but ALL use it (LC, TDF2, Quiros)
Eleggua, Orunmila (Irizarry)
Orishaoko, Ifá (Madan)
ALL Orisha (TDF, Diaz)

Odun Odi-owonrin, Okanran-obara, Ose-meji
(Quiros, Diaz, Irizarry, Madan, Orula.org)

NAME-SCIENTIFIC *Dioscorea alata* L. **See NOTE** (Roig, LC)
Dioscorea cayennensis subsp. *rotundata* (Poir.) J.Miège;
Dioscorea rotundata Poir. (Roig, Barros)

NAME-BRAZIL Inhame-São-Tomé (***Dioscorea alata***)
NAME-BRAZIL Inhame-branco, Inhame-de-água, Cará-branco, Cará-preto
Candomblé Jêje-Nagô Oxalá, Ogum Terra/Feminino (Barros)
Candomblé Ketu Iansã
Candomblé de Angola Inkosse, Zaze
Umbanda Exú, Oxalá, Ogum

NAME-Lucumí Ichu, Osúra (LC, TDF2)
Ichú, Ewura, Obisu, Osura (TDF)
Leka, Ichú, Ewura, Obisu **Ñame peludo** (TDF)
YORUBA Arùn fónfón, Ewùrà, Ègbodò ***Dioscorea alata*** (PV, CRC)
Àbáje, Isu funfun, Isu efùrù, Èfòn, Jànyìn jànyìn, Agogó, Wáwá jí,
Mùnú, Òpàràgà, Olótun iyangban, Oluku, Ogodomoyo, Òdò, Olonku,
Afegiagagake, Agbemo, Agemo okun, Ahune ***Dioscorea rotundata*** (PV)

NAME-CONGO Imbiku, Loato (LC)
Imbiko-Loato (TDF)
Kuo kua, Imbiko loato **Ñame peludo** (TDF)
PALO Imbiku

NAME-OTHER ***Dioscorea alata* L.** Water Yam (USDA)
Greater yam, Water yam, Purple yam (CRC)
Dioscorea cayennensis* subsp. *rotundata Guinea Yam (USDA)
Guinea yam, White Guinea yam, White yam (CRC)

USES		**DOES NOT** go to Osain (Omiero)	
		Although it belongs to Eleggua and/or Orishaoko, ALL	
		Orisha partake in it and is used as Addimu for them	(LC)
		The powder used by the Babalawo for the Oracle of Ifá is	
		made from the heart of the Ñame (Iyefa)	(LC)
		Many times, a Ñame will be used as a representation	
		of Eleggua by the front door of many a home	(LC)
		That a Ñame will grow and prosper spontaneously is a	
		portent of good fortune	(LC)
	Abakuá	Without Ñame, and initiate cannot be initiated	(LC)
	Candomblé Jêje-Nagô	it is the Addimú par-excellence for Oxalá	(Barros)
	Candomblé Ketu	The large leaves are used as towels for the cleansings	
		for Exú (obrigações de Exú)	
	Candomblé de Angola Inkosse	Planted in the temple (Axé) and honey is poured	
		over the roots.	
	Zaze	Initiation at the temple (assent Axé, feitura)	
	Umbanda	Offered as Addimú to Ogum, Oxalá and Exú.	
		Sacred plant for the Yoruba.	
	INDIA	**Dioscorea alata** Used in Ayurveda and Siddha	(CRC)

NOTE		Both of these species are considered Ñame by Juan Tomás Roig	
		Dioscorea alata originated in Tropical/Sub-tropical Asia	(CRC)
		Dioscorea rotundata **Poir.** originated in Tropical Africa	(CRC)

NOTE   **Why all the Orixá eat Ñame** by Lydia Cabrera

- One day Olofi had a gathering of all the Orisha, but Orunmila was but a poor yam farmer. Although all the other Orisha brought sumptuous gifts, all the Orunmila brought was his best-looking Ñame. All the Orisha laughed at his poor choice of a gift but Olofi, in a voice that was heard by everyone said "Ñame will be sacred". Time passed and there was a great famine and all lost their money and were going hungry. The Orisha then went to Orunmila to ask for yams in order to eat. Orunmila which had a good crop gave them Ñame so they could all eat. From then on, ALL Orisha eat Ñame.

NAME-CUBA	Ñame Volador, Ñame Cimarrón, Ñame de Monte	(Roig)
Owner	Changó (Quiros)	
Odun		
NAME-SCIENTIFIC	*Dioscorea bulbifera* L.	(Roig)
NAME-BRAZIL	Cará-moela, Cará-do-ar, Inhame-do-ar, Cará-voador, Cará-aéreo	
Candomblé Jêje-Nagô	Oxalá Terra/Feminino	(Barros)
CULTO DE NAÇÃO	Oxalá	
NAME-Lucumí	Ichu	(LC, TDF2)
YORUBA	Emìnà, Ewùrà esin, Dandan	(PV, CRC)
	Akan	(Barros)
NAME-CONGO	Imbíkua salálálá	(LC)
	Imbiko salalo	(TDF)
	Banga, Isaka, Dumbala, Mbila, Makambi, Sola-nkiti	(CRC)
PALO	Imblko Sala Lá Lá	
NAME-OTHER	Air Potato	(USDA)
	Air Potato, Aerial Yam, Bitter yam, Potato yam	(CRC)

USES

	The plant is a protector against Ndokis (flying witches)	(LC)
	With the yam, maleficent Afoches can be made	(LC)
Candomblé Jêje-Nagô	With the yam a powerful "Atín" (Afoche/powder)	
	is made for good luck	(Barros)
Umbanda	For Ebô for prosperity with Oxalá	
INDIA	Used in Ayurveda, Unani and Siddha	(CRC)

NAME-CUBA	Ocuje, O. Blanco, O. Macho, Bálsamo de María, Palo María	(Roig)
Owner	Mayombe (LC)	
	Changó (Diaz)	
Odun	Oturupon-ofun (Diaz, Madan, Orula.org)	

NAME-SCIENTIFIC	*Calophyllum brasiliense* var. *antillanum* (Britton) Standl.;	
	Calophyllum antillanum Britton	(Roig)

NAME-BRAZIL	Guanandi, Jacareúba	

NAME-Lucumí	Yenyé	(LC, TDF2)
YORUBA		

NAME-CONGO	Simano	(LC)
	Simanó	(TDF)

NAME-OTHER	Antille Calophyllum	(USDA)
	Brazil Beauty Leaf, Landim	
	Palo de María (PR); Baría, Malaguetta (DR);	
	Palo María (Venezuela), Bwa Marie, Dammarie (Creole Haiti)	(Duke's)

USES	Goes to Osain (Omiero)	
	Medicinal	
PALO	Sarayéyé in front of Nganga to detach bothersome spirits	(Diaz)

NOTE powo.science.kew.org and the plantlist.org list *Calophyllum antillanum* **Britton** as a synonym for *Calophyllum brasiliense* **var.** *antillanum* **(Britton) Standl.**; BUT gbif.org lists *Calophyllum brasiliense* **var.** *antillanum* **(Britton) Standl.** as a synonym of *Calophyllum antillanum* **Britton.** On the other hand; **Duke's** and **Elsevier** lists *Calophyllum brasiliense* **var.** *antillanum* **(Britton) Standl.** as a synonym for *Calophyllum brasiliense* **Cambess.**

NAME-CUBA	Ofón	(Roig)
Owner	Obatalá (LC, TDF2, Quiros)	
Odun		
NAME-SCIENTIFIC	*Vitex doniana* Sweet	(Roig)
NAME-BRAZIL	NOT found in Flora do Brasil	
NAME-Lucumí	Ofón, Ofún	(TDF2)
YORUBA	Òrì, Òrì nlá, Òrì odan	(PV, CRC)
NAME-CONGO	Meremiyé	(LC)
NAME-OTHER	Vitex, Meru-oak	(USDA)
	Black Plum, West African Plum	(CRC)
USES		
	Used during rituals to wash the reliquary of Obatalá	
	during the ceremony of initiation (Kari Ocha)	(LC)

NOTE   Per **IUCN Red List (IUCNredlist.org)** this tree is native to Africa and other than Africa, the other populations for these trees are located in the Seychelles and Cuba.

NAME-CUBA	Ojo de Buey, Ojo de Caballo	(Roig)
Owner	Changó (LC, TDF2, Quiros)	
Odun		
NAME-SCIENTIFIC	*Mucuna urens* (L.) Medik.	(Roig)
NAME-BRAZIL	Olho-de-boi, Mucunã	
Candomblé	Òsányìn (the leaves)	
Umbanda	Caboclos, Pretos-velhos	
NAME-Lucumí	Júmilli, Irúbaniyé	(LC)
	Júmíyí, Irúbaniyé	(TDF2)
YORUBA		
NAME-CONGO	Bambenga, Mera	(CRC)
NAME-OTHER	Oxeye Bean	(USDA)
	Horse-eye bean, Ox-eye bean, Sea bean	
	Ojo de Zamuro (Venezuela)	(CRC)

USES

	Used as a talisman for good luck and against evil-eye	(LC)
Candomblé	The leaves used for baths for the filhos of Òsányìn and for the cleansings of ritual items	
	Seeds used as amulets for luck and against evil-eye	
Umbanda	Used as decorations/necklaces for Caboclos and Pretos-velhos	
	The seed/s kept in a glass of water behind the door against Negative energies or the evil-eye	
Hoodoo/Root Magic (USA)	Sea beans carried as lucky pocket pieces	

NAME-CUBA	Ojo de Profeta	**See NOTE**	(LC)
	Ojo de Poeta, Anteojo de Poeta		(Roig)
Owner	Orula (LC, TDF2, Quiros)		
Odun			

| **NAME-SCIENTIFIC** | *Thunbergia alata* Bojer ex Sims | (Roig) |

| **NAME-BRAZIL** | Amarelinha, Carólia, Cipó-africano, Olho-de-poeta, Olho-preto, Suzana-dos-olhos-negros |

NAME-Lucumí	Mikembo	(LC)
	Réchéyeé	(TDF2)
YORUBA		

NAME-CONGO

| **NAME-OTHER** | Black-eyed Susan Vine | (USDA) |
| | Black-eyed Susan, Black-eyed Susan Vine | (CRC) |

USES

	For Use by Babalawo	
	The leaves for cleansing baths.	(LC)
	Medicinal	

NOTE Lydia Cabrera failed to name a particular species for this plant. The plant that was listed by Juan Tomás Roig in "Diccionario Botánico de nombres vulgares cubanos" was Ojo de Poeta. When this plant (***Thunbergia alata* Bojer ex Sims**) was checked against the listing for it in CRC (CRC World Dictionary of Medicinal and Poisonous Plants, Common Names, Scientific Names, Eponyms, Synonyms, and Etymology, 5 Volume Set) (Page 3734); the medicinal properties matched what Lydia Cabrera had written.

NAME-CUBA	Ojo de Ratón, Coralitos	(Roig)
Owner	Eleggua (LC, TDF2, Quiros)	
	Ifá (Madan)	
Odun	Oyekun-ofun (Quiros, Madan)	
NAME-SCIENTIFIC	*Rivina humilis* L.	(Roig)
NAME-BRAZIL	Rivina, Vermelinha, Ervas-dos-carpinteiros	
NAME-Lucumí	Módóbbo	(LC)
	Móddóbo	(TDF2)
YORUBA		
NAME-CONGO		
NAME-OTHER	Rougeplant	(USDA)
	Coral berry, Blood berry, Pepper bush, Rouge plant	(CRC)
USES	Goes to Osain (Omiero)	(Madan)
	Used to make a business fail	(LC)
	Used to make and/or destroy traps (trampas)	(Madan)

NAME-CUBA	Oreja de Palo, Guindavela, Palo Caballero	**See NOTE**	(LC)
	Oreja de Palo		(Roig)
Owner	Mayombe (LC)		
Odun			

NAME-SCIENTIFIC *Trametes maxima* (Mont.) A.David & Rajchenb.;
    Coriolus maximus (Mont.) Murrill   **See NOTE**   (Roig)

NAME-BRAZIL Specimens and info at Instituto de Botânica, São Paulo

NAME-Lucumí
  YORUBA

NAME-CONGO Gunda bela   (TDF)

NAME-OTHER White Rot Fungus   (uniport.org)

USES
  PALO With this Ewe, the spirit of a dead person and the necessary
      ancillary additions that "Paleros" use, a good talisman is made
      for protection.   (LC)

NOTE Although Lydia Cabrera lists this Ewe (Oreja de Palo) with two other synonyms; those same synonyms are used in the listing of Palo Caballero, which is totally different Ewe. This Ewe is a fungus where the other is an Angiosperm (plant)

NOTE This Ewe (***Coriolus maximus***) is a mushroom. Taxonomic info was found at GBIF - Global Biodiversity Information Facility; (**https://www.gbif.org/**)

NAME-CUBA	Orozuz de la Tierra, Orozuz	(Roig)
Owner	Ochún (LC, TDF2, Quiros, Diaz, Madan, Concordia)	
	Yemayá (TDF)	
	Obatalá (Irizarry)	
	Yemayá, Ochún (Menéndez)	
Odun	Ofun-irosun (Quiros, Diaz, Irizarry, Madan, Concordia, Orula.org)	
	Odi-ogunda (Quiros, Diaz, irizarrry, Concordia, Orula.org)	
	Ika-odi, Irete-iwori (Quiros, Diaz, Irizarry, Madan, Orula.org)	

NAME-SCIENTIFIC	*Phyla scaberrima* (Juss. ex Pers.) Moldenke;	
	Lippia dulcis Trevir.	(Roig)

NAME-BRAZIL	Erva-doce-dos-astecas, Arbusto-lipia	

NAME-Lucumí	Orosún kikio simawa, Eyéfoo	(LC)
	Orosú, Orosún Kíkio simawa	(TDF2)
YORUBA		

NAME-CONGO	Inmeyemo	(LC)
	Nmeyemo	(TDF)

NAME-OTHER	Honey Herb	(USDA)
	Aztec Sweet Herb, Lippia, Mexican Sweet Leaf	(Duke's)

USES	Goes to Osain (Omiero)	
	Used for ritual baths (Ebomisi) and Inche Osain	
	Medicinal	
	Used to make love potions and love baths	(Diaz)
	Baths for better luck and for increased financial gains	(Madan)
	This Ewe is used to clean the floors of places of illicit gain; i.e.- gambling parlors, etc.	(LC)
	When an amulet is made with this Ewe for men in illegal businesses, i.e.-gamblers, drug dealers, etc.; the amulet is name "Judas"	(LC)

NAME-CUBA	Ortiguilla, Ortiga	(Roig)
Owner	Babalú-Ayé (LC, Quiros, Diaz)	
	Babalú-Ayé, Ochosi (TDF2)	
Odun	Irosun-ika (Diaz)	

NAME-SCIENTIFIC	*Laportea cuneata* (A.Rich.) Chew; *Fleurya cuneata* (A.Rich.) Wedd.	(Roig)
	Laportea aestuans (L.) Chew	(Barros, PV)

NAME-BRAZIL	Urtiga-graúda, Urtiga-de-folha-grande, Cansanção-da-folha-grande	
Candomblé Jêje-Nagô	Exú, Ogum Fogo/Feminino	(Barros)
Candomblé de Angola	Aluvaiá	
Umbanda		

NAME-Lucumí	Ewe Né, Iná, Aiñá	(LC)
	Cheguere kue-kue, Ainá, Ewe Né, Iná, Iñá, Chequere Kuekue	(TDF2)
YORUBA	Òfià, Òfùèfùè, Ipè erin, Èsìsì pupa, Èfùyá, Ipò	(PV)
NAME-CONGO	Iyén	(LC)
	Iyen	(TDF)
	Kaololo, Toololo (***Laportea aestuans***)	(CRC)

NAME-OTHER	***Fleurya cuneate*** Weedy wood-nettle	(Wiki)
	Laportea aestuans West Indian wood nettle (florida.plantatlas.usf.edu	
	West Indian Nettle, Stinging Nettle. Nettle	(Duke's)

USES	**DOES NOT** go to Osain (Omiero)	
	Medicinal	
	To make a man impotent	(LC)
PALO	To make a powder (Afoche/Mpolo) to cause disputes and	
	bring about the destruction of a home/family	(LC)
Candomblé Jêje-Nagô	To prepare powders (afoche/Atín) with Exú.	
	To make Ogum mad	(Barros)
Candomblé de Angola	Aluvaiá Ebô for defense (Ebô de defensa) and Asssento Okutá	
Hoodoo/Root Magic (USA)	Nettle is a strong jinx braker	

NOTE	This plant (***Fleurya cuneata* (A.Rich.) Wedd.**) is native to Cuba and Hispaniola
	See: **http://powo.science.kew.org/taxon/urn:lsid:ipni.org:names:135478-2**

NAME-CUBA	Palma Cana, Guano Cana		(Roig)
Owner	Changó (Diaz)		
Odun	Irosun-iwori (Diaz, Orula.org)		
NAME-SCIENTIFIC	*Sabal maritima* (Kunth) Burret;		
	Sabal florida Becc.		(Roig)
NAME-BRAZIL	NOT listed in Flora do Brasil		
NAME- ANAGO	Abegudá, Ikó erí	**Palma**	(LC)
YORUBA			
NAME-CONGO			
BANTU	Maba munanfinda	**Palma Cana**	
	Lala	**Palma**	(LC)
Carabalí/Bríkamo	Ukano, Upanó	**Palma**	
	Ukano mambré	**Palma**	
	Ukano mambró	**Palma Macho**	(LC)
NAME-OTHER	No common name found. Endemic to Cuba and Jamaica		
	Bull Thatch Palm		(davesgarden.com)
USES	**DOES NOT** go to Osain (Omiero)		
	Medicinal		(Diaz, Quiros)

NOTE   *Sabal maritima* **(Kunth) Burret** is Native to Cuba and Jamaica
http://powo.science.kew.org/taxon/urn:lsid:ipni.org:names:224819-2
and listed as **Endemic** to Cuba and Jamaica
https://www.palmpedia.net/wiki/Sabal_maritima

NAME-CUBA	Palma Dátil, Dátil		(Roig)
Owner	Changó (Quiros)		
Odun	Odi-otura (Quiros, Madan, Orula.org)		
NAME-SCIENTIFIC	*Phoenix dactylifera* L.		(Roig)
NAME-BRAZIL	Tamareira, Datileira		
NAME- ANAGO	Okunká	**Dátil**	
	Abegudá, Ikó erí	**Palma**	(LC)
YORUBA			
NAME-CONGO			
BANTU	Lala	**Palma**	(LC)
Carabalí/Bríkamo	Ukano, Upanó	**Palma**	
	Ukano mambré	**Palma**	
	Ukano mambró	**Palma Macho**	(LC)
NAME-OTHER	Date palm		(USDA)
	Date, Date palm		(CRC)
USES			
	Medicinal		(Quiros)
INDIA	Used in Ayurveda, Unani and Siddha. Ritual: dried fruits used in different ceremonies, pujas and offerings		(CRC)

NAME-CUBA	Palma Real	(Roig)
Owner	Changó (TDF2)	
	Changó, Orula (Quiros, Madan)	
	Changó, Oggún, Orunmila (Irizarry)	
	Changó, Ibeyis (Diaz)	
	Oggún, Ochosi (Menéndez) **Cogollo de Palma**	
Odun	Odi-meji (Quiros, Irizarry, Diaz, Orula.org)	
	Irete-otura, Otura-irosun (Quiros, Diaz, Madan, Orula.org)	

NAME-SCIENTIFIC	*Roystonea regia (Kunth) O.F.Cook*	(Roig)

NAME-BRAZIL	Palmeira-real-de-Cuba, Palmeira-da-Flórida	

NAME-Lucumí	Ilé Changó, Orissá, Iggi Oppwé, Opé, Alábbi, Cefidiyé,	
	Eluwere, Oluwekón	(TDF2)
	Ono bri, Iggi mariwó, Alabbi	(TDF)

NAME-CONGO	Bakosola, Manga, Nkunia karondo	(TDF)
PALO	Maba	
	OWNER Siete Rayos	(Diaz)

NAME-OTHER	Royal Palm	(USDA)
	Cuban Royal Palm, Florida Royal Palm	(Elsevier)

USES	**DOES NOT** go to Osain (Omiero)	
	Used for home cleansings to refresh, and Ebomisi	(Diaz)
	Offerings to Changó placed at the foot of the palm tree.	
	The tender fronds used to make Mariwo to dress Oggún and	
	Other Orishas, and to adorn the Igbodú.	(Irizarry)
PALO	Roots and dirt from around tree go in the Nganga for Site Rayos	(Diaz)

NAME-CUBA	Palo Amargo, Palo Amarillo, Marigoncillo		(Roig)
Owner	Changó, Oggún (LC, TDF2, Quiros)		
NAME-SCIENTIFIC	*Picramnia reticulata* Griseb.		(Roig)
NAME-BRAZIL	NOT found in Flora do Brasil		
NAME-Lucumí	Iggi Kikán		(LC)
	Kikán, Iggi Kikán		(TDF2)
NAME-CONGO	Momboco		(LC)
	Nomboko		(TDF)
PALO	**PALO AMARGO**	Mómboco	
	OWNER	Zarabanda, Siete Rayos	(Nfinda)
NAME-OTHER USES	NO common name found. **Endemic to Cuba**		
	Plant is used without the bark for Orisha		(LC)
	Used to make someone's life miserable		(LC)
	In concoction, drunk to take out ingested Bilongo		(LC)
	Medicinal		
PALO	NOT to be used in all Ngangas. Only for Zarabanda and Siete Rayos		
	Good "palo" for Mpolo in case of problems with justice		
	or when you want to destroy someone.		
	To get rid of ingested Mpolo, a concoction of the bark, roots and		
	leaves is boiled and taken prior to morning meal.		(Nfinda)
	Can also be used for protection and to have victory		
	over your enemies		(Nfinda)
NOTE	This plant (*Picramnia reticulata* Griseb.) is **Endemic** to Cuba		(KewScience)
	There are no specimens photographed (actual specimens) in the Web		
	The only pictures are from collected specimens		
	The one shown is from the scan of specimen at the Moscow University Herbarium		
	See: **https://plant.depo.msu.ru/open/public/item/MW0576410**		
NOTE	There is an alternative species identified by Teodoro Díaz Fabelo and Juan Tomás Roig		

NAME-CUBA	Palo Amargo, Carbonero de Costa, Jayajabico		(Roig)
	Palo Amargo - 2		
Owner	Changó, Oggún (LC, TDF2, Quiros)		
Odun			

NAME-SCIENTIFIC	*Colubrina elliptica* (Sw.) Brizicky & W.L.Stern;		
	Colubrina reclinata (L'Hér.) Brongn.		(Roig)

NAME-BRAZIL	NOT found in Flora do Brasil

NAME-Lucumí	Iggi Kikán		(LC)
	Kikán, Iggi Kikán		(TDF2)
NAME-CONGO	Momboco		(LC)
	Nomboko		(TDF)
PALO	**PALO AMARGO**	Mómboco	
	OWNER	Zarabanda, Siete Rayos	(Nfinda)

NAME-OTHER	Soldier wood	(USDA)
	Naked wood, Soldier wood, West Indian green heart	
	Corazón de Paloma (DR, PR); Bwa mabi (Creole Haiti)	(Elsevier)

USES

	Plant is used without the bark for Orisha	(LC)
	Used to make someone's life miserable	(LC)
	In concoction, drunk to take out ingested Bilongo	(LC)
	Medicinal	
PALO	NOT to be used in all Ngangas. Only for Zarabanda and Siete Rayos	
	Good "palo" for Mpolo in case of problems with justice	
	or when you want to destroy someone.	
	To get rid of ingested Mpolo, a concoction of the bark, roots and	
	leaves is boiled and taken prior to morning meal.	(Nfinda)
	Can also be used for protection and to have victory	
	over your enemies	(Nfinda)

NAME-CUBA	Palo Arriero, Arriero		(LC)
	Arriero, Badana, Cordobán, Padero, Yagruma macho		(Roig)
Owner			
Odun			
NAME-SCIENTIFIC	*Schefflera morototoni* (Aubl.) Maguire, Steyerm. & Frodin;		
	Didymopanax morototoni (Aubl.) Decne. & Planch.		(Roig)
NAME-BRAZIL	Morototó, Mandioqueira, Matataúba, Para-pará, Sambacuim		(Elsevier)
NAME-Lucumí	Pikotó		(LC, TDF, TDF2)
ANAGO	Larí, Laro, Ogúgú, Ogúngú	**Yagrumo**	(LC)
	Ewe lari loró, Ewe loro	**Yagrumo – Hojas**	(LC)
YORUBA			
NAME-CONGO	Kuakari		(LC, TDF)
BANTU	Kukuanchala, Kukuan pela, Kukuasara,		
	Kuensala	**Arriero**	(LC)
	Kuakari	**Palo Arriero**	(LC)
NAME-OTHER	Matchwood		(itis.gov)
	Anonillo, Yagruma macho (DR); Palo de Yagua,		
	Yagruma macho (PR); Arriero, Yarumo macho (Vzla);		
	Bwa kano, Twompèt mal (Creole Haiti)		(Elsevier)
USES			
	Purification baths (baños de despojo) to banish negative		
	influences/energy		(LC)

NAME-CUBA	Palo Blanco, Gavilán		(Roig)
Owner	Osain (Quiros)		
Odun			
NAME-SCIENTIFIC	*Simarouba amara* Aubl.;		
	Simarouba glauca DC.		(Roig)
NAME-BRAZIL	Marupá-verdadeiro, Paparaúba-branca		
NAME-Lucumí	Iggi fún		(LC, TDF2)
YORUBA			
NAME-CONGO	Mussi mindola		(LC)
	Musi mundola		(TDF)
PALO	**PALO BLANCO**	Musi Mindola	
	OWNER	Tiembla Tierra, Mamá Chola	(Nfinda)
NAME-OTHER	Paradise Tree, Bitter-wood		(pfaf.org)
	Bitter Ash, Bitter Wood		
	Aceituno (PR); Palo Amargo (DR); Amargo (Venezuela);		
	Bwa blan, Bwa fwenn (Creole Haiti)		(Elsevier)
USES			
	Medicinal		
PALO	Good "palo" for works for people who are sick		
	Very good to use to get someone out of jail		(Nfinda)

NAME-CUBA		Palo Bobo	(LC)
		Palo Bobo de Cuba, Bagá	(Roig)
	Owner	Obatalá, Changó, Oggún (LC)	
		Obatalá (TDF2)	
		Abita, Eshú (Diaz)	**See NOTE**
	Odun	Ika-owonrin (Quiros, Orula.org)	

NAME-SCIENTIFIC	*Annona glabra* L.	(Roig)

NAME-BRAZIL		Araticum-do-brejo, Araticum-liso, Araticum-do-mangue	
Candomblé Bantu		**Angorô, Kaiá**	**See NOTE**

NAME-Lucumí			Inábiri, Iyúmo	(LC, TDF2)
YORUBA			Afe	(PV)
NAME-CONGO			Nkunia mbi machafio, Guaéko	(LC)
			Nkini-mbi, Mashafio, Guasko	(TDF)
	PALO	**PALO BOBO**	Nkuni mbi machafri, Guaéko	
		OWNER	Zarabanda, Siete Rayos, Lucero, Tiembla Tierra (Nfinda)	

NAME-OTHER	Pond apple	(USDA)
	Alligator apple, Custard apple, Anone (US)	
	Anona liso/de campo (Vzla); Kowosòl mawon (Creole Haiti)	(Elsevier)

USES		**ONLY** used in Regla Conga	
	PALO	This "palo" can be used for good or bad	
		A good "palo" to have when one has enemies. Used to make	
		powders (Afoche/Mpolo) where the enemy will never know	
		who caused his downfall.	(Nfinda)

NOTE	**ABITA**	It is the devil in Regla de Ocha
	Candomblé Bantu is the same as Candomblé de Angola or Candomblé de Congo	
	See:	**https://pt.wikipedia.org/wiki/Candomblé_bantu**
	Angorô, Kaiá are **Nkisi/Mikisi** in Candomblé de Angola; i.e.- deities.	
	See:	**https://pt.wikipedia.org/wiki/Nkisi**

NAME-CUBA	Palo Bomba	(LC)
	Palo de Bomba, Malagueta Blanca, Guabico de Sabana	(Roig)
Owner	Changó, Oggún (LC, TDF2, Quiros)	
Odun		
NAME-SCIENTIFIC	*Xylopia obtusifolia* (A.DC.) A.Rich.	(Roig)
NAME-BRAZIL	NOT found in Flora do Brasil	
NAME-Lucumí	Olúnipa	(LC, TDF2)
YORUBA		
NAME-CONGO	Mubón	(LC, TDF)
PALO	**Palo Cirio = PALO BOMBA**	(LC)
	PALO BOMBA Mubón	
	OWNER Zarabanda, Siete Rayos, Madre de Agua	(Nfinda)
NAME-OTHER	No common name found. Native to Cuba.	
	Obtuse-leaf Xylopia	(Elsevier)

USES

	Powders (afoche) made with this Ewe will KILL	(LC)
	Its only good for Malambo or Iká (doing BAD??)	(LC)
PALO	This "palo" is only good for doing misdeeds, but is recommended	
	that "Mayomberos" **NOT** to use it since this "palo" will	
	trick the one doing the deeds.	(Nfinda)

NOTE   *Xylopia obtusifolia (A.DC.) A.Rich.* is **ENDEMIC to Cuba**
      Xylopia obtusifolia (A.DC.) A.Rich. is listed as **ENDANGERED by BISSEA**

NOTE   Lydia Cabrera names another tree for this Ewe
      ***Annona squamosa* L.; *Xylopia glabra* L.** which is the ANON

NAME-CUBA	Palo Bronco	(LC)
	Palo Bronco de Monte, Cerezo	(Roig)
Owner	Osain, Oggún, Changó, Eleggua (LC)	
	Osain, Oggún, Changó (TDF2)	
	Osain, Obatalá (Quiros)	
Odun		
NAME-SCIENTIFIC	*Malpighia glabra* L.;	
	Malpighia biflora Poir.	(Roig)
NAME-BRAZIL	Acerola, Cerejeira-do-Pará, Cerejeira-de-Barbados, Cerejeira-das-Antilhas	
NAME-Lucumí	Moruambo	(TDF2)
YORUBA		
NAME-CONGO	Moruambo	(LC, TDF)
PALO	**PALO BRONCO** Muruambo	
	OWNER Ngurufinda, Lucero, Zarabanda, Siete Rayos	(Nfinda)
NAME-OTHER	Wild Crape Myrtle	(USDA)
	Barbados Cherry, Antillean Cherry	
	Cereza (PR); Semeruco (Venezuela);	
	Seriz, Seriz dayiti (Creole Haiti)	(Elsevier)

USES

Used as an amulet in the form of a cane in order to enter the woods or unknown places to collect Ewe   (LC)

PALO   The wood is used to prepare amulets in order to enter prohibited places. An amulet prepared of this wood will prevent from being attacked by witches, dark Eggun, animals and humans. It will guide the "Palero" through a safe path.   (Nfinda)

Hoodoo/Root Magic (USA)   Myrtle is a Love herb that can be used in mixtures with other herbs in love baths or incense.

NAME-CUBA	Palo Caballero, Cepa de Caballero		(Roig)
	Palo Caballero, Guinda Vela	**See NOTE**	(LC)
Owner	Changó (LC, TDF2, Quiros)		
Odun			
NAME-SCIENTIFIC	*Phoradendron quadrangulare* (Kunth) Griseb.;		(gbif.org)
	Phoradendron quadrangulare (Kunth) Krug & Urban		(Roig)
	Phoradendron rubrum Griseb. ex Eichler;		(gbif.org)
	Phoradendron rubrum (L.) Griseb.		(LC, Roig)
NAME-BRAZIL	Erva-de-passarinho (**Both**)		
NAME-Lucumí	Butekié		(TDF2)
YORUBA			
NAME-CONGO	Butekié		(LC, TDF)
PALO	**OWNER**	Marigwánga	(LC)
	PALO CABALLERO	Butekié	
	OWNER	Siete Rayos, Finda, Centella	(Nfinda)
BANTU	Butekié	**Palo Caballero** (Phoradendron rubrum)	(LC)
NAME-OTHER	*Phoradendron quadrangulare*	Quacimmila de canario	(USDA)
	Uáuá		(Hatian Cuban Creole)
	Phoradendron rubrum	Mahogany Mistletoe	(USDA)

USES

	Protects against witchcraft and bad influences	
	A small branch can be worn/kept as an amulet	(LC)
PALO	This "palo" cannot be absent from the Nganga	
	This "palo" has the power to save or to kill	
	A small branch can be worn/kept as an amulet to	
	ward off witchcraft and/or bad influences	(Nfinda)

NOTE   Lydia Cabrera notes *Phoradendron rubrum* **(L.) Griseb**. as the botanical name for Palo Caballero. Juan Tomás Roig notes that *Phoradendron rubrum* **(L.) Griseb**. is a synonym for *Phoradendron quadrangulare* **(Kunth) Krug & Urban**; when in reality they are both separate specimens. They are both types of **Mistletoe**

NAME-CUBA	Palo Cachimba, Víbona, Ramon de Vaca	(Roig)
Owner	Changó, Osain, Oyá (LC)	
	Changó (TDF2, Quiros)	
Odun		
NAME-SCIENTIFIC	*Dendropanax arboreus* (L.) Decne. & Planch.; **See NOTE**	
	Gilibertia arborea (L.) Marchal ex T.Durand & Pittier	(Roig)
	Gilibertia samydifolia (C.Wright ex Griseb.) Marchal	(Roig)
NAME-BRAZIL	Maria-molle	(Elsevier)
NAME-Lucumí	Achó Ikoko	(LC, TDF2)
YORUBA		
NAME-CONGO		
NAME-OTHER	Angelica Tree	(USDA)
	Palo de Pollo (PR); Ramón de Costa (DR);	
	Pama (Venezuela); Bwa nègès (Creole Haiti)	(Elsevier)
USES		
	Used to prevent lighting from hitting	(LC)

NOTE   Lydia Cabrera failed to name a species for this Ewe. Juan Tomás Roig has Víbona as a synonym for Palo Cachimba. Of the species listed under Víbona; two happen to be synonym for the same plant (***Dendropanax arboreus***)

NOTE   Per Lydia Cabrera in "Anagó - Vocabulario Lucumí"; the leaves of this tree are used by Babalawo's to make "**Yefá**" (the powder used on the Opón Ifá)

NAME-CUBA	Palo Café, Café Cimarrón, Pitajoní Cimarrón, Pitajoní Macho	(Roig)
Owner		
Odun		
NAME-SCIENTIFIC	*Amaioua corymbosa* Kunth	(Roig)
NAME-BRAZIL	NO common name found	
NAME-Lucumí	Iggifere, Apó	(LC)
	Iggi Fere, Apó	(TDF2)
YORUBA		
NAME-CONGO	Irínkao, Popolú	(LC)

| **PALO** | **PALO CAFÉ** | Irínkao, Popolú | |
| | **OWNER** | Lucero, Zarabanda | (Nfinda) |

| **NAME-OTHER** | Wild Coffee, Bastard Coffee | |
| | Canilla de Venado (Venezuela) | (Elsevier) |

USES

PALO
Like all incenses, the burning of this Ewe/" palo"
will drive all that is bad away.
It is the incense of old (negros de nación) that was
used to drive sickness away, purify the rooms where
sick people were and to drive away fetid odors that
carry other bad influences.
(LC, Nfinda)

NAME-CUBA	Palo Caja	(LC)
	Palo de Caja, Caja, Caja Común	(Roig)
Owner	Changó (LC, TDF2, Quiros, Diaz)	
	Babalú-Ayé (TDF)	
	Oyá (Menéndez)	
Odun	Irosun-meji (Diaz)	

| **NAME-SCIENTIFIC** | *Allophylus cominia* (L.) Sw. | | (Roig) |
| | *Allophylus africanus* P.Beauv. | **See NOTE** | (PV) |

| **NAME-BRAZIL** | DOES NOT occur in Brazil, per Flora do Brasil | |

NAME-Lucumí	Orín, Merémbe		(LC, TDF2)
	Biré		(TDF)
YORUBA	Àkànrò, Àkàrà àfín, Àkàrà èsù, Lánarí	(**Allophylus africanus**)	(PV, CRC)

NAME-CONGO	Ngüengue		(LC)
	Nguengué		(TDF)
	Umutwetwe, Wobyebye	(**Allophylus africanus**)	(CRC)
PALO	**PALO CAJA**	Nguengue	
	OWNER	Siete Rayos, Ngunrrunfinda	(Nfinda)

| **NAME-OTHER** | Bastard Cherry | |
| | Palo de Caja (DR); Kafe mawon (Creole Haiti) | (Elsevier) |

USES	Goes to Osain (Omiero)	
	Ritual baths (Ebomisi), cleansing baths. It kills witchcraft	(LC)
	Medicinal	
PALO	Recommended for cleansing baths and kills witchcraft	
	Very noble "palo" and very much used as medicinal	(Nfinda)

NOTE Both of this plant species are almost identical in looks and the name in Congo
per CRC (CRC World Dictionary of Medicinal and Poisonous Plants, Common Names,
Scientific Names, Eponyms, Synonyms, and Etymology, 5 Volume Set) is almost the
same as that listed by LC and TDF.

NAME-CUBA	Palo Cambia Voz, Palo Cambia Camino	(LC)
	Cuaba, Cuaba blanca, Cuaba de olor, Cuaba de sabana	(Roig)

Owner
Odun

NAME-SCIENTIFIC	*Amyris balsamifera* L.	(Roig)

NAME-BRAZIL	**NOT** found on Brazilian Flora Online	

| NAME-Lucumí | Kisíambolo | (TDF2) |
| **YORUBA** | | |

NAME-CONGO	Kisiambolo, Nkunia bodán súa	(LC)
	Nkunia bodánsúa	(Nfinda)
PALO	**PALO CAMBIA VOZ/CAMBIA CAMINO**　　Kisiambolo	
	OWNER　　　　Zarabanda, Mariwanga, Lucero	(Nfinda)

NAME-OTHER	Balsam Torchwood	(USDA)
	Guaconejo (DR); Sándalo de las Antillas (Venezuela)	
	Bwa chandèl (Creole Haití)	(Elsevier)

USES

	Medicinal	(LC)
PALO	"Palero" MUST pay in blood, or the "palo" will not work	
	Can either be for good or bad:	
	White Cuaba (Blanca) only used to do good	
	Black Cuaba (Negra) is for doing BAD　　**See NOTE**	(LC)
	This "palo" will make people change opinion or direction	
	This "palo" has great power and can either be used for good or bad	
	With a powder (Afoche) made from Cuaba, you can get	
	whatever you have requested/are seeking	(Nfinda)

NOTE　　**Cuaba Negra** – J. T. Roig has **NO** name for Cuaba Negra.
　　　　There is a **Cuaba Prieta** (Roig) which is the ***Erithalis fruticosa* L.**

NAME-CUBA	Palo Cenizo, Humo de Sabana	(LC)
	Cenizo, Humo, Abey Blanco, Encinillo	(Roig)
	Humo de Sabana, Guayabillo	(Roig)
Owner		

NAME-SCIENTIFIC	*Abarema obovalis* (A.Rich.) Barneby & J.W.Grimes;	
	Pithecellobium obovale (A. Rich.) C. Wright	(Roig)
	Chloroleucon mangense var. lentiscifolium (C.Wright) Barneby & J.W.Grimes;	
	Pithecellobium lentiscifolium C.Wright	(Roig)

| **NAME-BRAZIL** | NOT listed in Flora do Brasil | |

NAME-Lucumí	Igbeléfin	(LC)
ANAGO	Igbelefín	**Palo Cenizo, Humo de Sabana**	(LC)
NAME-CONGO	Nchúngo, Chúngora mifototo	(LC)
	Nshungo	**Palo Cenizo**	(TDF)
PALO	**PALO CENIZO, HUMO DE SABANA**	
	Nchúngo, Chúngora Mofototo	(Nfinda)

NAME-OTHER	**Pithecellobium obovale** NO common name found. Native to Cuba, Hispaniola	
	Obovate abarema (English); Encinillo (PR)	(Elsevier)
	Pithecellobium lentiscifolium NO common name found. Native to Cuba, Belize	
	Lentiscusleaf Manga chloroleucon	(Elsevier)

USES

| **PALO** | It is used to balance the powers of all the other "palos" in | |
| | the Nganga and talismans. | (Nfinda) |

NAME-CUBA	Palo Clavo	(LC)
	Palo del Clavo, Clavo de Especie, Árbol del Clavo	(Roig)
Owner	Oggún (LC, TDF2, Quiros)	

NAME-SCIENTIFIC	*Syzygium aromaticum* (L.) Merr. & L.M.Perry;	
	Eugenia caryophyllata Thunb.	(Roig)

NAME-BRAZIL	Cravo-da- Índia, Cravoáira, Craveiro-da-Índia		
Candomblé Jêje-Nagô	Oxum	Terra/Masculino	(Barros)
CULTO DE NAÇÃO	Oxalá, Oxum		
Umbanda	Oxalá, Oxum, **Ciganos**		**See NOTE**

NAME-Lucumí

NAME-CONGO

PALO	**PALO CLAVO**	Nkite	
	OWNER	Zarabanda	(Nfinda)

NAME-OTHER	Clove	(USDA)
	Cloves (US); Clavo de olor (South America)	(CRC)

USES

	Medicinal	
	To expulse ingested witchcraft (Bilongo)	(LC)
PALO	A concoction of the roots, bark and wood of this tree will expulse any ingested witchcraft. The powders (Afoche/Mpolo) made with this "palo" are very effective with problems with justice. It can take someone out of jai, or kill them.	(Nfinda)
Candomblé	Used as incense to attract positive people, things. Used in baths for women to attract men.	
Umbanda	Used in head cleansings (obrigações de Orí), ritual baths. Help in the development of "Mediums" with concentration. Help to remove (afastar) Eguns, purification and attraction of prosperity. Used to season the food of Orixás and spiritual entities.	
INDIA	Used in Ayurveda, Unani and Siddha	(CRC)
NOTE **Ciganos**	**Ciganos** are entities in the pantheon of Spiritual entities. See: **https://pt.wikipedia.org/wiki/Ciganos_na_Umbanda**	

NAME-CUBA	Palo Cochino, Palo de Cochino, Azucarero	(Roig)
Owner	Changó, Yemayá, Ochún (LC, Quiros)	
	Changó, Oggún (TDF2)	
Odun		

NAME-SCIENTIFIC	*Tetragastris balsamifera* (Sw.) Oken	(Roig)

NAME-BRAZIL	**NOT** found in Flora do Brasil	

NAME-Lucumí	Epotó, Iggiledé, Ewimamaro	(LC)
	Iggiledé, Ewímamaro, Iggiléde, Ewímaro, Epotó	(TDF2)
	Iggi lele	(TDF)
YORUBA		

NAME-CONGO	Fumasi		(LC, TDF)
PALO	**PALO COCHINO**	Fumasi	
	OWNER	Madre de Água, Siete Rayos	(Nfinda)

NAME-OTHER	Masa	(USDA)
	Hogwood, Balsam tetragastris	
	Abey, Amacey hembra (DR); Bwa kochon,	
	Bwa kochon mawon, Sikriye mòn (Creole Haiti)	(Elsevier)

USES

	The leaves for Ebó and ritual cleansings of persons and/or the household.	(LC)
PALO	Not a very important "Palo", but Madre de Água likes to use it.	
	A piece of the wood, made powder, will break-up groups/marriages	(Nfinda)

NAME-CUBA	Palo Diablo, Mostacilla, Mostaza, P... de Perro		(Roig)
Owner	Eshú (LC, TDF2, Quiros)		
Odun			
NAME-SCIENTIFIC	*Quadrella cynophallophora* (L.) Hutch.;		
	Capparis cynophallophora L.		(Roig)
NAME-BRAZIL	NOT found in Flora do Brasil		
NAME-Lucumí	Bieshu, Búrubú, Kinsonko		(LC)
	Bíeshu, Búrubú		(TDF2)
	Biashu		(TDF)
YORUBA			
NAME-CONGO	Mecuémbri, Wábí		(LC)
	Mekuembri		(TDF)
PALO	**PALO DIABLO**	Mecuémbri, Wábi	
	OWNER	Lucero	(Nfinda)
NAME-OTHER	Jamaican Caper		(USDA)
	Caper tree, Jamaican Caper		
	Bejuco Inglés (PR); Olivo Frijol (DR);		
	Bwa fetid, Bwa kaka (Creole Haiti)		(Elsevier)

USES

PALO	The powder (Mpolo/Afoche) made from this tree serves	
	as stimulant for the Nganga "Judías" during Holy Week	(LC)
	The maleficence of this tree is increased with the "menga"	
	(blood) fed directly to the roots since it begins to grow.	
	This "palo" is exclusively of Lugámbé/Lungombe (**Lukankazi**)	
	This "palo" only works with dark spirits; spirits that are crazy,	
	suicidal; dark souls, tormentors' souls.	(LC, Nfinda)

NOTE Lukankazi   Lugámbé/ Lugámbémbe/Lungombe   Is the Devil in Regla Congo
See: **https://es.wikipedia.org/wiki/Palo_(religión)**

NAME-CUBA	Palo Guitarra, Cateicillo, Collarete, Guairo Santo, Guayo Blanco	(Roig)
Owner	Obatalá, Changó, Oggún (LC, TDF2, Quiros)	
	Mayombe (TDF)	
Odun		
NAME-SCIENTIFIC	Citharexylum caudatum L.	(Roig)
NAME-BRAZIL	NOT found in Flora do Brasil	
NAME-Lucumí	Aláré	(LC, TDF2)
YORUBA		
NAME-CONGO	Osonko	(LC)
	Osanko	(TDF)
PALO		
NAME-OTHER	Juniper berry	(USDA)
	Fiddle wood, Juniper berry;	
	Café Clmarrón (DR); Higuerillo (PR); Kafe mawon (Creole Haiti)	(Elsevier)
USES		
	Medicinal	(LC)

NAME-CUBA	Palo Hacha	(LC)
	Cabo de Hacha, Guabán, Jubabán	(Roig)
Owner	Oyá (LC, Quiros)	
Odun		
NAME-SCIENTIFIC	*Trichilia hirta* L.	(Roig)
NAME-BRAZIL	Carrapeta, Catigua, Carra peta	(Elsevier)
NAME-Lucumí	Iggi Niká	(LC)
YORUBA	Ajígbagbó (***Trichilia sp.***)	(PV)
NAME-CONGO	Musi béle loasia	(LC)
PALO	**PALO HACHA** Imba	
	OWNER Centella	Nfinda)
NAME-OTHER	Broomstick	(USDA)
	Red Cedar (Belize); Breziyèt bata (Creole Haiti)	(Elsevier)
	Akika, Olomi oyallo (Nigeria)	(CRC)

USES	**DOES NOT** go to Osain (Omiero)	
	It is the battle tree of Oyá (Arbol de Guerra de Oyá)	
	Whenever you need Oyá to come fight (guerrear) for you,	
	this Ewé is used.	(LC)
PALO	It goes in the NE point of the "caldero"; which is the point	
	for Oyá. It is the principal "palo" of this point.	(TDF)
	Necessary "palo" in the Nganga for Centella.	
	This is a very strong "palo", and when the Palero knows	
	what he/she is doing, the results can be seen in hours.	(Nfinda)

NAME-CUBA	Palo Hediondo, Frijolillo	(Roig)
Owner		
Odun		
NAME-SCIENTIFIC	*Senna bicapsularis* (L.) Roxb.;	
	Cassia emarginata L. **See NOTE**	(Roig, LC)
NAME-BRAZIL	Canudo-de-pito, Aleluia, Pau-de-cachimbo	
NAME-Lucumí	Ikijara-jara	(LC, TDF2)
	Iki jara-jara, Olala tuya, Tarara, Anamó, Ayé iré, Maya yara	(TDF)
YORUBA	Sékésekè; Ìbòsí **(Cassia Sp.)**	(PV)
NAME-CONGO	Sekense, Bayé, Bitondo	(LC)
	Mbeutameiré	(TDF)
PALO	**PALO HEDIONDO** Sekense	(Nfinda)
NAME-OTHER	Christmasbush	(USDA)
	Yellow candlewood, Yellow Senna candlewood	
	Brisson (DR), Bruscamacho (Venezuela); Velamuerto (PR)	(Elsevier)
USES		
	To assist an earth-bound spirit, depart from a dying person,	
	Who refuses/cannot die, so it can pass on peacefully.	(LC)
PALO	Rarely used in Nganga	(Nfinda)

NOTE   There is another tree called **Palo Hediondo** per Jose Tomás Roig
 Ateleia gummifera **(DC.) D.Dietr.**; *Ateleia cubensis* **Griseb.**; and which is called
 Palo Hediondo, Hediondo, Bálsamo Hediondo, Canasí

NAME-CUBA	Palo Jeringa, Paraíso Francés, Bem, Acacia	(Roig)
Owner	Yemayá (LC, TDF2, Quiros)	
	Obatalá, Odudua, (Diaz)	
Odun	Otura-oturupon (Quiros, Diaz, Madan)	

NAME-SCIENTIFIC	*Moringa oleifera* Lam.	(Roig)

NAME-BRAZIL	Moringas, Acácia-branca, Árvore-rabanete-de-cavalo	
Tambor de Minas	Eggun, Oyá-Igbalé	

NAME-Lucumí	Tekén-teke	(TDF2)
YORUBA	Ewé ilé, Ewé ìgbálè, Ìdàgbà mánòyé, Ìdàgbà molóye	(PV, CRC)

NAME-CONGO

PALO	**PALO JERINGA**	Ngango	
	OWNER	Madre Agua	(Nfinda)

NAME-OTHER	Horse Radish Tree	(USDA)
	Horse radish tree, Ben, Ben tree, Drumstick tree	(CRC)

USES	Goes to Osain (Omiero)	
	Medicinal	
PALO	To prepare aphrodisiac powders to bring couples together	(LC)
	Necessary part of the Madre Agua Nganga.	
	Used for powders to help couples stay together when the	
	sexual fervor has diminished.	(Nfinda)

NOTE   Information on this tree (*Moringa oleifera*) was listed under the species *Moringa ovalifolia* **Dinter & A.Berger** in **CRC** (CRC World Dictionary of Medicinal and Poisonous Plants, Common Names, Scientific Names, Eponyms, Synonyms, and Etymology, 5 Volume Set)

NAME-CUBA	Palo Jicotea		(LC)
	Jicotea, Berijúa, Joban Blanco		(Roig, Elsevier)
Owner	Osain, Changó (LC, TDF2, Quiros)		
Odun	Ika-okanran (Quiros, Orula.org)		
NAME-SCIENTIFIC	*Sloanea amygdalina* Griseb.		(Roig)
NAME-BRAZIL	NOT found in Flora do Brasil		
NAME-Lucumí	Iki ayá ura		(LC)
	Ikí Ayá ura, Iggi Ayá Ura		(TDF2)
YORUBA			
NAME-CONGO			
PALO	**PALO JICOTEA**		
	OWNER	Ngurrunfinda, Siete Rayos	(Nfinda)
NAME-OTHER	Motillo		(USDA)
	Almondlike Burrwood		
	Chicarrón (DR); Motillo (PR)		
	Akoma, Chapo kare, Koma (Creole Haiti)		(Elsevier)
USES			
	Medicinal		
PALO	This "palo" speaks as if it was human when taken out		
	of the forest and united with other "palos" with same		
	strength and qualities.		(LC)
	A small piece of this "palo" with a "Mate Rojo" and other		
	"palos" are part of a very secure talisman (Resguardo)		
	of Changó.		(LC)

NOTE This tree (*Sloanea amygdalina* Griseb) is native to Cuba
This tree (*Sloanea amygdalina* Griseb) is listed as **CRITICAL ENDANGERED** by BISSEA

NAME-CUBA	Palo Malambo, Malambo, Cúrbana, Canela Blanca	(Roig)
	Palo Malambo, Árbol Malambo	(LC)
Owner	Osain (Diaz)	
Odun	Oturupon-irosun (Quiros, Diaz, Orula.org)	

| **NAME-SCIENTIFIC** | *Canella winterana* (L.) Gaertn.; | |
| | *Canella alba* Murray | (Roig) |

| **NAME-BRAZIL** | NOT found in Flora do Brasil | |

| **NAME-Lucumí** | Korokoyo | (TDF, TDF2) |
| **ANAGO** | Koro koyo   **Malambo** | (LC) |

NAME-CONGO	Nkunia mpeka, Korokollo	(LC)
	Nkunia mpejka	(TDF)
	Nkunia mpeka	(TDF2)
PALO	**PALO MALAMBO** Korollo	
	OWNER Lucero, Siete Rayos	(Nfinda)
BANTU	Nkunia mpeka **Árbol Malambo**	(LC)
	Koroyo, Malambo Mpeka, Nkunia Malambo **Palo Malambo**	(LC)

| **NAME-OTHER** | Wild Cinnamon | (USDA) |
| | Canela (DR, PR); Kanèl, Kanèl pwavre (Creole Haiti) | (Elsevier) |

USES	**DOES NOT** go to Osain (Omiero)	
	Medicinal	
PALO	This "palo" is very good at doing good, but it is also very good at	
	doing bad. It has a double personality	(LC)
	Although it is a "palo" that is very good when doing good, it works	
	best in a Nganga "Judía". The effects of this "palo" can be seen in	
	minutes and can kill or turn someone crazy in a matter of hours. (Nfinda)	

NOTE   Lydia Cabrera in "Vocabulario Congo" chooses *Croton malambo* H.Karst. for
Palo Malambo and *Croton malambo* H.Karst. or *Drimys winteri* J.R.Forst. & G.Forst.
for Árbol Malambo. Both of these plants are Native to South America.

NAME-CUBA	Palo Moro		(Roig)
Owner	Eleggua (LC, TDF2, Quiros)		
Odun	Oturupon-irosun (Quiros, Madan, Orula.org)		
NAME-SCIENTIFIC	*Psychotria obovalis* A.Rich.	**See NOTE**	(Roig)
	Psychotria glabrata Sw.;		
	Psychotria brownei Spreng.		(Roig)
NAME-BRAZIL	NOT found in Flora do Brasil		
NAME-Lucumí	Miñó		(LC, TDF2)
YORUBA			
NAME-CONGO	Dónsónko		(LC)
PALO	**PALO MORO**	Dónsónko	
	OWNER	Lucero, Zarabanda	(Nfinda)
NAME-OTHER	*Psychotria obovalis*	NO common name found. Native to Cuba	
	Psychotria brownei	Browne's Wild Coffee	(USDA)
		Glabrate Balsamo	(Elsevier)

USES	**DOES NOT** go to Osain (Omiero)
PALO	The earth around the base of this "palo" is used to take hold
	of a person's footsteps and thereby take hold of the "Guardian
	Angel" and dominate this person. A piece of this "palo" is also
	used for same purpose. (LC, Nfinda)
	A willing couple, willing to be together, can undergo this process
	and it is said their union will be long lasting, if not forever. (LC, Nfinda)

NOTE	Both of these plants are listed by Lydia Cabrera and Juan Tomás Roig
	as "Palo Moro"
NOTE	*Psychotria obovalis* **A.Rich.** is listed as native and endemic to Cuba
	Psychotria brownei **Spreng.** Is listed as native to Caribbean
	Information acquired at: **http://powo.science.kew.org/**

NAME-CUBA	Palo Mulato, Mulato, Yaicuaje, Guamacá, Anoncillo Cimarrón	(Roig)
Owner	Ochún (LC, TDF2, Quiros)	
Odun		
NAME-SCIENTIFIC	*Exothea paniculata* (Juss.) Radlk.	(Roig)
NAME-BRAZIL	NOT listed in Flora do Brasil	
NAME-Lucumí	Kukúnduku	(LC)
	Iggí Kukúnduku	(TDF2)
	Iggi Kukundukú	(TDF)
YORUBA		
NAME-CONGO	Potunkoro, Bandúndu	(LC)
	Bandundu, Potunkoro	(TDF)
PALO	**PALO MULATO** Potunkoro, Bandúndu	
	OWNER Mamá Chola	(Nfinda)
NAME-OTHER	Butterbough	(USDA)
	Butter bough, Butterbough inkwood	
	Anoncillo Cimarrón (DR); Guacaran (PR);	
	Bwa koulèv, Bwa milèt, Kenèp mawon (Creole Haiti)	(Elsevier)

USES

	Used in baths for cleansings from bad influences.	(LC)
	Medicinal	
PALO	This "palo" is as good when is good, and as bad when is bad.	(LC)
	When this "palo" is used with other ancillary items to make	
	a talisman, it has the power to attract and make silly	
	(embobecer). Much used by "ladies of the night" (prostitutes)	
	to attract and keep good paying clients.	(LC, Nfinda)
	When this "palo" is used, the effects are short in coming.	(Nfinda)

NAME-CUBA	Palo Negro, Palo Campeche, Palo de Campeche		(Roig)
	Palo Negro	**See NOTE**	(Roig, LC)
Owner	Eleggua, **Oggún-Achíbirí-Kí** (LC, TDF)	**See NOTE**	
	Eleggua (TDF2)		
Odun	Oyekun-ika (Quiros)		

NAME-SCIENTIFIC	*Haematoxylum campechianum* L.		(Roig)
	Lunania subcoriacea Britton & P.Wilson;		
	Lunania pachyphylla Urb.	**See NOTE**	(Roig, LC)

| **NAME-BRAZIL** | Campeche, Pau-de-campeche | (*Haematoxylum campechianum* L.) |

NAME-Lucumí	Iggi Erú (**LC, TDF**)	Iggí eru (**TDF2**)	
ANAGO	Igui erú	**Palo Negro**	(LC)
NAME-CONGO	Masensa, Mufuita (LC, TDF)		
PALO	**PALO NEGRO**	Mufuita	
	OWNER	Lucero, Zarabanda	(Nfinda)
BANTU	Musuita, Mufuita	**Palo Negro** (*Lunania pachyphylla* Urb.)	(LC)

NAME-OTHER	*Haematoxylum campechianum* L.	Bloodwood Tree	(USDA)
	Blackwood, Bloodwood tree		(CRC)
	Campeche Bloodwood tree; Palo Campeche (DR, PR);		
	Bwa kampèch, Kampèch (Creole Haiti)		(Elsevier)
	Lunania subcoriacea **Britton & P.Wilson**		
	NO Common name found. Native to Cuba		

USES

PALO	This "palo" is as black (dark, maleficent), as the heart	
	of this wood. It is a necessary "palo" since Lucero loves to	
	work with it. Also used by Zarabanda (**Oggún-Achíbirí-Kí**)	(LC, Nfnda)

NOTE Taxonomic information from Lydia Cabrera "Vocabulario Congo"

NOTE *Lunania subcoriacea* **Britton & P.Wilson** is listed as **VULNERABLE** by BISSEA

NOTE **Oggún-Achíbirí-Kí** Shibiriki/Echibiriki/Agibiri-ki is one of the avatars of Oggum.
- He is syncretized with St. Michael Archangel. He is very jealous of Changó over the love of Yemayá. He is very fierce, brave and of great courage, fighting mad and hot blooded. He is the creator of metal implements. (NBA)

  See: **https://sites.google.com/site/theyorubareligiousconcepts/oggun**
  https://es.wikipedia.org/wiki/Oggun

NAME-CUBA	Palo Ramón	(LC)
	Ramón, Ramón de Bestia, Ramón de Caballos	(Roig)
Owner	Mayombe (LC)	
	Oggún, Changó, Obatalá (LC from other sources)	
	Eleggua, Obatalá (Irizarry)	
Odun	Obara-okanran (Quiros, Orula.org)	
NAME-SCIENTIFIC	*Trophis racemosa* (L.) Urb.	(Roig)
NAME-BRAZIL	Feijãozinho-rasteiro	
NAME-Lucumí	Moluyaba	(TDF2)
YORUBA		
NAME-CONGO	Cuaribao, Nkitán kitán, Moluyaba, Nkento	(LC)
	Moluyaba, Molubaya, Nkitún-kitán, Kuria-bao, Nketo	(TDF)
PALO	**PALO Ramón** Mitón, Kitán, Moluyaba, Nkento	(Nfinda)
NAME-OTHER	White Ramoon	(USDA)
	White Breadnut, White Ramon, White Female Ramon	
	Ramón (PR); Ramón de Bestia (DR);	
	Bwa nèf, Bwa nèf ramo (Creole Haiti)	(Elsevier)
USES		
	Used in Ebomisi, Inche Osain and Ebó	(Irizarry)
	Medicinal	
PALO	Preferred "palo" of the Mayombero since it is excellent	
	in attaching the spirit of the Eggun in the Nganga	(Nfinda)
	This "palo" has the ability to talk	(LC)
	In order to use it for bad, it must be cut on Good Friday	(LC, Nfinda)

NAME-CUBA	Palo Rompe Hueso		(LC)
	Rompe Hueso, Aguedita Blanca, Aguedita Dulce,		
	Aguedita Macho, Sarnilla		(Roig)
Owner	Changó, Oyá, Ochún (LC, Quiros)		
	Changó, Oggún (TDF2)		
	Oggún, Eleggua (Irizarry)		
Odun	Ogunda-ejiogbe (Irizarry)		

| **NAME-SCIENTIFIC** | *Casearia sylvestris* Sw. | | (Roig) |

NAME-BRAZIL	São-Gonçalinho, Guaçatonga, Erva de bugre, Língua-de-telú		
Candomblé Jêje-Nagô	Oxossi	Terra/Masculino	(Barros)
NAÇÃO KETU	Oxossi		(Barros)
Candomblé de Angola	Inkosse		
Candomblé	Ogum, Oxossi	Terra/Masculino/Gùn	
CULTO DE NAÇÃO	Ogum, Oxossi		
Umbanda	Ogum, Oxossi		

NAME-Lucumí	Ichiegú, Borocoma	(LC)
	Ichiegú, Borokoma	(TDF2)
YORUBA	ALÉKÈSI	(Barros)

NAME-CONGO	Beberico, Kulombe		(LC)
	Beberiko, Kulombe		(TDF)
PALO	**PALO ROMPE HUESO**	Kulombe	
	OWNER	Siete Rayos, Centella, Zarabanda	(Nfinda)

NAME-OTHER	Crack-open	(USDA)
	Wildsage Casearia, Crack-open	
	Café Silvestre (PR); Cafetillo (DR); Pabito (Venezuela);	
	Papelit (Creole Haiti)	(Elsevier)

USES

Used in ritual baths (Ebomisi) and Inche Osain
Medicinal

PALO This "palo" has strong Eggun. When the Eggun possesses the
person; it can break his/her bones.   (LC)
When a cross is made of this "palo" in front of the Nganga, it
possesses a great mystery, an "Aché". Said cross will prevent
a tornado from causing damage to the home or plantings
in the field. When the tornado sees the cross, it will literally
head the other way.   (LC)
This "palo" is used when you want another person to be taken to
the next world (die/killed) by a tornado.   (Nfinda)

Candomblé Jêje-Nagô In gatherings (festas de Candomblé), it is very common
to see the temple covered in the leaves of this tree. It is done because
it is believed that the leaves of this tree have the power to repel
negativity (coisas negativas). It is also used where the **Iaô** (Iyawo/new
initiate) sleeps in order to protect them from bad influences and
dark spirits.   (Barros)

NAÇÃO KETU Oxossi is the patron of the Ketu nation and this Ewé has great
prestige since it belongs to Oxossi. It must always be present in
initiations, purification baths, sacrementation of ritual objects. It
is used as clothing (vestimenta) for Oxossi and Ossaim.   (Barros)

Candomblé de Angola Inkosse It is used in the cleansings (obrigações) of any
Aborixá, initiation, Assento Okutá, Abô and baths. It is good practice
to place a branch of this Ewé in a business, visible to anyone, as a
sign of defense.

Umbanda This Ewé is associated with Ogum and is considered to have great
magical powers, and as such the leaves SHOULD NOT be used as
incense or burned since it will bring bad luck   (Barros)
Used in baths, Amacis (ritual baths with herbs), Abôs (Omiero),
head cleansings (obrigações de Orí).

NAME-CUBA	Palo Santo, Guayacán blanco, Guayacancillo, Vera	(Roig)
Owner		
Odun		
NAME-SCIENTIFIC	*Guaiacum sanctum* L.	(Roig)
NAME-BRAZIL	Guaiaco, **Pau Santo**, Guaiacum	**See NOTE**
NAME-Lucumí		
YORUBA		
NAME-CONGO	Mpungu funán kunia	(LC)
PALO	**PALO SANTO** Mpungu funan kunia	
	OWNER Finda, Centella, Mama Chola, Siete Rayos	(Nfinda)
NAME-OTHER	Holywood	(USDA)
	Lignum Vitae, Holywood Lignum Vitae	
	Guayacán bastardo (DR); Guayacán de vera (PR)	
	Gayak blan, Gayak femèl, Gayak kadas (Creole Haiti)	(Elsevier)
USES		
PALO	It is the Holy Father of ALL "palos" in the forest	(LC)
	When the wood burns, it smells like burning flesh	(LC)
	Can ONLY be used for good.	
NOTE	In Brazil, there are several trees/species that are called **Pau Santo**	

NAME-CUBA	Palo Tengue	(LC)
	Tengue, Tengue Rojo, Tengue Amarillo, Abey Hembra	(Roig)
Owner	Mayombe (LC)	
	Eshú, Eleggua (Diaz)	
	Eshú (Madan)	
Odun	Owonrin-ika (Diaz, Madan)	
NAME-SCIENTIFIC	*Poeppigia procera* C.Presl	(Roig)
NAME-BRAZIL	Pintadinho	(Elsevier)
NAME-Lucumí	Adébesú	(LC, TDF2)
YORUBA		
NAME-CONGO	Nkita, Nkunia chéché cabinda	(LC)
	Kunia sheshe kabinda	(TDF)
	PALO TENGUE Nita, Nkunia Chache Cabinda	(Nfinda)
NAME-OTHER	Very tall Poeppigia	(Elsevier)
USES	**DOES NOT** go to Osain (Omiero)	
PALO	Is the strongest "palo" among all "palos" in the Nganga	(LC, Nfinda)
	Can be used for good or bad, but the results are excellent	(Nfinda)
	Used to dominate an enemy, and can make him an idiot	(Diaz)
PALO MONTE	This "palo" is used to do battle. It is both Mother and Father in Regla Conga; although this "palo" is "Judío".	
	This "palo" goes to all Nganga; the first is "Ceiba", the second is "Tengue" and the third is "Guayacán".	
	Used in purification baths in Regla Conga.	
NOTE	Lydia Cabrera has a separate listing for Tengue, but with different attributes	

NAME-CUBA	Palo Tocino	(LC)
	Tocino, Bejuco Cochino	(Roig)
Owner	Mayombe (LC)	
	Eshú, Eleggua (Diaz)	
Odun	Iwori-ofun (Diaz)	

| **NAME-SCIENTIFIC** | *Acacia tenuifolia* (L.) Willd.; | |
| | *Acacia paniculata* Willd. | (Roig) |

| **NAME-BRAZIL** | Angiquinho, Esperai, Espinheiro, Paú-de-fuso, Unha-de-gato | (Elsevier) |

| **NAME-Lucumí** | Ore | (LC, TDF2) |
| **YORUBA** | Èwòn ehoro | (***Acacia spp.***) | (PV) |

NAME-CONGO	Yigguayeo, Fúnkulere	(LC)
	Yiguayeo, Funkulebe	(TDF)
PALO	**PALO TOCINO**	Yigguayeo, Gunkulere	
	OWNER	Lucero, Centella, Siete Rayos, Saca Empeño	(Nfinda)

| **NAME-OTHER** | Slender leaf acacia | (Elsevier) |

USES	**DOES NOT** go to Osain (Omiero)	
	Medicinal	
PALO	It kills witches/witchcraft (mata brujo) and gives good fortune	(LC)
	Very good "palo" to do good. Powders (Afoche/Mpolo) made	
	for love matters and to counteract problems with justice	(Nfinda)
	Like with ALL thorns (Iru/Kerebende), the thorns of this tree	
	can either be used for protection or to do bad.	(LC)

NAME-CUBA	Palo Torcido, Torcido, Mano-Pilón, Lebrero		(Roig)
Owner	Eshú (LC, Quiros)		
	Eleggua (TDF2)		
Odun	Iwori-ofun (Quiros)		

NAME-SCIENTIFIC	*Mouriri valenzuelana* A. Rich.	**See NOTE**	(Roig)

NAME-BRAZIL	NOT found in Flora do Brasil

NAME-Lucumí	Otite, Mitónlo	(LC)
	Otite, Mitánlo	(TDF2)
YORUBA		

NAME-CONGO	Alubende diánfinda, Otutua		(LC)
	Alumbende, Dianfinda, Otutua		(TDF)
PALO	**PALO TORCIDO**	Alubende Diafianda, Otutua	
	OWNER	Lucero, Zarabanda	
	On occassion	Centella, Siete Rayos	(Nfinda)

NAME-OTHER	Valenzuela Mouriri	(CRC)

USES

PALO	Used to turn luck around (in a bad way)	
	It will turn the luck of your enemy where everything goes	
	wrong, and nothing that is done turns out right	(LC)

NOTE	Lydia Cabrera has a separate entry for **Mano-Pilón**, although
	it is the same species, it has different attributes
NOTE	This species (***Mouriri valenzuelana* A. Rich.**) is endemic to Cuba (KewScience)
	This species is listed as **Near Threatened** by BISSEA

NAME-CUBA	Palo Verraco, Yerba de Verraco		(Roig)
Owner	Yemayá (LC, Quiros)		
Odun			
NAME-SCIENTIFIC	*Hypericum styphelioides* A.Rich.		(Roig)
NAME-BRAZIL	**NOT** found in Flora do Brasil		
NAME-Lucumí	Teni-teni, Lédé		(LC)
	Sani		(TDF)
YORUBA			
NAME-CONGO	Fumasi, Dokiróngo		(LC)
	Dokirongo		(TDF)
PALO	**PALO VERRACO**	Fumasi, Dokirongo	
	OWNER	Mamá Chola, Madre de Água	(Nfinda)
NAME-OTHER	**Endemic to Cuba**, in the family of St. John's Wort		
USES			
PALO	Palo Verraco- The "Aafoche/Mpolo" prepared with this "palo" on top of Madre de Água is excellent for finding a job, money and even love.		(Nfinda)

NOTE This plant is listed as **ENDANGERED** by BISSEA
Distribution: Cuba (Pinar del Rio, Las Villas, Oriente, Isla de Pinos)
http://www.cybertruffle.org.uk/vinales/esp/hypericum_styphellioides.htm
PLANTAS DE VIÑALES

NAME-CUBA	Panetela	(Roig)
Owner	Ochún (Quiros, Diaz, Madan)	
	Ochún, Yemayá (Menéndez)	
Odun	Ika-odi (Quiros, Diaz, Madan, Orula.org)	
	Oyeku-irosun (Quiros, Diaz, Madan)	
NAME-SCIENTIFIC	*Phyllanthus angustifolius* (Sw.) Sw.;	
	Xylophylla angustifolia Sw.	(Roig)
NAME-BRAZIL	NOT found in Flora do Brasil	
NAME-Lucumí		
YORUBA		
NAME-CONGO		
PALO		
NAME-OTHER	Foliage Flower	(USDA)
	Foliage Flower	(Elsevier)
USES	Goes to Osain (Omiero) for Ochún, Yemayá	(Menéndez)
	Goes to Osain (Omiero)	(Diaz)
	To make perfumes for love and good luck	
	For baths for love and good luck	(Diaz)

NAME-CUBA	Papo de la Reina, Papo	(Roig)
	Papo de la Reina, Papito de la Reina, Zapatico de la Reina	(LC)
Owner	Ochún (LC, Quiros)	
	Ochún, Yemayá (TDF2, Diaz, Menéndez)	
Odun	Otura-ejiogbe (Diaz)	
NAME-SCIENTIFIC	*Bolusafra bituminosa* (L.) Kuntze;	
	Fagelia bituminosa (L.) DC.	(Roig)
NAME-BRAZIL	NOT found in Flora do Brasil	
NAME-Lucumí	Oyí, Batáyabá	(LC, TDF2)
YORUBA		

NAME-CONGO	Mukanda (LC)		
PALO	**PALO PAPITO/ZAPATICOS DE LA REINA**	Mukunda	
	OWNER	Tiembla Tierra	(Nfinda)

NAME-OTHER	Tar Pea	(I-Naturalist)

USES		
	Medicinal	(LC)
	Used in cleansings baths (leaves, stems and roots)	(LC, Nfinda)
	Also used in some amulets	(Nfinda)

NOTE This plant is native to South Africa
 See **https://npgsweb.ars-grin.gov/gringlobal/taxonomydetail.aspx?id=435796**
 and the name (Tar pea) is because the flower smells like tar.

NOTE There is another plant listed by Juan Tomás Roig under the name of Papito de la Reina
 which is **Centrosema plumieri Benth.** (gbif.org). It is known as "Fee fee" (USDA)

NAME-CUBA   Paragüita
                       Quitasolillo   (Roig)
    Owner   Yemayá (TDF2, Irizarry, Madan)
                       Yemayá, Olokun (Diaz)
                       Oggún, Ochosi, Yemayá, Ochún (Menéndez)
    Odun   Oyeku-ika, Ofun-ejiogbe (Diaz, Madan)

NAME-SCIENTIFIC   *Hydrocotyle umbellata* L.   (Roig)

NAME-BRAZIL   Erva-capitão, Acariçoba, Pára-sol, Chapéu-de-sapo
  Candomblé Jêje-Nagô Oxum   Água/Feminino/èró   (Barros)
  CULTO DE NAÇÃO   Oxum

NAME-Lucumí
  YORUBA   ABÈBÈ ÒSUN   (Barros)

NAME-CONGO

NAME-OTHER   Manyflower Marshpennywort   (USDA)
                       Pennywort, Shield pennywort   (CRC)
                       Dollar weed   (Web)

USES   Goes to Osain (Omiero)
                       Used for Ebomisi and home cleansings
  Candomblé Jêje-Nagô Used in Initiation rituals, Abô (Omiero), and ritual
                       baths for prosperity.   (Barros)
  CULTO DE NAÇÃO   Used in baths, Amacis (Ebomisi), Abô (Omiero),
                       ritual baths for prosperity, and head cleansings (obrigações de
                       cabeça). This Ewe is essential in **Ipeté de Oxum** (annual feast for
                       Oxum). See: **https://pt.wikipedia.org/wiki/Ipeté_de_Oxum**

NAME-CUBA	Paraíso, Paraíso Enano, Prusiana, Pulsiana		(Roig)
Owner	Changó (LC)		
	Changó, Obatalá, Orula (TDF2)		
	Changó, Obatalá, Ochún, Eleggua (Quiros)		
	Eleggua, Obatalá, Orula (Irizarry)		
	Changó, Oyá (Diaz)		
	Changó, Eleggua (Concordia)		
	Changó, Eleggua, Obatalá (Madan)		
	Changó, Agayú (Menéndez)		
Odun	Oyeku-okanran (Quiros, Irizarry, Diaz, Madan, Concordia, Orula.org)		
	Odi-ogunda (Quiros, Irizarry, Diaz, Concordia, Orula.org)		
	Odi-ika (Quiros, Irizarry, Diaz, Madan, Orula.org)		

NAME-SCIENTIFIC	*Melia azedarach* L.		(Roig)

NAME-BRAZIL	Cinamomo, Amargoseira, Pára-raio		
Candomblé Jêje-Nagô	Oiá	Ar/Masculino	(Barros)
Candomblé de Angola	Zaze		
Candomblé	Oiá, Xangô	Ar/Masculino/èró	
Umbanda	Iansã	Ervas Quentes	

NAME-Lucumí	Ibayo, Yiya		(LC)
	Ibayo, Yíya, Pakindé		(TDF2)
YORUBA	Afóforo òyìnbó, Eké òyìnbó, Eké ilè, Afóforo ìgbàlódé		(PV, CRC)
	IGÍ MÉSÀN		(Barros)

NAME-CONGO			
PALO	**PARAISO**	Yiya	
	OWNER	Siete Rayos	(Nfinda)

NAME-OTHER	Chinaberry	(USDA)
	Chinaberry tree, Bastard cedar, West Indian Lilac	(CRC)

USES		**DOES NOT** go to Osain (Omiero)	
		It's a sacred tree. It cleanses and provides protection	(LC)
		It is used in Sarayéyé, Paraldo and Ebomisi	
		Used to cleanse the home of dark spirits and influences	
	PALO	To use this Ewe, it must be paid for-to the tree or owner	(LC)
		Preferably, the branches of Paraíso should be picked on either a Monday or Friday, by pulling on the branch in an upward fashion.	(LC)
		Care must be taken by the owner of a Paraíso tree because when someone steals a branch, it could be stealing the well being and the luck of the person/home	(Nfinda)
		With the leaves, powders (Afoche/Mpolo) are made to be used to achieve your greatest desires.	(Nfinda)
	PALO MONTE	To clean the receptacle of the Guardian of the Patio	
	ESPIRITU CRUZADO	For Spiritual use and use in Spiritual Masses	
		Cleansings to draw out dark spirits and bad influences	
		Spiritual cleansings of people and homes.	
		Talismans for protection and good luck	
	Candomblé Jêje-Nagô	This Ewe is employed in the rituals of initiation and purification baths of the "filhos" of Oiá. The branches are used for cleansings of people and/or home.	(Barros)
		Participants in the Cult of Egúngún also use this Ewe	(Barros)
	Candomblé de Angola Zaze	Used for head cleansings (obrigações no Orí) for Omorixá in the Cult of **Omolokô**. **See NOTE**	
	Candomblé	Used in cleansings and initiation	

NOTE   Omolokô   Is a syncretic religion in Brazil having as base elements African religions, Spiritism and Amerindian religions
See: **https://pt.wikipedia.org/wiki/Omolokô**

NAME-CUBA	Paramí	**See NOTE**	(LC)
	Para Mí, Ponasí		(Roig)
Owner	Inlé (Quiros)		
	Ochosi, Yemayá (Irizarry)		
	Eleggua, Ochún (Diaz)		
	Yemayá (Madan)		
Odun	Oturupon-ose (Quiros, Irizarry, Diaz, Madan, Orula.org)		

| NAME-SCIENTIFIC | *Hamelia patens* Jacq. | (Roig) |

| NAME-BRAZIL | Mato-de-oração, Valmoura, Caraui-tanga, Ixicanan |

NAME-Lucumí
    YORUBA

NAME-CONGO	Kaguángaco		(LC)
	Kaguangako		(TDF)
PALO	**PALO PARAMI**	Kuguangaco	
	OWNER	Mamá Chola, Madre de Agua, Lucero	(Nfinda)

NAME-OTHER	Scarletbush	(USDA)
	Coralito (DR, Venezuela); Bálsamo Colorado (PR)	
	Koray, Koray wouj (Creole Haiti)	(Elsevier)

USES	Goes to Osain (Omiero)	
	Used for ritual baths (Ebomisi) and Inche Osain	
	Medicinal	
PALO	To possess, influence and own a person. This is done with this	
	Ewe and Amansa Guapo.	(LC)
	In love matters, these two Ewe (Parami & Amansa Guapo)	
	are infallible	(Nfinda)

| NOTE | Lydia Cabrera has a separate listing for Ponasí |

NAME-CUBA	Pastillo	(Menéndez)
	Pasto Labrado, Cambute, Alpargata, Sacasebo	(Roig)
Owner	Eleggua (TDF2, Menéndez)	
Odun		
NAME-SCIENTIFIC	*Paspalum notatum Flüggé*	(Roig)
NAME-BRAZIL	Grama-bahia, Grama-batatais, Grama-forquilha, Grama-mato-grosso	
NAME-Lucumí		
YORUBA		
NAME-CONGO		
PALO		
NAME-OTHER	Bahiagrass	(USDA)
	Common Bahia, Pensacola Bahia	(Wiki)
USES	Goes to Osain (Omiero) for Eleggua	(Menéndez)

NOTE Per se, there is NO plant called PASTILLO listed by Juan Tomás Roig.
The plant listed is the one that may have the highest probability.
The plant is listed as Pastillo in several websites, including in the book by
Migene González-Wippler-Santeria the Religion; with no scientific name.

NAME-CUBA	Pata de Gallina, Pata de Gallo, Grama de Caballo, Cambute	(Roig)
	Pata de Gallina, Yerba Pata de Gallina	(LC)
Owner	Eleggua (LC, TDF, Quiros)	
	Eleggua, Oggún, Ochún (TDF2)	
	Eshú (Madan)	
	Eleggua, Oggún, Ochosi (Diaz, Menéndez)	
Odun	Owonrin-iwori, Ose-ika (Quiros, Diaz, Irizarry, Madan, Orula.org)	
	Ika-ose, Irete-ejiogbe, Ofun-oyeku (Quiros, Irizarry, Orula.org)	

NAME-SCIENTIFIC	*Eleusine indica* (L.) Gaertn.	(Roig)

NAME-BRAZIL	Capim-pé-de-galinha, Pata-de-galinha, Capim-de-pomar, Capim-da-cidade	
Candomblé Jêje-Nagô	Oxum Água/Masculino	(Barros)
Candomblé	Ewá/Yewá	
Umbanda	Linha de Ibeije	

NAME-Lucumí	Ewe Erán, Dedé, Aráogu	(LC)
	Ewe Erá, Dedé, Aráogu, Oklepúesu,	
	Ewe Erán **Pata de Gallina**	(TDF2)
	Kotenembo, Ewe eran, Dengo, Tumayá,	
	Iyerán **Grama de Caballo**	(TDF2)
	Ewe Wrán, Dede, Arangú, Oklepuesu, Atikere,	
	Otari, Oklopuesú	(TDF)
YORUBA	Gbági, Gbégi, Esè kannakánná, Gbégidínà	(PV)

NAME-CONGO	Kimbánsa, Bebeke	(LC)
	Bebere, Minbansa	(TDF)
PALO	Bebeke Kimbasa Nsu Nkako	

NAME-OTHER	Indian Goosegrass	(USDA)
	Barnayard grass, Goosefoot grass, Indian goosegrass	(CRC)

USES	Goes to Osain (Omiero)	
	Goes to the Omiero for Eleggua and Oggún	(TDF2)
	Inche Osain	
	Medicinal	
PALO	To obtain a job with Eleggua	(LC)
	To tie the corners (amarrar las esquinas para Juego de Palo)	
	When the Palero/Mayombero is going to work, do an initiation, etc.; a special thing is done so that the police, or any one not convenient, realizes what is going on.	(LC)
Candomblé Jêje-Nagô	Used with other Ewe of Oxum for baths for health problems of the abdomen (problemas de barriga ou gravidez), baths for prosperity and cleansing ritual objects of the Orixá	(Barros)
INDIA	Used in Ayurveda and Siddha.	(CRC)

NAME-CUBA	Pega Pega, Amor Seco		(Roig)
Owner	Ibeyis (LC, Quiros)		
	Ochún, Ibeyis (Diaz)		
Odun	Ika-obara (Diaz)		

NAME-SCIENTIFIC	*Desmodium rigidum* (Elliott) DC.;		
	Desmodium obtusum (Willd.) DC.		(Roig)
	Desmodium adscendens (Sw.) DC.		(PV, Barros)

NAME-BRAZIL	Carrapicho-beiço-de-boi, Pega-pega, Picão, Picão-preto, Desmodio		
Candomblé Jêje-Nagô	Oxóssi	Terra/Masculino	(Barros)
CULTO DE NAÇÃO	Exú, Ogum, Oxóssi, Ossaim, Oxum		
Umbanda	Exú		

NAME-Lucumí	Kirimeco		(LC)
YORUBA	Èpà ìkúnígbó, Èpà ilè, Ògànsó dùndùn, Àjádìí		(PV)
	EWÉ ODE		(Barros)
NAME-CONGO	Inin Inago		(LC)
	Inin Inaro		(TDF)
PALO	**PALO PEGA PEGA**	Inin Inago	
	OWNER	Saca Empeño, Mamá Chola	(Nfinda)

| **NAME-OTHER** | *Desmodium rigidum* | Stiff ticktrefoil | (USDA) |
| | *Desmodium adscendens* | Zarzabacoa galana | (USDA) |

USES	Goes to Osain (Omiero)	
	The leaves and roots to unite broken marriages/relations	(LC)
	Medicinal	
PALO	Used to make marriages and relations last	(Nfinda)
Candomblé	Purification baths and as part of the Ewé of Oxossi	
	Used in "Ebós" to hold "weary" lovers or money that flees	
	(segurar o amante afastado ou dinheiro que foge)	
Umbanda	Ritual baths (Amacis), cleansing baths, as incense and as Abô	

NAME-CUBA	Pendejera, Pendenciera, Prendedera	(Roig)
Owner	Eshú (LC, Madan)	
	Eleggua (TDF2)	
	Eleggua, Eshú (Quiros, Diaz)	
Odun	Oyeku-meji, Irete-obara, Irete-ika (Quiros, Diaz, Madan, Orula.org)	
NAME-SCIENTIFIC	*Solanum torvum* Sw.	(Roig)
NAME-BRAZIL	NO common name found	
NAME-Lucumí	Isiami, Ewe Odúyafún, Inyelo	(LC)
	Isiami, Odúyafún, Inyelo	(TDF2)
YORUBA	Ikàn wéwé, Ikàn igún, Ìgbá yìnrìn elégùn	(PV, CRC)
NAME-CONGO	MIlisia	(LC, TDF)
NAME-OTHER	Turkey Berry	(USDA, CRC)
	Turkeyberry nightshade	
	Berenjena Cimarrona (DR, PR);	
	Amourèt (Creole Haiti)	(Elsevier)

USES		Goes to Osain (Omiero)	**See NOTE**
		Medicinal	
	PALO	Used to complicate judicial procedures against a high politician where the longer it takes, the more delays, the greater the problems I the judicial procedures benefit.	(LC)
	INDIA	Used in Ayurveda and Siddha	(CRC)

NOTE ONLY Pendejera/Pendejera Hembra goes to Osain. Pendejera Macho (*Solanum verbascifolium* L.) **DOES NOT** go to Osain. (Diaz)

NOTE See also **Pendejera Macho**

NAME-CUBA   Pendejera Macho, Pendejera Hedionda,
                          Prendedera Hedionda, Prendedera Macho   (Roig)
                     Pendejera Macho, Tabaco Cimarrón   (Roig)

          Owner
          Odun

NAME-SCIENTIFIC   *Solanum donianum* Walp.;
                              Solanum verbascifolium L.   (Roig)
                          Solanum erianthum D. Don   (Roig, PV, Barros)

NAME-BRAZIL   Fumo-bravo, Caiçara, Couvetinga, Capoeira-branca
          Candomblé Jêje-Nagô   Oxossi   Terra/Masculino/èró   (Barros)
          Candomblé de Angola   Mutalumbô

NAME-Lucumí
     YORUBA   Ewúro ìjèbú, Ìjèbú kògbìn, Òpeníníwùni   (PV)

NAME-CONGO

NAME-OTHER   *Solanum donianum*   Mullein Nightshade   (USDA)
                     Solanum erianthum   Potato Tree   (USDA)
                     Potato Tree, Wild Tobacco; Tabacón (DR);
                     Tabacón Felpado (PR); Amourèt mal (Creole Haiti)   (Elsevier)

USES   **DOES NOT** go to Osain (Omiero)
                     Unknown
          Candomblé Jêje-Nagô   Used in rituals of initiation for Oxossi. Used in
                     Agbo/Abô, purification baths and cleansings   (Barros)
          Candomblé de Angola   Mutalumbô -Used in head cleansings (obrigações no Orí)

NOTE   *Solanum verbascifolium* L. is **Unresolved** taxonomically in **theplantlist.org**;
                     but is a synonym for *Solanum donianum* **Walp**. In powo.science.kew.org and in
                     gbif.org

NAME-CUBA	Peonía, Peonía de Sto. Tomás, Peronía, Pepusa	(Roig)
Owner	Changó (LC)	
	Obatalá, All Orisha (TDF2)	
	Changó, Odudúa, Oggún (Quiros)	
	Eleggua, Changó, Agayú (Diaz)	
	Changó, Aña, Ochosi (Irizarry)	
	Eleggua, Changó, Oggún, Odudúa (Concordia)	
	Eshú, All Oricha (Madan)	
	Changó, Agayú, Oddúa (Menéndez)	
Odun	Odi-obara (Quiros, Diaz, Concordia, Madan, Orula.org)	
	Irete-irosun (Quiros, Irizarry, Madan, Orula.org)	

NAME-SCIENTIFIC	*Abrus precatorius* L.	(Roig)

NAME-BRAZIL	Jequiriti, Jiquiriti, Ervilha-do-rosário		
Candomblé Jêje-Nagô	Ossaim, Exú	Terra/Masculino/èró	(Barros)
Umbanda	Exú		(Barros)

NAME-Lucumí	Ewéréyeye, Iggereyeye, Cupa		(LC)
	Eguereyeye, Ewéréyeye, Iggereyeye, Cupá		(TDF2)
ANAGO	Egüere yeye, Ewereyéye, Iguereyeyé	**Peonía**	(LC)
	Chocho were yeye	**Peonía-the seeds**	(LC)
YORUBA	Aládùn, Mésénmésén, Makò, Mísínmisìn, Ojú ológbò,		
	Wérénjéjé, Pákùn obarìsà, Olátògégé, Adágbé,		
	Ewé aládùn, Mésénmésén ìtàkùn, Ojú eyelé		(PV)

NAME-CONGO	Bembari ngyengye, Ikegne, Mudjiri bisaye, Nguieguié	(CRC)
PALO		

NAME-OTHER	Rosary Pea	(USDA)
	Coral bead plant, Crab-eye plant, Jequirity seed	(CRC)

USES	Goes to Osain (Omiero)	
	Used in the Omiero for ALL Orisha	(TDF2)
	One of the 5 MOST important plants (Ewé) in the Omiero	
	The seeds are used to make "Elekes" (Collares) for Eleggua	(LC)
	The leaves of this Ewe are used in Omiero in order to replace	
	any possible missing Ewe in the Omiero	(Concordia)
	Roots are chewed in order to expel ingested witchcraft	(Concordia)
	Leaves used in baths and Inche Osain.	
	The SEEDS are used for noxious/maleficent witchcraft	(LC)

Candomblé Jêje-Nagô   This Ewe is part of the initiation (oró de iniciação) of all due to its association with Exú. It is used, mainly, as the first Ewe in Abô with the purpose, due to Exú Bara, to provide the initiate new and better paths after the initiation, which represents the birth of the initiate in a new life.   (Barros)
On the other hand, the seeds are used in maleficent witchcraft; and if someone were to step on them, it will generate fights and great disorder.   (Barros)

UMBANDA   The seeds are used to make necklaces which are used by the followers of Umbanda with the purpose to ward-off negative and envious people   (Barros)

INDIA   Used in Ayurveda, Unani and Siddha   (CRC)

Hoodoo/Root Magic (USA)   Rosary Peas crafted into amulets

NOTE   The seeds are **HIGHLY POISONOUS**

NOTE   Pataki in Odi-obara   **The pact of Obatalá and Iku (Death)**
- Obatalá had become disenchanted with all the disobedience of the world, so he decided to kill everyone in the world. For this he called Ikú (Death). Ikú came and began to kill everyone. When Obatalá saw that Ikú was about to take the life of one of his children, he went to see Orunmila. Orunmila checked with Ifá and told Obatalá to do Ebbó. Orunmila told Obatalá "If you want to save your children you have to find the Ewereyéye plant, which has the virtue of Olofi, Changó and Oyá, so that it can clean your children of all negative things". Obatalá then went and hid his children in the Ewereyéye bush and when Ikú passed, he did not see them. Seeing this, Obatalá was then able to save everyone from Ikú.

NAME-CUBA	Peregrina, Yuramira	(Roig)
Owner	Ochún (LC, TDF2, Quiros)	
Odun		
NAME-SCIENTIFIC	*Jatropha integerrima* Jacq.;	
	Jatropha diversifolia A.Rich.	(Roig)
NAME-BRAZIL	NOT found in Flora do Brasil	
NAME-Lucumí	Ero	(LC, TDF2)
YORUBA		
NAME-CONGO	Ntingoro	(LC)
	Ntangoto	(TDF)
PALO		
NAME-OTHER	Peregrina	(USDA)
	Peregrina, Spicy jatropha	(Wiki)
USES		
	For cleansings and for people that cry for no reason	(LC)

NOTE   ***Jatropha integerrima* Jacq.** Native Range is Cuba

           See: **http://powo.science.kew.org/taxon/urn:lsid:ipni.org:names:350290-1**

NAME-CUBA	Peregún, Bayoneta Africana	(LC)
	Bayoneta, Lirio Blanco	(Roig)
Owner	Obatalá (LC, TDF, TDF2, Quiros, Madan, Menéndez)	
	Oggún, Obatalá (Concordia)	
	Eleggua, Oggún (Irizarry)	
	All Orishas (Diaz)	
Odun	Ofun-ogunda (Quiros, Diaz, Irizarry, Madan, Orula.org)	
	Ogunda-meji (Diaz, Irizarry, Madan, Concordia)	
NAME-SCIENTIFIC	*Yucca gloriosa* L.	(Roig)
NAME-BRAZIL	Iúca	
Candomblé de Angola	Dandalunda	
NAME-Lucumí	Peregún, Denderé	(LC, TDF, TDF2)
YORUBA.	Pèrègún, Pèrègún lese (**REAL PEREGUN**-*Dracaena fragrans*)	(PV)
NAME-CONGO	Ngoooto	(LC)
	Ngooto, Peregún	(TDF)
NAME-OTHER	Spanish Bayonet, Spanish Dagger, Roman Candle (US)	
USES	Goes to Osain (Omiero)	
	One of the 5 MOST important plants (Ewé) in the Omiero	
	To protect against "Arayé" (tragedy, arguments, discord), Peregún	
	can be dried, or tosted, and made into a powder to blow on the	
	door, or anoint before going out.	(Concordia)
Candomblé de Angola	The flower spike used in head cleansings (obrigações no Orí)	

NOTE   There is a story that the reason Peregún has such a prominent position in this
religion is that Peregún, along with Ewereyeye, was there to witness the consecration
to Ocha of the first three priests of this religion.   (Concordia)

NAME-CUBA	Perejil		(Roig)
Owner	Ochún (LC, TDF2)		
	Ochún, Oyá, Eleggua (Quiros)		
Odun			

NAME-SCIENTIFIC	*Petroselinum crispum* (Mill.) Fuss;		
	Carum petroselinum (L.) Benth. & Hook.f.		(Roig)

NAME-BRAZIL	Salsa, Salsinha, Perrexil		
Candomblé Jêje-Nagô	Oxum, Exú	Água/Feminino	(Barros)

NAME-Lucumí	Isako, Iyádédé		(LC, TDF2)
	Sakú, Iyadedé, Isako		(TDF)
YORUBA	Ewé Obé		(Barros)

NAME-CONGO	Ntuoro, Vititi kamatuya		(LC)
	Ntuero, Bititi Kamaluya		(TDF)
PALO	Vititi Kumatuya		
	OWNER	Chola Guengue/Mamá Chola	(TDF)

NAME-OTHER	Parsley, Garden Parsley, Common Garden Parsley	(CRC)

USES

	Used for cleansings and cleansing baths.	(LC)
	Can be used to expel ingested witchcraft (Bilongo)	(LC)
	Used for financial gains and getting a job.	(LC)
Candomblé Jêje-Nagô	Parsley is used for cleansings	(Barros)
Candomblé Ketu	The food consumption of parsley is prohibited (**Èwó**) in the	
	Casas-de-santo of Ketu origin.	(Barros)

Hoodoo/Root Magic (USA) As opposed to European lore that parsley is associated with Protection, Love spells, Fertility or Death; it is used for money-drawing spells.

NAME-CUBA	Pica-Pica, Bejuco pica-pica	(Roig)
Owner	Eleggua, Babalú-Ayé (LC, TDF, TDF2, Quiros)	
	Eleggua (Irizarry)	
	Eleggua, Babalú-Ayé, Eshú (Diaz)	
	Babalú-Ayé, Eshú (Madan)	
Odun	Iwori-obara (Quiros, Irizarry, Madan, Orula.org)	

NAME-SCIENTIFIC	*Mucuna pruriens* (L.) DC.;	
	Stizolobium pruritum (Wight) Piper	(Roig)

NAME-BRAZIL	Feijão-da-flórida (the bean/plant)	Pó-de-mico (the bean casing)
Candomblé	Exú	
Umbanda	Exú-Mirim	

NAME-Lucumí	Sísi, Iseliyé, Rirá, Aguanará, Ainá	(LC)
	Sísi, Iseliyé, Rirá, Aguanará, Ainá, Aguanara	(TDF2)
	Sisi, Iseliyé, Birá, Aguanará, Ainá	(TDF)
YORUBA	Èjòkùn, Yèrèpè, Èèsìn, Èsìnsìn, Èsìse, Ewé iná, Ìrèpè, Wèrèpè	(PV, CRC)
NAME-CONGO	Ote	(LC, TDF)
	Abakwa, Abapa, Kapesa	(Duke's)
PALO	Nsontori	

NAME-OTHER	Velvet Bean	(USDA)
	Cowitch, Cowage, Florida Velvet bean	(CRC)

USES	**DOES NOT** go to Osain (Omiero)	
	Only used for bad	
PALO	With other ingredients used as a powder (Mpolo/Afoche)	
	to cause fights, mayhem	(LC)
Candomblé	Used for witchcraft with Exú	
Umbanda/Quimbanda	Used for witchcraft with Exú/Exú-Mirim	
Hoodoo/Root Magic (USA)	The BEAN used an amulet	
INDIA	Used in Ayurveda, Unani and Siddha (**NOT the casing**)	(CRC)

NOTE   For the purpose of usage, the part used is the casing of the bean

NAME-CUBA	Pimienta, Pimienta de Malagueta	(LC)
	Pimienta, Pimienta Gorda, P. de Clavo, P. de Jamaica	(Roig)
	Pimienta Negra, Pimienta Picante	(Roig)
Owner	Oggún (LC, TDF2, Quiros)	
Odun	Owonrin-ogunda (Quiros, Orula.org)	

| **NAME-SCIENTIFIC** | *Pimenta dioica* (L.) Merr. | (Roig) |
| | *Piper nigrum* L. | (Roig, Barros) |

NAME-BRAZIL	Pimenta-do-reino, Pimenta-preta, Pimenta-redonda	***Piper nigrum* L.**
Candomblé Jêje-Nagô	Exú	Fogo/Feminino	(Barros)
Umbanda	Xangô, Ogum, Egunitá, Oxossi, Exú,	
	Exú-Mirim, Pomba-gira, Baianos, Pretos-velhos	

| **NAME-Lucumí** | Atá | (LC) |
| **YORUBA** | Ata Dudu | (Barros) |

| **NAME-CONGO** | Esákukaku | (LC) |
| | Ndunga, Ndungo | (TDF) |

NAME-OTHER	***Pimenta dioica* (L.) Merr.**	Allspice	(USDA)
	Allspice, Jamaica Pepper (USA); Pimienta (DR, PR);	
	Malagueta (Venezuela); Pwa jamayik (Creole Haiti)	(Elsevier)
	***Piper nigrum* L.**	Black Pepper	(USDA)

USES

Widely used is spells/witchcraft (Bilongo, Afoche, Mpolo)
Both peppers used by a lovelorn lover to bring back and have
said lover under his/her control (LC)
PALO All types of pepper are used in the Chamba
Used in powders to cause mayhem, problems and even death (LC)
ESPIRITU CRUZADO Used to make and to win over (vencer) strong witchcraft
Candomblé Jêje-Nagô The fruit and leaves used in rituals with Exú (Barros)
Hoodoo/Root Magic (USA) **Allspice** berries draw good luck in business and gambling
INDIA ***Piper nigrum*** Used in Ayurveda, Unani, and Siddha. Ceremonial,
ritual: ingredient of Patra pooja in different religious pooja ceremonies (CRC)

NAME-CUBA	Pimienta China	**See NOTE**	(LC)
Owner	Oggún (LC, TDF2, Quiros)		
Odun			

NAME-SCIENTIFIC	*Zanthoxylum simulans* Hance	(Springer; V.4)

NAME-BRAZIL   Pimenta-de-Sichuan, Pimenta-chinesa

NAME-Lucumí	Osei	(LC, TDF2)
YORUBA		

NAME-CONGO	Tuólá	(LC)
	Tuola	(TDF)

NAME-OTHER	Szechuan Pepper, Chinese-pepper, Prickly Ash	(pfaf.org)
	Chinese Pepper, Sichuan Peppercorn, Szechuan Pepper	(Springer, V.4)

USES

	Medicinal	(LC)
PALO	Like ALL peppers, used extensively in Mayombe	
	to cause harm and mayhem	
	Used in Chamba	

NOTE   Lydia Cabrera failed to mention a plant species for this Ewe
Juan Tomás Roig **DOES NOT** list one

NAME	Pimienta de Brasil	
NAME-CUBA	Copal	(Roig, Elsevier's)
NAME-SCIENTIFIC	*Schinus terebinthifolia* Raddi	(Roig)

NAME-BRAZIL　Aroeira-vermelha, Aroeira-comum, Aroeira-pimenteira, Pimenta-rosa

Candomblé Jêje-Nagô	Ossaim, Ogum, Exú	Terra/Masculino	(Barros)
Candomblé de Angola	Inkosse, Mutalumbô, Kavungo		
CULTO DE NAÇÃO	Ogum, Ossaim, Exú, Xangô		
Umbanda	Ogum, Oxossi		

NAME-Lucumí
　　YORUBA　　ÀJÓBI, ÀJÓBI OILÉ, ÀJÓBI PUPA　　　　　　　(Barros)
NAME-CONGO

NAME-OTHER	Brazilian Pepper Tree	(USDA)
	Brazilian pepper tree, Christmas berry	
	Pimienta de Brasil (DR, PR)	
	Pimienta del Brasil (Venezuela)	(Elsevier's)

USES　　　　　　　**NOT USED** in Cuba

Candomblé Jêje-Nagô　Ewe belongs to Ogum in the morning; in the afternoon it belongs to Exú. Also used to dress Ossaim. The branches are used in cleansing Ebô.

The leaves of this tree are used in the ritual sacrifice of all four-legged animals.

Candomblé de Angola　Inkosse　　Used for head cleansings (obrigações no Orí) and for a discharge bath, with other Ewe, in an open crossroad at Zero hours.

　　　　　　　Mutalumbô　Used for head cleansings (obrigações no Orí)
　　　　　　　Kavungo　Used for head cleansings (obrigações no Orí)

Umbanda　Used in the ritual sacrifice of four legged animals in Ebô. Also used as incense, cleansings, head cleansings (obrigações de cabeça), strong discharge baths, in the consecration and purification of the Otanes and religious objects.

NOTE　　This tree is listed as **Category I** in the Florida Exotic Pest Plant Council of the Invasive Plants List (**www.fleppc.org**). This is a Legally Prohibited plant in Florida.

NAME-CUBA   Pimienta de Guinea   **See NOTE**   (Roig)
   Owner
   Odun

NAME-SCIENTIFIC   *Xylopia aethiopica* (Dunal) A.Rich.   (Roig, PV)
                         Xylopia aromatica (Lam.) Mart.   (Barros)

NAME-BRAZIL   Pimenta-da-África   ***Xylopia aethiopica***
                     Pimenta-de-macaco; P.-de-negro, P.-de-bugre, Pindaíba ***Xylopia aromatica***
   Candomblé Jêje-Nagô   Ossaim   Terra/Masculino   (Barros)
   Umbanda

NAME-Lucumí   Atáre   (LC)
   YORUBA   Èèrù, Èèrunje, Olórin   (PV, CRC)
                     BEJEREKUN   (Barros)

NAME-CONGO   Nsa Nkako   (TDF)
                    Bongando, Botongo, Kani, Kuba-kuba, Sange   (CRC)
   PALO   Ndundo Guiare

NAME-OTHER   ***Xylopia aethiopica***   Ethiopian Pepper   (USDA)
                          African pepper, Alligator pepper, Guinea pepper   (CRC)
                    Xylopia aromatica   Monkey Pepper   (USDA)
                          Fragrant Xylopia; Fruta de Burro (Venezuela)   (Elsevier)

USES
   Candomblé Jêje-Nagô   The name of Bejerekun is used for similar species.
                             It's uses are extensive with different Orixá. It is used in some
                             for Abô, Initiation of "filhos-de-santo" and in the preparation
                             of powders (pó) with beneficial ends.   (Barros)

NOTE   Although this Ewe is called Guinea Pepper/Pimienta de Guinea, this is NOT
                    the one used for rituals in Cuba and Brazil. This pepper is referred to
                    as Senegal Pepper, Grains of Selim and Ethiopian Pepper. The REAL
                    Pimienta de Guinea is ***Aframomum melegueta*** **K.Schum**. which are
                    commonly called Grains of Paradaise.

NAME-CUBA	Pimienta de Guinea	**(REAL)**	(LC)
Owner	ALL Orisha use it		
Odun			

NAME-SCIENTIFIC	*Aframomum melegueta* K.Schum.	(Barros, PV)

NAME-BRAZIL	Pimenta-da-costa, Grãos-do-paraíso, Pimenta-da-Guiné		
Candomblé Jêje-Nagô	Ossaim	Fogo/Masculino	(Barros)
Candomblé de Angola	Aluvaiá, Lembá		
CULTO DE NAÇÃO	Exú, Ossaim		

NAME-Lucumí	Atáre	(LC)
YORUBA	Ataare, Òbùró, Ata, Ata ire, Atayé, Atayé liya (Abéòkuta),	
	Atayé isa, Atayé ìjobì, Atayé rere, Etalúyà (ìjèbú)	(PV)

NAME-CONGO	Nsa Nkako	(TDF)
	Mebongabonga, Ndoango ya banganga, Tosekele	(CRC)
PALO	Ndundo Guiare	

NAME-OTHER	Melegueta Pepper	(USDA)
	Grains of paradise, Guinea pepper, Melegueta pepper	(CRC)

USES	Goes to Osain (Omiero)
	Necessary for initiation (Kari Ocha)
	Used in almost ALL rites in Regla Ocha
	Necessary for the immolation of ALL four-legged animals
	Necessary for Eggun Rituals
PALO	Used in Chamba and Mayombe rituals
	Used to cause problems and mayhem

Candomblé Jêje-Nagô   This type of pepper has various uses in the rituals of
Orixá, being used for **Borí/Ebori**, in the initiations of some Orixá,
the rituals of Ossaim and to make Ebbó. It is commonly chewed
by the priests when they are making requests to the Orixa because
it is credited that the seeds have the power of purification.   (Barros)

Candomblé de Angola   **Aluvaiá**   It is used as offerings to the Orixá
Lembá   It is offered to Exú and all the other Orixá in
cleansings (obrigações). Also used in **Obori/Ebori**, chewed with Obi (Kola)
and Orogbo (*Garcinia kola*) for the offering of Olórí of the Iyawó.

CULTO DE NAÇÃO   When the grains of paradise are chewed, it gives force to
prophetic words (whether good or bad). They provide protection to
both the physical and spiritual body. Used in Ebós (sacrifices or offerings
to the Orixá). Used in head cleansings (obrigações de cabeça),
powders (pó), initiation and magics.

Hoodoo/Root Magic (USA)   Grains of Paradise are protective and lucky, but
can also be used in jinxing.

NOTE   **Borí/Ebori**   The feeding of the mythical head. The sacrificing of the animals to
the Orixá during initiation.
See: **https://pt.wikipedia.org/wiki/Ebori**

NAME-CUBA	P. de Gato	(LC)
	P. de Negro, Dicha, Brazo Poderoso, Mata del Cáncer	(Roig)
Owner	Eleggua, Oggún (LC, TDF2, Quiros)	
Odun		

NAME-SCIENTIFIC	*Dieffenbachia seguine* (Jacq.) Schott	(Roig)

NAME-BRAZIL	Comigo-ninguém-pode, Cano-de-mudo, Aningapara		
Candomblé Jêje-Nagô	Ifá, Exú	Fogo/Feminino	(Barros)
CULTO DE NAÇÃO	Exú		
Umbanda	Exú, Ogum		

NAME-Lucumí		
YORUBA	WOMOBÚ FUNFUN	(Barros)

NAME-CONGO

NAME-OTHER	Dumbcane	(USDA)
	Dumb cane, Mother-in-Law-plant, Spotted dumbcane	(CRC)
	Mata Puerco (DR)	(Elsevier)

USES

PALO	The whole plant used to take the virility of a man, and	
	thereby make him impotent for a long time, if not forever	(LC)
Candomblé Jêje-Nagô	Used in initiations and other religious matters	(Barros)
Umbanda	Used against the evil-eye and envy. One of the Ewe in the "Vasos de 7 Ervas" that should be placed at the entrance homes, businesses, and temples. This Ewe helps in the strengthening and spiritual cleaning of the environment. Also used in cleansing baths and as incense.	

NAME-CUBA	Pino, Pino Hembra, Pino Blanco, Pino de Cuba		(Roig)
Owner	Changó (LC, TDF2, Quiros, Madan)		
Odun	Irosun-owonrin (Quiros, Madan, Orula.org)		
NAME-SCIENTIFIC	*Pinus tropicalis* Morelet	**See NOTE**	(Roig)
NAME-BRAZIL	NOT found in Flora do Brasil		
NAME-Lucumí	Okilán, Orúkoñikán, Yémao (LC, TDF2)		
YORUBA			
NAME-CONGO	Búndumoyé		(LC)
	Búndomoyé		(TDF)
PALO	**PINO**	Búndomoyé	
	OWNER	Siete Rayos, Nsasi Nkita	(Nfinda)
NAME-OTHER	NO common name found. Endemic to Cuba		
	Tropical Pine		(Elsevier)

USES

Medicinal
When the Pine tree is planted for purposes of luck, the
owner will plant it and sacrifice to it at the time of planting;
and as the pine tree grows, so does the luck of the owner.
The owner must "feed" it yearly and NEVER let anyone else
cut a branch from it (it will cut his luck and wellbeing)   (LC)

Hoodoo/Root Magic (USA)   Pine is a spiritual cleanser. Because it is
evergreen, it also draws steady money. Keeping a perfect
unopened pine cone in the home will provide for fertility,
long life, good health and ward off the Evil Eye.

NOTE   *Pinus tropicalis* **Morelet** is listed as **VULNERABLE** by IUCN Red list
Pinus tropicalis **Morelet** is **ENDEMIC** to Cuba   (KewScience)

NOTE   Lydia Cabrera listed both species under Pino.

NAME-CUBA	Pino, Pino Macho, Pino Amarillo		(Roig)
Owner	Changó (LC, TDF2, Quiros, Madan)		
Odun	Irosun-owonrin (Quiros, Madan, Orula.org)		

NAME-SCIENTIFIC	*Pinus caribaea* Morelet	**See NOTE**	(Roig)

NAME-BRAZIL	NOT found in Flora do Brasil

NAME-Lucumí	Okilán, Orúkoñikán, Yémao (LC, TDF2)
YORUBA	

NAME-CONGO	Búndumoyé		(LC)
	Búndomoyé		(TDF)
PALO	**PINO**	Búndomoyé	
	OWNER	Siete Rayos, Nsasi Nkita	(Nfinda)

NAME-OTHER	Caribbean Pine	(USDA)
	Caribbean Pine, Black Pine, Cuban pine	
	Pino Blanco (PR), Pino (DR); Bwa pen (Creole Haiti)	(Elsevier)

USES

Medicinal
When the Pine tree is planted for purposes of luck, the
owner will plant it and sacrifice to it at the time of planting;
and as the pine tree grows, so does the luck of the owner.
The owner must "feed" it yearly and NEVER let anyone else
cut a branch from it (it will cut his luck and wellbeing)   (LC)

Hoodoo/Root Magic (USA)   Pine is a spiritual cleanser. Because it is
evergreen, it also draws steady money. Keeping a perfect
unopened pine cone in the home will provide for fertility,
long life, good health and ward off the Evil Eye.

NOTE   Lydia Cabrera listed both species under Pino.

NAME-CUBA	Piña Blanca	(LC)
	Piña, Piña Blanca, Piña Cubana, Piña de la Habana	(Roig)
Owner	Obatalá (LC, TDF2) (Quiros - **Piña Blanca**)	
	Ochún (TDF)	
	Ibeyis (Quiros – **Piña**)	
	Eggun, Ochún, Ibeyis (Irizarry)	
Odun	Owonrin-irete (Irizarry, Orula.org)	

NAME-SCIENTIFIC *Ananas comosus* (L.) Merr.;
Ananas ananas (L.) H.Karst. ex Voss   (Roig)

NAME-BRAZIL Abacaxi, Abacaxizeiro, Ananás-Selvagem, Abacaxí-Do-Mato, Gravatá
Candomblé Jêje-Nagô Iyábas, Ibeije   Terra/Feminino   (Barros)
Candomblé de Angola Vunge
Umbanda Oxossi, Obaluaê

NAME-Lucumí	Egboibo, Oppóyibo	(LC)
	Egboibo, Opóyibo	(TDF2)
YORUBA	Eékún ahùn, Ekúnkún ahùn, Ekúnkún, Ògèdè òyìnbó,	
	Òpè òyìnbó, Òpeyìbó, Òpòn Òyìnbó	(PV, CRC)
NAME-CONGO	Merentén, Mingue	(LC)
	Matoko, Niná, Miengué, Mienke	(TDF)
	Langa Ngbandi	(Springer, v.1)

NAME-OTHER Pineapple   (USDA)
USES

    Used as Addimu for Orishas
    Used for head cleansings (rogación de cabeza)   (LC)
    Medicinal
Candomblé Jêje-Nagô Used as Addimú for Iyábas (female Orixá) and during
    Apanan Erê (initiation). It is **Èwó for Obaluaiè**   (Barros)
    In Africa, the leaves were used in order to get money/wealth,
    and as protection against evil; BUT the fruit was used in bad magic
    (trabalho para matar o amante da esposa)   (Barros)
Candomblé de Angola Vunge Èwó for Obaluaiè; fruit used for Apanan Erê
Umbanda **Èwó for Omolú/Obaluaiè**
INDIA Used in Ayurveda, Unani and Siddha   (CRC)

NAME-CUBA	Piña de Ratón, Piña Ratón, Piña Cimarrona,	
	Piña de Cerca, Maya	(Roig)
Owner	Eleggua (LC, TDF)	
	Eleggua, Orula (Quiros)	
Odun		
NAME-SCIENTIFIC	*Bromelia pinguin* L.	(Roig)
NAME-BRAZIL	Gravatá, Gravatá-commun, Gravatá-do-gancho	(Duke's)
NAME-Lucumí	Omó iggi Boíbo, Maimai	(LC, TDF)
YORUBA		
NAME-CONGO		
NAME-OTHER	Pinguin	(USDA)
	Pinguin, Wild Pineapple	(CRC)
	Maya cimarrona (DR), Piñuela (PR);	
	An-nan'na pengwen, Bayonèt pengwen (Creole Haiti)	(Duke's)
USES		
	Medicinal	(LC)

NAME-CUBA	Piña de Salón, Piña de Adorno	(LC)
Owner	Ochún (LC, TDF2)	
Odun		
NAME-SCIENTIFIC	*Ananas ananassoides* (Baker) L.B.Sm.;	
	Ananas nanus (L.B.Sm.) L.B.Sm.	
NAME-BRAZIL	Ananás-de-raposa	
NAME-Lucumí	Iyé, Koroyima, Ogbá eweko	(LC)
	Yyé, Koroyima, Ogbá eweko	(TDF2)
YORUBA		
NAME-CONGO	Maba nlónbe (LC)	
NAME-OTHER	Dwarf Pineapple, Pink Pineapple	(LLIFLE)
USES		
	Used as a Protective Talisman	(LC)

NOTE   The use of plants, in this case the dwarf pineapple; is ingrained in the lives of the believers in this religion. Said ornamental plants can hide under the roots magical talismans hidden there to protect the home/person/family/business. Said plants are taken care off, fed, and treated as special items. Lydia Cabrera goes on to say that said plants can have an adverse effect on the person/family/home/business if the plant is not kept up and is let to wither and/or die.

NAME-CUBA	Piñi-Piñi	(LC)
	Piñipiñi, Raíz de indio, Raíz de añil	(Roig)
Owner	Eshú (LC, TDF2, Quiros)	
Odun		
NAME-SCIENTIFIC	*Morinda royoc* L.	(Roig)
NAME-BRAZIL	NOT found in Flora do Brasil	
NAME-Lucumí		
YORUBA		
NAME-CONGO		
PALO	**OWNER** **Cachica**	(LC)
NAME-OTHER	Redgal	(USDA)
	Royoc Indian Mulberry, Redgal, Wild pine	(Elsevier)
USES	ONLY used to do bad	(LC)
PALO	Just like "Guao", this is a truly malevolent plant.	
	It is so malevolent, that it will poison the person that	
	has made a pact with **Cachica** in order to use it.	(LC)
NOTE **CACHICA**	Cachica, aka Cáddian pémbe, aka Kaddianpémbe, aka Taita Cochano	
	He is The Devil. See: **https://es.wikipedia.org/wiki/Palo_(religión)**	

NOTE   The reason the devil/negative entity has so many names, it is because it is not prudent to mention the Devil by name.

NAME-CUBA	Piñón de Botija, Piñón Botija, Piñón Criollo, Piñón Purgante		(Roig)
Owner	Eleggua, Changó (LC, Diaz)		
	Eleggua, Changó, Obatalá (TDF2)		
	Eleggua, Changó, Obatalá (Quiros)		
	Changó, Obatalá, Eggun (Irizarry)		
	Eleggua, Obatalá, Babalú-Ayé (Menéndez)		
	Changó, Obatalá, **Aña** (Madan)		**See NOTE**
Odun	Irosun-meji; Obara-otura (Quiros, Diaz, Irizarry, Madan, Orula.org)		

NAME-SCIENTIFIC	*Jatropha curcas* L.		(Roig)

NAME-BRAZIL	Pinhão-branco, Pinhão, Pinhão-de-purga, Maduri-graça, Peão, Pião		
Candomblé Jêje-Nagô	Ogum, Oxossi, Oiá	Fogo/Feminino	(Barros)
Candomblé de Angola	Aluvaiá		
Candomblé	Ogum, Oxossi, Oyá, Xangô	Fogo/Feminino/Gùn	
CULTO DE NAÇÃO	Ogum, Oxossi, Oyá, Xangô, Exú		
Umbanda	Exú		
Odun	Otura-ose, Ofun-meji, Iwori-meji, Osa-meji, Odi-meji		(PV)

NAME-Lucumí	Addó, Alumofó, Akanu		(LC)
	Akunu, Alumofó, Addó, Oddo, Oloboluyo, Ewé tuyé,		
	Alabo tuye, Yínyere Rompe, Kinbansa Buenas Horas,		
	Olodotuyo, Akunu, Olé Iyé, Tebe		(TDF2)
	Olobo, Tuyo		(TDF)
YORUBA	Olóbòntujè, Ìyálóde, Làpálàpá lá, Ewé ibò, Bòtujè,		
	Bòtujè ubo, Lóbòtujè		(PV)

NAME-CONGO	Puluka, Masorosi		(LC)
	Peluka, Masorose		(TDF)
	Mebondo, Mobondo		(CRC)
PALO	Ekeni		
OWNER		Centella	

NAME-OTHER		Cuban physic nut, Barbados nut, Purging nut	(CRC)
		Piñón Purgante, Tartago (PR), Piñón (DR)	
		Fey medsen, Gran Medsinye (Creole Haiti)	(Elsevier)

USES

DOES NOT go to Osain (Omiero)
Has ability to expel any ingested "Bilingo"   (LC)
To cleanse the door if you feel a witchcraft (Bilongo)
has been thrown in your doorsteps.   (LC)
Leaves put inside he shoes in a cross will prevent any
witchcraft/negative energy from entering your body   (LC)
Principal Ewé in Abikú Ceremony and used
in Eggun rituals   (Irizarry)
For ritual baths (Ebomisi) and cleansings
Medicinal

PALO   NOT part of the Nganga since this "palo" has the ability to
ward-off the spirits that inhabit the Nganga.
Only used by Mayombero (Palero) for his own defense

Candomblé   **Jêje-Nagô**   dedicated to **Iansã Òrun**, the patron of Eguns.
The branches for cleansings and ritual baths
for "filhos" of Iansã, Ogum and Oxossi   (Barros)

Casa-das-Minas Maranhão   Used for ritual baths for
luck and prosperity   (Barros)

Candomblé de Angola   Used with "Aroeira" (*Schinus terebinthifolia* Raddi –
Brazilian Pepper tree) for strong bath applied at the crossroads
(para banho forte aplicado em encruzilhada)

Umbanda   Used in strong cleansing baths, much the same as "Aroeira", an
Ewe that breaks jinxes and can be substituted in certain cases in
sacrifices to Exú. Also used in cleansings and Ebós

NOTE   **Aña**   Is an **Irunmole** of percussion instruments; i.e.- **Batá drums**
Irunmoles   are the manifestation of the power of nature
See: **https://es.wikipedia.org/wiki/Irunmoles**

NAME-CUBA	Piñón de Pito, Piñón de Cerca, Piñón de Cuba	(Roig)
Owner	Eleggua (LC, Quiros)	
	Eleggua, Yemayá (TDF2)	
	Eleggua, Babalú-Ayé (Diaz)	
Odun	Irosun-meji, Obara-unle, Obara-otura (Diaz)	
NAME-SCIENTIFIC	*Erythrina berteroana* Urb.	(Roig)
NAME-BRAZIL	NOT found in Flora do Brasil	
NAME-Lucumí	Eféke, Yirin	(LC)
	Yirín, Eléke	(TDF2)
YORUBA		
NAME-CONGO	Fosóganko	(LC)
PALO	Puluka	
NAME-OTHER	Coralbean	(cabi.org)
	Coral bean, Bertero Coral Bean	
	Brucal (DR); Machete (PR); Brikal (Creole Haiti)	(Elevier)
USES	**DOES NOT** go to Osain (Omiero)	
	To wash the religious items of Eleggua	
	Used for cleansings	
	Medicinal	(LC)
PALO	Used for work in "palo"	
	Cleansings NOT to be done in front of Nganga	(Diaz)
Hoodoo/Root Magic (USA)	The bean crafted into an amulet	

NOTE	The seeds are **HIGHLY POISONOUS**

NAME-CUBA	Piñón Lechoso		(LC, EcuRed)
	Piñón de Botija, Piñón Botija, Piñón Criollo, Piñón Purgante		(Roig)
Owner	Eshú, Oggún (LC, Quiros)		
	Eleggua, Oggún (TDF2)		
Odun			

NAME-SCIENTIFIC	*Jatropha curcas* L.		(Roig)

NAME-BRAZIL	Pinhão-branco, Pinhão, Pinhão-de-purga, Maduri-graça, Peão, Pião		
Candomblé Jêje-Nagô	Ogum, Oxossi, Oiá	Fogo/Feminino	(Barros)
Candomblé de Angola	Aluvaiá		
Candomblé	Ogum, Oxossi, Oyá, Xangô	Fogo/Feminino/Gùn	
CULTO DE NAÇÃO	Ogum, Oxossi, Oyá, Xangô, Exú		
Umbanda	Exú		

NAME-Lucumí	Ewera, Adó		(LC)
	Adó, Addó, Ewé-ra		(TDF2)
ANAGO	Obutuyé, Olobo tuyo	Piñón	(LC)
YORUBA	Olóbòntujè, Ìyálóde, Làpálàpá lá, Ewé ibò,		
	Bòtujè, Bòtujè ubo, Lóbòtujè		(PV)

NAME-CONGO	Masorosi, Pulúka	(LC)
PALO		

NAME-OTHER	Barbados nut	(USDA)
	Cuban physic nut, Barbados nut, Purging nut	(CRC)
	Piñón Purgante, Tartago (PR), Piñón (DR)	
	Fey medsen, Gran Medsinye (Creole Haiti)	(Elsevier)

USES		
	Used to counteract love spells	(LC)
BRAZIL	See: Piñón de Botija	

NAME-CUBA	Piscuala	(Roig)
Owner	Changó, Oyá (LC, Diaz)	
	Changó (TDF2, Quiros)	
	Changó, Ochún (Irizarry)	
Odun	Obara-otura (Diaz, Irizarry, Quiros, Orula.org)	
NAME-SCIENTIFIC	*Combretum indicum* (L.) DeFilipps;	
	Quisqualis indica L.	(Roig, PV)
NAME-BRAZIL	Jasmim-da- Índia	
NAME-Lucumí	Mómón	(LC)
	Momón	(TDF2)
YORUBA	Ògan funfun, Ògan igbó	(PV, CRC)
NAME-CONGO		
PALO		
NAME-OTHER	Rangoon creeper	(USDA)
	Burma creeper, Chinese honeysuckle, Rangoon creeper	(CRC)
USES	Goes to Osain (Omiero)	
	Medicinal	(LC)

NAME-CUBA	Pitahaya, Flor de Cáliz	(Roig)
Owner	Changó (LC, TDF2)	
	Changó, Babalú-Ayé (Quiros)	
	Ifá (Madan)	
Odun	Odi-ogunda (Quiros, Orula.org)	
	Iwori-meyi (Madan)	
NAME-SCIENTIFIC	*Hylocereus trigonus* (Haw.) Saff. ;	
	Hylocereus triangularis (L.) Britton & Rose	(Roig)
NAME-BRAZIL	Pitaya-vermelha, Pitaia, Cato-barse, Cardo-ananaz, Rainha-da-noite	
NAME-Lucumí	Esogi	(LC)
	Esogí	(TDF2)
YORUBA		
NAME-CONGO	Belóngo	(LC)
PALO	Belóngo	
NAME-OTHER	Strawberry pear	(USDA)
	Pitahaya, Dragon fruit	
USES		
	The flower and fruit make **Changó Oniyo** happy	(LC)
	Medicinal	(LC)
NOTE	**Changó Oniyo**/Changó Obbañá – El rey de los Ilúbatá (Añá),	
	los tambores	(NBA)

NAME-CUBA	Platanillo de Cuba, Pimienta de Costa, Canilla de Muerto		(Roig)
Owner	Changó (LC, TDF2)		
	Changó, Odudua, Ochún (Quiros)		
	Changó, Ibeyis, Ochún (Irizarry)		
	Changó, Agayú (Diaz)		
	Changó, Odudua, Ochún, Asojuano (Concordia)		
	Changó, Odudua (Madan)		
	Changó, Agayú, Oddúa, Yemayá, Ochún (Menéndez)		
Odun	Odi-obara (Quiros, Irizarry, Diaz, Concordia, Madan, Orula.org)		
	Ejiogbe-ose (Irizarry, Diaz, Concordia, Madan)		

NAME-SCIENTIFIC	*Piper aduncum* L.		(Roig)

NAME-BRAZIL	Aperta-ruão, Pimenta-de-fruto-ganchoso, Tapa-buraco, Jaborandi-falso		
Candomblé Jêje-Nagô	Oxum	Terra/Masculino	(Barros)
Candomblé de Angola	Zaze		
Candomblé Ketu	Xangô		
CULTO DE NAÇÃO	Oxum, Oxalá		

NAME-Lucumí	Olúbbo	(LC, TDF2)
YORUBA	ÌYÈYÉ	(Barros)

NAME-CONGO	Esakuselu	(TDF)

NAME-OTHER	Higuillo de Hoja Menuda	(USDA)
	Hooked Pepper, Spiked Pepper; Anisillo (DR),	
	Cordoncillo Negro (Vnzla); Higuillo (PR), Bwa siwo (Creole Haiti)	(Elsevier)

USES	Goes to Osain (Omiero)	
	Used for cleansings, ritual baths (Ebomisi) and Ebbó	
	Medicinal	
	Can be used to make a slave of someone (amarre) or to be	
	made into a powder to make someone leave your home	(LC)
Candomblé Ketu	Head cleansings (obrigações no Orí)	
CULTO DE NAÇÃO	Head cleansings (obrigações no Orí), Initiation, Abô	

NAME-CUBA	1. Plátano, P. Indio, P. Macho, P. Burro, P. Johnson, P. Manzano (Roig)	
	2. Plátano Congo, P. Enano, P. Hembrita, P. Dátil	(Roig)
Owner	Changó (LC, TDF, TDF2, Diaz, Madan)	
	Changó, Agayú (Quiros)	
	Changó, Eleggua, Eggun (Irizarry)	
Odun	Otura-irete (Quiros, Irizarry, Diaz, Madan, Orula.Org)	
	Osa-ejiogbe (Quiros, Irizarry, Madan, Orula.org)	

NAME-SCIENTIFIC	1. *Musa × paradisiaca* L.	(Roig)
	2. *Musa acuminata* Colla	(Roig)

NAME-BRAZIL 1. Bananeira, Banana-da-terra, Banana-ouro, Banana-prata, Banana-São-Tomé
NAME-BRAZIL 2. Banana-d'água, Banana maçã

Candomblé Jêje-Nagô	Oxalá, Oxum, Logun Edé, Oxumaré, Ibeije	Água/Masculino	(Barros)
Casa das Minas/Maranhão	Ìrókò/Loko	Água/Masculino	(Barros)
Candomblé Ketu	Oxum		
Candomblé de Angola	Aluvaiá, Angorô, Zaze, Vunge		
Umbanda	Exu, Ogum		

NAME-Lucumí	Oggedé	(LC)
	Ogguedé, Ewe Agguddé	(TDF2)
	Ogedé (TDF)	
YORUBA	1. Ògèdè, Ògèdè abo, Ògèdè lóbóyò, Ògèdè òmìnì, Àgbagbà	(PV, CRC)
	2. Ògèdè-ntiti, Òyìnbó	(PV, CRC)

NAME-CONGO	Makondo			(LC)
Plátano Indio	Makondo Minganga	**P. Enano**	Mbaka	
P. Guineo	Biékere, Ntiba			(LC)
Makondo, Makocho, Makodo				(TDF)
1. Iko, Leka				(CRC)
2. Ikondo a betika, Makondo ma betika, Tshetika				(CRC)
PALO **Plátano**	Makondo	**P. Verde**	Bule	
P. Enano	Mekondo Mbaka	**P. Guineo**	Makondo Biekerere	
P. Hembra	Makondo Nkento	**P. Indio**	Makondo Mingonga	
P. Macho	Makondo Yákala			

NAME-OTHER	1. Banana, Eating Banana, Sweet Banana, Plantain	(CRC)
	2. Banana, Chinese Dwarf Banana	(CRC)

USES		**DOES NOT** go to Osain (Omiero)	
		Fruit for Addimu for the Orishas, but Changó and Yánsa like it most (LC)
		Used for cleansing baths (LC)
		Used for Eggun rituals and Inche Osain (Irizarry)
		The whole raceme of bananas **NECESSARY** when requesting
		something from Changó, or for religious occasions for Changó.
		The stalk of the banana tree used in the exchange of life (cambio
		de cabeza) of a sick person. Done by Babalawo or Palero (LC)
		Plantains used to calm Changó (LC)

PALO Plátano Morado/ Plátano Indio and Plátano Manzano
are Èwó **for Mayombero** (LC)

Candomblé Jêje-Nagô The flower stalk of the banana tree (Associated with Oxum)
are used for Ebós and religious works to resolve love or health problems
Banana-da-terra is **Èwó of Xangô and Aganju**
Banana-d'água is **Èwó for Oxalá and Oiá.**
Banana-prata and Banana-ouro, fresh, offered as Addimú to Iabás.
The trunk of the banana tree used in Abikú rituals (Barros)

Candomblé Ketu Leaves used to cover tortoise shell (Ajapá) in the
offerings to the Orixá

Candomblé Jêje **Èwó for Lembá (Exú)**

Candomblé de Angola Aluvaiá Leaves used in sacrifices (Erankó), and the
preparation of food (Addimu). The flower stalk used as Ebô

Angorô, Zaze Leaves used to cover the tortoise shell in the
offerings to the Orixá

Vunge **Èwó for Xangô.** Used in Apanan Erê

Candomblé Used as Addimu for Oxossi, Ibeije, Jemanjá, Nanna, Obá, Oxum,
Xangô and Iansã.
Èwó of Oxossi (Banana-d'água, Banana maçá, Banana-prata);
Iemanjá (Banana-figo); **Obaluaiè** (Banana-prata)

Candomblé Jêje **Èwó of Lembá/Exú** (Banana-d'água)

Umbanda Used as Addimu for Exú and Ogum

INDIA *Musa × paradisiaca* L. Used in Ayurveda, Unani and Siddha.
Sacred plant, fruits used in religion and magico-religious beliefs,
ceremonial, ritual: ingredient of Patra pooja in different religious
pooja ceremonies; garland of leaves used while removing bad
spirit from a man; evil spirits staying around the plant during
the night; a bunch of ripened fruits given as an offering to deities
before sowing seeds (CRC)

NAME-CUBA	Pomarrosa, Manzana de Cuba, Manzana de Rosa, Manzana	(Roig)
Owner	Ochún (LC, TDF2, Diaz, Irizarry, Madan)	
	Ochún, Oggún (Quiros)	
Odun	Okanran-ogunda (Quiros, Irizarry, Madan, Orula.org)	

NAME-SCIENTIFIC	*Syzygium jambos* (L.) Alston;	
	Jambosa jambos (L.) Millsp.	(Roig)

NAME-BRAZIL	Jambo, Jambeiro-rosa, Jambo-amarelo		
Candomblé Jêje-Nagô	Oxum	Terra/Feminino	(Barros)
Candomblé Ketu	Ogum		
Candomblé de Angola	Inkosse		
Umbanda	Oxum		

NAME-Lucumí	Yilebo, Echicacho	(LC)
	Yílebo, Echicacho	(TDF2)
YORUBA	IGI ÈSO PUPA	(Barros)
NAME-CONGO	Colomafa	(LC)
PALO	**POMARROSA** Colomafa	
	OWNER Mamá Chola	(Nfinda)

NAME-OTHER	Malabar Plum	(USDA)
	Malabar Plum, Rose Apple	(CRC)

USES	Goes to Osain (Omiero)	
	Kills witchcraft (mata brujo)	(LC)
	Used for ritual baths (Ebomisi) and cleansings	
	Medicinal	
PALO	**Èwó for Mayombero**, specially with Nganga "Judía". It will drive away the spirits that live in the Nganga.	(LC)
Candomblé Jêje-Nagô	Used to create powders (pó) in order to repel anything that is negative.	(Barros)
Candomblé Ketu	Used in any head cleansings, Abô and purification baths	
Candomblé de Angola	Used in any head cleansing (obrigações no Orí)	
INDIA	Used in Ayurveda and Unani	(CRC)

NAME-CUBA	Ponasí, Para Mí	(Roig)
Owner	Changó, **Nsasi** (LC, Madan)	
	Changó (TDF2)	
	Changó, Babalú-Ayé (Quiros, Diaz)	
	Changó, Oggún (Irizarry)	
Odun	Ose-ofun, Ofun-otura (Quiros, Irizarry, Diaz, Madan, Orula.org)	
NAME-SCIENTIFIC	*Hamelia patens* Jacq.	(Roig)
NAME-BRAZIL	Mato-de-oração, Valmoura, Caraui-tanga, Ixicanan	
NAME-Lucumí **YORUBA**	Nfita Sunda Mogna	(TDF2)
NAME-CONGO **PALO**	Nfita-súnda-mocna Nfita Sinda Moana	(LC)
NAME-OTHER	Scarletbush	(USDA)
	Coralito (DR, Venezuela); Bálsamo Colorado (PR)	
	Koray, Koray wouj (Creole Haiti)	(Elsevier)
USES	Goes to Osain (Omiero)	
	Used for cleansing baths, Sarayéyé	(LC)
	Used for ritual baths (Ebomisi) and Inche Osain	
	Medicinal	
NOTE	Lydia Cabrera has a separate listing for Paramí	
Nsasi	Nsasi (also known as **Siete Rayos**, **Nsazi**, or **Mukiamamuilo**) is the mpungo who rules over thunder, fire, virility, spell-casting and justice in Regla Conga. He is Changó in the Regla Ocha.	

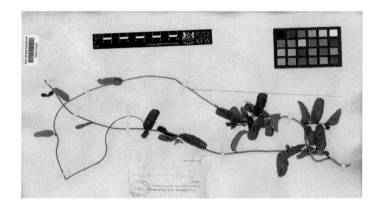

NAME-CUBA	Pringa Hermosa	See NOTE	(LC)
	Pringamoza, Ortiga		(Roig)
Owner	**Ochún Panchacara** (LC, TDF2)	See NOTE	
	Ochún (Quiros)		
Odun			

| NAME-SCIENTIFIC | *Platygyna hexandra* (Jacq.) Müll.Arg.; | | |
| | *Platygyna urens* P.Mercier | See NOTE | (Roig) |

| NAME-BRAZIL | NOT found in Flora do Brasil | |

NAME-Lucumí	Okerere	(LC)
	Okorere	(TDF2)
YORUBA		
NAME-CONGO	Nakato	(LC)
PALO	Nfula Feinó	

| NAME-OTHER | NO common name found. Native to Cuba and Haiti |

USES

Powder (Afoche) made to include in a talisman/amulet which		
is given to prostitutes to protect them from mistreatment	(LC)
Powder (Afoche) made to physically destroy (make them look		
like a monster) an unfaithful lover/wife/spouse	(LC)

NOTE   Lydia Cabrera failed to name a scientific name for this plant.
Juan Tomás Roig has the plant in question; but with a slight change in name.

NOTE   Lydia Cabrera denotes the name of Ochún as **Ochún Panchacara**. The only
approximation is **Ochún Agandara**. She is an avatar of Ochún. She lives sitting
in a chair. Included with her attributes is a lock and a lot of Ñame.
She is born in the Odun Ika-odi   (NBA)

Platygyna hexandra **(Jacq.) Müll.Arg** is **NATIVE** to Cuba and Haiti
See: **http://powo.science.kew.org/taxon/urn:lsid:ipni.org:names:354933-1**

NAME-CUBA	Prodigiosa, Siempreviva, Hoja Bruja, Inmortal, Víbora	(Roig)
Owner	Obatalá, Changó (TDF2)	
	Obatalá, Eleggua (Quiros, Concordia)	
	Obatalá (Diaz, Madan)	
	Obatalá, Ochosi, Odudua, Aña (Irizarry)	
	Oggún, Ochosi, Obatalá, Yemayá, Ochún (Menéndez)	
Odun	Oyeku-okanran, Okanran-ofun (Quiros, Diaz, Irizarry, Madan, Orula.org)	
	Ogunda-ofun (Concordia)	

NAME-SCIENTIFIC	*Bryophyllum pinnatum* (Lam.) Oken	(Roig)

NAME-BRAZIL	Folha-da-fortuna, Folha-grossa, Folha-da-vida, Sempre-viva		
Candomblé Jêje-Nagô	Ifá, Oxalá, Xangô	Água/Feminino	(Barros)
Candomblé Ketu	Exu, Oxalá		
Candomblé de Angola	Aluvaiá, Zaze, Lembá		
Umbanda	ALL Orixa		

NAME-Lucumí	Ewe Odundu	(Irizarry)
	Ewe Dun dun	(Concordia, Madan)
YORUBA	Àbámodá, **Erú òdúndún**, Kantíkantí, Kóropòn **See NOTE**	(PV)

NAME-CONGO	Djokaka, Mayama, Ndjoa, Nzua, Tebete, Tsui	(CRC)

NAME-OTHER	Cathedral Bells	(USDA)
	Air plant, Tree of Life, Resurrection plant, Never Die, Miracle Leaf	(CRC)

USES	Goes to Osain (Omiero)
	One of the 5 MOST important plants (Ewé) in the Omiero
	Used for head cleansings (Ebori Eleda), ritual baths (Ebomisi)
	Used for spiritual assistance
	Used for Eggun rituals
	Medicinal

Candomblé Jêje-Nagô   Although some believe that this Ewe belongs to Xangô, it is used in other Orixá, confirming the African tradition that this Ewe belongs to "Orixá-funfun" which with few exceptions said Orixás are associated with either Oxalá or Ifá.

A characteristic of this Ewe is that the leaves sprout multiple plants, thereby being associated with prosperity and therefore being used in Initiation rituals, Abô, purification baths and the cleaning/cleansing of the ritual items of the Orixá.   (Barros)

Candomblé Ketu   Used in ALL head cleansings (obrigações de cabeça), ritual baths for cleansing and/or discharge (banhos de limpeza ou descarrego), and Abô for any "filho-de-santo".

Candomblé de Angola **Aluvaiá**   The flowers and leaves used for ritual baths
                        Zaze   Used for head cleansings (obrigações no Orí)
                        Lembá   Used for head cleansings (obrigações no Orí)
of ALL Omorixá since this is a principal Ewe for Oxalá

Umbanda   This Ewe represents increased prosperity and Axé (Aché). It placates negative energies. It cannot be absent from rituals of initiation, offerings, ritual baths, and the purification of ritual objects.

INDIA   Used in Ayurveda. Magic, ritual: leaves in bath for bewitchment.   (CRC)

NOTE Erú òdúndún   This Ewe is named **Erú òdúndún** which translates to "slave to òdúndún" since it is subordinate to òdúndún it can replace it in rites.
Òdúndún is *Kalanchoe crenata* (Andrews) Haw.

NOTE   **Pataki of Ogunda-ofun** Obatalá and the Siempreviva plant.   (Concordia)
- In the land that Ewe DunDun lived, he was considered a weak plant and everyone stepped on him. He got tired of this treatment and went to see Obatalá to ask him for a blessing. Obatalá proclaimed that Ewe DunDun would from then on live forever. Obatalá had a neighbor that would not leave him alone, so in gratitude Ewe DunDun went to talk to the neighbor to leave Obatalá in peace. The neighbor got bothered and ripped Ewe DunDun into a thousand pieces and said "Let Obatalá cure you". The neighbor left, but when he came back to the house, he found it completely covered by Ewe DunDun. The neighbor then got mad and grabbed a machete and hacked Ewe DunDun into a million pieces and threw it out in the sun to burn. The next morning, when he opened the door, he found a mountain of Ewe DunDun blocking his path. He became so furious that he began ripping the plant out of the ground and threw it in the river to rot. When the neighbor came back that afternoon, Ewe DunDun covered the entire river, where only Ewe DunDun knew where the land ended and the river began. When the neighbor ran to the river to rip Ewe DunDun, he fell into the muddy shores and drowned.

NAME-CUBA	Quiebra Hacha, Caguairán	(Roig)
Owner	Oggún, Oyá (LC, Quiros)	
	Oggún (TDF2)	
Odun	Owonrin-ika (Quiros, Orula.org)	

NAME-SCIENTIFIC	*Guibourtia hymenaeifolia* (Moric.) J.Léonard;	
	Copaifera hymenaeifolia Moric.	(Roig)

NAME-BRAZIL   NOT listed in Flora do Brasil

NAME-Lucumí	Edú, Iggi, Elé, Arudiki	(LC)
	Eddú, Arúdikí	(TDF2)
YORUBA		

NAME-CONGO	Mbele múkua nkerete	(LC)
	Mole lenuka, Mole nuka, Mobele neuka, Musi bele loasia	(TDF)
PALO	**QUIEBRA HACHA** Mbele Mukua Nketete	
	OWNER Zaranamda, Centella	(Nfinda)

NAME-OTHER	NO common name found. Native to Cuba	
	Membranous-leaf Guibourtia	(Elsevier)

USES

	Oggún likes to work with this Ewe.	(LC)
PALO	Prefered "palo" for all those that have Nganga of Zarabanda and Centella.	
	This "palo" usually is used for bad.	
	It is excellent for making powders (Afoche/Mpolo); and these	
	Powders usually are used to cause mayhem/tragedies	(Nfinda)

NOTE   *Guibourtia hymenaeifolia* **(Moric.) J.Léonard** is **NATIVE** to Cuba
       See: **http://powo.science.kew.org/taxon/urn:lsid:ipni.org:names:1080531-2**

NAME-CUBA	Quimbombó	(Roig)
Owner	Changó (LC, TDF, TDF2)	
	Changó, Orishaoko (Quiros)	
	Changó, Agayú (Diaz)	
	Changó, Eleggua, Orishaoko, Ochun (Irizarry)	
	Changó, Oyá, Orishaoko (Madan)	
Odun	Irete-oturupon (Quiros, Madan)	

NAME-SCIENTIFIC	*Abelmoschus esculentus* (L.) Moench;	
	Hibiscus esculentus L.	(Roig)

NAME-BRAZIL   Quiabo, Quingombô, Gombô, Quibombô, Quigombó
  Candomblé Jêje-Nagô   Xangô, Oiá, Iemanjá, Oxossi, Oxumaré, Ibeije   (Barros)
  Candomblé   Culto Egúngún, Òrò (Baba-Ègun), Exú, Ifá, Ogum, Xangô, Obaluaiè, Oxalá

NAME-Lucumí	Lilá, Alilá	(LC, TDF2)
	Kimbombó, Okró, Pkola, Alilá	(TDF)
YORUBA	Ìlasa, Ilá, Ìlasadò, Erúlá (irúlá), Ìròkò	(PV, CRC)

NAME-CONGO	Gondei, Bañé	(LC)
	Molondrón, Ngungo, Ngueso, Dongo-dongo, Kingambó,	
	Nguido, Kingombó	(TDF)
	Ngaingai, Umvumba	(CRC)
Sierra Leone	Bonde, Bondei	(CRC)
PALO	Gondei	

NAME-OTHER	Okra	(USDA)
	Okra, Common Okra, Lady's Finger	(CRC)

USES	**DOES NOT** go to Osain (Omiero)	
	Used to undo the damage done by Bilongo	(LC)
	Used for ritual baths (Ebomisi), cleansings (Ebori Eledá),	
	Paraldo and Inche Osain	(Irizarry)
PALO	NOT used by Mayomberos because the hexes would	
	slide-off (resbalan); i.e.-fail.	(LC)

Candomblé Jêje-Nagô   Used in food offerings to the Orixás.

i.e.: Amalá de Xangô for Xangô; Caruru das Crianças for Ibeije; Amalá with okra cut in slices for Iansã; Amalá fried without seeds for Oxumaré; and Adjàbó (an offering which is prepared with cut green okra, some honey and olive oil and which is beaten with the hands) which is used to ask something of Xangô, this offering is also used in a bath which has great success in fighting demands.   (Barros)

Candomblé It is a food offering in the Culto Egúngún.

When it is offered to Exú and Ifá it is for the purpose to accelerate a better financial condition.

When it is offered to Ogum, it is because of a manifested confrontation.

When it is offered to Xangô, it is to attack or appease any threat that has yet to manifested itself.

For Obaluaiè it is offered pounded in order to accelerate the progress of wealth and prosperity.

For Oxalá its function is to appease any aggressive force or situation. That is, the Ilà has characteristics that are to advance something, to slide, to slip in or out of a situation.

It is **Èwó of Ogum**.

Umbanda It is **Èwó of Ogum**.

INDIA Used in Ayurveda and Unani.   (CRC)

NAME-CUBA	Quita Maldición sin Espinas/de Babalao, Fosforito (**Vernacular**)	
	Yerba de Sapo	(LC)
	Oro Azul, Hierba de Sapo	(Roig)
Owner	Eleggua, Obatalá, Ibeyis (Quiros)	
	Eleggua, Obatalá (Diaz)	
	Obatalá (Irizarry)	
	Osain, ALL Orisha (Madan)	
Odun	Otura-okanran, Irete-iwori (Quiros, Madan, Orula.org)	
	Okanran-ose, Otura-ofun, Odi-ogunda (Quiros, Orula.org)	

| **NAME-SCIENTIFIC** | *Phyla nodiflora (L.) Greene* | (Roig) |

| **NAME-BRAZIL** | NO common name found | |

NAME-Lucumí	Ewe Pólo, Okuale	(LC)
	Ewé Shewerekuekue; Ewé Shewekekuekue	**See NOTE**
ANAGO YORUBA	Ewekuolo **Yerba de Sapo**	(LC)

| **NAME-CONGO** | Nfina Ñokapémbe | (LC) |

| **NAME-OTHER** | Turkey Tangle Fogfruit | (USDA) |
| | Cape weed, Turkey tangle, Fog fruit, Daisylawn | (CRC) |

USES	**DOES NOT** go to Osain (Omiero)	
	To make Omiero to clean Otanes to remove curse,	
	prior to consecrating the Otanes in regular Omiero;	
	NOT done by ALL Santeria Houses	(Diaz)
	Used in ritual bath (Ebomisi) to remove curse (Maldición)	(Irizarry)
INDIA	Used in Ayurveda, Unani and Siddha	(CRC)

NOTE   These are the two types of Quita Maldición

Ewé Ayé/Ewé Ayo   **Guacalote** - Commonly called Quita Maldición, Quita Maldición de Santero, Quita Maldición con espina.

Ewé Shewerekuekue   Quita Maldición, Quita Maldición de Babalao

NAME-CUBA	Rabo de Gato, P. de Gato	(Roig)
Owner	Eleggua, Ibeyis (LC, Quiros)	
	Eleggua (TDF2, Madan)	
	Eleggua, Ibeyis, Oggún, Ochosi (Diaz)	
	Eleggua, Eggun (Irizarry)	
Odun	Otura-ejiogbe (Quiros, Diaz, Irizarry, Madan)	
NAME-SCIENTIFIC	*Achyranthes aspera* L.	(Roig)
NAME-BRAZIL	Fia-ponto, Folha-galo, Folha-ponto, Mato-bana, Papué	(Wiki)
NAME-Lucumí		
YORUBA	Abòro, Èpà abòro	(PV, CRC)
NAME-CONGO		
NAME-OTHER	Devil's Horse Whip	(USDA)
	Colic weed, Devil's horse whip, Rough chaff flower	(CRC)
USES	Goes to Osain (Omiero)	
	Used to tie (amarrar) the fetus before is born, as a form	
	of vengeance, where the new-born baby will be under the	
	power of the enemy.	(LC)
	Used for Inche Osain and Paraldo	(Irizarry)
INDIA	Used in Ayurveda, Unani and Siddha. Used in religion and magico-religious beliefs: for safe delivery of pregnant mother; plant infusion given as bath in sickness which is believed to be due to ghost; ingredient of Patra pooja in different religious pooja ceremonies, in Ganesh-pooja; dried inflorescence used by orthodox Hindus in sacred pyres.	(CRC)

NAME-CUBA	Rasca Barriga	(LC)
	Rascabarriga, Arraiján	(Roig, Elsevier)
Owner	Eleggua (LC, Quiros)	
	Eleggua, Oggún, Orula (Diaz)	
Odun	Otura-ika (Diaz, Orula.org)	

| **NAME-SCIENTIFIC** | *Espadaea amoena* A.Rich. | (Roig) |

| **NAME-BRAZIL** | NOT found in Flora do Brasil | |

NAME-Lucumí	Omá, Eká ore	(LC)
YORUBA		
NAME-CONGO	Lunga kuma, Wangará	(TDF)
BANTU	Kumayanga nfita	(TDF)
PALO	**RASCA BARRIGA** Ngumbe	
	OWNER Lucero	(Nfinda)

| **NAME-OTHER** | NO common name found. Native to Cuba | |
| | Pleasing Espadea | (Elsevier) |

USES	**DOES NOT** go to Osain (Omiero)	
	To hit Eleggua during ceremony of Kari Ocha	(LC)
	Used in the changing of head (Cambio de Cabeza,	
	Cambiar Vida) ceremony. **See NOTE**	(LC)
PALO	Rarely used in Regla Conga	(Nfinda)
	"Palo" put in Nganga to scourge the enemy	(Diaz)

NOTE   *Espadaea amoena* **A.Rich.**

Its native range is Cuba (Kew Science)
See: **http://powo.science.kew.org/taxon/urn:lsid:ipni.org:names:862786-1**
It is Endemic to Cuba (Fairchild Tropical Botanical Garden)
See: **http://www.virtualherbarium.org/research/JewelsCaribbean.html**
Photographs from "Plants of Viñales"
See: **http://www.cybertruffle.org.uk/vinales/eng/espadea_amoena.htm**

NOTE   **Cambio de Cabeza/Cambiar Vida**   It is a ceremony where a sick person's life is
exchanged for an inanimate object (a doll, a stump from the banana tree)
so that Ikú (death) is satisfied.

NAME-CUBA	Raspa Lengua	(LC)
	Raspalengua, Ranilla	(Roig)
Owner	Eleggua (LC, TDF2, Quiros, Irizarry, Madan)	
	Eleggua, Changó (Diaz)	
Odun	Ose-obara (Quiros, Diaz, Irizarry, Madan)	
NAME-SCIENTIFIC	*Casearia hirsuta* Sw.	(Roig)
NAME-BRAZIL	NO common name found	
NAME-Lucumí	Ewe Elenú, Yeréobo	(LC)
	Elenú, Yereobo	(TDF2)
YORUBA		
NAME-CONGO	Nkanga, Nkúfindula, Luékeloni	(LC)
NAME-OTHER	Crackopen	(USDA)
	Wild Coffee, White Wattle	(Elsevier)
USES	**DOES NOT** go to Osain (Omiero)	
	Used for Ebomisi, Inche Osain and Ebó	(Irizarry)
	Used in powders (Afoche) to win legal problems	(LC)
	Used to silence gossipy people	(LC)

NAME-CUBA	Reseda	(Roig)
Owner	Yemayá (LC, TDF2)	
	Yemayá, Inlé (Quiros)	
	Yemayá, Ochún (Diaz, Madan)	
	Ochún (Irizarry)	
Odun	Oturupon-owonrin (Quiros, Diaz, Madan, Orula.org)	

NAME-SCIENTIFIC	*Reseda odorata* L.	(Roig)

NAME-BRAZIL	Reseda, Resedá	

NAME-Lucumí	Dincuyero	(LC)
	Díncuyeró	(TDF2)
YORUBA		

NAME-CONGO		
PALO	Dínkuyero	

NAME-OTHER	Mignonette	(USDA)

USES	Goes to Osain (Omiero)	
	Used against cockroaches	(LC)
	Medicinal	
	Used in love baths and aphrodisiac perfumes	(Diaz)
	Used for ritual baths (Ebomisi) and Inche Osain	(Irizarry)

NOTE There is another plant listed by Juan Tomás Roig under Resedá and Resedá Francesa (please note the accent) which is **Lawsonia inermis L.; Lawsonia alba Lam.** (gbif.org) which is known as Henna (USDA)

NAME-CUBA	Retama, Salvia Cimarrona, Vitoriana	(Roig)
Owner	Babalú-Ayé (LC, TDF2, Quiros, Madan)	
	Ochún (Irizarry)	
Odun	Oturupon-meji (Quiros, Irizarry, Madan, Orula.org)	
NAME-SCIENTIFIC	*Neurolaena lobata* (L.) R.Br. ex Cass.;	
	Neurolaena lobata (L.) R.Br.	(Roig)
NAME-BRAZIL	NOT found in Flora do Brasil	
NAME-Lucumí	Chachara, Ewe ale	(LC)
	Chachara, Ewe ale, Teikoyo	(TDF2)
YORUBA		
NAME-CONGO	Teicollo, Nkorimánfo	(LC)
NAME-OTHER	Sepi	(USDA)
	Jackass Bitters, Bitterwood	
	Caballón (DR), Sepi (PR); Tabac zombi (Creole Haiti)	(Duke's)

USES

Used for ritual baths (Ebomisi) and Inche Osain
Used to invoke/ when saying the prayer of the "**Ánima Sola**"
(The Lonely Soul in Purgatory)   **See NOTE**   (LC)
Medicinal

NOTE **Ánima Sola** or **Ánimas del Purgatorio**   Catholic tradition of praying for the souls in
Purgatory. Also imbedded into the Santeria, Voodoo (Haitian, Dominican,
Louisiana) and Afro-Brazilian religions.
See: **https://en.wikipedia.org/wiki/Anima_Sola**

NOTE Per Duke's (Duke's Handbook of Medicinal Plants in Latin America; CRC Press), the
leaves of this plant are used widely for the control of sugar in the blood in patients
suffering from Diabetes II (Diabetes-Adult onset)

NAME-CUBA	Revienta Caballos	(Roig)
Owner	Oyá (LC, Quiros)	
Odun		

NAME-SCIENTIFIC	*Hippobroma longiflora* (L.) G.Don;	
	Isotoma longiflora (L.) C.Presl	(Roig)

NAME-BRAZIL	Jasmim-da-Itália, Arrebenta-boi, Cega-olho	
Candomblé Jêje-Nagô	Oxalá, Oxum	Água/Masculino	(Barros)
Umbanda		

NAME-Lucumí	Erán opani chi, Mansokato	(LC)
YORUBA		

NAME-CONGO	Fita fwa kómbo, Efínloro	(LC)

NAME-OTHER	Madamfate	(USDA)
	Frog's flower	
	Tibey, Guibey (DR)	(Duke's)

USES

Only used to do bad.
Used to make a good poison (LC)

Candomblé Jêje-Nagô The leaves are used in the initiation rites and Abô of the "filhos" of Oxum; and for prosperity baths for ALL "filhos de santo". (Barros)

NOTE Although the leaves are considered medicinal, a drop of latex in the eye/s can cause blindness (CRC)

NAME-CUBA	Roble	(LC)
	Roble de Magriñá, Roble Maquiligua, Maculiso, Maquiligua	(Roig)
Owner	Changó, Agayú (Diaz)	
	Oggún, Orunmila (Irizarry)	
	Oggún, Mayombe (Madan)	
Odun	Oturupon-owonrin (Quiros, Diaz, Irizarry, Madan, Orula.org)	
	Owonrin-oyeku (Quiros, Irizarry, Madan, Orula.org)	
NAME-SCIENTIFIC	*Tabebuia heterophylla* (DC.) Britton;	
	Tabebuia pentaphylla Hemsl.	(Roig)
NAME-BRAZIL	NOT listed in Flora do Brasil	
NAME-Lucumí **YORUBA**	Akogí	(LC, TDF2)
NAME-CONGO	Talaví	(LC)
NAME-OTHER	White Cedar	(USDA)
	Cuban Pink Trumpet tree, Pink Manjack, White Cedar	(CRC)
	Roble Blanco (DR), Apamate, Roble Negro (Venezuela)	(Elsevier)
USES	Goes to Osain (Omiero)	
	Medicinal	
	Used to consecrate the **Opon Ifá**	(Irizarry)
PALO	This wood can ONLY be used for good	(LC)

NOTE   *Tabebuia pentaphylla* Hemsl. Is listed under *Tabebuia rosea* (Bertol.) A.DC.
in Elsevier's (Elsevier's Dictionary of Trees: Volume 1: North America; 1st Edition 2005)

Opon Ifá   **Opon Ifá** is the divination tray used by the Babalawo
See: **https://en.wikipedia.org/wiki/Opon_Ifá**

NAME-CUBA	Romerillo, Romerillo Blanco		(Roig)
Owner	Ochún, Ochosi (TDF2)		
	Ochún, Oggún, Inlé (Quiros)		
	Ochún (Diaz)		
	Ochún, Eleggua, Obatalá, Eggun (Irizarry)		
	Ochún, Eleggua (Madan)		
	Oggún, Ochosi (Menéndez)		
Odun	Odi-osa (Quiros, Diaz, Irizarry, Madan, Orula.org)		
	Oyekun-ika (Quiros, Diaz, Irizarry, Madan)		

| **NAME-SCIENTIFIC** | *Bidens pilosa* L. | | (Roig) |

NAME-BRAZIL	Picão-preto, Picão, Pico-pico, Fura-capa		
Candomblé Jêje-Nagô	Exú, Oxum	Terra/masculino/Gùn	(Barros)
CULTO DE NAÇÃO	Exú, Oxum, Ifá		
Umbanda	Exú, Iemanjá, Ogum, Pretos-velhos		
ODUN	Odi-Meji, Ogbe-ofun		(PV)

NAME-Lucumí			
YORUBA	Elésin máso, Akésin máso, Oyà, Malánganran, Abéré olóko,		
	Agamáyàn, Agaran mòyàn, Àgbèdè dudu oko, Ajísomobíàlá		(PV, CRC)

| **NAME-CONGO** | Bulangu, Potambili | | (CRC) |

| **NAME-OTHER** | Hairy Beggarticks | | (USDA) |
| | Beggar's Ticks, Burr Marigold, Black Jack | | (CRC) |

USES	Goes to Osain (Omiero)	
	Goes to the Omiero of Ochún	(TDF2)
	Flowers used for bath to remove Ogu (Bilongo/witchcraft)	(Irizarry)
	Leaves used for Ebomisi, Inche Osain and Paraldo	(Irizarry)
	Medicinal	
Candomblé Jêje-Nagô	the leaves used in the initiation for Exú	
	Leaves attributed to witchcraft (feitiços) with Oxum	(Barros)
Umbanda	Used in ritual baths, Amacis, cleansings and to break hexes (witchcraft) and send them back in the Cult of Ifá.	
INDIA	Used in Ayurveda, Unani and Siddha	(CRC)

NAME-CUBA	Romero		(Roig)
Owner	Yemayá (LC, Diaz)		
	Yemayá, Babalú-Ayé (TDF2)		
	Yemayá, Odudua (Quiros)		
	Ochún (Irizarry, Madan)		
Odun	Owonrin-irete (Quiros, Diaz, Irizarry, Madan)		

NAME-SCIENTIFIC	*Rosmarinus officinalis* L.		(Roig)

NAME-BRAZIL	Alecrim, Rosmaninho, Alecrim-da-horta		
Candomblé Jêje-Nagô	Oxalá	Ar/Masculino	(Barros)
Candomblé de Angola	Lembá		
CULTOS DE NAÇÃO	Oxalá, Oxossi		
Umbanda	Xangô, Ogum, Omolú, Iemanjá		

NAME-Lucumí	Ewé Ré, Ewé Págwábimá	(LC, TDF2)
YORUBA	EWÉRÉ	(Barros)
NAME-Abakuá	Ifán mkere	(LC)
PALO	Sererú	

NAME-OTHER	Rosemary, Common Rosemary	(CRC)

USES	DOES NOT go to Osain (Omiero)	
	Used for ritual baths (Ebomisi)	
	A tea made from the leaves and the prayer to San Ramon Neonato (Raymond Nonnatus) will facilitate the birth for women about to give birth.	(LC)
	Used for cleansing and purification baths to attract good luck, money and harmony	(Diaz)
	Medicinal	
Candomblé Jêje-Nagô	Used as part of purification baths and incense	
Candomblé de Angola	Used in Amacis, Ebori, Abô, incense	
Umbanda	Used in baths, Amacis, Abô, head cleansings and incense	
Hoodoo/Root Magic (USA)	Used to ward-off evil in the home, and bring good luck in family matters.	

NAME-CUBA	Rompe Camisa Macho, Damiana	(Roig)
Owner	Oggún (Diaz)	
	Asojuano (Irizarry)	
	Osain (Madan)	
Odun	Ofun-osa (Quiros, Diaz, Irizarry, Madan)	

NAME-SCIENTIFIC	*Turnera diffusa* Willd. ex Schult.	(Roig)

NAME-BRAZIL	Damiana	
Umbanda	Oxum	Ervas Mornas

NAME-Lucumí
    YORUBA

NAME-CONGO

NAME-OTHER	Damiana	(USDA)
	Damiana, Mexican Damiana	(CRC)
	Oreganillo, Orégano Cimarrón (DR)	(Duke's)

USES	**DOES NOT** go to Osain (Omiero)	
	Purification baths to break hexes and solve problems	
	Home cleansings	(Diaz)
	Eggun Rituals, Paraldo	(Irizarry)
	Medicinal	
Hoodoo/Root Magic (USA)	Leaves used for luck in love affairs	

NAME-CUBA Rompezaragüey, Albahaquilla, Filigrana de Sabana (Roig)
Owner Changó (LC, Madan)
Changó, Eleggua, Ochosi (TDF2)
Changó, Ochún, Ibeyis (Quiros)
Changó, Elegguá, Babalú-Ayé (Diaz)
Ibeyis, Yemayá, Oggún, Asojuano, Ochosi (Irizarry)
Oggún, Ochosi, Babalú-Ayé (Menéndez) **Rompezaragüey**
Yemayá, Ochún (Menéndez) **Filigrana**
Odun Irete-iwori, Odi-ogunda (Quiros, Diaz, Irizarry, Madan, Orula.org)

NAME-SCIENTIFIC *Chromolaena odorata* (L.) R.M.King & H.Rob.;
Eupatorium odoratum L. (Roig)
Ageratum conyzoides L. (Barros, Camargo)

NAME-BRAZIL Erva de São João, Mentrasto, Catinga-de-bode, Picão-roxo
Candomblé Jêje-Nagô Xangô, Orumilá Fogo/Feminino (Barros)
Candomblé de Angola Zaze
Candomblé Exú, Oxum Terra/Masculino **Èwé Abéré Olóko**
Candomblé Nagô Xangô Airá Fogo/Masculino/Gùn **Èwé Arún Sánsán**
Odun Ogbe-osa, Ika-oyeku, Ika-ogunda (PV)

NAME-Lucumí Tabaté (LC)
Tabaté, Rompe Dió, Tabé, Ján (TDF2)
YORUBA Àrún sánsán, Ími exú, Ako yúnyun (*Ageratum conyzoides* L.) (PV)
NIGERIA Awolowo, Ebe-ighoedo (CRC)

NAME- CONGO Ntema dián finda (LC)
PALO **Rompezaragüey** Ntema Duán Finda
OWNER Siete Rayos, Remolino (Nfinda)
OWNER Tiembla Tierra **Regla Kimbisa**

NAME-OTHER	Jack in the Bush		(USDA)
	Bitterbush, Jack in the Bush, Triffid Weed		
	Cariaquillo Santa Maria (PR), Zaragüey (DR)		
	Guérit tout, Guérit vite (Creole Haiti)		(Duke's)

USES Goes to Osain (Omiero)
For cleansing and purification baths (de despojo)
to remove any witchcraft or hexes   (LC)
Ritual baths (Ebomisi), Inche Osain and Paraldo
For cleansings, to remove obstacles and impediments
To protect the home against evil   (LC)

PALO Used in the initiation baths for purification required in
most Regla Conga religions/branches.   (LC)

Candomblé Jêje-Nagô Considered one of the best Ewé for defense. Per Pierre Verger
its purpose is to combat witchcraft sent by Ìyàmi (witches).

Candomblé de Angola Used for head cleansings (obrigações no Orí)

Candomblé **Èwé Abéré Olóko** It's an Ewé that can be used for good or bad

Candomblé Nagô **Èwé Arún Sánsán** Used for the initiation of Airá. Used
in defense baths, cleansings and protection (trabalhos de proteção)

PALO MONTE Ritual baths, cleansings (rompimientos), initiation
baths and to remove physical damages
Protection for followers (hijos) of Mamá Chola.

ESPIRITISMO CRUZADO Ritual baths, remove spiritual damages, cleansings.
Can be used for good or bad.

NOTE Abre Camino and Rompezaragüey are used interchangeably. Roig lists them as the same family of plants although in the religion they are ***different.***
Juan Tomás Roig lists several plants under Rompezaragüey. They are:

- ***Vernonanthura menthifolia* (Poepp. ex Spreng.) H.Rob.;** *Vernonia menthifolia* **Less.**; which is listed as occurring **ONLY** in Cuba (gbif.org)
- ***Trixis inula* Crantz;** *Eupatorium ageratifolium* **DC.** (gbif.org)
- ***Koanophyllon villosum* subsp.** *Villosum;* *Eupatorium villosum* **Sw.** (gbif.org); which is listed here under Abre Camino

NAME-CUBA	Rosa		(Roig)
	Rosa de Jericó (*Rosa gallica* var. *centifolia*)		(Roig, LC)
Owner	Ochún (LC, TDF2, Quiros)		
Odun	Ika-owonrin (Orula.org)		

NAME-SCIENTIFIC	*Rosa indica* L.	(Roig)
	Rosa centifolia L.	(Roig)
	Rosa centifolia L.; *Rosa gallica* var. *centifolia* (L.) Regel	(Roig)

NAME-BRAZIL Rosa-branca, Rosa-amarela, Rosa-vermelha, Rosa

Candomblé Jêje-Nagô	Oxalá, Jemanjá	Ar/Feminino	Rosa-branca	(Barros)
	Oxum, Oiá, Obá	Ar/Feminino	Rosa-vermelha	(Barros)
	Iabás	Ar/Feminino	Rosa-amarela	(Barros)
Umbanda	Iemanjá, Oxalá		Rosa-branca	
	Oxum, Iansã, Omolú		Rosa-amarela	
	Iabás, Erês		Rosa-cor-de-rosa	
	Iansã, Oxum, Nanã, Ciganas, Pomba-gira		Rosa-vermelha	
	Iemanjá, Ogum		Rosa-azuis	
	Pomba-gira, Nanã, Omolú		Rosa-negra	

NAME-Lucumí YORUBA	Idón, Dido	(LC, TDF2)
NAME-CONGO		
NAME-OTHER	Rose	

USES

	Used for love baths to attract.	
	Used for baths of **Iowó** – to attract money, financial gain	(LC)
Candomblé Jêje-Nagô	Used in the ornamentation of the altars of the Orixás	(Barros)
Candomblé de Angola	Feitura (inital rites of initiation) and head cleansings (obrigações no Orí)	
Umbanda	Used for purification baths	(Barros)
Hoodoo/Root Magic (USA)	Rose symbolize love, romance, sexual attraction.	
	Rose-hips as a symbol of good luck	
INDIA	Used in Ayurveda, Unani and Siddha. Sacred plant: ceremonial, ritual, ingredient of Patra pooja in different religious pooja ceremonies (**Rosa × damascena Mill.**; i.e.-Cabbage Rose, Hundred petal rose)	(CRC)

NAME-CUBA	Rosa de Jericó
Owner	Ochún (Diaz)
Odun	Oyekun-iwori (Diaz, Orula.org)

NAME-SCIENTIFIC	*Selaginella lepidophylla* (Hook. & Grev.) Spring	(Wiki)
	Anastatica hierochuntica L.	(Wiki)

NAME-BRAZIL   Planta-da-ressurreição, Rosa-do-deserto, Rosa-de-Jericó
     Selaginella lepidophylla

NAME- YORUBA
NAME- CONGO

NAME-OTHER	*Selaginella lepidophylla*	False Rose of Jericho,	
	Resurrection Plant, Resurrection Moss		(Wiki)
	Anastatica hierochuntica **L.**	Rose of Jericho,	
	Myriam's flower, St. Mary's Flower		(CRC)

USES

Used in rites to invoke luck and fortune   (Wiki)
Used widely because of the fact that the plant is dried and
when water is added, it will become green again.
Associated with the resurrection and a new beginning.
Used, specially in the Spiritual field (both Afro-Cuban and Afro-
Brazilian) for the purpose of cleansing of spaces of negative energies,
to advert the Evil-Eye and Envy, to gain new opportunities and to
increase financial well-being. Usually accompanied, on a weekly basis,
by the Prayer to the Rose of Jericho
Hoodoo/Root Magic (USA)   They are kept in shops to draw money in, and usually
watered on Fridays with a recital of Psalms.

NOTE   In the Afro-Caribbean and Afro-Brazilian communities, when you refer to the
"Rose of Jericho", you are referring to *Selaginella lepidophylla* which is a desert
plant that originates in the Mexican dessert. This plant can survive without a root basis.
The **real/true Rose of Jericho** is *Anastatica hierochuntica*, comes from the
Arabian Peninsula and the African dessert. This plant NEEDS its root to come back
to life. It is sold as a dried ball with its root stalk attached. (see last picture)

NAME-CUBA	Rosa Francesa, Adelfa	(Roig)
Owner	Yewà (LC, TDF2, Quiros)	
	Ochún, Oyá (Irizarry)	
Odun	Ika-owonrin (Quiros, Irizarry, Madan, Orula.org)	
NAME-SCIENTIFIC	*Nerium oleander* L.	(Roig)
NAME-BRAZIL	Oleandro, Loandro-da-índia, Loureiro-rosa, Adelfa, Flor-de-São-José	
NAME-Lucumí	Tetelí, Didekeré	(LC, TDF2)
YORUBA		
NAME-CONGO	Meni-meni, Impoiko, Konkosoti wango ubécon	(LC)
NAME-OTHER	Oleander	(USDA)
	Ceylon Rose, Common Oleander	(CRC)

USES

	Ritual baths (Ebomisi)	
INDIA	Used in Ayurveda. Ceremonial, used in religion and magico-religious beliefs: ingredient of Patra pooja in different religious pooja ceremonies, in Ganesh-pooja; flowers used for religious worships	(CRC)

NOTE   This is a highly **POISONOUS** tree/shrub. Even dried, the leaves remain **TOXIC**

NAME-CUBA	Ruda		(Roig)
Owner	Changó (LC, TDF2, Diaz)		
	Changó, Inlé (Quiros)		
	Eggun (Irizarry)		
Odun	Osa-ofun (Irizarry, Diaz, Orula.org)		

NAME-SCIENTIFIC	*Ruta graveolens* L.		(Roig)
	Ruta chalepensis L.	**See NOTE**	(Roig, LC)

NAME-BRAZIL	Arruda, Arruda-macho (folhas graúdas), Arruda-fémea (folhas miúdas)		
Candomblé Jêje-Nagô	Exú	Fogo/Feminino	(Barros)
Candomblé Ketu	Exú		
Candomblé de Angola	Aluvaiá, Mutalumbô		
CULTO DE NAÇÃO	Exú		
Umbanda	Oxalá, Omolú, Oxossi, Iemanjá, Pretos-velho		

NAME-Lucumí	Atopá kún		(LC)
	Otopá kún		(TDF2)
ANAGO	Atopá kumí, Ewe atapú	**Ruda**	(LC)
	Ewe atópá kún	**Ruda Cimarrona** (Ruta chalepensis L.)	(LC)
YORUBA	ÀTOPÁ KUN	(Ruta graveolens L.)	(Barros)
	Àtópákun ako	**Male Rue**	
	Àtópákun abo	**Female Rue**	(deJagun)

NAME-CONGO

NAME-OTHER	*Ruta graveolens* **L.**	Common Rue	(USDA)
		Rue, Common rue, Garden rue, Herb of repentance	(CRC)
	Ruta chalepensis **L.**	Fringed rue	(USDA)

USES	For Osain (Omiero) **ONLY** for Babalú-Ayé	(Diaz)
	The house where this plant grows, prevents the visit	
	of Ndoki (Flying witches); it can kill them	(LC)
	Can be used to make works for binding someone (trabajo	
	de amarre) and which are hard to undo	(LC)
	Used for cleansings, Inche Osain and Paraldo	(Irizarry)
	Can be used to expel ingested witchcraft (Bilongo)	(Diaz)

Candomblé Jêje-Nagô   Used to protect against the evil-eye and envy.
A branch od rue on the ear is used against the evil eye.
A branch of Rue in a glass of water on the left side of the
entrance prevents malignant spirits from entering the home.
In Territorio Jêje-Nagô of Bahia and Rio de Janeiro, this Ewé is
NOT used because "é um **Èwó de nação**".   (Barros)

Candomblé Ketu   Used in rituals because Exú indicates that this Ewe is good
against the evil eye. **Arruda-folhas miúdas** used in Ebori, cleansing and
discharge baths. The wood of the Rue is crafted into amulets.

Candomblé de Angola Aluvaiá   **Arruda-folhas graúdas** are used against the
evil eye and envy. With the wood, amulets and Figa are crafted.

        Mutalumbô   **Arruda-folhas miúdas** are used for head
cleansings (obrigações no Orí), the making of amulets and/or Figa
from the wood of the Rue plant.

Umbanda   One of the Ewe necessary for the "Vaso de 7 Ervas" which is placed
at the entrance of a home, temple, business in order to protect the
location against the evil eye, negative energies and envious people.
This Ewe is used in spiritual cleansings, discharge baths, incense, Amacis,
head cleansings (obrigações de cabeça), cleansings, initiation and the
cleansing of ritual objects.
It is believed that this Ewe has natural spiritual properties for defense
and protection.

Hoodoo/Root Magic (USA)   Rue is an herb of protection and cleansing. It is also used
to help in love and health. Used for protection against the Evil-Eye,
breaking and reversing a jinx and in cleansing a home when used as an incense.

INDIA   Used in Ayurveda, Unani and Siddha.   (CRC)

NOTE   *Ruta chalepensis* **L.** is listed by Lydia Cabrera ("El Monte") and Juan Tomás Roig
("Plantas Medicinales, Aromáticas o Venenosas de Cuba") as the scientific name for
"Ruda".
Juan Tomás Roig in "Diccionario Botánico de nombre vulgares Cubanos" lists
Ruta chalepensis **L.** as a synonym for *Ruta graveolens* **L.**
Ruta chalepensis **L.** is listed as an accepted species in powo.science.kew.org,
theplantlist.org and in gbif.org

NAME-CUBA	Sábila		(Roig)
Owner	Yemayá (LC, TDF2, Quiros, Irizarry)		
	Obatalá (Diaz)		
Odun	Irosun-irete (Irizarry, Diaz, Orula.org)		

NAME-SCIENTIFIC	*Aloe vera* (L.) Burm.f.		(Roig)

NAME-BRAZIL	Babosa, Aloe		
Candomblé Jêje-Nagô	Ogum, Omolú	Terra/Masculino	(Barros)
Candomblé Ketu	Obaluaiè		
Candomblé de Angola	Inkosse, Kavungo		
Umbanda	Obaluaiè		

NAME-Lucumí

YORUBA	Ipòlerin, Ipè erin	(*Aloe spp.*)	(PV)
	IPÒLERIN		(Barros)

NAME-CONGO

NAME-OTHER	Barbados Aloe	(USDA)
	Aloe Vera, Barbados Aloe, Common Aloe	(CRC)

USES	**DOES NOT** go to Osain (Omiero)	
	Will keep-out evil if put behind the door	(LC)
	Used for Ebomisi, Ebó, and Addimu	(Irizarry)
	Medicinal	
Candomblé Jêje-Nagô	Used in initiation rituals and baths for filhos Omolú	(Barros)
Candomblé Ketu	Discharge baths	
Candomblé de Angola **Inkosse, Kavungo**	Used as incense with other Ewé for depuration.	
Umbanda	Used as incense and discharge baths	
Hoodoo/Root Magic (USA)	Bitter Aloe (*Aloe ferox* **Mill**.) powder is used to stop gossip, slander and backtalking	
INDIA	Used in Ayurveda, Unani and Siddha	(CRC)

NAME-CUBA	**Sacu-Sacu**, Malanguilla	See NOTE	(LC)
	Quitasol Chino, Paragüita		(Roig)
Owner	Inlé, Osain (LC, TDF2, Quiros)		
	Inlé, Changó, Mayombe (Madan)		
Odun	Oturupon-odi (Quiros, Madan, Orula.org)		
NAME-SCIENTIFIC	*Cyperus alternifolius* L.		(Roig, Quiros)
NAME-BRAZIL	Sombrinha-chinesa		
NAME-Lucumí	Sácú-sácú, Saku-Saku		(TDF2)
YORUBA	Èwà òsanyìn, Ìyáfún, Ajípàte **(*Cyperus sp.*)**		(PV)
NAME-CONGO			
NAME-OTHER	Umbrella flatsedge		(cabi.org)
	Umbrella Plant, Umbrella Palm		(CRC)
USES	**DOES NOT** go to Osain (Omiero)		
PALO	Used by Mayombero since with this "palo"		
	the **Nfumbe** (the spirit that inhibit the ritualized		
	bones in the Nganga) will not leave the Nganga		(LC)
	Used for love matters		(LC)

NOTE   Lydia Cabrera only mentions the name/names of this Ewe.
This listing is for "Sacu-Sacu", and the scientific name was provided
by Dalia Quiros-Moran and pictures in the Internet

NOTE   Although Lydia Cabrera uses the names of these plants interchangeably, they
have been separated. Sacu-Sacu and Malanguilla under their own listings

NAME-CUBA	Sagú, Sagú Cimarrón, Yuquilla	(Roig)
Owner	Ibeyis (LC, Quiros)	
Odun		

NAME-SCIENTIFIC	*Maranta arundinacea* L.	(Roig)

NAME-BRAZIL	Araruta, Agutiguepe, Araruta-caixulta, Araruta-comum	
Candomblé Jêje-Nagô	Ibeije Terra/Feminino	(Barros)
Umbanda		

NAME-Lucumí
  YORUBA

NAME-CONGO

NAME-OTHER	Arrowroot	(USDA)
	Arrowroot, Indian Arrowroot, St. Vincent Arrowroot	(CRC)
	Araru (DR); Maranta (PR); Guate (Venezuela);	
	Alloyo (Creole Haiti)	(Duke's)

USES

	Used for cleansing baths	(LC)
	Medicinal	
Candomblé Jêje-Nagô	Used in purification baths, specially for "very thin" children. Offered to Ibeije in Eborí of head cleansing to fortify the head (obrigação de fortalecimento de cabeça)	(Barros)
Hoodoo/Root Magic (USA)	Arrow Root powder is good in certain gambling spells, but only in conjunction with other ingredients.	

NAME-CUBA	Salvadera, Aba, Haba	(Roig)
Owner	Eleggua (LC, TDF)	
	Eleggua, Changó, Obatalá (TDF2)	
	Obatalá (Diaz)	
	Todos los Orishas (Madan)	
	Oggún, Ochosi (Menéndez)	
Odun	Ose-oyeku, Oworin-ejiogbe (Madan, Diaz, Irizarry)	
	Ogbe-ika (Madan, Diaz)	
NAME-SCIENTIFIC	*Hura crepitans* L.;	
	Hura brasiliensis Willd.	(Roig)
NAME-BRAZIL	Açacu, Assacú, Árvore-do-diabo	
Umbanda	Obatalá	
Odun	Ejiogbe-meji, Ogunda-irete	
NAME-Lucumí	Abáa, Ewe gúnna, Arónica	(LC)
	Abáa, Ewe Gúnna, Arónika	(TDF2)
	Abáa,	(TDF)
	Ewé Abonla	(Madan)
YORUBA	Erú bùjé, Èwé bùjé	(PV)
NAME- CONGO	Finli	(LC, TDF)
PALO	**Salvadera**	
OWNER	Ta Kañeñe (Cobayende)	(Nfinda)
NAME-OTHER	Sandbox Tree	(USDA)
	Sandbox Tree, Possum Wood (USA)	
	Havilla, Javilla (PR); Javilla (DR); Ceibo Amarillo (Colombia)	
	Ceiba Blanca, Javillo (Vzla); Bwa djab, Bwis sab (Creole Haiti)	(Elsevier)
USES	Goes to Osain (Omiero)	
	Used for ritual baths (Ebomisi) and Inche Osain (protection amulets, talismans)	
	Used for people running from justice	
	After the funeral home or cemetery, participants are cleansed with it.	
PALO MONTE	Ritual baths, house cleansing & "Rompimientos"	
ESPIRITISMO CRUZADO	Cleansings, "Rompimientos" & Ritual baths	

NAME-CUBA	Salvia, Salvia Morada	(LC)
	Salvia, Salvia Común, S. de Playa, S. del País, S. Cimarrona	(Roig)
Owner	Babalú-Ayé (LC, TDF2)	
	Babalú-Ayé, Odudua (Quiros)	
	Babalú-Ayé, Obatalá (Diaz)	
	Asojuano, Odudua (Madan)	
	Oddúa (Menéndez)	
Odun	Owonrin-osa, Oturupon-meji, Irete-irosun (Quiros, Diaz, Madan, Orula.org)	
	Irosun-irete, Iwori-osa, Ogunda-ika (Diaz, Madan, Orula.org)	
	Otura-okanran (Quiros, Madan, Orula.org)	

NAME-SCIENTIFIC	*Pluchea odorata* (L.) Cass.;	(Roig)
	Pluchea purpurascens (Sw.) DC.	
	Pluchea sagittalis (Lam.) Cabrera	(Barros)

NAME-BRAZIL	Quitoco, Tabacarana, Madrecravo, Lucera, Erva-lucera, Lucero	
Candomblé Jêje-Nagô	Obaluaiè	Terra/Masculino	(Barros)
Candomblé Ketu	Obaluaiè, Nanã	
Candomblé de Angola	Kavungo	
Umbanda	Jemanjá, Ibeije, Obaluaiè, Nanã	

NAME-Lucumí
  YORUBA
NAME-CONGO

NAME-OTHER	*Pluchea odorata*	Sweet Scent	(USDA)
		Salt Marsh Fleabane, Sweet Scent	(CRC)
	Pluchea sagittalis	Wingstem Camphorweed	(USDA)

USES	Goes to Osain (Omiero)	
	Used for cleansings and Sarayéyé	(Diaz)
	Medicinal	
Candomblé Jêje-Nagô	Used in discharge baths, from neck down	(Barros)
Candomblé Ketu	Used in discharge and cleansing baths	
Candomblé de Angola	Used in discharge baths	
Umbanda	Used in cleansing and discharge baths, head cleansings	
	(obrigações de cabeça), and spiritual cleansings	

NAME-CUBA	Salvia de Castilla	(Roig)
Owner	Obatalá (LC, Quiros)	
	Obatalá, Ochún (TDF2)	
	Obatalá, Eggun (Irizarry)	
Odun	Ogunda-oyeku (Irizarry)	

NAME-SCIENTIFIC	*Salvia officinalis* L.	(Roig)

NAME-BRAZIL Sálvia, Sálvia-das-boticas, Sálvia-dos-jardins, Sálvia-verdadeira

Candomblé Jêje-Nagô	Oxalá	Água/Masculino	(Barros)
Umbanda	Oxalá, Obaluaiè, Nanã	Ervas Morna	

NAME-Lucumí	Kiriwi	(LC, TDF2)
YORUBA	Ikiriwí	(Barros)

NAME-CONGO	Vitití Leká	(LC)
	Bititi Leka	(TDF)

NAME-OTHER	Kitchen Sage	(USDA)
	Sage, Common Sage, True Sage, Garden Sage	(CRC)

USES	Goes to Osain (Omiero)	(Irizarry)
	Used as incense, ritual baths (Ebomisi), Inche Osain and Paraldo.	
Candomblé Jêje-Nagô	Since it belongs to Oxalá, it is used for baths for all. Also used as incense to purify	(Barros)
Umbanda	Used as incense with other Ewe to purify	
Hoodoo/Root Magic (USA)	Sage enhance wisdom, protects against the Evil Eye, purifies the air, gives strength to women, and is a good addition to any reversing mojo bag or candle spell.	

NAME-CUBA	San Diego, San Diego Blanco, Flor de San Diego, Inmortal		(Roig)
Owner	Eleggua (LC, TDF)		
Odun	Obara-iwori (Quiros, Orula.org)		
NAME-SCIENTIFIC	*Gomphrena globosa* L.		(Roig)
NAME-BRAZIL	Perpétua-roxa, Suspiro-roxo, Imortal, Suspiro-branco		
Candomblé Jêje-Nagô	Exú	Fogo/Masculino	(Barros)
Umbanda			
NAME-Lucumí	Maitoko		(LC)
YORUBA	Amúewú wáyé (*Gomphrena celosioides* **Mart**.)		(PV)
	ÈKÈLEGBÀRÁ		(Barros)
NIGERIA	Kandiri		(CRC)
NAME-CONGO	Fóyinkaro		(LC)
	Maitoko		(TDF)
NAME-OTHER	Common Globe Amaranth		(USDA)
	Bachelor's Button, Globe Amaranth		(CRC)
	Havana, Santoma (DR)		
USES			
	Ritual baths (Ebomisi) to banish evil		(Quiros)
	Has a great secrets of Eleggua.		(LC)
	Medicinal		
Candomblé Jêje-Nagô	Use for initiation (assentamentos) of Exú.		
	Religious works related to Exú.		(Barros)

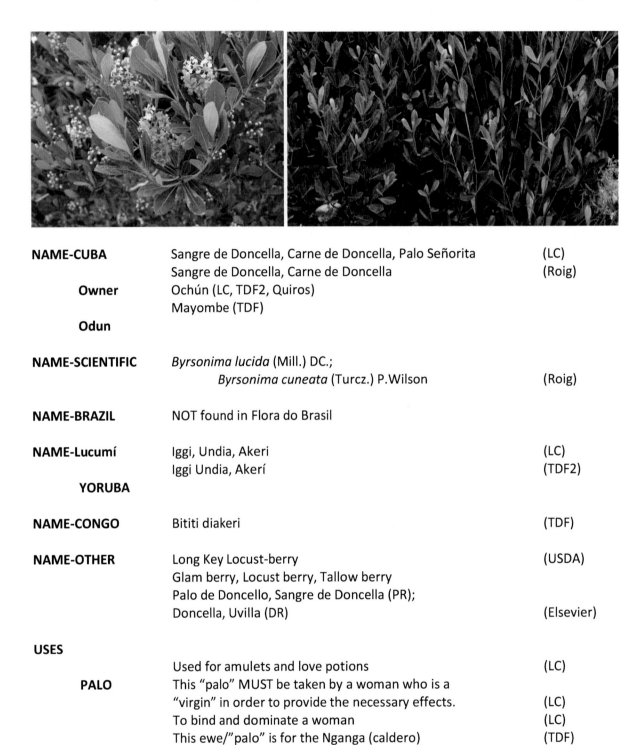

NAME-CUBA	Sangre de Doncella, Carne de Doncella, Palo Señorita	(LC)
	Sangre de Doncella, Carne de Doncella	(Roig)
Owner	Ochún (LC, TDF2, Quiros)	
	Mayombe (TDF)	
Odun		
NAME-SCIENTIFIC	*Byrsonima lucida* (Mill.) DC.;	
	Byrsonima cuneata (Turcz.) P.Wilson	(Roig)
NAME-BRAZIL	NOT found in Flora do Brasil	
NAME-Lucumí	Iggi, Undia, Akeri	(LC)
	Iggi Undia, Akerí	(TDF2)
YORUBA		
NAME-CONGO	Bititi diakeri	(TDF)
NAME-OTHER	Long Key Locust-berry	(USDA)
	Glam berry, Locust berry, Tallow berry	
	Palo de Doncello, Sangre de Doncella (PR);	
	Doncella, Uvilla (DR)	(Elsevier)
USES		
	Used for amulets and love potions	(LC)
PALO	This "palo" MUST be taken by a woman who is a	
	"virgin" in order to provide the necessary effects.	(LC)
	To bind and dominate a woman	(LC)
	This ewe/"palo" is for the Nganga (caldero)	(TDF)

NAME-CUBA	Sapote, Zapote, Níspero	(Roig)
Owner	Ibeyis (LC)	
	Ochún (TDF2)	
	Ibeyis, Oggún (Quiros)	
	Ibeyis, Ochún (Diaz)	
Odun	Ejiogbe-oyeku (Quiros, Diaz, Orula.org)	
	Ofun-irosun (Diaz, Orula.org)	

NAME-SCIENTIFIC	*Manilkara zapota* (L.) P.Royen;	
	Achras zapota L	(Roig)
	Manilkara multinervis (Baker) Dubard	(PV)

NAME-BRAZIL	Sapotizeiro, Sapodilho, Sapota, Sapoti		
Candomblé Jêje-Nagô	Ibeije	Fogo/Masculino/Gùn	(Barros)
Umbanda	Jemanjá		

NAME-Lucumí	Nekigbé	(LC)
YORUBA	Emidó, Ako emidó	(PV, CRC)
	NEKIGBE	(Barros)

NAME CONGO	Kobanko		(LC)
	Nfurú, Nfurie, Kpuru		(TDF)
PALO	**SAPOTE**	Kobanko	
	OWNER	Siete Rayos	(Nfinda)

NAME-OTHER	Sapodilla	(USDA)
	Sapodilla balata, Beef apple	
	Sapodilla (PR); Nisperillo (DR);	
	Nispero (Venezuela); Sapoti (Creole Haiti)	(Elsevier)

USES	Goes to Osain (Omiero)	
	Fruit used as ritual food offering (Addimú)	
	The leaves ground and mixed with wood/charcoal ashes	
	will nullify any witchcraft (matan una brujería)	(LC)
PALO	Used for Ngangas and personal protection.	
	Belongs to Siete Rayos	
	With a tea made from the leaves, you can nullify any	
	hex (brujería) that was ingested.	
	With the leaves a powder (Afoche/Mpolo) can be made	
	to remove any obstacles in our lives.	(Nfinda)
Candomblé Jêje-Nagô	The fruit much appreciated by Ibeije as Addimú.	
	The fruit offered as Addimú to Iabás (female Orixás).	
	The leaves pulverized blown inside house to ward off spells	(Barros)
Candomblé	The fruit is **Èwó of Exú**	
	The fruit is **Èwó for Candomblé practitioners**	
Umbanda	The fruit is **Èwó for Umbanda practitioners**.	

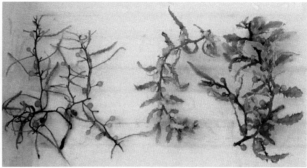

NAME-CUBA	Sargazo, Sargazo Común, Uva de Mar	(Roig)
Owner	Yemayá (LC)	
	Yemayá, Babalú-Ayé (TDF2, Diaz)	
	Yemayá, Ochún, Eleggua (Quiros)	
	Oró, Eleggua (Irizarry)	
	Yemayá, Olokun (Madan)	
	Babalú-Ayé (Menéndez)	
Odun	Osa-ose (Diaz, Madan, Orula.org)	
	Osa-ejiogbe (Irizarry)	

NAME-SCIENTIFIC	*Sargassum bacciferum* (Turner) C.Agardh;		
	Sargassum vulgare C.Agardh	**See NOTE**	(Roig)

NAME-BRAZIL	Sargaços, Musgo-marinho
Candomblé de Angola	Kaiá
Candomblé	Jemanjá
Umbanda	Jemanjá, Linha dos Marinheiros

NAME-Lucumí	Ayaráyeré	(LC, TDF2)
YORUBA		

NAME-CONGO	
PALO	Nfita Kalunga
OWNER	Madre Agua, Mamá Chola

NAME-OTHER	Sargassum

USES	Goes to Osain (Omiero)	
	Used in Ebomisi and Inche Osain	
	Used for Eggun Rituals	(Irizarry)
Candomblé de Angola	Used for head cleansings (obrigações no Orí)	
Candomblé	Head cleansings (obrigações no Orí) and cleansings baths	

NOTE	Taxonomic information from AlgaeBase
See:	**http://www.algaebase.org/search/species/**

NAME-CUBA	Sasafrás, Sasafrás del País	(Roig, Duke's)
Owner	Babalú-Ayé (TDF2)	
	Oyá (Diaz)	
Odun	Ofun-oyekun (Madan, Orula.org)	
	Odi-ose, Ofun-otura (Diaz, Madan)	
	Ejiogbe-okanran (Quiros)	
NAME-SCIENTIFIC	*Bursera graveolens* (Kunth) Triana & Planch.	(Roig)
NAME-BRAZIL	Pau-santo, Madeira-santa, Ibiocaí, Vera, Verahood	
NAME-Lucumí		
YORUBA		
NAME-CONGO		
NAME-OTHER	Strong Smelling Bursera	(Elseveir)
	Palo Santo (Spanish)	
USES	**DOES NOT** go to Osain (Omiero)	(Quiros, Diaz)
	Goes to Osain (Omiero)	(Madan)
	Medicinal	(LC)
	Used for Sarayéyé	(Diaz)

NAME-CUBA	Saúco Amarillo	(Roig)
Owner	Ochún (TDF2)	
	Osún (TDF)	
	Olokun, Oggún (Quiros)	
	Ochún (Diaz)	
	Ochún, Eleggua, Obatalá (Madan)	
Odun	Osa-otura (Diaz, Madan)	
NAME-SCIENTIFIC	*Tecoma stans* (L.) Juss. ex Kunth;	
	Stenolobium stans (L.) Seem.	(Roig)
NAME-BRAZIL	Ipê-de-jardim, Amarelinho, Guarã-guarã, Ipê-amarelo-de-jardim	
NAME-Lucumí		
YORUBA		
NAME-CONGO	Kundumba	(TDF)
NAME-OTHER	Yellow Trumpet Bush	(USDA)
	Florida Yellow Trumpet, Yellow Elder, Yellow Trumpet	
	Roble Amarillo (PR, DR); Fresnillo (Venezuela);	
	Chevalye, Flè senpiè, Tèk (Creole Haiti)	(Elsevier)
USES	Goes to Osain (Omiero)	
	Goes to the Omiero of Ochún	(TDF2)
	Used for cleansing the home	
	Baths for luck and love	(Diaz)

NAME-CUBA	Saúco Blanco		(Roig)
Owner	Obatalá (TDF2, Quiros)		
	Obatalá, Odudua (Diaz)		
	Obatalá, Ochún (Irizarry)		
	Obatalá, Eleggua, Ochún (Madan)		
Odun	Osa-otura (Diaz, Madan)		

NAME-SCIENTIFIC	*Sambucus canadensis* L.	**See NOTE**	(Roig)
	Sambucus nigra L.		(Barros)

NAME-BRAZIL	Sabugueiro		
Candomblé Jêje-Nagô	Obaluaiè	Fogo/Masculino	Barros)
Candomblé Ketu	Obaluaiè		
Candomblé de Angola	Kavungo		
Umbanda	Oxossi		

NAME-Lucumí		
YORUBA	ÀTÒRÌNÀ	(Barros)
NAME-CONGO		

NAME-OTHER	American Black Elderberry	(USDA)
	Florida Elder, American Black Elder, American Elderberry	
	Saúco Blanco (DR)	(Elsevier)

USES	Goes to Osain (Omiero)	
	Used for purification baths and Inche Osain	
Candomblé Jêje-Nagô	Leaves used for initiation rituals, offerings and purification baths for filhos of Obaluaiè	(Barros)
Hoodoo/Root Magic (USA)	The dried berries, leaves or roots of Elder are carried by some as protection and to ward-off both natural and unnatural illness	

NOTE	In theplantList.org and powo.science.kew.org, *Sambucus canadensis* **L.** is listed as an accepted species. Elsevier and USDA lists *Sambucus canadensis* **L.** as a synonym for *Sambucus nigra* **subsp.** *canadensis* **(L.) Bolli**

NAME-CUBA	Sensitiva, Vergonzosa, Dormidera		(Roig)
Owner	Yewá (LC)		
	Yewá (TDF2)	**Sensitiva, Vergonzosa**	
	Oggún (TDF2)	**Adormidera, Vergonzosa**	
	Ochosi (Diaz)		
	Eshú, Eleggua, Yewá (Irizarry)		
	Osain (Madan)		
	Oggún, Ochosi (Menéndez)	**Dormidera**	
Odun	Odi-osa, Otura-ika (Quiros, Diaz, Irizarry, Madan, Orula.org)		

NAME-SCIENTIFIC	*Mimosa pudica L.*	(Roig)

NAME-BRAZIL	Dormideira, Sensitiva, Malícia-de-mulher, Dorme-dorme		
Candomblé Jêje-Nagô	Exú, Oiá	Fogo/Masculino	(Barros)
Candomblé de Angola	Matamba		
Candomblé Ketu	Iansã		
Candomblé	Exú, Oiá, Oxumarê, Yewá		
Umbanda	Iansã		
ODUN	Ejiogbe-meji, Ejiogbe-irosun, Otura-ogunda		(PV)

NAME-Lucumí	Eran kumi, Eran Loyó, Omimi, Yaránimó		(LC)
	Eran kumi, Eran Loyó, Omini, Yaránímó **Sensitiva, Vergonzosa**		(TDF2)
	Ewe Erúkumú, Erunkumí	**Adormidera, Vergonzosa**	(TDF2)
YORUBA	Patonmó, Pamámó àlùro, Paìdímó		(PV)
	Ápèjé		(Barros)

NAME-CONGO	Morí-víví		(LC)
	Atangaow, Fombalikoko		(Duke's)
PALO	Milisia		
	OWNER	Garufinda	**Regla Kimbisa**

NAME-OTHER	Shame Plant	(USDA)
	Sensitive plant, Humble plant, Shame bush, Shame plant	(CRC)
	Morir vivir (DR); Sensitiva (PR);	
	Féy lan domi, Mouri-lévé (Creole Haiti)	(Duke's)

USES		**DOES NOT** go to Osain (Omiero)	
		Goes to the Omiero of Oggún (**Adormidera, Vergonzosa**)	(TDF2)
		For cleansings and purification	(LC)
		Used for spells, perfumes in love matters	(LC)
		To calm enemies, or for love spells	
	PALO	With this Ewe anything can be achieved. Only the one without thorns (Female) is used. Male plant (w/ thorns) is no good (with thorns is **Mimosa hostilis (C.Mart.) Benth.**)	(LC)
	Candomblé Jêje-Nagô	This Ewe is used to facilitate a trance of the filhos de santo. Used for some initiations of Exú (em outras ocasiões e utilizada para assentar Exú) and in other religious works.	(Barros)
	Candomblé de Angola	Main Ewe for ritualistic initiation bath (banho de feitura) Also used to cover embarrassing situations (apaziguar situação embaraçosa).	
	Candomblé	This Ewe is used to facilitate a trance of the filhos de santo	
	ESPIRITU CRUZADO	For cleansings and spiritual work (obras espirituales)	
	Hoodoo/Root Magic (USA)	Called **Shame Brier** or **Sensitive Brier**. Used for: to shame an enemy into leaving you alone, to get a job, or to get a lawsuit against you dropped	
	India	Used in Ayurveda and Siddha. Magic, ritual: water extract of root is given to children to ward off evil spirits.	(CRC)

NAME-CUBA	Seso Vegetal, Árbol del Seso, Akee de África	(Roig)
Owner	Obatalá (LC, TDF2, Irizarry, Diaz)	
	Obatalá, Babalú-Ayé (Quiros)	
	Obatalá, Asojuano (Concordia)	
	Orunmila (Madan)	
Odun	Odi-otura (Quiros, Diaz, Irizarry, Madan, Orula.org)	
NAME-SCIENTIFIC	*Blighia sapida* K.D.Koenig	(Roig)
NAME-BRAZIL	Akee, Ackee	
NAME-Lucumí	Ewe Ayire **Leaves**	(Irizarry)
	Igi Ayire **Branches/Sticks**	(Irizarry)
YORUBA	Isin, Isin jíje, Isin oká, Isin òdàn	(PV, CRC)
NAME-CONGO		
NAME-OTHER	Akee	(USDA)
	Ackee, Akee, Akee Apple, Vegetable Brain	(CRC)
USES	**DOES NOT** go to Osain (Omiero)	
	For head cleansings (Ebori Eledá), especially in case	
	of dementia and/or mental problems	(LC)
	Used in Ebó	
	Used in rituals of Asojuano/Babalú-Ayé	(Concordia)

NAME-CUBA	Siguaraya, Ciguaraya, Siguaraya de Costa	(Roig)
Owner	Changó, Eleggua (LC, TDF, Irizarry)	
	Changó, Eleggua, Yemayá (TDF2, Diaz)	
	Changó, Eleggua, Babalú-Ayé (Quiros)	
	Changó (Madan)	
	Changó, Agayú (Menéndez)	
Odun	Ejiogbe-ogunda (Madan)	

NAME-SCIENTIFIC	*Trichilia havanensis* Jacq.	(Roig)

NAME-BRAZIL	NOT found in Flora do Brasil

NAME-Lucumí	Atori	(LC, TDF, TDF2)
YORUBA	Ajígbagbó (*Trichilia sp.*)	(PV)

NAME-CONGO   Ionso, Tinso, Ebora, Nsimba diam finda   (LC)
                 Tingo ebeta, Neiba, Dian finda, Tinso, Inso, Mbora nsimba dian finda   (TDF)
PALO   **SIGUARAYA/CIGUARAYA**   Inso, Tinso, Ebora, Nsimba dian finda
            OWNER   Lucero, Siete Rayos   (Nfinda)
            OWNER   Madre de Agua, Siete Rayos   **Regla Kimbisa**
            OWNER   Sarabanda   **Espiritismo Cruzado**

NAME-OTHER   Havana bitter-wood, Bastard lime
                  Hiede-hiede, Yede-yede (DR); Verdenaz (Venezuela);
                  Bwa loray (Creole-Haiti)   (Elsevier)

USES   Goes to Osain (Omiero)
            Used for ritual baths (Ebomisi), cleansings
            (Sarayéyé), Inche Osain and for religious cleansings
            and purifications of the home   (LC)
            Ciguaraya will break/nullify ALL hexes/witchcraft
            Used to expel ingested witchcraft (Bilongo/Murúbba)   (LC)
            The resin the tree produces can be used as incense   (LC)
            Medicinal

PALO	It's called "Rompe-Camino, Tapa-Camino & Abre-Camino (Close/destroy the path, Cover the path, Open the path) Because the "**fúmbi**" (Nfumbe) will close the road to the enemy (Rompe Camino); will hide the path to his owner (Tapa Camino) from the enemy; and will open the road to his owner (Abre-Camino) away from the enemy	(LC)
	It is the principal "palo" in the Nganga of Lucero and Siete Rayos.	(Nfinda)
PALO MONTE	The leaves are used to open and close paths, and destroy negative energy. The tree is considered an anti-witch and a talisman for the sons of Mamá Chola.	
ESPIRITU CRUZADO	Spiritual cleansings, ritual baths and cleansings of the home/house.	
	For the spiritual fundament (Fundamento) of Sarabanda	

NOTE	**Regla Kimbisa**	It is one of the types/branches in **Regla Congo**
	Regla Congo	Comprises of Palo Monte, Palo Mayombe, Palo Congo, Brillumba and Kimbisa
	See:	**https://es.wikipedia.org/wiki/Palo_(religión)**

NAME-CUBA	Siguaraya Macho	(Roig)
Owner	Changó, Eleggua (Diaz)	
Odun	Ofun-meji, Ofun-obara (Diaz)	

NAME-SCIENTIFIC	*Trichilia pallida Sw.*	(Roig)
NAME-BRAZIL	Baga-de-morcego	
NAME-OTHER	Gaita	(USDA)
	Pale Bitterwood	
	Caracolí (DR); Caraolillo (PR); Dombou (Creole Haiti)	(Elsevier)

NAME-CUBA	Soplillo, Abey, Frijolillo, Tamarindillo	(Roig)
Owner	Ochún (LC, TDF2, Quiros)	
	Ochún, Obatalá (Diaz)	
Odun	Ejiogbe-ose, Ose-meji, Ose-ejiogbe (Diaz)	
NAME-SCIENTIFIC	*Lysiloma latisiliquum* (L.) Benth.;	
	Lysiloma bahamensis Benth.	(Roig)
NAME-BRAZIL	NOT found in Flora do Brasil	
NAME-Lucumí	Aki	(LC)
	Akí	(TDF2)
YORUBA		
NAME-CONGO		
NAME-OTHER	False Tamarind	(USDA)
	Horseflesh tree (PR); Candelón (DR)	(Elsevier)
USES	Goes to Osain (Omiero)	
	Medicinal	(LC)
PALO	Must be in Nganga of Tiembla Tierra and Mamá Chola	(Diaz)
	Powder (Afoche/Mpolo) made at the Nganga to expel	
	someone from their work and/or home.	(Diaz)

NAME-CUBA	Tabaco	(Roig)
Owner	Osain, Eleggua, Oggún, Ochosi (LC, Quiros)	
	Osain, Eleggua, Oggún (TDF2)	
	Osain, Eleggua, Oggún, Ochosi, Guerreros (TDF)	
	Eleggua, Oggún, Ochosi, Chango, Eggun (Irizarry)	
Odun	Ogunda-ejiogbe (Quiros, Irizarry)	

NAME-SCIENTIFIC	*Nicotiana tabacum* L.		(Roig)

NAME-BRAZIL	Tabaco, Fumo, Erva-santa		
Candomblé Jêje-Nagô	Oxalá	Ar/Feminino	(Barros)
CULTO DE NAÇÃO	Omolú, Exú		
Umbanda	Xangô (in some temples)		

NAME-Lucumí	Ewe Etába, Achá	(LC)
	Ewe Etába, Achá, Ewe Etaba	(TDF2)
	Ewe etaba, Ashá, Ewe tabá	(TDF)
YORUBA	Tábà, Tàbà èsù	(PV, CRC)
	ETÁBÀ, ASÁ	(Barros)

NAME-CONGO	Sunga	(LC)
	Nsunga, Sunga	(TDF)
	Fumu, Laanga, Maanga, Mbuli	(CRC)

NAME-OTHER	Cultivated Tobacco	(USDA)
	Tobacco, Common tobacco, Bosotho tobacco	
	Tabaco de Oler (DR); Tabac (Haiti)	(Duke's)

USES	**DOES NOT** go to Osain (Omiero)	
	Tobacco smoke used in Sarayéyé, Eggun Rituals	
	Leaves used in Ebomisi, Inche Osain, Paraldo	(Irizarry)
	ALL Eggun rituals include Tobacco and/or Tobacco smoke	
PALO	Used in different rites as Cigars or Cigar smoke	

PALO MONTE   The cigar smoke used over the signatures (firmas) before
starting to work with the Nganga
The concoction of the leaves used to strengthen the Nganga
ESPIRITU CRUZADO   Tobacco is used in ALL rites and ceremonies
The cigar smoke is used to start the spiritual mass in order
to make it more propitious for the spirits to come through
The cigar smoke used for cleansings and to keep away dark entities.
Candomblé Jêje-Nagô   The leaves used in the initiation and Abô of the
"filhos de santo" of Oxoguiãn (an avatar of Oxalá).
The rolled tobacco (fumo-de-rolo) used in different offerings to
Odú, Ossaim, Exú, Caboclos, Pretos-velhos and Vodum. Cigars are
Much appreciated by Exú and Caboclos. Cigarettes are offered to
Exú Pomba-gira in Umbanda centers.   (Barros)
Candomblé Ketu/Candomblé Ijexá   Fumo-de-rolo   **Èwó for Ossaim**
Umbanda   Used in discharge and purification baths, incense and initiations.
Much used by Pretos-velhos in curative cleansings.
Hoodoo/Root Magic (USA)   Tobacco is a Native American spiritual incense often
burned as an offering when making a request. In Hoodoo it is also
used to control people and situations.
OTHER   Ritual, magical: pulverized tobacco as magical repellent against
hostile demons.   (CRC)

NAME-CUBA	Tamarindo		(Roig)
Owner	Obatalá (LC, TDF2)		
	Oyá (TDF2)	**Tamarindo (muerto)**	
	Obatalá, Oyá (Quiros, Diaz)		
	Oyá, Eggun (Irizarry)		
	Oyá (Madan, Menéndez)		
Odun	Irete-okanran (Quiros, Irizarry, Diaz, Orula.org)		
	Osa-okanran, Otura-obara (Quiros, Irizarry,		

NAME-SCIENTIFIC	*Tamarindus indica* L.		(Roig)

NAME-BRAZIL	Tamarineiro, Tamarindo, Tamarindeiro, Tamarineira, Tamarina		
Candomblé Jêje-Nagô	Oxalá, Xangô	Ar/Masculino	(Barros)
Candombe de Angola	Lembá		
Candomblé	Oxumarê; Oxossi (in some casa-de-santo)		
CULTO DE NAÇÃO	Xangô, Oxalá		
Umbanda	Omolú, Xangô		

NAME-Lucumí	Iggi Iyágbón		(LC, TDF2)
	Ewé Ayen	**Leaves**	(Irizarry)
	Igi Odan	**Branches/Sticks**	(Irizarry)
YORUBA	Àjàgbon		(PV, CRC)

NAME-CONGO	Mukwaya, Musisi, Muskishi, Tchwa		(Duke's)
	Tomi		(CRC)
PALO	**TAMARINDO**	Nfinyagbo	
	OWNER	Tiembla Tierra	(Nfinda)

NAME-OTHER	Tamarind	(USDA)
	Tamarind, Indian date, Indian tamarind	(CRC, Duke's)
	Tamaren, Tamaren fran (Creole Haiti)	(Duke's)
	Tamarindo (Mexico)	(CRC)

USES		Goes to Osain (Omiero)	
		Nuestra Señora del Carmen (Our Lady of Mt. Carmel) first	
		appeared in a Tamarind tree in Santa Clara	(LC)
		Branches under pillow used for restful sleep/dreams	(LC)
		The tree goes to sleep at 3:00pm, branches should be picked	
		before 3:00 pm	(LC)
		Used for Ebomisi, Inche Osain and as Addimu	(Irizarry)
		Medicinal	
	PALO	A powder (Afoche/Mpolo) made with the tamarind "palo"	
		is of great destructive power to the "Palero" since it will greatly	
		diminish his/her power, and never be the same	(Nfinda)

Candomblé Jêje-Nagô   Sacred tree of Oxalá, sometimes called "Igi Iwín"
Some priests also associate the tamarind tree to Xangô, and use
the leaves in cleansings and purification baths.   (Barros)

Candombe de Angola   Sacred tree of Oxalá. Used in head cleansings
(obrigações no Orí) of all Omorixá.

Umbanda   Used in Amacis (ritual herbal baths-Ebomisi), Abô (Omiero),
head cleansings (obrigações de cabeça) and cleansings.

INDIA   Used in Ayurveda, Unani and Siddha. Used in religion and
magico-religious beliefs: plant meant for the construction
of God's temple, so wood not recommended to be used as
a housing material.   (CRC)

NAME-CUBA		Tengue, Tengue Rojo, Tengue Amarillo, Abey Hembra	(Roig)
		Tengue, Árbol Tengue	(LC)
	Owner	Eshú (LC, Quiros, Madan)	
		Eleggua (TDF2)	
		Eshú, Eleggua (Diaz)	
		Babalú-Ayé (Menéndez)	
	Odun	Owonrin-ika (Diaz, Madan)	

NAME-SCIENTIFIC	*Poeppigia procera* C.Presl	(Roig)

NAME-BRAZIL	Pintadinho	(Elsevier)

NAME-Lucumí			Songa, Labari	(LC, TDF2)
NAME-CONGO			Inkita, Linga, Nkuni, Chéché Cabinda	(LC)
			Tengue	(TDF)
BANTU			Kunia sheshe cabinda	(TDF)
PALO	**OWNER**		Tiembla Tierra	(TDF)
	TENGUE		Inkita, Linga, Nkuni, Cheche Cabinda	
	OWNER		Lucero	(Nfinda)
NAME-OTHER			Very tall Poeppigia	(Elsevier)

USES		**DOES NOT** go to Osain (Omiero)	
		With Tengue all sorts of "trabajos" can be done; i.e.- the enemy	
		Is made dumb (se idoitiza al enemigo), obstacles are made	
		surmountable (se allanan los obstáculos) and the imposible	
		is done (se obtiene lo imposible)	(LC)
	PALO	Is the strongest "palo" among all "palos" in the Nganga	(LC, Nfinda)
		This "palo" fights, takes down and destroys (pelea, tumba y	
		desbarata); but at the same time, it can fix, enliven and harmonize	
		(arregla, recompone and armoniza)	(LC)
		Can be used for good or bad, but the results are excellent	(Nfinda)
	PALO MONTE	This "palo" is used to do battle. It is both Mother and Father	
		in Regla Conga; although this "palo" is "Judío".	
		This "palo" goes to all Nganga; the first is "Ceiba", the second	
		is "Tengue" and the third is "Guayacán".	
		Used in purification baths in Regla Conga.	

NOTE	Lydia Cabrera has a separate listing for Palo Tengue, but with different attributes

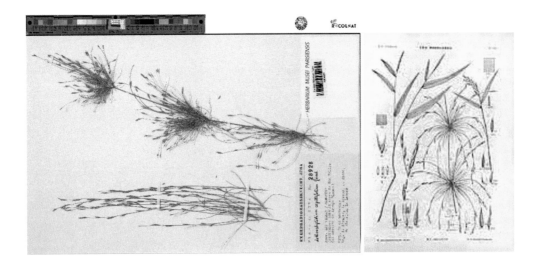

NAME-CUBA	Tibisí, Tibisí Grande	(Roig)
Owner	Changó (LC, Quiros)	
Odun		
NAME-SCIENTIFIC	*Arthrostylidium farctum* (Aubl.) Soderstr. & Lourteig;	(gbif.org)
	Arthrostylidium capillifolium Griseb.	(Roig)
NAME-BRAZIL	NOT listed in Flora do Brasil	
NAME-Lucumí		
YORUBA		
NAME-CONGO	Koroleo, Igbe Kambo	(LC)
NAME-OTHER	Old-Man's Beard	(USDA)
USES		

Made into a powder, it is scattered anywhere a person
wants to be "the flavor of the month", to increase visibility
of a person; i.e.- a politician, musician, etc.   (LC)

NOTE   On Kew Science, this species is listed as:
Tibisia farcta (Aubl.) C.D.Tyrrell, Londoño & L.G.Clark;
Arthrostylidium capillifolium Griseb
Arthrostylidium farctum (Aubl.) Soderstr. & Lourteig
Both being synonyms with and its native range of Caribbean to French Guiana.

NOTE   This Ewe is a type of tall grass, much like a thin bamboo like grass.

NAME-CUBA	Titonia	(Roig)
Owner	Ochún (LC, TDF2, Quiros)	
Odun		
NAME-SCIENTIFIC	*Tithonia rotundifolia* (Mill.) S.F.Blake	(Roig)
NAME-BRAZIL	Girassol-mexicano, Margarida-mexicana, Margaridão	
NAME-Lucumí	Seréiye	(LC, TDF2)
YORUBA		
NAME-CONGO	Monikuana	(LC)
NAME-OTHER	Clavel de Muerto	(USDA)
	Red Sunflower, Mexican Sunflower	(Wiki)
USES		
	Used powdered in the front door to keep unwanted guests from visiting	(LC)

NAME-CUBA	Tomate, Tomate Americano, Tomate de Riñón,	
	Tomate placero, Tomate Criollo	(Roig)
Owner	Changó, Ibeyis (LC, Quiros)	
	Changó (TDF2, Madan)	
Odun	Oturupon-irete, Irete-Oturupon (Quiros, Orula.org)	

| **NAME-SCIENTIFIC** | *Lycopersicon esculentum* Mill. | (Roig) |

NAME-BRAZIL	Tomate, Tomateiro		
Candomblé Jêje-Nagô	Oxumarê, Caboclos	Água/Feminino	(Barros)
Umbanda			

NAME-Lucumí	Ichomá, Icán	(LC)
	Ichomá, Ikán	(TDF2)
	Ikare, Ibefú, Ishomé, Ikán, Ikane	(TDF)
YORUBA	Sekúnwin, Ekúe, Tòmátì, Tùmátì	(PV, CRC)

NAME-CONGO	Korogóndo	(LC)
	Korongodo	(TDF)
	Makayama	(CRC)

| **NAME-OTHER** | Garden Tomato | (USDA) |
| | Tomato, Love Apple, Gold Apple | (CRC) |

USES

Medicinal

Candomblé Jêje-Nagô	As part of food offerings to Oxumarê	(Barros)
Umbanda	Used in differing offerings, mainly to Caboclos	(Barros)
Candomblé-de-Caboclo	Used in differing offerings, mainly to Caboclos	(Barros)
Candomblé de Angola	Used in differing offerings, mainly to Caboclos	(Barros)
Batuque do Rio Grande do Sul	Used in the preparation of delicacies for Oxum and Xangô.	(Barros)

NAME-CUBA	Tomate de Mar		(LC)
	Boja, Poja, Guacalote		(Roig)
Owner	Changó, Agayú (Menéndez)		
Odun			
NAME-SCIENTIFIC	*Entada gigas* (L.) Fawc. & Rendle;		
	Entada scandens (L.) Benth.		(Roig)
NAME-BRAZIL	Fava-de-Xangô, Coração-do-mar		
Candomblé Jêje-Nagô	Xangô	Terra/Masculino	(Barros)
Umbanda			
NAME-Lucumí	Icán Olókun		(LC)
YORUBA	Agbaà		(PV)
	OLIBÉ		(Barros)
NAME-CONGO	Korogóndo di kalunga, Foronkó		(LC)
NAME-OTHER	Nicker Bean		(USDA)
	Elephant Creeper, Sea Bean, Sea Heart		(CRC)

USES

There are male and female beans. When put in water, the one that floats is female and the one that sinks is male. The female one is used by men and vice-versa.

Used for hemorrhoids. (LC)

Used as a talisman/amulet.

PALO Used in "palo"

Candomblé Jêje-Nagô The bean used ritualistically in the initiation of Xangô. (Barros)

Hoodoo/Root Magic (USA) Sea beans carried as lucky pocket pieces

INDIA Used in Ayurveda and Siddha. (CRC)

NAME-CUBA	Toronjil, Torongil			(Roig)
Owner	Obatalá, Ochún, Babalú-Ayé (Diaz)			
	Asojuano (Irizarry)			
Odun	Ika-irete (Diaziaz)			

NAME-SCIENTIFIC	*Mentha × piperita* L.;			
	Mentha × citrata Ehrh.			(Roig)
	Melissa officinalis L.			(LC)

NAME-BRAZIL	Levante-miúda, Menta-do-levante			
Candomblé Jêje-Nagô	Oxum, Iemanjá	Água/Feminino	(Barros)
Candomblé	Oxum, Jemanjá, Oxalá	Água/Feminino/Gùn	

| **NAME-Lucumí** | Ewetúni | | | (LC, TDF2) |
| **YORUBA** | ERÉ TÚNTÚN | | | (Barros) |

NAME-CONGO

| **NAME-OTHER** | Bergamot Mint | (USDA) |
| | Bergamot Mint, Lemon mint, Lime mint, Orange mint | (Wiki) |

USES
  Goes to Osain (Omiero)
  Important plant in Omiero of Babalú-Ayé/Asojuano (Diaz, Irizarry)
  Used for ritual baths (Ebomisi)
  Medicinal

Candomblé Jêje-Nagô Always used in combination with other Ewe
for purification baths or incense to attract good fortune.
Since it is used with many Orixá, a lot of the "pais-de-santo"
claim that it belongs to Oxalá.
This Ewe is also indicated in the making of the Amassis/Amacis
(ritual herb bath) used to wash the divinatory shells (Barros)

Hoodoo/Root Magic (USA) Mint breaks jinxes, purifies people, and protects money.

NAME-CUBA   Toronjil de Menta, Menta Piperita,
                                    Yerba Buena de olor de pimienta   (Roig)

    Owner
    Odun

NAME-SCIENTIFIC   *Mentha × piperita* L.   (Roig)

NAME-BRAZIL   Hortelã-pimenta, Hortelã, Hortelã-menta
    Candomblé Angola   Aluvaiá
    Umbanda

NAME-Lucumí
    YORUBA

NAME-CONGO

NAME-OTHER   Peppermint   (USDA)
                                    Brandy Mint, Lamb Mint, Peppermint   (CRC)

USES
    Candomblé Angola   Aluvaiá   Planted around of the temple for Exú
        Used in ritual baths and initiation (Assento Erê Exú)
    Hoodoo/Root Magic (USA)   Mint breaks jinxes, purifies people, and protects money.
    INDIA   Used in Unani   (CRC)

NAME-CUBA	Travesera, Abre Camino, Albahaca de Sabana, Albahaquilla	(Roig)
Owner	Eleggua, Changó (LC, TDF2, Quiros)	
Odun		
NAME-SCIENTIFIC	*Koanophyllon villosum* (Sw.) R.M.King & H.Rob.;	
	Eupatorium villosum Sw.	(Roig)
NAME-BRAZIL	NOT found in Flora do Brasil	
NAME-Lucumí	Afosi	(LC)
	Afosí	(TDF2)
YORUBA		
NAME-CONGO		
NAME-OTHER	Florida Keys thoroughwort	(USDA)
	Jack-Ma-Da, Bitter Sage, Thoroughwort	(levypreserve.org)
	Thoroughwort, Boneset	

USES

For defense or to close the pathway of an enemy.
Make the enemy's life unbearable   (LC)

Hoodoo/Root Magic (USA)   Boneset opposes unnatural illness and snakes.
Used for protection: to ward off jinxing and illness
Used for ritual cleansing: baths and incense

NOTE   This plant is listed as Abre Camino. As such, it has completely different use and attributes.

NAME-CUBA	Trébol	(Roig)
Owner	Obatalá (LC, TDF2, Quiros, Diaz, Madan)	
Odun	Otura-meji (Quiros, Diaz)	
	Iwori-irete (Madan)	
NAME-SCIENTIFIC	*Trifolium repens* L.	(Roig)
NAME-BRAZIL	Trevo-branco, Trevo-coroa-de-rei, Trevo-da-Holanda, Trevo-ladino	
NAME-Lucumí	Ewé Etámerí	(LC, TDF2)
YORUBA		
NAME-CONGO	Kánda tatu	(LC)
PALO	Kándatatu	
NAME-OTHER	White Clover	(USDA)
	White Clover, Dutch Clover, Ladino Clover	(CRC)
USES	**DOES NOT** go to Osain (Omiero)	
	It makes Obatala wrathful/choleric	(LC)
	Used for ritual baths (Ebomisi)	(Diaz)
	Used for Ebomisi, Inche Osain	(Irizarry)

NAME-CUBA	Trébol de Agua, Trébol Criollo	(Roig)
Owner	Yemayá (LC)	
Odun		
NAME-SCIENTIFIC	*Nymphoides grayana* (Griseb.) Kuntze;	
	Limnanthemum grayanum Griseb.	(Roig)
NAME-BRAZIL	Coração-piloso	
NAME-Lucumí	Ewé Etámerí	(LC)
ANAGO	Irituto, Ochú miri, Oyóro, Oyóuro, Oyuoro	**Flor de Agua**
	Ewe egbodo	**Planta de Agua** (LC)
YORUBA		
NAME-CONGO	Kánda tatu	(LC)
NAME-OTHER	Floating Heart	(USDA)
	Gray's Floating Heart	(FL Dept. Agriculture)
USES		
	Medicinal	(LC)

NAME-CUBA	Tripa de Jutia, Alambrillo	**See NOTE**	(LC)
	Jutia, Alambrillo, Bejuco San Pedro de flor amarilla		(Roig)
Owner	Eleggua (LC, Quiros)		
Odun			

NAME-SCIENTIFIC	*Stigmaphyllon sagraeanum* A. Juss.	(Roig)

NAME-BRAZIL   NOT listed in Flora do Brasil

NAME- ANAGO	Eki ni ki, Ewe ochibatá	**Alambrillo**	(LC)
YORUBA			

NAME-CONGO

NAME-OTHER	Sagra's Amazon Vine	(florida.plantatlas.usf.edu)
	Pour Man Strength, Seven Man Strength	(levyprreserve.org)

USES

This Ewe is used to cover Eleggua when you want
to get him mad in order to resolve a difficult
but important situation.   (LC)

NOTE   Lydia Cabrera failed to denote a particular plant species. There is no
listing in Juan Tomás Roig under "Tripa de Jutia". There is a listing for
"Jutia", which is also known as "Bejuco San Pedro de flor amarilla". A
Bejuco is a vine/creeper/climber and those plants listed as "Tripa de .." are
also vines/creepers/climbers. Hence, the decision to use the plant "Jutia"
as the plant in question.

NAME-CUBA	Tuatua, Túba-Túba	(LC)
	Tuatúa, Toatúa, Frailecillo, San Juan de Cobre	(Roig)
Owner	Obatalá (LC, Madan, Diaz)	
	Obatalá, Yemayá (TDF2, Quiros)	
	Yemayá (Irizarry)	
	Yemayá, Ochún (Menéndez)	
Odun	Okanran-otura (Madan, Quiros, Diaz, Orula.org)	
	Iwori-oturupon (Madan, Quiros, Diaz, Irizarry)	

| **NAME-SCIENTIFIC** | *Jatropha gossypiifolia* L. | (Roig) |

NAME-BRAZIL	Pinhão-roxo, Pinhão-de-purga, Pinhão-bravo, Maranhão		
Candomblé Jêje-Nagô	Ogum, Oxossi, Oiá	Fogo/Feminino	(Barros)
Candomblé de Angola	Inkosse		
Candomblé	Ogum, Oxossi, Oyá, Xangô	Fogo/Feminino/Gùn	
CULTO DE NAÇÃO	Oyá, Xangô		
Umbanda	Exú, Iansã		
ODUN	Osa-meji, Ogunda-ika (PV)		

NAME-Lucumí	Túatúa, Tuba-tuba	(TDF2)
YORUBA	Làpálàpá pupa, Bòtúje pupa, Lóbòtúje, Olóbóntúje,	
	Ako làpá làpá	(PV)

| **NAME-CONGO** | | |
| **PALO** | Ntíngoro | |

NAME-OTHER	Belly Ache Bush	(USDA)
	Spanish Physic nut, Belly-ache bush, Black physic nut	
	Higuerito Cimarrona, Tátua (DR); Sibidigua (Venezuela)	
	Médicinier Rouge (Haiti)	(Elsevier)

USES		Goes to Osain (Omiero)	
		The roots and leaves, in a tea, for cleansing bath	(LC)
		To make religious items for Obatalá	(LC)
		Used for home/personal cleansings and purification	
		Used for ritual baths (Ebomisi)	
		Medicinal	

Candomblé   **Jêje-Nagô**   dedicated to **Iansã Òrun**, the patron of Eguns.
The branches for cleansings and ritual baths
for "filhos" of Iansã, Ogum and Oxossi   (Barros)

Casa-das-Minas Maranhão   Used for ritual baths for
luck and prosperity   (Barros)

Candomblé de Angola   Used with "Aroeira" (*Schinus terebinthifolia* **Raddi** –
Brazilian Pepper tree) for strong bath applied at the crossroads
(para banho forte aplicado em encruzilhada)

Umbanda   Used against the evil-eye, cleansing baths, cleansings and used
at the entrance of residences as protection

INDIA   Used in Ayurveda and Siddha
Magico-religious beliefs: leaf a component of hot bath
taken to get rid of evil Spirits; the presence of the plant
repels evil divinities, tawar, azana; tribal wear some pieces
of root as protective measure from pox.   (CRC)

NOTE   **Iansã Òrun**   **Oyá Igbalé, Oya Ygbale, Iansã do Balé** is an avatar of Iansã/Oyá
See: **https://pt.wikipedia.org/wiki/Oyá_Igbalé**

NAME-CUBA	Tuna	**See NOTE**	(LC)
	Tuna Mansa, Tuna de Castilla		(Roig)
Owner	Obatalá, Changó (TDF2)		
	Obatalá (LC, Quiros, Diaz)		
	Oggún, Ochosi, Changó (Irizarry)		
Odun	Iwory-ejiogbe (Diaz)		

NAME-SCIENTIFIC	*Opuntia ficus-indica* (L.) Mill.	(Roig)
	Opuntia cochenillifera (L.) Mill.	(Barros, KewSciece)
	Euphorbia lactea Haw.	(LC)

NAME-BRAZIL	Palmatória-de-Exú, Tabaibeira, Figueira-tuna, Figo-do-inferno		
Candomblé Jêje-Nagô	Exú, Ossaim	Fogo/Feminino	(Barros)
Candomblé de Angola	Aluvaiá		
Umbanda	Exú		

NAME-Lucumí	Egún, Weggún, Ikikigún	(LC)
	Egún, Weggún, Ikikigún, Ewe Egún Fun	(TDF2)
YORUBA		
NAME-CONGO		
LUANGO	Kunanso	(TDF)

NAME-OTHER	*Opuntia ficus-indica*	Barbary Fig	(USDA)
		Barbary fig, Burbank's spineless cactus, Prickly pear	(CRC)
	Opuntia cochenillifera	Cochineal nopal cactus	(USDA)

USES	**DOES NOT** go to Osain (Omiero)	
	Medicinal	
Candomblé Jêje-Nagô	Usually planted where Exú is located	
	Used macerated in water to wash religious articles of Exú	
	The fruit is given as Addimu to Ossaim	(Barros)

NOTE   Lydia Cabrera denotes *Euphorbia lactea* **Haw.** as being the plant in question, when in reality it is the "**Cardón, Tuna de Cruz**", and with no possible relation to what she states the medicinal uses are. Juan Tomás Roig does name the proper plants as to the two uses that she proposes.
See "Tuna Brava" for the one with spines.

NAME-CUBA	Tuna Brava, Tuna Espinosa, Tuna Silvestre, Tuna Colorada	(Roig)
Owner	Obatalá (LC, Quiros, Diaz)	
	Oggún, Ochosi, Changó (Irizarry)	
Odun	Ejiogbe-okanran (Diaz, Irizarry)	

NAME-SCIENTIFIC	*Opuntia dillenii* (Ker Gawl.) Haw.	(Roig)
	Opuntia stricta (Haw.) Haw.;	
	Opuntia dillenii (Ker Gawl.) Haw.	(CRC)

NAME-BRAZIL	Piteira-brava (Portuguese name, none found for Brazil)	

NAME-Lucumí	Egún, Weggún, Ikikigún	(LC)
YORUBA		
NAME- LUANGO	Kunanso	(TDF)

NAME-OTHER	Erect Prickly Pear	(USDA)
	Common prickly pear, Eltham Indian fig, Spiny pest pear	(CRC)

USES	**DOES NOT** go to Osain (Omiero)	
	To keep enemies away, it is hung behind the door	(LC)
	Also planted Infront of the home to keep enemies away	
INDIA	Used in Ayurveda	(CRC)
Hoodoo/Root Magic (USA)	The spines of ANY cactus are used for jinxing	

NOTE   Pataki for Ejiogbe-okanran   **La Tuna Brava** or **How the Tuna got its spines**
- There was a time when the Tuna had no spines. It lived among the big and small and whenever they passed next to it, they would knock its sons down and trample it. So, Tuna went to see Orunmila with the problem. Orunmila did **Osode** (checked with Ifá) and told Tuna had to do Ebó. Immediately Orunmila did small cuts all over Tuna and put **Eyebale** (blood sacrifice) and inserted needles in each cut. With time, the sons that came also had needles and no one would get near Tuna. Tuna found itself alone and found that the best place to be was in the desert, but was not happy being alone with all her sons. Time went by and Orunmila had a war, and remembering what he had done to Tuna, went to see Tuna for help in the war. Tuna would not hear anything about it. Orunmila had to remind Tuna of what he had done, so Tuna had no other choice than accompany Orunmila. (Irizarry)

NAME-CUBA	Tuya, Tuya de Oriente, Tuya Enana Compacta	(Roig)
	Árbol de la Vida, Tuya	(LC)
Owner	Obatalá, Oddúa (LC, Quiros)	
	Obatalá (TDF2)	
Odun		
NAME-SCIENTIFIC	*Platycladus orientalis* (L.) Franco;	
	Thuja orientalis L.	(Roig)
NAME-BRAZIL	Arborvitae (árvore-da-vida), Tuia-compacta, Tuia-da-china	
NAME-Lucumí	Anñúa	**Árbol de la Vida**	(LC)
	Annúa	**Árbol de la Vida**	(TDF2)
YORUBA		
NAME-CONGO		
BANTU	Matende (LC)	**Tuya**
NAME-OTHER	Oriental arborvitae	(USDA)
	Chinese arbor-vitae, Oriental arbor-vitae	(CRC)
USES		
	Medicinal	(LC)

NAME-CUBA	Uña de Gato, Zarza Blanca, Zarzaparrilla Cimarrona,	
	Uña de Gavilán	(Roig)
Owner	Mayombe (Madan)	
Odun	Iwori-ofun (Quiros, Madan)	

| **NAME-SCIENTIFIC** | *Celtis iguanaea* (Jacq.) Sarg.; | |
| | *Momisia iguanaea* (Jacq.) Rose & Standl. | (Roig) |

NAME-BRAZIL   Cipó-farinha-seca, Cipó-laranjinha, Grão-de-galo, Gumbixava

NAME-Lucumí
    YORUBA

NAME-CONGO
| **PALO** | **PALO Uña de Gato** | Masangró | (Nfinda) |

| **NAME-OTHER** | Iguana Hackberry | (USDA) |
| | Maíz Tostado (Venezuela) | (Elsevier) |

USES
	This is a maleficent Ewe	(LC)
	Mixed in a powder (Afoche), it can blind a person	(LC)
PALO	Used to hex a person/someone	(Nfinda)

NOTE   Lydia Cabrera lists Zarza Blanca as a separate entry with different attributes

NAME-CUBA	Uva Caleta, Uva de Caleta, Uvero	(Roig)
Owner	Changó (TDF2)	
	Yemayá, Oggún (Quiros)	
	Yemayá, Obatalá (Diaz)	
	Oyá (Irizarry)	
	Oyá, Oggún (Madan)	
Odun	Ika-irete (Quiros, Diaz, Irizarry, Madan, Orula.org)	
NAME-SCIENTIFIC	*Coccoloba uvifera* (L.) L.	(Roig)
NAME-BRAZIL	Uva-da-praia	
NAME-Lucumí		
YORUBA		
NAME-CONGO		
NAME-OTHER	Sea Grape	(USDA)
	Seagrape, Common sea grape, Pigeon wood	
	Uva Caleta (DR); Uva de la Mar (PR);	
	Uva de Playa (Venezuela);	
	Rezen fè, Rezen lamè (Creole Haiti)	(Elsevier)
USES	Goes to Osain (Omiero)	
	Used for cleansings and Sarayéyé	(Diaz)
	Used for ritual baths (Ebomisi)	(Irizarry)
	The trunk used for the initiation of a "hijo" of Oyá	(Web)

NAME-CUBA	Uva Gomosa, Uvita, Ateje Amarillo, Saúco, Varía Blanca		(Roig)
Owner	Ochosi (TDF2)		
	Obatalá, Yemayá (Diaz)		
	Yemayá (Madan)		
Odun	Ika-irete (Quiros, Diaz, Madan, Orula.org)		

NAME-SCIENTIFIC	*Cordia dentata* Poir.;	(gbif)
	Cordia alba (Jacq.) Roem. & Schult.	(Roig)
	Trema micranthum (L.) Blume;	(powo, Barros)
	Cordia alba (Jacq.) Roem. & Schult.	(Roig)

NAME-BRAZIL	Pau-Pólvora, Crindiúva, Candiuba		
Candomblé Jêje-Nagô	Oxalá, Oiá	Ar/Masculino	(Barros)

NAME-Lucumí
   YORUBA
NAME-CONGO

NAME-OTHER	*Cordia alba*	NO common name found.
	Angel Flower	(caymanflora.org)
	Cordia dentata/Trema micranthum	Jamaican nettletree (USDA)
	White Manjack; Capá Blanca (PR); Muñeco Blanco (DR);	
	Torare Amarillo (Vzla); Bwa chik (Creole Haiti)	(Elsevier)

USES	Goes to Osain (Omiero)	
	Used for baths and ritual baths (Ebomisi). Used for home cleansings	
	Used to make Omiero to wash the shells of the Orisha	(Diaz)
	Medicinal	
Candomblé Jêje-Nagô	This is a very positive Ewe and can be used	
	by ANY "filho de santo" for baths, cleansings, etc.	(Barros)

NOTE   *Cordia alba* (Jacq.) Roem. & Schult. Is a synonym of **Trema** *micranthum (L.) Blume* per powo.science.kew.org and an accepted name in theplantlist.org; **BUT** on gbif.org, Elsevier and CRC its listed as a synonym of *Cordia dentata* Poir.

NAME-CUBA	Vacabuey, Bacabuey, Paralejo Macho, Chaparro	(Roig)
Owner	Changó (LC, TDF2, Quiros)	
Odun		
NAME-SCIENTIFIC	*Curatella americana* L.	(Roig)
NAME-BRAZIL	Sambaíba-de-Minas-Gerais, Cajueiro-bravo-do-campo, Cajueiro-bravo	
NAME-Lucumí		
YORUBA		
NAME-CONGO		
NAME-OTHER	Sandpaper Tree, Rough-leaf tree	
	Aparalejo (DR); Chaparro (Venezuela);	
	Kiratèla (Creole Haiti)	(Elsevier)
USES		
	Used for maleficent purposes	
	Used in a lamp to destroy a person	(LC)

NAME-CUBA	Vainilla Amarilla	(Roig)
Owner	Ochún (LC, TDF2, Quiros)	
Odun		

NAME-SCIENTIFIC	*Encyclia fucata* (Lindl.) Schltr.;	
	Epidendrum fucatum Lindl.	(Roig)

NAME-BRAZIL NOT found in Flora do Brasil
Candomblé Jêje-Nagô
Umbanda   Iansã, Oxum (flores amarelas); Oxossi (Flores-do-campo)

NAME-Lucumí
YORUBA

NAME-CONGO

NAME-OTHER	Butterfly orchid	**(Encyclia Sp.)**	(USDA)
	Brown Veined Encyclia		(cattleya.wikidot.com)

USES

	To feed amulets of Ochún		(LC)
Umbanda	Used for discharge baths and baths for prosperity		
	Iansã, Oxum	All yellow flowers, including orchids	
	Oxossi	Flowers from the jungle/forest; which Orchids are.	

NOTE   This is **NOT** a Vanilla Orchid.
This orchid's habitat is Cuba, Bahamas and Hispaniola
The flowers of Encyclia fucata are fragrant and smell of vanilla
See: **http://cattleya.wikidot.com/encyclia-fucata**

NAME-CUBA	Vainilla Rosada	(Roig)
Owner	Ochún (LC, TDF2, Quiros)	
Odun		

NAME-SCIENTIFIC	*Psychilis atropurpurea* (Willd.) Sauleda;	
	Epidendrum atropurpureum Willd.	(Roig)

NAME-BRAZIL NOT found in Flora do Brasil
Candomblé Jêje-Nagô
  Umbanda Nanã Buruquê (flores na cor roxa);   Oxossi (flores-do-campo)

NAME-Lucumí
  YORUBA

NAME-CONGO

NAME-OTHER	Peacock orchid **(Psychilis Sp.)**	(USDA)
	The Dark Purple Psychilis	(orchidspecies.com)

USES

	To feed amulets of Ochún destined for men	(LC)
Umbanda	Used for discharge baths and baths for prosperity	
	Nanã Buruquê Flowers that are pink/lilac	
	Oxossi Flowers from the jungle/forest; which	
	Orchids are.	

NOTE This is **NOT** a Vanilla Orchid.
  This orchid's habitat is Haiti and Dominican Republic (Cuba??)
  See: **http://www.orchidspecies.com/psyatropurpurea.htm**

NAME-CUBA	Valeriana	
SPANISH	Valeriana común, Valeriana de las boticas, Valeriana medicinal	(Wiki)
Owner	Ochún, Obatalá (Diaz)	
	Ochún, Oggún (Irizarry)	
Odun	Owonrin-odi (Quiros, Irizarry, Orula.org)	
	Osa-ejiogbe (Diaz, Madan)	

NAME-SCIENTIFIC   *Valeriana officinalis* L.   (Wiki)

NAME-BRAZIL   Valeriana, Erva-valeriana, Amantila, Bardo-selvagem, Erva-gata

Candomblé Jêje-Nagô

Umbanda	Oxumaré, Obá, Ogum, Obaluaê, Omolú	Ervas Quentes

NAME-Lucumí

     YORUBA

NAME-CONGO

NAME-OTHER	Garden Valerian	(USDA)
	Garden Heliotrope, All-Heal, Cut-Heal, English Valerian	

USES	Goes to Osain (Omiero)	
	Used for baths for luck and love	(Diaz)
	Used ritual baths (Ebomisi) and for "lamps" (lamparas)	(Irizarry
Umbanda	For baths and incense. Harmonizes, attracts prosperity and protects against negativity.	
Hoodoo/Root Magic (USA)	Vandal root has a dual reputation for evil and protection Used to jinx and enemy, for uncrossing jinxes, to stop unwanted visitors and stop marital fighting.	

NAME-CUBA	Varita de San José, Vara de José, Altea	(Roig)
Owner	Obatalá (LC, TDF2, Quiros, Madan)	
Odun	Ose-osa (Quiros, Madan)	

NAME-SCIENTIFIC	*Alcea rosea* L.;	
	Althaea rosea (L.) Cav.	(Roig)

NAME-BRAZIL	Altéia, Malva-rosa, Malvarisco	
Candomblé Angola	Aluvaiá, Mutalumbô, Angorô, Matamba, Dandalunda, Kaiá, Zumbarandá, Lembá
Candomblé	Nanã, Oxum, Oxumarê, Yansã, Jemanjá
Umbanda	Nanã, Oxum, Oxumarê, Yansã, Jemanjá

NAME-Lucumí	Ofún dara, Didefún	(LC, TDF2)
YORUBA		
NAME-CONGO		
NAME-OTHER	Hollyhock	(USDA)
	Antwerp hollyhock, Garden hollyhock, Hollyhock	(CRC)

USES

	For cleansings (despojos y rogaciones)	(LC)
	For ritual cleansings (Sarayéyé)	(Quiros)
Candomblé	Cleansing baths for filhos-de-santo, and purification of the stones (Assento Okutá) for Nanã, Oxum, Oxumarê, Yansã, Jemanjá	
Umbanda	Cleansing baths for filhos-de-santo, and purification of the stones (Assento Okutá) for Nanã, Oxum, Oxumarê, Yansã, Jemanjá	
Candomblé Angola	**Aluvaiá, Lembá** Ritual baths	
	Mutalumbô, Lembá Head cleansings (obrigações no Orí)	
	Angorô, Matamba, Dandalunda, Kaiá, Zumbarandá Purification of the stones (Assento Okutá)	
Hoodoo/Root Magic (USA)	Used for medicinal and spiritual healing, to soothe, comfort and bring spiritual assistance	

NAME-CUBA	Vence Batalla, Palo Vence Batalla, Vence Guerra, Bejuco Carabalí	
	Ofón Criollo, Roble Guayo, Roble Güiro	(Roig)
Owner	Oggún, Changó (Diaz)	
	All Orisha (Madan)	
	Obatalá (Nfinda)	
	Babalú-Ayé (Menéndez) **Bejuco Carabalí**	
Odun	Okanran-odi, Owonrin-osa (Diaz, Madan, Orula.org)	
NAME-SCIENTIFIC	*Vitex divaricata* Sw.	(Roig, Nfinda)
NAME-BRAZIL	Not found in Flora do Brasil	
NAME-Lucumí		
YORUBA		
NAME-CONGO		
PALO	**PALO VENCE BATALLA**	(Nfinda)
BANTU	Nkunia kema tenda **Palo Vence Guerra**	(LC)
NAME-OTHER	Higuerillo	(USDA)
	White Fiddle Wood, Fiddle wood	
	Pendula, Pendula Blanca (PR)	
	Higuerillo, Higuerillo Cimarrón (DR)	
	Totumillo (Venezuela); Bwa leza (Creole Haiti)	(Elsevier)
USES	Goes to Osain (Omiero)	
	Used during initiation (Kari Ocha) and to wash	
	religious items of Obatalá	(Nfinda)
PALO	Powder (afoche/Mpolo) made to destroy someone	(Nfinda)
	Cannot be absent from the Nganga.	
	Used to win disputes/wars.	(Diaz)
NOTE	**Bejuco Carabalí** denoted as a Synonym for Vence Guerra by Lázara Menéndez	

NAME-CUBA	Vencedor, Palo Vencedor, Bálsamo	(Roig)
Owner	Mayombe (TDF)	
	Obatalá (Irizarry)	
	Yemayá, Changó (Diaz)	
Odun	Okanran-odi (Quiros, Irizarry, Diaz, Madan, Orula.org)	
NAME-SCIENTIFIC	*Zanthoxylum flavum* subsp. *pistaciifolium* (Griseb.) Reynel;	
	Zanthoxylum pistaciifolium Griseb.	(Roig)
NAME-BRAZIL	NOT found in Flora do Brasil	
NAME-Lucumí	Ewe Ashegun	(Irizarry)
YORUBA		
NAME-CONGO	Vencedor	
PALO	**PALO VENCEDOR**	(TDF)
NAME-OTHER	*Zanthoxylum pistaciifolium* **Griseb**	
	NO common name found. Native to Cuba	
	Zanthoxylum flavum subsp. *pistaciifolium* **(Griseb.) Reynel**	
	West Indian Satinwood	(USDA)
USES	Goes to Osain (Omiero)	
	Used for Ebomisi and Inche Osain	(Irizarry)

NOTE	This plant *Zanthoxylum flavum* subsp. *pistaciifolium* **(Griseb.) Reynel** is Native to Cuba
	See: **https://www.gbif.org/species/7524374**
	And its native range is Cuba
	See: **http://powo.science.kew.org/taxon/urn:lsid:ipni.org:names:77175391-1**
	This plant is listed as **CRITICAL ENDANGERED** by BISSEA
NOTE	Picture is of *Zanthoxylum flavum*

NAME-CUBA	Verbena, Verbena Francesa		(Roig)
Owner	Yemayá (LC, TDF2, Quiros, Irizarry, Diaz, Madan, Concordia)		
	Oyá (TDF2)	**Verbena-las Hojas**	
	Yemayá, Ochún (Menéndez)		
Odun	Owonrin-irete, Ika-odi (Quiros, Diaz, Irizarry, Madan, Orula.org)		

NAME-SCIENTIFIC   *Verbena officinalis* L.   (Roig)

NAME-BRAZIL	Verbena, Erva-de-fígado, Erva-sagrada, Urgebão, Verbena-sagrada		
Candomblé Jêje-Nagô	Jemanjá	Água/Feminino	(Barros)
Candomblé de Angola	Matamba		
CULTO DE NAÇÃO	Jemanjá		
Umbanda	Ibeije, Jemanjá, Xangô, Iansã		

NAME-Lucumí	Ewe orukán, Orriyo		(LC)
	Ewe Orukán, Orroyo	**Verbena**	(TDF2)
	Ewe Orroyokán, Orroyo	**Verbena-las Hojas**	(TDF2)

NAME-CONGO

PALO	**OWNER**	Madre Agua, Mamá Chola	**PALO MONTE**

NAME-OTHER	Herb of the Cross	(USDA)
	Common verbena, European verbena, Common vervain	(CRC)
USES	Goes to Osain (Omiero)	
	For the Omiero of Yemayá	(Concordia)
	Used for ritual baths (Ebomisi)	
	If this Ewe is picked before sunrise on June 24th, a powerful amulet/talisman can be made to achieve your heart's desire	(LC)
PALO MONTE	Always planted outside, or in the house, to keep away evil/evil eye	
ESPIRITU CRUZADO	Used spiritually and the planted shrub to keep away evil/evil eye.	
Candomblé Jêje-Nagô	this Ewe is used to make a powder (pó) and for baths to attract good luck. This powder can be used in anything that needs to be better (que se quiera melhorar)	(Barros)
Candomblé de Angola	Used for head cleansings (obrigações no Orí)	
Umbanda	This Ewe is associated with repelling psychic attacks, negativity, melancholy, and negativity while attracting wellbeing. Used as incense, in Amacis, head cleansings (obrigações de cabeça), and ritual baths.	
Hoodoo/Root Magic (USA)	Verbena is a love and protective herb that is considered helpful in many conditions; i.e.- Breaking a Jinx, Against Evil, For Love-Drawing, For Happy Marriage.	

NAME-CUBA	Verdolaga, Verdolaga Verdadera		(Roig)
	Verdolaga, Verdolaga de España		(LC)
Owner	Yemayá (LC, TDF2, Madan)		
	Yemayá, Eleggua (Quiros)		
	Yemayá, Ochún, Obatalá (Diaz)		
	Yemayá, Ochún (Concordia)		
	Yemayá, Ochún, Eleggua, Obatalá, Orula (Irizarry)		
	Changó, Agayú, Yemayá, Ochún (Menéndez)		
Odun	Ose-irosun (Quiros, Diaz, Irizarry, Concordia, Madan, Orula.org)		
	Odi-obara, Oturupon-irete (Quiros, Diaz, Irizarry, Madan, Orula.org)		

NAME-SCIENTIFIC	*Portulaca oleracea* L.		(Roig)

NAME-BRAZIL	Beldroega, Beldroega-verdadeira, Portulaca		
Candomblé Jêje-Nagô	Oxalá	Água/Feminino	(Barros)
Candomblé Ketu	Exú, Obaluaiè		
Candomblé de Angola	Aluvaiá, Kavungo		

NAME-Lucumí			
ANAGO	Euro, Ewe euro	**Verdolaga de España**	(LC)
YORUBA	Pápásan, Ségunsétè, Sémolésè, Akórélówó		(PV, CRC)

NAME-CONGO	Baselesele, Poli, Selesele	(CRC)

NAME-OTHER	Little Hogweed	(USDA)
	Purslane, Common purslane, Garden purslane, Pig weed	(CRC)
	Verdolaga (Spanish); Poupyé komen (Creole Haiti)	(Duke's)

USES	Goes to Osain (Omiero)	
	One of the 5 MOST important Ewe in the Omiero	
	To refresh Orishas, specially Yemayá	(LC)
	For home cleansings to attract good fortune	(LC)
	Used for **Aché Lenu** (the power of speech) where an Orisha	
	will be able to talk through the Olorisha (Santero/a)	(Concordia)
	Used to wash the Jutía (Hutia, bush rat)	
	Used in **Ituto** (death rites for Olorisha)	(Irizarry)
	Part of food offerings (Addimú) to the Orishas	
	Used in ritual baths (Ebomisi) and Inche Osain	(Irizarry)

Candomblé Jêje-Nagô   Like all Ewe that belong to Oxalá, this Ewe
can be used by any "filho-de-santo" for any Orixá.   (Barros)

Candomblé Ketu   Used in the purification of the stones
(Assento Okutá) of the Orixás, especially those of Exú

Candomblé de Angola   **Aluvaiá, Kavungo**   Assento Okutá

Hoodoo/Root Magic (USA)   Purslane wards off evil and enhances divinatory
powers, but it is rarely used alone.

INDIA   Used in Ayurveda, Unani and Siddha.   (CRC)

NAME-CUBA	Verdolaga Francesa		(Roig)
	Verdolaga, Verdolaga Ordinaria		(LC)
Owner	**per Lydia Cabrera-the same as Verdolaga**		

NAME-SCIENTIFIC *Talinum paniculatum* (Jacq.) Gaertn. (Roig)

NAME-BRAZIL Língua-de-vaca, Bênção-de-deus, Xanã
   Candomblé Jêje-Nagô   Xangô, Oxum   Água/Feminino/èró (Barros)
   Candomblé de Angola   Angorô

NAME-Lucumí
   ANAGO   Barakusa   **Verdolaga** (Talinum paniculatum) (LC)
   YORUBA   Gbúre òsun   (***Talinum sp.***) (PV)
            EWÉ GBÚRE ÒSUN (Barros)
NAME-CONGO

NAME-OTHER   Jewels of Opar (USDA)
               Fame Flower, Jewels of Opar (CRC)

USES   **per Lydia Cabrera-the same as Verdolaga**
   Candomblé Jêje-Nagô   Used in the preparation of food offerings
               (Addimu) for Orixás, specially for **Xangô-Barú** who
               does not eat/hates okra (Barros)
   Candomblé   Used for Abô, purification baths and food offerings to **Xangô-Barú**
   Candomblé de Angola   Used for head cleansings (obrigações no Orí),
               initiation, baths and Assento Okutá

NOTE **Xangô Barú**   One of the avatars of Xangô. In Cuba is Changó Lubbe Bara Lubbe (NBA)
             See: **https://pt.wikipedia.org/wiki/Xangô**

NAME-CUBA	Vetiver		(Roig)
Owner	Ochún (LC, TDF2, Quiros)		
Odun			

NAME-SCIENTIFIC	*Chrysopogon zizanioides* (L.) Roberty;	
	Anatherum zizanioides (L.) Hitchc. & Chase	(Roig)

NAME-BRAZIL   Vetiver, Capim-vetiver, Capim-de-cheiro, Grama-cheirosa

NAME-Lucumí	Orúfiri, Kurubí		(LC)
	Orúfirí, Kurubí		(TDF2)
ANAGO	Ewe eta merí, Orufirí	**Vetiver**	(LC)
YORUBA			

NAME-CONGO
   PALO

NAME-OTHER	Vetivergrass	(USDA)
	Cuscus Grass, True Vetiver, Vetiver, Vetiver Grass	(CRC)

USES

Roots used to keep insects away (repellent)

Medicinal   (LC)

Hoodoo/Root Magic (USA)   Roots soaked in Cologne and sprinkled on the bed for marital faithfulness. Roots burned in charcoal to reverse jinxes, or placed in cash registers to draw business

INDIA   Used in Ayurveda, Unani and Siddha   (CRC)

NAME-CUBA	Víbora	(Roig)
Owner	Eshú (LC, Quiros)	
	Eleggua (TDF2)	
Odun		
NAME-SCIENTIFIC	*Bryophyllum pinnatum* (Lam.) Oken;	
	Kalanchoe pinnata (Lam.) Pers.	(Roig)
	Bryophyllum calycinum Salisb.	(LC)

NAME-BRAZIL	Folha-da-fortuna, Folha-grossa, Folha-da-vida, Sempre-viva		
Candomblé Jêje-Nagô	Ifá, Oxalá, Xangô	Água/Feminino	(Barros)
Candomblé Ketu	Exu, Oxalá		
Candomblé de Angola	Aluvaiá, Zaze, Lembá		
Umbanda	ALL Orixá		

NAME-Lucumí	Ewe, Nioka, Fátu-Fátu, Fukororoko, Móngao		(LC)
	Nioka, Fátu-Fátu	**Palo Víbora**	(TDF2)
YORUBA	Àbámodá, Erú òdúndún, Kantíkantí, Kóropòn		(PV)

NAME-CONGO	Djokaka, Mayama, Ndjoa, Nzua, Tebete, Tsui	(CRC)
NAME-OTHER	Cathedral Bells	(USDA)
	Air plant, Tree of Life, Resurrection plant,	
	Never Die, Miracle Leaf	(CRC)
USES		
	Used to cause mayhem and confusion in someone's life	(LC)
	This plant is only good to do bad.	(LC)
BRAZIL	Refer to **Prodigiosa**	

NOTE   This Ewe is just one more case where it is listed with different names and different attributes. This plant is the the same as "**Prodigiosa**", except that it has a different scientific name which is a synonym for the scientific name of Prodigiosa.

NAME-CUBA	Vicaria, Vicaria Blanca, Vicaria Morada, Purísima	(LC)
	Vicaria, Vicaria Blanca, Purísima	(Roig)
Owner	Obatalá (LC, TDF2, Quiros, Diaz, Irizarry, Madan)	
Odun	Irete-odi (Quiros, Diaz, Irizarry, Madan, Orula.org)	

NAME-SCIENTIFIC	*Catharanthus roseus* (L.) G.Don;	
	Vinca rosea L.	(Roig)

NAME-BRAZIL	Vinca, Boa-noite, Maria-sem-vergonha, Vinca-de-Madagáscar		
Candomblé Jêje-Nagô	Oxalá	Ar/Feminino	(Barros)
Umbanda			

NAME-Lucumí
YORUBA
SIERRA LEONE Flawah   (CRC)

NAME-CONGO

NAME-OTHER	Madagascar Periwinkle	USDA)
	Vinca, Periwinkle, All-day flower, Old Maid, Cape periwinkle	(CRC)

USES	**DOES NOT** go to Osain (Omiero)	
	Used in ritual baths (Ebomisi)	
	Used to refresh the eyes	
	Medicinal	
Candomblé Jêje-Nagô	Used in purification baths and cleansings.	
	Used to refresh the eyes of those who engage in divination.	
	Oxalá owns both the white and pink/purple varieties	(Barros)
Hoodoo/Root Magic (USA)	Periwinkle leaves are reputed to enhance	
	conjugal felicity, pleasure and happiness.	
INDIA	Used in Ayurveda	(CRC)

NAME-CUBA	Vigueta, Vigueta Hembra, Vigueta de Cocina, Hicaquillo	(Roig)
Owner	Changó (LC, TDF2, Quiros)	
Odun		
NAME-SCIENTIFIC	*Chione venosa* var. *cubensis* (A.Rich.) David W.Taylor;	
	Chione cubensis A.Rich.	(Roig)
NAME-BRAZIL	NOT found in Flora do Brasil	
NAME-Lucumí	Fórumbo	(LC, TDF2)
YORUBA		
NAME-CONGO		
PALO		
NAME-OTHER	NO common name found. Native to Cuba and Hispaniola	
	Cuban chione	(Elsevier)
USES		
	Used in fortifying baths	
	Medicinal	(LC)

NOTE

- *Chione venosa* var. *cubensis* **(A.Rich.) David W.Taylor** is an Intraspecific Taxa of *Chione venosa* **(Sw.) Urb.** per theplantlist.org
- *Chione venosa* **(Sw.) Urb.**is listed as **ENDANGERED** by BISSEA
- *Chione cubensis* **A.Rich**. is listed as a synonym for *Chione venosa* **var.** *cubensis* **(A.Rich.)** by gbif.org (and shows it as being **Endemic** to Cuba)

NAME-CUBA	Vinagrillo, Mariposa, Trébol Silvestre	(Roig)
Owner	Yemayá (TDF2)	
	Eshú/Eleggua (Quiros)	
	Obatalá (Irizarry, Madan)	
Odun	Osa-oyeku (Quiros, Irizarry, Madan, Orula.org)	
NAME-SCIENTIFIC	1. *Oxalis corniculata* L.	(Roig)
	2. *Oxalis violacea* L.	(Roig)
NAME-BRAZIL	1. Erva-azeda, Erva-azeda-de-folha-pequena, Trevo-azedo	
	2. NOT found in Flora do Brasil	
NAME-Lucumí YORUBA	Ewe Orawe	(Irizarry)
NAME-CONGO PALO	Lopeto, Ngongua (*Oxalis corniculata* L.)	(CRC)
NAME-OTHER	*Oxalis corniculata* L. Creeping Wood Sorrel	(USDA)
	Creeping Lady's sorrel, Creeping wood sorrel	(CRC)
	Oxalis violacea L. Violet wood sorrel	(USDA)
USES		
	Used in ritual baths (Ebomisi) and Inche Osain	(Irizarry)
NOTE	Both plants listed under Vinagrillo by Juan Tomás Roig	

NAME-CUBA	Violeta, Violeta Silvestre	(Roig)
Owner	Yemayá (LC, TDF2, Quiros)	
Odun		

NAME-SCIENTIFIC	*Viola odorata* L.	(Roig)

NAME-BRAZIL	Violeta, Violeta-de-cheiro, Viola, Viola-roxa, Violeta-de-jardim	
Umbanda	Iemanjá, Nanã, Xangô	

NAME-Lucumí	Lúko	(LC, TDF2)
ANAGO	Kuye kuyé **Violeta**	(LC)
YORUBA		

NAME-CONGO
    PALO

NAME-OTHER	Sweet Violet	(USDA)
	Common violet, English violet, Garden violet, Sweet violet	(CRC)

USES

	Medicinal	(LC)
Umbanda	Used for baths, Amacis, head cleansings (obrigações de cabeça), and initiation (assentamento)	
Hoodoo/Root Magic (USA)	Violet is considered a Love herb	
INDIA	Used in Ayurveda and Unani	(CRC)

NAME-CUBA	Yaba, Yaba Colorada, Moca, Yabá	(Roig)
Owner	Changó, Oggun (LC, Diaz)	
	Changó (TDF2)	
	Mayombe (TDF)	
	Changó (Quiros)	
Odun	Ejiogbe-ose (Diaz)	
NAME-SCIENTIFIC	*Andira inermis* (Wright) DC.;	
	Andira jamaicensis (Wright) Urb.	(Roig)
NAME-BRAZIL	Acapurana, Angelim-morcegueira, Angelim-morce-quiera	(Elsevier)
NAME-Lucumí	Iggi soiku, Yaba	(LC)
	Soiku, Yaba	(TDF2)
NIGERIA	Daluhi, Gwaska, Ikong ebonko	(CRC, Elsevier)
NAME-CONGO	Nkasa Kadiampemba	(LC)
	Yaba	(TDF)
NAME-OTHER	Cabbage Bark Tree	(USDA)
	Bastard Mahogany, Cabbage Bark, Cabbage Angelim	
	Palo de Burro (DR); Moca Blanca (PR);	
	Cochenilla (Venezuela); Bwa palmis (Creole Haiti)	(Elsevier)
USES	**DOES NOT** go to Osain (Omiero)	
	This is an all-around bad tree, maleficent.	(LC)
	Oggún uses this tree to blind when fighting; so that	
	the enemy does not see him coming.	(LC)
PALO	Used with Nganga Judía to make powders (Mpolo)	
	to blind/cause blindness	(LC)
NOTE	The smoke the wood of this tree produces **CAN/DOES** cause blindness	(CRC)

NAME-CUBA	Yagruma, Yagruma Hembra		(Roig)
Owner	Obatalá (LC, Madan)		
	Obatalá, Changó (TDF2)		
	Obatalá, Oyá, Yemayá (TDF)		
	Obatalá, Oyá (Quiros)		
	Obatalá, Oyá, Yemayá, Oggún, Changó (Irizarry)		
	Obatalá, Orunmila (Diaz)		
	Oyá (Menéndez)		
Odun	Ika-oturupon (Quiros, Diaz, Irizarry, Madan, Orula.org)		
	Odi-ika, Obara-odi (Quiros, Irizarry, Orula.org)		

| **NAME-SCIENTIFIC** | *Cecropia peltata* L. | | (Roig) |

NAME-BRAZIL	Umbaúba, Embaúba, Imbaúba, Árvore-da-preguiça		
Candomblé Jêje-Nagô	Ossaim, Xangô	Terra/Feminino	(Barros)
Candomblé de Angola	Zaze, Matamba		
CULTO DE NAÇÃO	Jemanjá, Ossaim, Nanã (**BRANCA**)		
	Xangô, Oyá/Iansã, Nanã (**ROXA**)		
Umbanda	Obaluaiè (some Umbanda Temples)		

NAME-Lucumí	Iggi oggugú, Láro		(LC)
	Iggi Oggurú láro		(TDF2)
	Ogugu, Ewe loro, Gungua, Oggorú laro, Ekeboro,		
	Gum-gum, Mishora		(TDF)
YORUBA	ÀGBAÓ		(Barros)

NAME-CONGO	Matiti, Kandólao, Moratafo, Feniliyé		(LC)
	Kankolao, Feniliye, Moratafo		(TDF)
PALO	**YAGRUMA**	Matiti, Kandolao, Moratafo	
	OWNER	Tiembla Tierra	(Nfinda)

NAME-OTHER	Trumpet Tree, Snakewood, Congo pump, Wild pawpaw	(pfaf.org)
	Trumpet Tree, Congo Pump, Snakewood	(CRC)
	Yagrumo (PR, DR, Venezuela); Bwa twompèt (Creole Haiti)	(Elsevier)

USES
        DOES NOT go to Osain (Omiero)
        Used in ritual baths (Ebomisi) and Inche Osain
        Used in Paraldo and cleansings (rogaciones)   (Irizarry)
        Used in Ituto (funerary rites for dead Olorishas) Ceremony   (Madan)
        Medicinal

PALO
        This tree is associated with death since it is the perch of
        Susundamba (the owl), who is the messenger of death.   (LC, Nfinda)
        Since it is one of the tallest trees in the forest (if not the
        tallest), this is where the Nfumbi (the spirit of the Nganga)
        as well as the owl, can see the coming of an enemy.   (LC)

Candomblé Jêje-Nagô The leaves of this tree are used in ritual baths of
        purification for the "filhos" of Xangô.
        In the 'Casas-de-Santo", it is not unusual to see fruit offerings
        for Ossaim placed over the leaves of this tree.
        When "Mateiros" (Yerberos) go into the forest to collect Ewe,
        it usually involves leaving an offering at the base of this tree
        for Ossaim so that they can collect the Ewe with Ossaim's
        blessing; otherwise, they may not be able to find the Ewe
        they are looking for.   (Barros)

Candomblé de Angola Zaze   cleansings and **Obori/Ebori**
               Matamba   since the leaves are silvery (suas folhas
        são prateadas) they are used in cleansings and **Obori/Ebori**

Umbanda
        Used in Amacis, Abô, ritual baths, cleansings, Ebós and
        head cleansings (obrigações de cabeça).

NOTE **Obori/Ebori**   Rites that a neophyte who wants to be initiated into the religion
        must undergo. The Orí (head) is the first Orisha that is done.
        See: **https://pt.wikipedia.org/wiki/Ebori**

NOTE   This tree is included in the "**100 of the World's Worst Invasive Alien Species**"
        in the Global Invasive Species Database.
        See: **http://www.iucngisd.org/gisd/100_worst.php**

NOTE   There is another tree listed by Juan Tomás Roig as **Yagruma Macho** which is Palo Arriero

NAME-CUBA	Yamao, Yamagua, Yamagua Colorada, Llamao, Llamagua	(Roig)
Owner	Eleggua (TDF2, Menéndez)	
	Mayombe (TDF)	
	Eleggua, Yemayá, Ochún (Quiros)	
	Eleggua, Yemayá (Irizarry)	
	Eleggua, Ochún (Diaz)	
	Yemayá (Madan)	
Odun	Okanran-ofun (Diaz, Irizarry, Madan, Orula.org)	
	Owonrin-ejiogbe (Quiros, Irizarry, Orula.org)	

NAME-SCIENTIFIC *Guarea guidonia* (L.) Sleumer;
Guarea trichilioides L. (Roig)

NAME-BRAZIL Bilreiro, Carrapeta, Jitó, Gitô, Carrapeta-verdadeira, Carrapeteira

Candomblé Jêje-Nagô	Xangô	Fogo/Feminino	(Barros)
Candomblé de Angola	Katendê, Zaze		
Umbanda	Iansã		

NAME-Lucumí	Fendébillo	(LC, TDF2)
YORUBA	ÌPÈSÁN	(Barros)

NAME-CONGO	Nkita, Morinbánkuo, Machucho		(LC)
	Mkita morimbankuo, Fendebillo, Machuecho-kúo,		
	Moshusho, Morumbakua		(TDF)
PALO	**OWNER**	Centella Ndoki	(TDF)
	PALO YAMAO/YAMAGUA	Nkita, Mrinbankuo, Machucho	
	OWNER	Mamá Chola, Madre de Agua	(Nfinda)

NAME-OTHER	American Muskwood	(USDA)
	American muskwood, Alligator wood	
	Guaraguao, Guayabilla (PR); Cabima, Cedro Macho (DR);	
	Cabimbo, Cedro Dulce (Venezuela); Bwa wouj (Creole Haiti)	(Elsevier)

USES	**DOES NOT** go to Osain (Omiero)	
	Goes to the Omiero of Eleggua	(TDF2)
	Used to find ground water (dowsing rod/stick)	(LC)
	Used for ritual baths (Ebomisi) and Inche Osain	(Irizarry)
PALO	This "palo" is called YAMAO because it is used to call	(LC)
	Used in a powerful love spell to call back a lorn-lost lover, who will return obediently	(LC, Nfinda)
	Also used in a spell called the "Talismán de Portugalete" to call money/wealth into one's home	(LC)
	To call upon Xangô to destroy an enemy	(LC)
	It is a required "palo" in all Nganga	(Nfinda)

Candomblé Jêje-Nagô   Used in baths of protection, prosperity, and initiation baths. The branches used in cleansings. The ÌPÈSÁN is praised in the songs to Ossaim during the ritual of **sasányìn** (Osaín/Omiero) as the tree that denied its fruit to the sorceresses/black birds (Iyábas) when they landed on the tree; I.e.- the tree is considered a powerful deterrent against witchcraft/spells/hexes. (Assim se explica o fato dela ser considerada poderosa protetora contra feitiço)   (Barros)

Candomblé de Angola Katendê   Baths to the head (banho no Orí) in order to develop clairvoyance

           Zaze   Head cleansings (obrigações no Orí)

Umbanda   Cleansing and purification baths

NAME-CUBA	Yarey		(Roig)
Owner	Changó (LC, TDF2, Quiros)		
Odun	Otura-irosun (Quiros, Madan, Orula.org)		

| **NAME-SCIENTIFIC** | *Copernicia molinetii* León | **see NOTE** | (Roig) |
| | *Copernicia Sp.* | | (LC) |

| **NAME-BRAZIL** | NOT listed in Flora do Brasil |

NAME-Lucumí	Opé		(TDF2)
ANAGO	Opé	**Yarey** (*Copernicia Sp.*)	
	Abegudá, Ikó erí	**Palma**	(LC)
YORUBA			

NAME-CONGO	Goroguáyo, Mábba, Diba		(LC)
BANTU	Mamba	**Palma Yarey**	
	Gorowayo	**Yarey**	(LC)
Carabalí/Bríkamo	Awarionké	**Yarey**	
	Ukano mambré	**Palma**	
	Ukano, Upanó	**Palma**	
	Ukano mambró	**Palma Macho**	(LC)

| **NAME-OTHER** | No common name found. Native to Cuba | (powo.science.kew.org) |
| | Blue yarey palm, Cana palm, Cuban wax palm | (CRC) |

USES

	Used to change the color of the skin of a person in order	
	to evade justice/capture	(LC)
PALO	NOT used	(LC)

NOTE *Copernicia molinetii* **León** is listed under *Copernicia hospita* **Mart.** In CRC (CRC World Dictionary of Palms: Common Names, Scientific Names, Eponyms, Synonyms, and Etymology (2 Volume Set); Umberto Quattrocchi, 02/22/2017)

NAME-CUBA	Yaya, Yaya Hembra, Y. Común, Y. del Monte, Y. Mansa, Y. Prieta (Roig)			
	Yaya, Palo Muerto		(Hodge Limonata)	
Owner	Changó (LC, TDF2, Madan)			
	Mayombe (TDF)			
	Changó, Eleggua (Quiros)			
	Changó, Agayú (Diaz)			
	Changó, Oggún (Irizarry)			
	Babalú-Ayé (Menéndez)			
Odun	Osa-irete (Quiros, Diaz, Irizarry, Madan, Orula.org)			
	Irosun-otura (Quiros, Diaz, Irizarry, Madan)			
NAME-SCIENTIFIC	*Oxandra lanceolata* (Sw.) Baill.		(Roig)	
NAME-BRAZIL	NOT found in Flora do Brasil			
NAME-Lucumí	Yáyá, Echi		(LC)	
	Yáayá, Echi		(TDF2)	
NAME-CONGO	Koromeni, Mbékese		(LC)	
	Koroweni, Mbekosé		(TDF)	
PALO	**PALO YAYA**	Koromeni, Mbekese		
	OWNER	ALL Nganga		(Nfinda)
	PALO MUERTO		**PALO MONTE**	
	YAYA **OWNER**	Zarabanda	**ESPIRITU CRUZADO**	
NAME-OTHER	Black Lancewood		(USDA)	
	Black lancewood, West Indian lancewood			
	Haya Blanca (PR); Yaya Boba (DR); Bwa lans (Creole Haiti)		(Elsevier)	
USES	**DOES NOT** go to Osain (Omiero)			
	Used for ritual baths (Ebomisi) and Inche Osain		(Irizarry)	
	The leaves, alone, for Lustral baths		(LC)	
PALO	This "palo" is used for both good and bad. It will destroy ANY			
	witchcraft, but will also kill and destroy		(LC)	
	It is a "palo" necessary for ALL Nganga		(LC, Nfinda)	
	Yaya is female and is used with Guayacán (which is male)			
	for love matters		(Nfinda)	
PALO MONTE	Used to fight. Necessary for all Nganga. Lives with Guayacán			
ESPIRITU CRUZADO	Necessary "palo" for spiritual Nganga of Zarabanda			

NAME-CUBA	Yaya Cimarrona	(Roig)
Owner	Changó (Quiros)	
	Mayombe (TDF, Madan)	
	Changó, Agayú (Diaz)	
Odun	Irosun-otura, Osa-irete (Diaz, Madan)	
NAME-SCIENTIFIC	*Mouriri myrtilloides* subsp. *acuta* (Griseb.) Morley;	
	Mouriri acuta Griseb.	(Roig)
NAME-BRAZIL	NOT found in Flora do Brasil	
NAME-Lucumí	Yáyá, Echi	(LC)
NAME-CONGO	Koromeni, Mbékese	(LC)
	Koroweni, Mbekosé	(TDF)

| **PALO** | **PALO YAYA CIMARRONA** | Koromeni, Mbekese | |
| | **OWNER** | Nsasi | (Nfinda) |

NAME-OTHER	Acute blueberrylike Mouriri	(Elsevier)
USES		
	Medicinal	
PALO	Used by all Nganga	
	An IMPORTANT "palo" for the Nganga, cannot be missing	(LC)
	To fight and win, there is no equal	(LC, Nfinda)
	It cures ALL that is bad.	

NOTE This plant *Mouriri myrtilloides* subsp. *acuta* **(Griseb.) Morley**
is listed in Kew Science with a native range of Cuba.
See: **http://powo.science.kew.org/taxon/urn:lsid:ipni.org:names:164579-2**
And per gbif.org and Elsevier, it is located **ONLY** in Cuba.

NOTE The only photo for this tree was found at "The Encyclopedia of Life"
See: **https://eol.org/pages/5428155**

NAME-CUBA	Yedra, Yedra del País, Hiedra, Ensalada de Obispo		(Roig)
	Yedra, Hiedra		(Roig)
Owner	Obatalá (LC, Quiros, Diaz, Madan)		
	Oyá (TDF2)	**Yedra**	
	Changó (TDF2)	**Ensalada de Obispo**	
	Obatalá, Odudúa, Ochún (Irizarry)		
	Oddúa (Menéndez)	**Ensalada de Obispo**	
Odun	Otura-obara (Quiros, Irizarry, Orula.org)		
	Ejiogbe-obara (Diaz, Madan)		

NAME-SCIENTIFIC	*Anredera vesicaria* (Lam.) C.F.Gaertn. ;	
	Boussingaultia leptostachya Moq.	(Roig)
	Anredera spicata J.F.Gmel.	(LC)
	Ficus pumila L.	(Roig)

NAME-BRAZIL — NOT found in Flora do Brasil

NAME-Lucumí	Itako	(LC, TDF2)
	Ewe Alukerese (Madan)	
YORUBA		

NAME-CONGO

NAME-OTHER	***Anredera vesicaria***	Texas Madeira Vine	(USDA)
	Cuban Ivy, Climbing false buckwheat		(CRC)
	***Ficus pumila* L.**	Climbingfig	(USDA)

USES	Goes to Osain (Omiero)	
	Used for ritual baths (Ebomisi) and Inche Osain	
	It removes "bad ideas" (quita las malas ideas)	(LC)
	Since the Ivy lives on top of another, not easily ejected,	
	a "trabajo" is done to unite lovers.	(LC)
	Medicinal	

NAME-CUBA	Yerba Bruja, Yerba Paraná, Paraná, Yerba Pará, Yerba del Pará	(Roig)
Owner	Yemayá (LC, TDF2, Madan)	
	Yemayá, Eleggua (Quiros)	
	Ochosi (Diaz)	
Odun	Obara-okanran, Irete-irosun (Quiros, Madan, Orula.org)	
	Oyeku-ika, Ofun-ejiogbe (Diaz)	

NAME-SCIENTIFIC	*Brachiaria mutica* (Forssk.) Stapf;	
	Panicum purpurascens Raddi	(Roig)

NAME-BRAZIL	Capim-angola, Capim-bengo	

NAME-Lucumí	Ewe Ichocho	(LC)
	Iwe Ichócho	(TDF2)
YORUBA		

NAME-CONGO	Yerba Bruja	(TDF)

NAME-OTHER	Para Grass	(USDA)
	Para Grass, Buffalo grass, California grass, Scotch grass	

USES	**DOES NOT** go to Osain (Omiero)	
	To call upon the spirit of a person who is far away	
	To do a spell (amarre) to women who are not faithful to	
	their husband.	(LC)
	This Ewe in powder form is very powerful; the leaves are	
	used to wash down doors/door-ways for protection	(TDF)
PALO	Ewe used with Nganga to keep the law away	(Diaz)

NAME-CUBA	Yerba Buena, Hierba Buena	(Roig)
Owner	Yemayá (LC, TDF2, Quiros)	
	Yemayá, Changó, Asojuano (Irizarry, Madan)	
	Yemayá, Ochún (Diaz, Menéndez)	
Odun	Osa-irosun (Madan, Quiros, Diaz, Irizarry, Orula.org)	

NAME-SCIENTIFIC	1. *Mentha nemorosa* Willd.	(Roig)
	2. *Mentha × verticillata* L.; *Mentha × sativa* L.	(LC)
	3. *Mentha spicata* L.	(Roig)

NAME-BRAZIL	Menta, Hortelã, Hortelã-de-horta, Hortelã-comum	***Mentha spicata* L.**
Candomblé Ketu	Oxalá	
Candomblé de Angola	Zaze, Lembá	
CULTO DE NAÇÃO	Oxalá, Oxossi, Iansã	
Umbanda	Oxalá, Oxossi, Iansã	

NAME-BRAZIL	Levante, Alevante, Hortelã-silvestre	***Mentha spicata* L.; *Mentha viridis* (L.) L.**
Candomblé	Oxum, Iemanjá, Oxalá	
Candomblé de Angola	Zaze, Matamba, Lembá	
CULTO DE NAÇÃO	Oxum, Iemanjá, Oxalá, Xangô	
Umbanda	Oxalá, Xangô, Omolú, Iemanjá, Ogum, Oxossi, Exú	

NAME-Lucumí	Efirin ewe ka, Amasi	(LC)
	Efirín Ewe Ka, Amasí	(TDF2)
YORUBA	EWÉ ERÉ TUNTÚN (*Mentha spicata*)	
NAME-CONGO		

NAME-OTHER	***Mentha nemorosa* Willd**	Mint	(USDA)
	***Mentha × verticillata* L.; *Mentha × sativa* L.**	Cuban Mint	
	***Mentha spicata* L.**	Garden Mint, Mint, Spearmint	(CRC)

USES	Goes to Osain (Omiero)
	Used in aromatic baths, ritual baths (Ebomisi) and Inche Osain
	Used in cleansings; i.e.- personal, home, business
Hoodoo/Root Magic (USA)	Mint breaks jinxes, purifies people, and protects money.

Mentha spicata **L.**

Candomblé Ketu	Head cleansings (obrigações de cabeça) for ALL Orixás since it is used for Oxalá.
Candomblé de Angola	Head cleansings (obrigações no Orí) for ALL Orixás.
Umbanda	Baths, head cleansings (obrigações de cabeça), ritual cooking and harmonization of the chakras.
	This Ewé provides prosperity and emotional equilibrium.

Mentha spicata **L.;** *Mentha viridis* **(L.) L.**

Candomblé de Angola	**Zaze**	Head cleansings (obrigações no Orí)
	Matamba, Lembá	Baths, **Amassi, Abô**
Umbanda		This Ewe has the power to lift mediums to the Astral Plane
		Baths, **Amassi, Abô**

NOTE	**Amassi**	Ritual baths with different Ewe
		See: **https://pt.wikipedia.org/wiki/Banho_de_ervas**
	Abô	Sacred water, Omiero
		See: **https://pt.wikipedia.org/wiki/Águas_sagradas**

NAME-CUBA   Yerba Caimán   (Roig)
    Owner   Yemayá, Ochún (LC, TDF2, Quiros)

NAME-SCIENTIFIC   *Persicaria glabra* (Willd.) M.Gómez;
                    Polygonum portoricense Bertero ex Endl.   (Roig)
               Persicaria maculosa Gray; *Polygonum persicaria* L.   (Barros)

NAME-BRAZIL   Erva-de-bicho, Cristas, Erva-das-pulgas, Erva-pessegueira, Persicária
    Candomblé Jêje-Nagô   Exú, Obaluaiè   Água/Masculino   (Barros)
    BATUQUE   Xapanã
    Candomblé de Angola   Lembá

NAME-Lucumí   Ewe dó   (LC)
                   Ewedó   (TDF2)
    YORUBA   ERÓ IGBIN   (***Polygonum persicaria* L.**)

NAME-CONGO   Nséke gándo, Bámba (LC)
                   Nseeke guando, Bamba (TDF)

NAME-OTHER   *Persicaria glabra*   Dense Flower Knotweed   (USDA)
                        Smooth Smartweed   (CRC)
               Persicaria maculosa   Spotted Ladysthumb   (USDA)

USES
               Medicinal
    Candomblé Jêje-Nagô   Used in the cleansing of ritual objects of Exú
               Some houses attribute this Ewe to Obaluaiè and its used for baths,
               specially to people with skin problems.   (Barros)
    BATUQUE   Used in ritual baths for filhos of Xapanã   (Barros)
    Candomblé de Angola   Used for initiation (**Feitura**) for any Omorixá

NOTE **Feitura**   One of the steps of the neophyte need for initiation
               See: **https://pt.wikipedia.org/wiki/Fazer_a_cabeça**
    BATUQUE   It's a general form to denominate Afro-Brazilian religions in the South of Brazil
               See: **https://pt.wikipedia.org/wiki/Batuque_(religião)**

NAME-CUBA	Yerba de Garro, Garro Blanco	(Roig)
	Yerba Garro	(Menéndez)
Owner	Obatalá (Diaz)	
	Eleggua, Oyá, Oró (Irizarry)	
	Oyá (Menéndez)	
Odun	Obara-iwori (Quiros, Diaz, Irizarry, Orula.org)	
NAME-SCIENTIFIC	*Spermacoce tenuior* L.	(Roig)
NAME-BRAZIL	Does NOT occur in Brazil per Flora do Brasil	
NAME-Lucumí		
YORUBA		
NAME-CONGO		
PALO		
NAME-OTHER	Slender False Buttonweed	(USDA)
USES	Goes to Osain (Omiero) for Oyá	(Menéndez)
	Goes to Osain (Omiero)	(Diaz)
	Used for Inche Osain	(Irizarry)
NOTE	This plant (*Spermacoce tenuior* L.) is listed under *Spermacoce remota* Lam. in CRC	

NAME-CUBA	Yerba de Garro, Garro Morado	(Roig)
	Yerba Garro	(Menéndez)
Owner	Oyá (Menéndez)	
Odun	Obara-iwori (Orula.org)	
NAME-SCIENTIFIC	*Spermacoce laevis Lam.*;	
	Borreria laevis (Lam.) Griseb.	(Roig)
NAME-BRAZIL	No common name found	
NAME-Lucumí		
YORUBA		
NAME-CONGO		
PALO		
NAME-OTHER	Buttonweed	(levypreserve.org)
USES	Goes to Osain (Omiero) for Oyá	(Menéndez)
NOTE	This plant was chosen to be listed in the plants for Oyá	
	since is called "Garro Morado" and is a color syncretic with Oyá.	

NAME-CUBA	Yerba de Guinea, Yerba de Guinea Tanganyka,	
	Yerba de Guinea Hembrita, Guinea Gigante	(Roig)
Owner	Babalú-Ayé (LC, TDF, TDF2, Quiros, Menéndez)	
Odun		
NAME-SCIENTIFIC	*Panicum maximum* Jacq.	(Roig)
NAME-BRAZIL	Capim-colonião, Capim-coloninho, Capim-milhã, Capim-guiné	
		(agrolink.com.br)
NAME-Lucumí	Okoerán eránguini, Edi-edi	(LC)
	Okoerán, Erankíni, Edé-edi	(TDF2)
	Okoerán, Edi-edi, Otarí	(TDF)
YORUBA	Ikin, Ikin iruke, Iran akun, Kooko, Eru oparun	(CRC)
NAME-CONGO	Vititi, Mariare, Maóma, Boolóngo	(LC)
	Kumasasi, Kumaria-ria, Bititi dengo, Mariare,	
	Kumarabia, Bolongo	(TDF)
NAME-OTHER	Guinea Grass	(USDA)
	Bush Buffalo grass, Common Buffalo grass, Guinea grass	(CRC)
USES	Goes to the Omiero of Babalú-Ayé	(TDF2)
	Medicinal	
	At the beginning of Spring, to make an Omiero to wash Changó	(LC)
INDIA	Used in Siddha	(CRC)

NAME-CUBA	Yerba de la Niña, Azulejo, Llorón		(Roig, Duke's)
Owner	Ochún (TDF2, Diaz)		
	Ochún, Oggún (Quiros)		
	Ochún, Aña (Irizarry)		
	Obatalá (Madan)		
	Ochún, Yemayá (Menéndez)		
Odun	Oyeku-ogunda (Quiros, Diaz, Irizarry, Madan)		
NAME-SCIENTIFIC	*Phyllanthus niruri* L.		(Roig)
NAME-BRAZIL	Quebra-pedra, Arrebenta-pedra, Erva-pombinha		
Candomblé Jêje-Nagô	Ossaim, Oxumaré	Terra/Masculino	(Barros)
CULTO DE NAÇÃO	Ossaim, Oxumarê		
Umbanda	Xangô, Oxossi		
NAME-Lucumí	Ewe Néne, Ewe Náni		(LC, TDF2)
YORUBA	Èyìn olobe funfun, Aáwé, Lénkosùn	(*Phyllanthus sp.*)	(PV)
	EWÉ BOJUTÒNA, EWÉ ÍYEMÍ		(Barros)
NAME-CONGO			
NAME-OTHER	Gale of the Wind		(USDA)
	Stonebreaker, Hurricane weed, Creole Senna, Gale-wind grass		
	Yaquillo (PR); Quininito (DR); Lavandero (Venezuela);		
	Quinquina du Pays (Haiti)		(Duke's)
USES	**DOES NOT** go to Osain (Omiero)		
	Cleansing baths and home cleansings		(LC)
	Ritual baths (Ebomisi) and cleansings (despojos)		(Irizarry)
	To make powder (afoche) to bind a lover		(Diaz)
	Medicinal		
Candomblé Jêje-Nagô	Used in the rituals of initiation, Abô, purification baths for the filhos of Ossaim, Oxumaré, Nanã and Obaluaiè		
Umbanda	Cleansing baths to release negative energies		

NAME-CUBA	Yerba de la Sangre, Mierda de Gallina, Papita	(Roig)
Owner	Yemayá (LC)	
	Yemayá, Oggún (TDF2, Diaz)	
	Yemayá, Ochún (Quiros)	
	Eleggua, Asojuano (Madan)	
	Oggún, Ochosi (Menéndez)	
Odun	Irete-meji, Ose-oturupon (Diaz, Madan)	
NAME-SCIENTIFIC	*Cordia bullata* var. *globosa* (Jacq.) Govaerts;	
	Cordia globosa (Jacq.) Kunth	(Roig)
NAME-BRAZIL	NOT found in Flora do Brasil	
NAME-Lucumí	Eweyé	(LC)
	Eweye, Eweyé	(TDF2)
YORUBA		
NAME-CONGO		
NAME-OTHER	Curaciao Bush	(USDA)
	Bloodberry, Butterfly-sage, Curacao bush	(fnps.org)
USES	Goes to Osain (Omiero)	
	Goes to the Omiero of Oggún	(TDF2)
	Used in purification baths and home cleansings	(Diaz)
	Medicinal	

NAME-CUBA	Yerba de la Vieja, Contrayerba	(Roig)
Owner	Babalú-Ayé (TDF2)	
	Babalú-Ayé, Ochún, Oggún, Inlé, Eleggua (Quiros)	
	Ochún (Diaz)	
	Ochún, Asojuano (Irizarry)	
Odun	Obara-irosun (Quiros, Irizarry)	
	Oyeku-ogunda (Diaz)	
NAME-SCIENTIFIC	*Flaveria trinervia* (Spreng.) C.Mohr	(Roig)
NAME-BRAZIL	NO common name found	
NAME-Lucumí	Ewe Abguá	(LC, TDF2)
	Agbá, Durugbó	(TDF)
YORUBA		
NAME-CONGO	Kiámboba	(LC)
	Kiamboba	(TDF)
NAME-OTHER	Clustered Yellowtops	(USDA)
	Cluster Flower	(CRC)
USES	Goes to Osain (Omiero)	
	Goes to the Omiero of Babalú-Ayé	(TDF2)
	For ritual baths for love and luck	(Diaz)
	Ritual baths (Ebomisi), Inche Osain and Ebó	(Irizarry)
	Medicinal	

NAME-CUBA		Yerba de Plata		(LC)
		Yerba de la Plata, Corazón de Hombre		(Roig)
	Owner	Obatalá (Quiros)		
	Odun			

| **NAME-SCIENTIFIC** | *Peperomia pellucida* (L.) Kunth | | (Roig) |

NAME-BRAZIL		Oriri, Oriri-de-Oxum, Alfavaquinha-de-cobra, Erva-de-jabuti		
	Candomblé Jêje-Nagô	Oxalá, Oxum	Água/Feminino	(Barros)
	Candomblé de Angola	Dandalunda, Kaiá		
	Candomblé Ketu	Oxum		
	CULTO DE NAÇÃO	Oxum, Oxalá		

| **NAME-Lucumí** | Ewe Sádádá | (LC) |
| **YORUBA** | Rinrin | (PV, CRC) |

NAME-CONGO

| **NAME-OTHER** | Man to Man | (USDA) |
| | Crow's foot, Shinning bush, Soldier parsley | (CRC) |

USES

Medicinal

Candomblé Jêje-Nagô   This is a fundamental Ewe. It is used for all rituals of initiation, periodic cleansings (obrigações periódicas) and in Abô for all Orixá. This Ewe also has to do with sight both medicinal and religiously since it is associated with **Oxum Opará** which is syncretized as Santa Luzia (St. Lucy)   (Barros)

Candomblé de Angola   Dandalunda, Kaiá   Head cleansings (obrigações no Orí)

Candomblé Ketu   It is used in ALL cleansing baths and obrigações de Orí

CULTO DE NAÇÃO   Used in head cleansings (obrigações de cabeça), spiritual cleansing baths, and cleansing of ritual objects.

NOTE   Oxum Opará   **Oxum Opará/Apará** is an avatar of Oxum. She uses a fan (abebé/abanico) and a scythe (alfange/guadaña). She is accompanied by Oyá and Ogum.
See: **https://pt.wikipedia.org/wiki/Oxum**

NAME-CUBA	Yerba de Santa Bárbara, Santa Bárbara, Ruda Cimarrona	(Roig)
Owner	Changó (LC, TDF2, Quiros)	
	Eggun (Madan)	
	Changó, Agayú (Menéndez) **Ruda Cimarrona**	
Odun	Osa-ofun (Quiros, Madan, Orula.org)	
NAME-SCIENTIFIC	*Dalea carthagenensis* (Jacq.) J.F.Macbr.;	
	Dalea domingensis DC.	(Roig)
NAME-BRAZIL	NOT found in Flora do Brasil	
NAME-Lucumí	Ewe Chango	(TDF2)
ANAGO	Atopá Kuní, Ewe atópa kún **Ruda Cimarrona**	(LC)
YORUBA		
NAME-CONGO		
NAME-OTHER	Cartagena Prairie Clover	(USDA)

USES

	Used in a ritual, with other Ewe of Changó, to
	guarantee success in an endeavor, or over enemies.
	This ritual is heavily participatory by the person requiring
	the favor from Changó. (LC)

NOTE   Lydia Cabrera lists **Ruta chalepensis L.** as the scientific name for "Ruda Cimarrona" in "Anagó – Vocabulario Lucumí". **Ruta chalepensis L.** happens to be one of the two scientific names for "**Ruda**". The above listed information is correct as to the plant names.

NOTE   The Infraspecific Taxa of **Dalea carthagenensis (Jacq.) J.F.Macbr.;** **Dalea carthagenensis var. floridana (Rydb.) Barneby** is **CRITICAL ENDANGERED** in the State of Florida. It is the Florida Prairie Clover. See: **https://www.fnai.org/FieldGuide/pdf/Dalea_carthagenensis_var_floridana.pdf**

NAME-CUBA	Yerba Díez del Día	(LC)
	Díez del Día, Verdolaga de las Díez, V. de Playa, V. de Sabana	(Roig)
Owner	Oggún (LC, TDF2)	
	Oggún, Eleggua, Yemayá (Quiros)	
	Oggún, Eleggua (Irizarry)	
	Yemayá (Madan)	
	Oggún, Ochosi (Menéndez)	
Odun	Oturupon-odi (Quiros, Irizarry, Madan, Orula.org)	
	Otura-ofun (Quiros, Irizarry, Madan)	
NAME-SCIENTIFIC	*Portulaca pilosa* L.	(Roig)
NAME-BRAZIL	Amor-crescido	
NAME-Lucumí		
YORUBA		
NAME-CONGO		
NAME-OTHER	Kiss Me Quick	(USDA)
	Chisme, Rose purslane, Shaggy portulaca, Hairy pigweed	(llifle.com)
USES		
	Used for ritual baths (Ebomisi)	Irizarry
	First Ewe the **Ęgbado** picked to make Kari Ocha	(LC)
	Medicinal	
NOTE Ęgbado	**Ęgbado** now **Yewa** A tribe of the Yoruba people	
	See: **https://en.wikipedia.org/wiki/Yewa**	

NAME-CUBA	Yerba Fina, Grama, Grama Cimarrona, Hierba de la Bermuda	(Roig)
Owner	Ochún (LC)	
	Eleggua (TDF2)	
	Eleggua, Oggún (TDF)	
	Eleggua (Madan, Diaz, Quiros, Concordia)	
	Eleggua, Oggún, Ochosi, Obatalá (Irizarry)	
	Eleggua (Menéndez)	**Yerba Fina**
	Yemayá, Ochún (Menéndez)	**Grama**
Odun	Owonrin-otura (Irizarry, Quiros, Orula.org)	
	Ejiogbe-irete (Madan, Diaz)	

| **NAME-SCIENTIFIC** | *Cynodon dactylon* (L.) Pers. | (Roig) |

| **NAME-BRAZIL** | Capim-de-burro, Grama-seda, Grama-bermudas, Capim-fino | |
| **Candomblé Jêje-Nagô** | Xangô, Oxum | Terra/Masculino | (Barros) |

NAME-Lucumí	Cotonembo, Ewé Eran, Dengo, Elúggúé, Tumayá, Iyeraán	(LC)
	Era Namo	(TDF2)
	Ewé Eran, Dengo, Katonembo, Eleggúa, Tumayá, Iyerán	(TDF)
ANAGO	Dengo	**Grama Cimarrona** (*Cynodon dactylon*)
	Ayinaro, Eran omó, Ewe amó, Oyí naro	**Hierba Fina**
	Ewe erán	**Yerba Grama**	(LC)
YORUBA	Koóko ìgbá	(PV, CRC)

NAME-CONGO	Nfita solanki, Guandi, Indónso	(LC)
	Nfita solanki, Guandi, Sundí, Inidenso	(TDF)
PALO	Nfita Kinbansa	
BANTU	Nfita solanki	**Grama** (*Cynodon dactylon*)
	Nfita kimbansa	**Grama**	(LC)

NAME-OTHER	Bermudagrass	(USDA)
	Bahamas Grass, Bermuda Grass	

USES   Goes to Osain (Omiero)
One of the 5 MOST important plants (Ewé) in the Omiero
Medicinal

Candomblé   Used for baths to balance (com finalidade de equilibrar a vida da pessoa)

PALO MONTE   Used for bindings (amarres), and powders (Afoche/Mpolo)
With it, the Mayombero makes sure that no unwanted guests come
while at work (amarrar las cuatro esquinas para Juego de Palo)

ESPIRITU CRUZADO   Spiritual works and "rompimientos"

INDIA   Used in Ayurveda, Unani and Siddha; Used in religion and magico-religious
beliefs: spiritual, ceremonial: symbol of peaceful and long life, sacred to
Hindus; ingredient of Patra pooja in different religious pooja ceremonies, in
Ganesh-pooja; plants used as offerings to Lord Buddha, aerial parts in
worship, leaves used in wedding rituals   (CRC)

NAME-CUBA	Yerba Hedionda, Hedionda	(Roig)
Owner	Eleggua (TDF2)	
	Eleggua, Changó (Quiros)	
	Changó, Orunmila (Madan)	
	Eggun, Eshú (Irizarry)	
Odun	Osa-irete (Madan, Quiros, Irizarry, Orula.org)	
	Owonrin-iwori, Okanran-otura (Quiros, Irizarry, Orula.org)	

NAME-SCIENTIFIC	*Senna occidentalis* (L.) Link; *Cassia occidentalis* L.	(Roig)

NAME-BRAZIL	Fedegoso, Fedegoso-verdadeiro, Mangerioba, Mata-pasto, Mamangá	
Candomblé Jêje-Nagô	Obaluaiè Fogo/Masculina	(Barros)
Candomblé de Angola	Aluvaiá	
Candomblé	Oyá, Obaluaiè Terra/Masculino/Gùn	
CULTO DE NAÇÃO	Exu, Obaluaiè Oyá, Egúngún **Fedegoso-branco**	
Umbanda	Xangô, Oxossi	

NAME-Lucumí	Jara-jara	(LC, TDF2)
	Iki jara-jara, Olala tuya, Tarara, Anamó, Ayé iré, Maya yara	(TDF)
YORUBA	Abo réré, Réré, Adáwérésewéré, Ògànlara	(PV, CRC)
NAME-CONGO	Mbeutameiré	(TDF)
PALO	**OWNER** Lucero	

NAME-OTHER	Septicweed	(USDA)
	Fetid Cassia, Stinking Pea	

USES	Goes to the Omiero of Eleggua	(TDF2)
	Inche Osain	
Culto Egúngún	in Bahia, in the Cult Egúngún; it is used as and Ewé of defense against maleficent entities (entidades maléficas).	
Candomblé	Ritual and defense baths	
Candomblé Jêje-Nagô	Used in cleansings and purification baths	
Candomblé de Angola	Cleansings of the home (sacudimento de casa)	
Umbanda	Defense baths, head cleansings (obrigações de cabeça), cleansings.	
INDIA	Used in Ayurveda and Siddha. Ritual, magico-religious beliefs: a bath in hot water containing pieces of its roots to ward off evil spirits.	(CRC)

NAME-CUBA	Yerba Jicotea	(LC)
	Hierba de jicotea, Nelumbio, Ova blanca	(EcuRed)
	Ova Blanca, Flor de Agua, Nelumbio Blanco	(Roig)
Owner	Changó (LC, TDF2, Quiros)	
Odun		

| **NAME-SCIENTIFIC** | *Nymphaea ampla* (Salisb.) DC. | Roig) |

NAME-BRAZIL Nymphaea, Ninfeia
  Culto aos Orixás Oxum, Iemanjá, Oyá, Obá, Nana, Ewá; Oxalá (**ninfeia branca**)

NAME-Lucumí	Okoñanígbo, Ewe Ayá, Ilíncale		(LC)
	Okañanígbo, Ewe Ayá, Ilincale		(TDF2)
ANAGO	Irituto, Ochú miri, Oyóro, Oyóuro, Oyuoro	**Flor de Agua**	
	Oyóuro	**Lirio de Agua**	
	Ewe ti	**Lirio Acuático**	(LC)
YORUBA	Ewé ÒSÍBÀTÁ		

| **NAME-CONGO** | Mofóroyo, Nflú (LC) |
| **PALO** | |

| **NAME-OTHER** | Dotleaf waterlily | (USDA) |

USES

  To make Changó work. Ewe of many secrets   (LC)

NAME-CUBA	Yerba Luisa		(Roig)
Owner	Ochún (LC, TDF2, Quiros, Diaz, Madan)		
	Eleggua (Irizarry)		
Odun	Okanran-meji (Quiros, Irizarry, Madan, Orula.org)		
NAME-SCIENTIFIC	*Aloysia citriodora* Palau;		
	Aloysia triphylla (L'Hér.) Britton		(Roig)
NAME-BRAZIL	Limonete, Lúcia-lima, Erva-Luísa, Verbena-cidrada, Cidrão, Cidrão-de-árvore		
Candomblé Jêje-Nagô	Oxum, Jemanja	Água/Feminino	(Barros)
Umbanda	Oxum		

NAME-Lucumí
    YORUBA

NAME-CONGO

NAME-OTHER	Lemon Beebush	(USDA)
	Lemon Verbena, Lemon-scented Verbena	(Duke's, CRC)
USES	Goes to Osain (Omiero)	
	Baths for prosperity and love	(Diaz)
	Ritual baths (Ebomisi)	(Irizarry)
	Medicinal	
Candomblé Jêje-Nagô	baths and incense for good luck	(Barros)
Umbanda	Used in Amacis, Abô and ritual baths.	
Hoodoo/Root Magic (USA)	Lemon Verbena clears away unwanted things	

NAME-CUBA	Yerba Maravedí	(Roig)
Owner	Ochún (LC, TDF2, Quiros)	
Odun		
NAME-SCIENTIFIC	*Crossopetalum uragoga* (Jacq.) Kuntze;	
	Myginda uragoga Jacq.	(Roig)
NAME-BRAZIL	NOT found in Flora do Brasil	
NAME-Lucumí	Banaíbana, Mocoloimao, Tenkennia	(LC)
	Banaibana, Mocoloimao, Yenkennia	(TDF2)
YORUBA		
NAME-CONGO		
NAME-OTHER	NO common name found. Native to Cuba	
	Snake Berry	(Flora of the Cayman Islands)
USES		
	For ritual baths (Ebomisi) and home cleansings	(LC)
	A talisman/amulet is made with this Ewe for thieves	
	and prostitutes for luck in their endeavors	(LC)

NOTE	This plant, ***Myginda uragoga* Jacq.** distribution is Cuba	(Tropicos.org)

NAME-CUBA	Yerba Mora, Mora	(Roig)
Haitian	Lamá (name used by Haitian immigrants in Camagüey)	
OWNER	Oggún, Yemayá (LC, TDF2, Diaz)	
	Oggún (Irizarry)	
	Oggún, Yemayá, Ochún, Eleggua (Quiros)	
	Oggún, Ochosi (Menéndez)	
ODUN	Ose-otura (Quiros, Irizarry, Diaz)	

NAME-SCIENTIFIC	*Solanum americanum* Mill.; *Solanum nigrum* L.	(Roig)

NAME-BRAZIL	Maria-preta, Erva-moura, Mata-cavalo, Pimenta-de-galinha, Araxixu,	
Candomblé Jêje-Nagô	Obaluaiyé Terra/Masculino/Gùn	(Barros)
Candomblé de Angola	Aluvaiá, Kavungo, Zaze	
CULTO DE NAÇÃO	Omolú	
Umbanda	Obaluaiyé, Xangô	
ODUN	ÒFÙN MÉJÌ (PV)	

NAME- Lucumí	Atoré, Efodá	(LC)
	Atoré, Efodá, Ewé Atoré, Epodú	(TDF2)
YORUBA	Èwé Ègùnmò, Ègùmò, Agunmo gàra, Òdú	(PV, CRC)
NAME-CONGO		
NAME-OTHER	Black Nightshade	(USDA)
	Common nightshade, Deadly nightshade, Inkberry	(CRC)

USES	**DOES NOT** go to Osain (Omiero)	
	Spiritual baths; food offerings (Ochinchin) for Eggun	
	Taboo (**Èwó**) for children of Ochún	(Quiros)
	Used to baptize the Lode-stone (Piedra Imán)	(Diaz)
Candomblé Jêje-Nagô	Ritual baths of protection and cleansings	
Candomblé de Angola	**Aluvaiá** Ritual baths and home/personal cleansings	
	Kavungo Ritual baths to discharge negative energies	
	Zaze Head cleansings (obrigações no Orí)	
Umbanda	Cleansing baths, Amacis, Abô, cleansing Ebô	

NAME-CUBA	Yúa, Ayúa, Ayúa Macho, Ayúa Amarilla, Ayuda,	
	Ayuda Macho, Ayuda Amarilla	(Roig)
Owner	Oggún (LC, Quiros, Diaz)	
Odun	Oturupon-ose (Diaz, Madan)	
NAME-SCIENTIFIC	*Zanthoxylum martinicense* (Lam.) DC.	(Roig)
NAME-BRAZIL	NOT found in Flora do Brasil	
NAME-Lucumí	Elegún, Iggi oro	(TDF)
YORUBA	Èègùn (*Zanthoxylum viride*)	(PV)
NAME-CONGO	Lúnga-kuma	(LC)
	Lungá-kuma	(TDF)
PALO	**Yúa, Ayúa** Lunga-kuma	
	OWNER Zarabanda	(Nfinda)
NAME-OTHER	White Prickly Ash	(USDA)
	Martinique prickly-ash, White Hercules, White Mary	
	Ayúa Macho, Espino (DR); Ayúa, Cenizo (PR);	
	Bwa penn, Bwa pine blan (Creole Haiti)	(Elsevier)
USES	**DOES NOT** go to Osain (Omiero)	
	ONLY used in Palo Monte	
PALO	The talisman/amulet made from this "palo" are very secure	(LC)
	The spines are used to craft amulets/talismans	(Diaz)
	As a general rule, this "palo" is used to cause mayhem,	
	and destroy	(LC, Nfinda)
	The tree itself used for a love hex/witchcraft	(LC)

NAME-CUBA	Yuca, Yuca Agria, Yuca Dulce, Yuca Blanca, Yuca Cristalina, Yuca Cartagena		(Roig)
Owner	Oggún (LC, TDF2)		
	Oggún, Orishaoko (Quiros)		
	Oyá (Menéndez)		
Odun	Odi-osa (Quiros)		

NAME-SCIENTIFIC *Manihot esculenta* Crantz   (Roig)

NAME-BRAZIL Mandioca, Mandioca-doce, Mandioca-mansa, Mandioca-amarga

Candomblé Jêje-Nagô	Exú, Xangó	Fogo/Masculino	(Barros)
CULTO DE NAÇÃO	Oxossi, Caboclos		
Umbanda	Oxossi, Caboclos		

NAME-Lucumí	Kokomadoco, Ibagguddán, Baggudán	(LC)
	Ibgguddán	(TDF2)
YORUBA	Ègé funfun, Ègé òkè, Ègé, Gbàgùúdá, Ègé gbokogbàglà, Gbàjadà, Pákí, Gbágùúdá dále joró, Gbágùúdá funfun, Gbágùúdá pupa, Ègé kàragbá, Ègé gbokogbàglà, Ègé Olówókúnbó, Ègé atú, Lánàsé	(PV CRC)

NAME-CONGO	Nkumbia, Mandioka, Maddiaka, Mayoko	(LC)
	Mandioko, Nkaba, Mayaka mongolo, Nkunia kerebende, Marioko, Mandioko makongo	(TDF)
	Ayaka, Mikele, Mokele, Saka saka	(CRC)

NAME-OTHER	Cassava	(USDA)
	Bitter cassava, Sweet cassava, Manioc, Tapioca	(CRC)

USES

	Used as Ebó and Addimu for Orisha	
	The **BEST** counter to any hex/witchcraft	(LC)
Candomblé Jêje-Nagô	Used cooked as Addimu for Exú and Xangô	(Barros)
Candomblé Ketu	Tapioca is **Èwó of Oxum**	
Umbanda	Ritualistic food, offerings (Addimu) and Ebós	
	Must avoid (Quizila/**Èwó**) because it **belongs to Egun**	
INDIA	Used in Ayurveda and Siddha. Ceremonial, ritual: root juice in ritual baths to treat sterility in women	(CRC)

NAME-CUBA	Zarza, Zarza Uña de Gato	(Roig)
	Zarza, Árbol de Espinas	(LC)
Owner	Oggún (LC, Quiros, Diaz, Madan)	
Odun	Iwori-okanran (Quiros, Madan)	
NAME-SCIENTIFIC	*Pisonia aculeata* L.	(Roig)
NAME-BRAZIL	Espora-de-galo	
NAME-Lucumí **YORUBA**	Egún iggi Egún	(LC)
NAME-CONGO	Nkunia ntuta, Nkunia kerebende, Mpuko, Tilinkó	(LC)
	Nkunia ntuta	(TDF)
NAME-OTHER	Pull-back	(USDA)
	Cockspur, Devil's Claw, Pull-back-and-hold	
	Escambrón (PR); Uña de Gato (DR);	
	Krók chen (Creole Haiti)	(Elsevier)

USES	**DOES NOT** go to Osain (Omiero)	
	This Ewe is the "shirt" of Oggún (it is used to cover him).	
	It is used in all ceremonies of this Orisha.	(LC)
	This Ewe is also used to cover Eleggua and Babalú-Ayé	(LC)
	In case of epidemics, all offerings and monetary rights for	
	Babalú-Ayé are deposited in/on this tree	(LC)
	With the spines of this tree and other items an amulet is made	
	(called **Agongó Nigué**) to achieve anything.	(LC)
	Used for home and personal cleansings	(Diaz)
	Medicinal	

NAME-CUBA	Zarza Blanca, Uña de Gato, Uña de Gavilán	(Roig)
Owner	Oggún, Eshú (LC)	
	Oggún, Eleggua (TDF2)	
	Oggún, Ochosi (Quiros)	
Odun		
NAME-SCIENTIFIC	*Celtis iguanaea* (Jacq.) Sarg.;	
	Momisia iguanaea (Jacq.) Rose & Standl.	(Roig)
NAME-BRAZIL	Cipó-farinha-seca, Cipó-laranjinha, Grão-de-galo, Gumbixava	
NAME-Lucumí	Tilinko fún	(TDF2)
YORUBA		
NAME-CONGO		
NAME-OTHER	Iguana Hackberry	(USDA)
	Maíz Tostado (Venezuela)	(Elsevier)

USES

This Ewe can make an innocent person, or a person in the
"right" in a court case get embroiled and loose the case/his
rights in a court of law through his own doing.   (LC)

NOTE   Lydia Cabrera lists Uña de Gato as a separate entry with different attributes

NAME-CUBA	Zarzaparrilla	(Roig)
	Zarzaparrilla, Bejuco Lucumí	(TDF2)
Owner	Changó, Orishaoko (LC)	
	Changó (TDF2)	**Zarzaparrilla**
	Babalú-Ayé, Yemayá (TDF2)	**Bejuco Lucumí**
	Changó (Quiros, Diaz)	
	Ochún, Ibeyis, Asojuano (Irizarry)	
	Changó, Orishaoko (Madan)	
	Ochún, Ibeyis (Madan)	
	Oggún, Ochosi (Menéndez)	
Odun	Osa-obara, Irete-oyeku (Quiros, Diaz, Madan, Orula.org)	

NAME-SCIENTIFIC   *Smilax havanensis* Jacq.   (Roig)

NAME-BRAZIL   NOT found in Flora do Brasil

NAME-Lucumí	Atéwé Edín, Atéke din	(LC, TDF2)
ANAGO	Ateke din, Atewedún **Zarzaparrilla**	(LC)
YORUBA		

NAME-CONGO

NAME-OTHER	Everglades Greenbrier	(USDA)
	Bell Apple	(CRC)

USES	**DOES NOT** go to Osain (Omiero)	
	Goes to the Omiero of Babalú-Ayé	(TDF2)
	To make Changó mad in order to make him work/	
	resolve a problem or a request	(LC)
	Used for Ebomisi, Inche Osain and Paraldo	(Irizarry)
	Medicinal	
PALO MONTE	Mayomberos use this "palo" for the preparation of the Nganga	
ESPIRITU CRUZADO	Used for cleansings and to ward-off negative influences	

Shorthand for References used:

- **LC**   Lydia Cabrera; "El Monte"; "Anagó: Vocabulario Lucumí"; "Vocabulario Congo"; "La Lengua Sagrada de los Ñañigos", "Vocabulario Congo – Edición revisada por I. Castellanos"
- **TDF**   Teodoro Diaz Favelo; "Diccionario de la Lengua Conga Residual en Cuba"
- **TDF2**   Teodoro Díaz Fabelo; "Lengua de Santeros (Guiné Góngorí)"
- **Quiros**   Dalia Quiros-Moran; "Guide to Afro-Cuban Herbalism"
- **Diaz**   José Carlos Diaz; "The Plants of Santería and the Regla de Palo Monte"
- **Irizarry**   William J. Irizarry; "Ewé Osaín"
- **Concordia**   Maria "Oggunbemi" Concordia; "Ritual Use of Plants in Lucumí Tradition"
- **Madan**   Marcelo Madan; "Enciclopedia de las Hierbas de Ifá"
- **Roig**   Juan Tomás Roig; "Diccionario Botánico de nombres vulgares cubanos", "Plantas Medicinales, Aromáticas o Venenosas de Cuba"
- **Barros**   Jose Flávio Pessoa de Barros, Eduardo Napoleão; "Ewé òrìsà"
- **PV**   Pierre Fatumbi Verger; "Ewé: O uso das plantas na sociedade Iorubá"
- **NBA**   Natalia Bolívar Aróstegui; "Los Orishas en Cuba", "Orishas del Panteón AfroCubano"
- **Menéndez**   Menéndez, Lázara (2009); Estudios Afro-Cubanos; Volume 3
- **CRC**   Quattrocchi, Umberto; "CRC World Dictionary of Medicinal and Poisonous Plants"; "CRC World Dictionary of Palms"
- **Elsevier's**   Grandtner, Miroslav M.; "Elsevier's Dictionary of Trees: Volume 1: North America"; "Elsevier's Dictionary of Trees: Volume 2: South America"
- **Duke's**   Duke, James A.; "Duke's Handbook of Medicinal Plants in Latin America"
- **Hoodoo/Root**   Catherine Yronwode; "Hoodoo Herb and Root Magic"
- **Palo Monte & Espiritismo Cruzado**   Ileana Hodge Limonata; "El uso de las plantas en la Regla Conga y el Espiritismo Cruzado"
- **Osain/Omiero**   Unless otherwise noted, information garnered from José Carlos Diaz.
- **BISSEA**   BISSEA-Jardín Botánico Nacional; "Lista Roja de la Flora de Cuba"
- **IUCN**   The IUCN Red List of Threated Species;   https://www.iucnredlist.org/
- **gbif.org**   Global Biodiversity Information Facility;   https://www.gbif.org/
- **USDA**   https://plants.usda.gov/
- **The Plant List**   http://www.theplantlist.org/1/
- **Kew Science**   http://powo.science.kew.org/
- **Flora do Brasil**   http://floradobrasil.jbrj.gov.br/
- **Algae Base**   http://www.algaebase.org/
- **Plants of Viñales**   http://www.cybertruffle.org.uk/vinales/eng/
- **Orula.org**   http://www.orula.org/ - Odun of Ifá
- **Nfinda**   https://nfinda.wordpress.com/category/palos-fuertes/
- **EcuRed**   https://www.ecured.cu/EcuRed:Enciclopedia_cubana
- **Wiki**   https://www.wikipedia.org

In Cuba, the religion of the African slaves evolved into several religions/religious concepts. These are:

- Regla de Ocha/Ifá   of Lucumí/Yoruba ancestry.
- Reglas Congas   of Bantu ancestry. These are broken up into
    - Regla de Palo Monte
    - Palo o Regla Mayombe
    - Regla Kimbisa
        - Shamalongo   Influences by Ocha and Espiritismo Cruzado
        - Santo Cristo del Buen Viaje- Created by Andrés Facundo Petit
    - Biyumba
    - Musunde or Musundí
    - Brillumba or Vrillumba
        - Brillumba Ndoki   Nganga Judía
    - Espiritismo Cruzado   Influenced by Allan Kardec/Spiritism
- Sociedad Abakuá   from the Calabar region of present-day Nigeria. Secret MALE society
- Iyessá   much like Regla de Ocha, now mainly seen in Matanzas, Cuba
- Arará   from the kingdoms of Arada, Ardra and Jakin. Now mostly in Matanzas

In Brazil, much the same occurred with the religions the slaves brought and which have evolved into:

- Candomblé
    - Nagô origin   Yoruba descendants from Nigeria, Benin and Togo; language is Yoruba
        - Nação ketu   Ketu Nation
        - Nação Ijexá   Iyessá Nation
        - Nação efon   Efon Nation
    - Jêje Origin   Ewe-fon descendants from Benin and Togo; language is Fongbe
        - Nação Jêje-mahi   Jêje -Maji Nation
        - Nação Jêje-savalu   Jêje-Savalu Nation
        - Nação Jêje-Nagô or Nagô-vodum   Orisha cult with Jêje rites
    - Bantu Origin   Bakongo/Umbundo descendants from Angola, and Congo
        - Nação congo-angola or Nação angola   Congo-Angola Nation
        - Candomblé de Caboclo Syncretic religion with Bantu and Ameridian religions
- Umbanda   Brazilian religion that syncretizes Christian and African religions (Magia Branca)
    - Umbanda Tradicional
    - Primado de Umbanda
    - Umbanda de Nação or Umbanda Mista
    - Umbandomblé
    - Umbanda Esotérica
    - Umbanda Astrológica
    - Umbanda Sagrada
    - Umbanda da Magia Divina
    - Umbanda Omolocô/Omolokô
    - Umbanda Crística

- Quimbanda   Brazilian origin and identified with the "Left side" of Umbanda (Magia Negra)
- Xangô de Pernambuco   Afro-brazilian religion
    - Xangô do Recife
    - Xangô do Nordeste
    - Nagô Egbá
- Tambor de Mina do Maranhão

In the United States, due to the lack of permissiveness from the slave owners, the religions that now exist are not as rich as those of the Caribbean or Brazil. These are:

- Hoodoo   African folkloric practices and beliefs with American Indian botanical knowledge
    - Hoodoo   disambiguation of Hudu-a tribe and language of Ewe, Togo and Ghana
    - Conjuration
    - Conjure
    - Witchcraft
    - Root Work
    - Candle Burning
    - Tricking
- Obeah   Much the same as Hoodoo

Hoodoo uses the magical techniques that originated in Africa without any of the religion. There is no presence of the Nkisi, Orishas or Loa of Africa and most practitioners are Protestant Christians and some Catholic practitioners who will invoke a saint.

The Sacred Divinities of Regla Ocha and their syncretism with Catholic Entities.

Supreme Beings

OLOFI

- Olofi is GOD, and came into being from nothing.
- He created the world, the orishas, the animals and mankind. He retired and does not partake an active role; although nothing can be achieved without his knowledge and help.
- All offerings (Addimu, Ebó) to the Orishas are said to end at his feet; that is why there is a saying "El Ebó llegó a Olofi" (The Ebó reached Olofi).
- He uses all Orishas to act as intermediaries/messengers; but only uses Osun as the messenger for death.

OLODDUMARE   **Olódùmarè**

- Oloddumare is the universe with all its elements. He is the manifestation of the material and the spiritual in everything that exists.
- He is everywhere, in all our acts, in the wisdom of Olofi and the goodness of all Orisha. He is also in the actions of Eshú, because Oloddumare is comprised of both good and bad.
- In the immensity that is Oloddumare, the Ará-Onú is also located. Ará-Onú is that part of the heavens where all the Eggun go to rest.

OLORUN   **Olórun**

- Olorun is the Sun, the most concrete, permanent and visible of the material manifestation of that which is Olofi and Oloddumare.
- It is the vital force for existence. Without it there would be no day or night, the waters would not move, crops would not grow, animals would not be born. He is the substance in this terrestrial plane.

The Warriors/The Guardian Orishas (Los Guerreros)

ELEGGUA   **ÈṢÙ ẸLẸGBÁRA**

- Elegguá is the Orisha with the keys to destiny. He can open or close the doors to either happiness or misfortune. He is the first to be prayed to and the first to eat. He is the "smallest/youngest" of all Orisha, but the biggest in rank after Olofi (God)
- Eleggua-Eshú constitute the mystic pair of the inevitable relation between the positive and the negative. When one behaves according to Divine law, he manipulates the forces of good, **ire**, and grants blessings. If, on the contrary, one behaves unduly, he opens the path for the evil forces such as **ofo, ikú, arún, eyó** (loss, death, disease, tragedy) amongst others and due punishment is rendered.
- He is the guardian of the door. He has 21 paths/avatars, although some say that he has as many as 121 paths/avatars.

- Syncretized with El Niño de Atocha (Holy Infant of Atocha), San Antonio de Padua (St. Anthony of Padua) and the Ánima Sola (Anima Sola or Lonely Soul).

OGGUN　　　　　　　ÒGÚN

- Oggún is from Iyesá Modduń, Nigeria. He is the Orisha of Iron and War. He is violent, but clever.
- He is the owner/god of minerals, the mountains and of metal implements. He is the patron of metal-workers, mechanics and soldiers. He is also the owners of the keys, the chains and the jails.
- In order for animal sacrifices to be done that involve a knife; the Olorisha/Iyalorisha must undergo a second initiation (called "Pinaldo") in order to wield the knife of Oggún.
- Oggún also possesses several paths/avatars
- Syncretized with San Pedro (Saint Peter), San Pablo (Paul the Apostle), San Juan Bautista (John the Baptist), San Miguel Arcángel (Saint Michael Archangel).

OCHOSI　　　　　　　ỌṢỌỌSÌ

- Ochosi is the patron of those that have problems with justice. He protects all those who are persecuted unjustly and punishes the guilty. He is a magician, clairvoyant, a warrior, a hunter and a fisherman.
- Ochosi has no paths/avatars.
- Syncretized with San Norberto (St. Norbert of Xanten) and San Alberto (Saint Albert the Great/Albert of Cologne/Albertus Magnus). In Santiago de Cuba he is syncretized with San Humberto (Saint Hubertus); who is the patron saint of hunters.

OSUN/OZUN

- Osún/Ozun is the Orisha that acts as the messenger for Obatalá and Olofi.
- He is received at the time one receives "Los Guerreros", but is NOT an Orisha that one possesses. He is the representation of the head of the person that receives it and as such, it is kept in a high place and should it fall, it is a portent of misfortune that needs to be addressed immediately. Represented by a cup with a rooster on top who is ever vigilant.
- Syncretized with the cane (bastón) of San Francisco (which represents the head, the soul) (Saint Francis of Paula), La Divina Providencia (Devine Providence), and San Juan Bautista (John the Baptist).

Orishas of Creation

ODDUA/ODUDUA/ODUDUWA　　　　ODÙDUÀ

- Oddúa/Odudúa/Oduduwa was the first king (Ooni of Ile-Ife) of the unified kingdom of Oyo. His progeny went on to create several kingdoms/dynasties; i.e.- the Owu kingdom (by the son of Obatalá and a daughter of Oddúa), The Ketu kingdom (by a son of his favorite wife), the kingdom of Ila-Yara (by his first legitimate son), the kingdom of Oyo-Ile (by his youngest son and father of Changó – Alaafin of Oyo). After his death he was deified into the Yoruba pantheon.

- He represents the mysteries and secrets of death, he is Orisha fúnfún (white/pure Orisha), owner of solitude and androgynous. He is the creator of moral rectitude, justice and truth.
- Syncretized with El Nombre de Jesús (the Name of Jesus) and with El Santísimo Sacramento (the Blessed Sacrament/Eucharist).

OBATALA   **ỌBÀTÁLÁ**

- Oba Obatalá was a king in Ife who was deposed by Oduduwa. His son went on to create the Owu kingdom.
- Obatalá is the creator of the earth (from the sea- he used a shell full of sand and a rooster to spread the earth as it was poured out), and the sculptor of man. He is the owner of all heads (todas las cabezas) and until an Orisha claims one, they belong to Obatalá.
- He is the intermediary between Orishas and a lover of peace. He alone can placate the anger of Changó and Oggún. All Orisha respect him. He is the owner of all that is white and is the oldest of the Orisha fúnfún.
- He has 16 paths or avatars, and half are male and the other female (although some say is close to 50 paths/avatars).
- Syncretized with La Virgen de las Mercedes/Virgen de la Merced (Our Lady of Mercy) and Jesús Nazareno (Jesus of Nazareth).

Orishas of Nature

OSAIN   **ÒSANYÌN**

- Osaín is the owner of the forest/nature and all the plants that grow in it. All of the plants have a different "Aché" (magical power) that is used in the different rituals for the Orishas. In effect, he is the owner of all the pharmacology that comes from plants in the forest, whether it is to heal or kill.
- The traditional healer-orisha who dwells in the forest. All of nature is at his disposal. Osaín is an indispensable orisha, for without his help, worship of the other orishas would not be possible. Without the necessary herbs provided by an Olú Osaín, the consecration of an orisha would be impossible. Osaín is the god of traditional medicine. All herbs the world-over are his property and it is he that provides them for the salvation of humankind. He also shares them with the other orishas.
- Phenomenal or grotesque in appearance, he is described as small in size, with only one eye, one hand, one foot, a tiny ear which enables him to hear an ant crawling miles away, and the other, larger than his head, through which he hears absolutely nothing. According to legend, he was not born so. His grotesque appearance is due to a conflict he encountered with Orúnmilá whereby the latter used Osaín's own magic to disfigure him so.
- Osaín has sixteen paths/avatars
- Syncretized with San Silvestre (Pope Sylvester/Saint Sylvester) and San Antonio Abad (Saint Anthony Abbot/Anthony the Great).

ORISHA OKO   **Òrìṣà-Okô**

- Orisha Oko is the deity of the earth, agriculture and the harvest.
- He is responsible for the harvest since without the harvest, the world would not eat; thereby considered and revered as an Orisha for fertility when women are unable to have children.
- Syncretized with San Isidro Labrador (Isidore the Laborer).

IROKO

- Irokó is the orisha of abundance and prosperity. He is believed to reside in the irokó tree—West African teak—but because of this tree's absence in Cuba, he is associated with the Ceiba. He lives in the foliage of the Ceiba with his wife Abomán and sister Ondó.
- All Orisha receive their offerings at the Ceiba/Irokó. All Eggun live in the Ceiba/Irokó.
- It is a very old Orisha which is no longer ordained (asentado) in Cuba.
- Syncretized with the Inmaculada Concepción (Immaculate Conception)

Orishas of Maternity

YEMAYA   **YEMỌJÁ**

- Yemayá is the Orisha of maternity. She governs everything pertaining to women; childbirth, conception, parenting, child safety, love, and healing. She oversees deep secrets, ancient wisdom, the moon, sea shells, and the collective unconscious. According to myth, when her waters broke, it caused a great flood creating rivers and streams and the first mortal humans were created from her womb.
- She is said to be able to cure infertility in women, and cowrie shells represent her wealth. She does not easily lose her temper, but when angered she can be quite destructive and violent, as the flood waters of turbulent rivers.
- Yemayá has 7 paths or avatars, although more are listed by Lydia Cabrera and by Natalia Bolívar Aróstegui.
- Syncretized with La Virgen the Regla (Our Lady of Regla)

IBEYIS   **Ìgbejì**

- Ibeyis are the patron Orisha of twins. They are the sons of Changó and Ochún, but raised by Yemayá. They are considered the patron of all children.
- The first twin born is named Taiwó—go out and taste the world. The second twin is called Kehindé—I shall follow. If the former indicates to the latter that life is a pleasant affair, Kehindé follows suit and is born. Taiwó is considered the youngest Ibejí and Kehindé is the older of the two.
- For inexplicable reasons, the Yoruba people have the highest incidence of twin births in the world.
- Syncretized with Santos Cosme y Damián (Saints Cosmas and Damian) when both are male; Santa Justa y Santa Rufina (Saints Justa and Rufina) when both are female

Orishas of the Waters

OCHUN   **ÒŞUN**

- Ochún was the princess consort of Changó, Alaafin of Oyo. She is also the Orisha of the Osun river in Nigeria.
- Ochún is the Yoruba Venus. The goddess of love, sexuality, beauty, and feminine flirtatiousness; patron of a river in Nigeria that bears her name.
- Nothing is impossible for Ochún. She is very kind, but can become very vindictive and rancorous when she encounters opposition. When she cries, she does so out of joy; when she laughs, she does so out of anger.
- The bees are her greatest friends that produce honey, the element that allows her to conquer all obstacles and tribulations.
- She has several paths/avatars; not all being the flirtatious, happy-go lucky type.
- Syncretized with La Virgen de La Caridad del Cobre (Our Lady of Charity)

OLOKUN   **Olóòkun**

- Olokun is the Orisha of the sea in its most terrifying aspect, he is the owner of the depths of the sea and all that it encompasses and contains.
- Olokun is represented as a mermaid carrying a mask (Somú Gagá/Somúgagá) in one hand and a snake (Akaró) in the other; representing Life and Death respectively.
- Olokun is androgynous; although some say he is a hermaphrodite (due to a Pattaki of Olokun and Orishaoko)
- There is NO syncretization.

INLE/ERINLE   **ÍNLÈ**

- Inle/Erinlé is the Orisha of health and medical healing.
- He is supposed to have had a relationship with Yemayá and after learning all her secrets, she cut his tongue out and for that reason he talks only through Yemayá's shells.
- Ochún and Inle had a son, Loggún-Eddé
- His inseparable companion is his brother, Abbata.
- Syncretized with El Arcángel Rafael (Archangel Rafael)

Orishas of the Fire

CHANGO   **ŞÀNGÓ**

- Changó was the third Alaafin of Oyo (Emperor of the kingdom of Oyo, Nigeria).
- Changó is the god of fire, lighting, thunder, war, of the Batá (drums), dance, music and virility.
- He is both one of the most venerated and most feared of the Orishas.
- Changó has many paths/avatars. He was both benign or violent; rich and poor.
- Syncretized with Santa Bárbara (Saint Barbara)

AGGAYU SOLA   **Aginjù Solá**

- Aggayú-Solá is the god of the volcano, the desert and of the arid earth.
- He is the protector of the travelers.
- He has several paths/avatars.
- Syncretized with San Cristóbal (Saint Christopher) – Patron Saint of Havana.

Orisha od Divination

ORULA/ORUNMILA   **ÒRÚNMÌLÀ**

- Orula is the Orisha wisdom, knowledge and divination.
- He possesses the secret of Ifá through which it allows humanity (and orishas) to know their future and how to affect it.
- Syncretized with San Francisco de Asís (Saint Francis of Assisi)

Orishas of Health and Death

OYA YANSA   **ỌYA YÁNSÀN**

- Oyá Yansá is the orisha of winds, lightning, and violent storms, death and rebirth.
- She is the owner of the Niger river (known as Odo-Ọya) because it traditionally has nine (9) tributaries.
- She is the owner of the cemetery
- She loves to fight and is always next to Changó in any battle; and is able to use the lightning bolt
- She has 23 paths/avatars
- Syncretized with La Virgen de la Candelaria (Our Lady of Candelaria), La Virgen del Carmen (Our Lady of Mount Carmel) and Santa Teresa de Jesús (Saint Teresa of Ávila)

OBBA   **ỌBÁ**

- Obba is the Orisha of the Oba river near Igbon, Nigeria.
- She is traditionally identified as the third wife of Changó.
- She is the owner of lakes and lagoons and guardian of the tombs in the cemetery after she was repudiated by Changó for cutting her ear.
- Syncretized with Santa Rita de Casia (Saint Rita of Cascia), Santa Catalina de Siena (Saint Catherine of Siena) and La Virgen del Carmen (Our Lady of Mount Carmel)

YEWA   **Yèwá**

- Yewá is the Orisha of the Yewá river, a trans-boundary river between the Republic of Benin and Nigeria, running along the Bight of Benin.
- She is the Orisha of the grave. She lives inside the cemetery within the tombs and the dead and is in charge of giving the bodies of the deceased to Oyá.
- She is very caste/pure and demands the same from her followers

- She has several paths/avatars.
- Syncretized with Nuestra Señora de los Desamparados (Our Lady of the Forsaken), Nuestra Señora de Monserrate (Our Lady of Montserrat/Virgin of Montserrat), La Virgen de los Dolores (Our Lady of Sorrows) and Santa Clara de Asís (Saint Clare of Assisi).

NANA BURUKU   **NÀNÁ BÙKÙÚ**

- The cult of Naná Burukú is of Fon, Ewe, Ashanti and Mahi (i.e.-Arará) descent.
- Due to a conflict with Oggún, her sacrifices (and cutting) can only be done with a knife that is not metal; the usual case being a knife made out of bamboo.
- She assumes the form of a snake and lives among the rivers and marshlands within the bamboo stands.
- In the Yoruba cult she is considered the grandmother of all Obatalá.
- Like Obatalá she is both male and female.
- Syncretized with Santa Ana (Saint Anne, mother of Mary and grandmother of Jesus)

BABALU AYE   **OBALUAÊ**

- Babalú-Ayé is an Orisha strongly associated with epidemics, infectious disease and healing.
- He is a much revered and venerated Orisha, but which has the terrible power of sickness and the ability to cure it.
- Venerated in Africa by the Yoruba, Fon and Ewe people.
- He has several paths/avatars.
- Syncretized with San Lázaro (Lazarus the Leper from the Gospel of Luke)

Other Deities and Orishas

EGGUN

- Eggun represent the spirit of our forefathers (African ancestors), ancestors, dead Babalawos, dead Babalochas and Iyalochas, dead family members and those spirits that decide to help us in our lives.
- In ALL houses (Ocha temples), the first to be saluted and mentioned are the Eggun.
- In ALL ceremonies, they are the first to be fed, although separate from the Orisha.
- The Eggun can be consulted by way of the Obí (coconut), Spiritual Mass and with the shells of Eleggua.
- There is a saying about the Eggun: "Ikú lobi ocha: Eggun gave life to Ocha"

ABITA

- Abita is considered a Yoruba minor deity.
- Per se; the Yoruba do not have a dichotomy as to Good and Evil. What they have is that there are both positive and negative forces and some are more inherently negative.
- Abita is the manifestation of all that is bad, and its vast power.
- Syncretized with El Diablo/Lucifer (the Devil, Lucifer)

The Sacred Divinities of Regla Conga and their syncretism with Catholic and Yoruba Entities.

Supreme Beings

Nzámbi, Nsambi, Sambia, Nsambiampungo, Pungun Sambia, Sambia Liri, Sambia Surukuru, Sambi Bilongo
- It is the Supreme being, the creator of the Universe. He embodies all that is good.
- He is syncretized with Olofi/Olorun in Yoruba mythology.

Lungombe, Lukankanse, Kadiampembe, Lukankazi
- Negative entity. Per se; the Congo religion has NO Devil, just an entity that represents the negative aspects and actions in the world.
- He is syncretized with the Devil in Catholic beliefs and with Abita in Yoruba mythology

Mpungus

Nkuyu Nfinda, Lucero, Lucero Mundo, Nkuyo, Mañunga, Lubaniba
- Deity of the pathways, who can open or close them.
- As **Remolino Cuatro Vientos and Lucero Mundo** he represents the good benefits in the force of the wind.
- As **Viento Malo, Nkuyo** (El Ánima Sola/Elegguá Alaguana) he represents the bad in the force of the winds.
- Syncretized with El Niño de Atocha in Catholic beliefs and with Eleggua/Eshú in Yoruba mythology.

Siete Rayos, Nsasi, Mukiamamuilo, Mukiama Muilo, Nkita Kitán
- He is the God of lighting and fire. He also represents all the imperfections and virtues in humanity as well as male virility.
- He is syncretized with Santa Bárbara in Catholic beliefs and with Changó in Yoruba mythology.

Sarabanda, Zarabanda, Rompe Monte, Pungo Dibudi, Mpúngu Mbüudi
- God of metals (forge, etc.), work and fire.
- He is syncretized with San Pedro in Catholic beliefs and Oggún in Yoruba mythology.

Watariamba, Nkuyo Watariamba, Pajarito, Surumba Mukalla, Nguatariamba Enfumba Bata, Saca Empeño, Cabo Rondo, Vence Batalla
- He is the God of the Hunt and order.
- He is syncretized with San Juan Bautista in Catholic beliefs and with Ochosi in Yoruba mythology.

Lufo Kuyu
- The union of Oggún and Ochosi in one

Baluandé, Madre de Agua, Kisimbi Masa, Mamá Kalunga, Mamá Umba, Mbumba Mamba, Mboma, Nkita Kiamasa, Nkita Kuna Masa, Nkita Kuna Mamba, Pungo Kasimba
- Goddess of the water and fertility. She represents the forces of the water and maternity.
- Syncretized with La Virgen de Regla in Catholic beliefs and with Yemayá in Yoruba mythology.

Choya Wengue, Mamá Chola, Chola Wengue
- Goddess of pleasure and wealth. She represents the forces of wealth and carnal pleasure.
- Syncretized with La Virgen de La Caridad del Cobre in Catholic beliefs and with Ochún in Yoruba mythology.

Mariwanga, Centella Ndoki, Pungu Mama Wanga, Mpungu Mamá Wánga, Mariwara, Mama Linda, Campo Santo, Kariempebe,
- Guardian of the door between life and death. She represents the force of death.
- Syncretized with Santa Teresa de Jesús/Virgen de la Candelaria in Catholic beliefs and with Oyá Yánsa in Yoruba mythology.

Tiembla Tierra, Iña Ñaába, Mama Kengue, Ma Kengue, Yeyé, Pandilanga
- God of wisdom, knowledge and justice.
- He is syncretized with La Virgen de La Merced/Virgen de las Mercedes in Catholic beliefs and with Obatalá in Yoruba mythology.

Gurunfinda, Sindaula Ndudu Yambaka Bután Séke, Sindaula Ndudu Yambaka Butá Nseke
- He is the God of the forest and ALL the plants that grow in it. He represents the force of vegetation in all its forms.
- Syncretized with San Norberto or San Silvestre in Catholic beliefs and with Osain in Yoruba mythology.

Brazo Fuerte, Quendú, Bola del Mundo, Cabo de Guerra
- God of the volcano and the desert
- Syncretized with San Cristóbal in Catholic beliefs and Aggayú-Solá in Yoruba mythology

Kobayende, Cobayende, Pata Llaga, Tata Kañeñe, Tata Pansua, Mpungu Fútila, Pungún Fútila, Pungu Nfútilla, Pungu Mfútila, Tata Fumbe, Tata Funde, Tata Nfumbe
- He is the God of sickness and pestilence. He represents the force of sickness and pestilence.
- He is syncretized with San Lazaro in Catholic beliefs and with Babalú-Ayé in Yoruba mythology.

Nsambia Munalembe, Tonde, Cuatro Vientos, Kimbabula, Kabanga, Madioma, Mpungo Lomboán Fula, Mpungo Lombua Mfula, Daday, Munalendo, Padre Tiempo
- God of divination.
- Syncretized with San Francisco de Asís in Catholic beliefs and Orula/Orunmila in Yoruba mythology.

Mayúmbo Moúngu Mpúngu
- The twins, yet not the playful ones from Yoruba mythology.
- Mayúmba - Nkisi that causes madness, sadness
- Mpúngu - Nkisi that cures it
- Syncretized with Santos Cosme y Damian in Catholic beliefs and with Ibeyis in Yoruba mythology

Nkita Kinseke, Nkita Minseke
- Not a particular Nkisi, but those Nkisi that live in the jungles, the plains.

Nkita Kiamasa, Nkita Kiamamba
- Not a particular Nkisi, but those Nkisi that live in the water.

The Sacred Divinities of Yoruba pantheon in Brazil and their syncretism with Catholic Entities.

OLODUMARE   **Olódùmarè/Olórun**

- Above the Orixá reigns a supreme god, Olodumaré, whose etymology is doubtful.
- Olodumaré lives in a dimension, parallel to ours known as Òrun (Òrun is the spiritual world, whereas Àiyé is the physical world; everything that exist in Òrun exists in Àiyé through the Òrun -Àiyé dual existance) and also known as Olórun.
- It is a distant god, inaccessible and indifferent to the prayers and destiny of men. It's out of reach of human understanding. He created the orishas to govern and oversee the world. It is to them, then, that men should direct their prayers and make offerings.
- Olodumaré, however, agrees to judge any disagreements that may arise between the Orixá.

OBATALÁ   **OBATALÁ/OXALÁ/ÒRÌṢÀNLÁ/ỌBÀTÁLÁ**

- Òrìsànlá or Obàtálá, "The Great Òrìsà" or "The King of White Cloth", in Yoruba mythology, is the creator of the world, of men, animals and plants. It was the first Orixá created by Olodumaré and is considered the greatest of all Orixás.
- Obatalá is the direct son of Olórun the creator of the universe. Once Olórun created the universe and the earth, after thousands of years he decided to give life to the earth and sent his direct son "Obatalá" to this end to the land that until then was composed of water. Coming with the bag of earth Obatalá brought with him a guinea fowl that was responsible for spreading the earth over the waters, thus forming the earth over the water, after creating the mounds etc ... Obatalá created the vegetables, animals and finally of the creation itself "earth" with the help of Nanã shaped the human being with the clay and with its breath gave life to the human being.
- Oxalá is a generic name for the Orixá funfun (White). As such, there are 154 paths/avatars
  - Of note is that Orixá Okô is considered an avatar (i.e.- Òrìṣá in Okô)
- Syncretized with Senhor do Bonfim na Bahia (Lord of Bonfin of Bahia)

ORUNMILÁ   **ÒRÚNMÌLÀ**

- Orunmilá is in the tradition of Ifé the first companion and "Chief Counselor" of Odùduà upon his arrival in Ifé.
- Despite their high positions, Orunmilá and Olodumaré, consults Ifá on certain ceremonies, to know what their fate holds.
- Two systems allow the Babalawo to find the sign of Ifá that is being sought, the key to the problem presented by the consultant. One of them is the Ikin Ifá and the other is the Ọpẹlẹ Ifá.

EXU ELEGBARÁ   **ÈṢÙ ẸLẸGBÁRA**

- Exú is an orisha of multiple and contradictory aspects, which makes it difficult define it coherently.
- Of irascible character, he likes to arouse dissension and disputes, to provoke accidents and calamities public and private. It is crafty, rude, vain, indecent, to such an extent that the early missionaries, frightened by these characteristics compared it to the devil.
- However, Exú has his good side and, if he is treated with consideration, reacts favorably, being helpful. If, on the contrary, people become forgetting to offer sacrifices and offerings, you can expect all catastrophes
- Exú proves to be, perhaps, in this way the most human. Not completely bad, not completely good.
- He has 7 paths/avatars or 21 paths/avatars, depending on the "Casa de Santo"

OGUM   **ÒGÚN**

- Ogum in Brazil is known, above all, as the God of warriors.
- He is the Lord of iron, war, agriculture and technology
- Ogum possesses several paths/avatars
- Syncretized with São Jorge (Saint George of Cappadocia) in Rio de Janeiro and with Santo Antônio de Pádua (Saint Anthony of Padua) in Bahia

OXÓSSI   **ỌṢỌỌSÌ**

- Oxóssi is the Orixá of hunting, forests, animals, abundance, sustenance
- In Bahia it is said that he was once King of Ketu, where he was once worshipped.
- Ochosi has several paths/avatars.
- Syncretized Arcanjo Miguel (Saint Michael Archangel) in Pernambuco and with São Jorge (Saint George of Cappadocia) in Bahia.

OSSAIM   **ÒSANYÌN**

- Ossaim is the deity of medicinal and liturgical plants. Its importance is fundamental, since no ceremony can be performed without his presence, he being the holder of Axé (power, energy, force), indispensable even to the gods themselves
- Each orisha has its leaf, but only Ossaim holds its secrets. And without the leaves and their secrets there is no Axé, so without it no ceremony is possible.
- There is a saying: "Cosi Ewé, Cosi Orixá: Without leaves, there is no Orixá"

XANGÔ   ṢÀNGÓ

- Xangô was the third Alaafin of Oyo (Emperor of the kingdom of Oyo, Nigeria).
- Xangô is the Orixá of lightning, thunder, large electrical charges and fire. He is virile and bold, violent and righteous; He punishes liars, thieves and evildoers.
- Many Orixá have a relationship with the Egunguns but he is the only one who truly exercises power over the dead.
- Xangô has many paths/avatars.
- Syncretized with Santo António (Saint Anthony of Padua) and São Jerônimo (Saint Jerome)

IEMANJÁ   YEMỌJÁ

- Iemanjá whose name derives from Yèyé ọmọ ẹjá ("Mother whose children are fish"), is a deity of the Ẹgbá people and the Orixá of fertility; originally associated with rivers and their confluence into the ocean.
- Iemanjá is the daughter of Olóòkun, a male god in Benin and a female goddess in Ifé.
- She is called the "Mother of all Orixá" and represents the female parent power; it is she who gives birth to us, a deity that is universal motherhood, the Mother of the World.
- Yemayá has several paths/avatars.
- Syncretized with Nossa Senhora da Imaculada Conceição (Immaculate Concepction) in Bahia and with Nossa Senhora dos Navegantes (Our Lady of Navigators/Our Lady of Seafarers) in Rio Grande and Porto Alegre.

OXUM   ÒṢUN

- Oxum is the Orixá of the Osun river in Nigeria and second wife of Xangô.
- She is the Orixá who reigns over the fresh water of rivers, being considered the mistress of beauty, river water, love, and closely linked to wealth, vanity, and feminine power.
- Oxum is called Ìyálóòde, title given to the most important woman in the town
- She has several paths/avatars.
- Syncretized with Nossa Senhora das Candeias (the Virgin of Candelaria) and with Nossa Senhora dos Prazeres (Our Lady of Prazeres/Pleasures) in Bahia

OYA YANSA   ỌYA YÁNSÀN

- Oiá or Iansã is the orisha of winds, lightning, and violent storms.
- She is associated with the cult of Egun; where she is commissioned to receive them from Xangô in order to guide them to one of the nine heavens, according to their deeds.
- She is usually revered before Xangô, like the personified wind that precedes the storm
- She has many paths/avatars
- Syncretized with Santa Bárbara de Nicomédia (Saint Barbara) in Bahia

OBÁ   **ỌBÁ**

- Obá is the Orisha of the Obá river and third wife of Xangô
- Obá represents the raging waters of rivers and the strong confluence of the waters of the rivers and the salt water of the ocean. She also controls mud, standing waters, mud sludge and floods.
- Obá is an energetic, strong and feared female Orixá, stronger than many male Orixá and said to have won a fight with Oxalá, Oyá, Oxumarê, Exú e Orumilá; thereby representing the masculine aspect of women (physically)
- Obá cut her ear at the behest and trickery of Oxum, and served it to Xangô.
- Syncretized with Santa Catarina (due to the many Saint Catherine's, it can be Saint Catherine of Siena, Saint Catherine of Alexandria, Saint Catherine of Bologna or Saint Catherine of Genoa)

NANÃ BURUKU   **NÀNÁ BURUKU/NÀNÁ BÙKÙÚ/NÀNÁ BRUKUNG**

- Nanã Buruku is the Orixá rain, mangroves, swamp, mud, mistress of death, and responsible for entry (reincarnation) and exit (disincarnating) portals
- Like Obaluaiyê, she is of Mahi origin and prior to Odùduà and its religious system
- Sacrifices to Nanã cannot be done with metal implements.
- Syncretized with Santa Ana, mãe de Maria (Saint Anne, mother of Mary and grandmother of Jesus)

OBALUAÊ   **OMOLU/XAPANÃ/ỌBALÚAYÉ/ỌMỌLU/ṢÀNPÒNNÁ**

- Obaluaiyê (King and Owner of the Earth), Omolu (King and owner of Life) are the names generally given to Xapanã, god of smallpox and contagious diseases, whose name is dangerous to be pronounced. Better defined, he is the one who punishes the evildoers and insolents giving/sending to them the smallpox.
- He demands respect and gratitude even when he claims a victim, and so people sometimes honor him with the name of praise Alápa-dúpé, which means "He who dies and is grateful for it."
- He is of Mahi origin and prior to Odùduà and its religious system
- Syncretized with São Roque (Saint Roch/Rocco) in Bahia and São Sebastião (Saint Sebastian) in Recife and Rio de Janeiro

OXUMARÉ   **ÒṢÙMÀRÈ**

- Oxumarê is the Orixá of wealth and fortune and represented by the rainbow and a snake.
- He is the symbol of continuity and permanence and sometimes is represented as the serpent that coils and bites its own tail
- He is both masculine and feminine and is of Mahi origin.
- Syncretized with São Bartolomeu (Bartholomew the Apostle)

IBEJI   **Ìgbejì**

- Ibeji is a conjunction of two Yoruba words: Ibi (birth) and Eji (two).
- Ibeji are the twin Orixá of life and protector of twins.
- The first is named Taiwo and the second Kahinde. The Yuruba believe that it was Kehinde who had Taiwo oversee the world, hence the hypothesis that he was the older brother.
- Because they are twins, they are associated with the principle of duality; being children, they are linked to everything that starts and begins: the source of a river, the birth of human beings, the germination of plants, etc.
- Syncretized with Santos Cosme e Damião (Saints Cosmas and Damian)

ÍNLÈ-ÍBUÀLÁMÒ   **Erinlẹ-Ibùalámọ**

- Inlé is of Ijexá origin, named for the river Erinlẹ
- He is a young hunter, and has his cult on the banks of the river Erinlẹ. He is known as an elephant hunter; the ivory is his business.
- Ibaluama is an old hunter, and has his cult in the deep waters of the river Erinlẹ
- Both are associated with qualities/paths/avatars for Oxóssi in Brazil

LOGUNEDE   **Lógunẹde**

- Logunedé is of Ijexá origin
- He is the son of Oxum Ipondá and Oxóssi Ibualama. According to legends, he lives six months in the woods hunting with Oxossi and six months in the rivers fishing with Oxum.
- Syncretized with São Expedito (Saint Expeditus) in Bahia.

IROCO   **IROKO**

- Iroco is an Orixa and treated as such, especially in houses of Ketu origin.
- For the Yoruba, the Iroco tree is the home of Abikú children's spirits.
- The worship of Iroco is one of the most popular in the Yoruba land and relations with this deity are almost always based on exchange: a request made, when answered, must always be paid because one should not risk displeasing Iroco, as he usually pursues those who owe

IYEWA   **Yèwá**

- Iyewa is the Orisha of the Yewá river, a trans-boundary river between the Republic of Benin and Nigeria, running along the Bight of Benin.
- Iyewa is also known as the lady of possibilities, possessing the power of invisibility and mimicry.
- She has few followers in Brazil due to the complexity of the rituals. Mostly seen in old houses/temples in Bahia where the last initiation was done was in 1981 after more than 30 years ago.

AJE SALUGA   **Ajé Salúgá/Ajê Xalugá**

- Ajê Salugá is a feminine African orisha
- She is the Orixá of wealth, harmony, owner of the prosperity of the world
- She is a calm, harmonious and patient orisha.

IYAMI AJE   **Ìyáàmi-Ajé/ Ìyáàmi Oxorongá**

- Iyami-Ajé (My Witch Mother) it is the sacralization of the mother figure, so its worship is enveloped by many taboos.
- Its great power is because it keeps the secret of creation (giving birth).
- The power of great mothers is expressed among the orishas by Oxum, Iemanjá, and Nanã Buruku, but the power of Iyá-Mi is manifest in every woman, who, not by chance, in almost every culture, is considered taboo.

The main Minkisi (plural of Nkisi) in Brazil.

Aluvaiá, Pambu Njila, Vangira, Maviletanga

- Lord of the roads and crossroads, lord of fertility and guardian of the home.
- Intermediary between other Mkisi and humanity.
- Some cults say that there is a female version called Panjira or Vanjira
- Syncretized with Exú

Nkosi, Roxo Mukumbi, Panzuá, Xauê

- Nkisi of war and Lord of the dirt roads, Nkisi of iron and forge, Lord of metals and patron of blacksmiths
- Syncretized with Ogum

Mukongo

- it encompasses the energies of hunters, cattle breeders, herders and those who live deep in the woods, dominating the parts where the sun does not penetrate.

Kabila

- Nkisi linked to the forest. He is a shepherd/hunter who also takes care of the herds for Mutalambô
- Syncretized with Oxóssi

Mutalambô, Lembaranguange, Teleku-mpensu

- Nkisi hunter, who lives in forests and mountains, is the Nkisi of abundance and abundant food.
- Syncretized as Oxóssi.

Gongobira or Ngongobila

- Nkisi of sensuality, wealth, abundance, fishing and hunting
- Syncretized with Logun Edé

Katendê

- Lord of the forests and sacred leaves. Lord of divine alchemy.
- Syncretized with Ossaim

Nzazi, Kambarangunange

- It is lightning itself and fire, lord of justice among human beings
- Syncretized with Xangô

Kavungo, Kafungê or Kafunjê, Kingongo, Kafundeji

- Nkisi of smallpox, skin diseases, health and death
- Syncretized with Obaluaiyê/Omolu

Hongolo or Angorô (MALE); Angoroméa or Zingalumbondo (FEMALE)

- Nkisi that aids communication between humans and deities. It is a type of snake that has a very characteristic color on its leather and similar to the color of the rainbow.
- Syncretized with Oxumarê

Kindembu, Tempo

- Lord of time and the seasons.
- Nkisi of transformations, which guides his nomadic people through his white flag, so everyone, no matter how far away, can join the leader, because his flagpole is so high that it can be seen from anywhere.
- Syncretized with Irôko/Loko

Kaiangô

- It is the energy of the wind, that is, Kaiangô is the wind itself. It is the manifestation arising from the cooling of the earth as the magma cooled and the rains took place. Command the Nvumbe (spirits of those who have died) through their winds, guiding them to the proper place for each
- Syncretized with Oyá/Iansã

Matamba, Bamburucenda, Nunvurusemavula

- Lady of the tempests and the storms.
- Commands the Nvumbe (spirits of the dead)
- Syncretized with Oyá/Iansã

Kisimbi, Samba Nkisi, Mina Lugando

- Nkisi of lakes and rivers. The great mother.
- The representation fertility, maternity, female womb, wealth, family
- Syncretized with Oxum

Dandalunda, Ndanda Lunda

- Considered the lady of fertility and the moon.
- Lady of riches linked to gold, female tantrums, fertility, labor, and birth
- Syncretized with either Oxum or Jemanjá

Kaitumba, Kayaya, Kok'eto

- Female Nkisi of the saltwaters, seas, oceans

Nzumbarandá, Nzumba, Zumbarandá, Ganzumba

- It is the oldest of the Nkisi, it is related to the mud that appears in the ravines on rainy days.
- Syncretized with Nanã Buruku.

Nvunji, Nvungi, Wunji, Vungi, Wunje, Wunge

- It is the youngest of the Nkisi. t is the deity of play, of joy, its regency is linked to childhood. Represents youth, the joy of youth
- Syncretized with Ibeji

Lembá Dilê, Lembarenganga, Jakatamba, Nkasuté Lembá, Gangaiobanda

- First Nkisi created by Zambi. His color is white.
- Syncretized with Oxalá

Nzambi, Zambi, Nzambi Mpungu, Zambiapongo, Zambiampungu, Zambuipombo, Zambe-o-pombo, Zambiapungo, Zamiapombo, Zamuripongo, Zâmbi

- Supreme god. Creator of everything.
- Syncretized with Olórun/Olódùmarè

EWE that belong to each Orisha (to make Omiero *); per Teodoro Díaz Fabelo "Lengua de Santeros (Guiné Góongorí); 1956".

PLANT NAME-CUBA	SCIENTIFIC NAME	PAGE#
ELEGGUA		PAGE#
Abre Camino, Filigrana	Koanophyllon villosum (Sw.) R.M. King & H. Rob.	3
Aceitero	Zanthoxylum flavum Vahl	12
Agalla de Costa	Randia aculeata L.	16
Aguacatero Blanco	Persea americana Mill.	19
Ají Chileno	Capsicum annuum L.	24
Ají de China	Solanum havanense Jacq.	25
Ají Güagüao	Capsicum baccatum L.	27
Albahaca de Hoja Ancha	Ocimum basilicum L.;	38
Alcanfor	Cinnamomum camphora (L.) J.Presl	41
Almácigo	Bursera simaruba (L.) Sarg.	44
Aretillo	Savia sessiliflora (Sw.) Willd.	69
Aroma Amarilla, Aroma Olorosa	Acacia farnesiana (L.) Willd.	70
Aroma Uña de Gato	Pithecellobium unguis-cati (L.) Benth.	73
Artemisa	Ambrosia artemisiifolia L.	75
Atikuánla/**Atipolá Macho** *	Boerhavia diffusa L.	83
Bejuco Colorado	Serjania diversifolia (Jacq.) Radlk.	100
Bejuco Guaro	**Fischeria crispiflora K.Schum.**	**N/A**
Bejuco Jimagua, Parra Cimarrona	Vitis tiliifolia Humb. & Bonpl. ex Schult.	110
Bejuco Lombriz	Philodendron consanguineum Schott	112
Bejuco Prieto	Serjania subdentata Juss. ex Poir.	117
Bejuco Sabanero	Stigmaphyllon diversifolium (Kunth) A. Juss.	118
Bejuco San Pedro	Stigmaphyllon diversifolium (Kunth) A. Juss.	119
Bejuco Verraco	Chiococca alba (L.) Hitchc.	122
Bibona/Vibona	Dendropanax arboreus (L.) Decne. & Planch.	126
Bija	Bixa orellana L.	127
Carraspita	Iberis odorata L.	189
Caumao	Petesiodes clusiifolium (Sw.) Kuntze	192
Cayaya	Tournefortia bicolor Sw.	194
Chamico	Datura stramonium L.	204
Chichicate	Urera baccifera (L.) Gaudich. ex Wedd.	209
Croto/s	Codiaeum variegatum (L.) Rumph. ex A.Juss.	238
Curujey	**VARIOUS**	247
Ébano Carbonero	Diospyros crassinervis (Krug & Urb.) Standl.	255
Escoba Cimarrona	Abutilon trisulcatum (Jacq.) Urb.	260
Espartillo *	Sporobolus indicus (L.) R.Br.	262
Espinillo	Parkinsonia aculeata L.	265
Espuela de Caballero	Jacquinia aculeata Mez	266

Flor de Agua/Lechuguilla	Pistia stratiotes L.	374
Gambute, Gambutera	Brachiaria platyphylla (Munro ex C.Wright) Nash	287
Gateado	Brosimum alicastrum Sw.	288
Grama de Caballo *	Eleusine indica (L.) Gaertn.	494
Guabico/Guabico de Costa	Xylopia obtusifolia Hook.f. & Thomson	299
Guajaca	Tillandsia usneoides (L.) L.	308
Guao	Comocladia dentata Jacq.	318
Guayaba	Psidium guajava L.	323
Guayabillo	Pithecellobium lentiscifolium C. Wright	325
Irú	**?????**	**N/A**
Itamo Real	Euphorbia tithymaloides L.	350
Lengua de Vaca	Sansevieria hyacinthoides (L.) Druce	375
Maloja/Maíz	Zea mays L.	387
Mastuerzo	Lepidium virginicum L.	419
Meloncillo	Melothria pendula L.	426
Mije	**Eugenia rhombea (O.Berg) Krug & Urb.**	**N/A**
Ñame/Ñame de Cuba	Dioscorea cayennensis subsp. rotundata (Poir.) J.Miège	440
Ojo de Ratón	Rivina humilis L.	447
Palo Diablo	Quadrella cynophallophora (L.) Hutch.	469
Palo Moro	Psychotria obovalis A.Rich./Psychotria glabrata Sw.	476
Palo Negro	Haematoxylum campechianum L.	478
Palo Torcido	Acacia tenuifolia (L.) Willd.	485
Palo Víbora/Víbora	Bryophyllum pinnatum (Lam.) Oken	608
Pastillo	Paspalum notatum Flüggé	493
Pata de Gallina *	Eleusine indica (L.) Gaertn.	494
Pendejera	Solanum torvum Sw.	497
Pica-Pica	Mucuna pruriens (L.) DC.	504
Picha de Gato/P. de Negro	Dieffenbachia seguine (Jacq.) Schott	511
Piñi-Piñi	Morinda royoc L.	517
Piñón Botija	Jatropha curcas L.	518
Piñón Criollo	Jatropha curcas L.	518
Piñón de Pito	Erythrina berteroana Urb.	520
Piñón Lechoso	Jatropha curcas L.	521
Rabo de Gato	Achyranthes aspera L.	536
Raspa Lengua	Casearia hirsuta Sw.	538
Rompezaragüey	Chromolaena odorata (L.) R.M.King & H.Rob.	546
Salvadera	Hura crepitans L.	556
Siguaraya	Trichilia havanensis Jacq.	570
Tabaco	Nicotiana tabacum L.	573
Tengue	Poeppigia procera C.Presl	577
Travesura/Travesera	Koanophyllon villosum (Sw.) R.M.King & H.Rob.	584
Tripa de Jutia	Stigmaphyllon sagraeanum A. Juss.	587
Varía/Baría	Cordia gerascanthus L.	91

Genjibre	Zingiber officinale Roscoe	290
Grajo	Eugenia axillaris (Sw.) Willd.	294
Granadillo	Brya ebenus (L.) DC.	296
Guabari	**??????**	**N/A**
Guao	Comocladia dentata Jacq.	318
Guayabillo	Chloroleucon mangense var. lentiscifolium (C.Wright) …	325
Guisaso de Caballo	Xanthium strumarium L.	331
Jagüey	Ficus membranacea C.Wright.	354
Jocuma	Sideroxylon foetidissimum Jacq.	365
Maíz	Zea mays L.	387
Manopilón	Mouriri valenzuelana A. Rich.	409
Palo Amargo	Picramnia reticulata Griseb.	454
Palo Bomba	Xylopia obtusifolia (A.DC.) A.Rich.	459
Palo Bronco	Malpighia glabra L.	460
Palo Cavo/Palo Clavo	Syzygium aromaticum (L.) Merr. & L.M.Perry	467
Palo Cochino	Tetragastris balsamifera (Sw.) Oken	468
Palo Guitarra	Citharexylum caudatum L.	470
Palo Rompe Hueso	Casearia sylvestris Sw.	480
Pata de Gallina *	Eleusine indica (L.) Gaertn.	494
Picha de Gato/P. de Negro	Dieffenbachia seguine (Jacq.) Schott	511
Pimienta	Pimenta dioica (L.) Merr.	505
Pimienta China	Zanthoxylum simulans Hance	506
Pimienta Negra	Piper nigrum L.	505
Piñón Lechoso	Jatropha curcas L.	521
Quiebra Hacha	Guibourtia hymenaefolia (Moric.) J.Leonard	532
Tabaco	Nicotiana tabacum L.	573
Yerba de la Sangre *	Cordia bullata var. globosa (Jacq.) Govaerts	630
Yerba Díez del Día	Portulaca pilosa L.	634
Yerba Mora	Solanum americanum Mill.	641
Yuca	Manihot esculenta Crantz	643
Zarza Blanca	Celtis iguanaea (Jacq.) Sarg.	645

OSUN   **PAGE#**

Albahaca Cimarrona	Ocimum gratissimum L.	35
Daguilla	**Lagetta lagetto (Sw.) Nash**	**N/A**

OSAIN   **PAGE#**

Ají Agujeta	Capsicum baccatum L.	23
Ají de China	Solanum havanense Jacq.	25
Ají Güagüao	Capsicum baccatum L.	27
Artemisa	Ambrosia artemisiifolia L.	75

Palo Manajú/Manajú	Garcinia aristata (Griseb.) Borhidi	403
Pegojo	Tabernaemontana citrifolia L.	343
Romerillo	Bidens pilosa L.	543
Rompezaragüey	Chromolaena odorata (L.) R.M.King & H.Rob.	546
Uva Gomosa	Cordia alba (Jacq.) Roem. & Schult.	595
Yankoró	**????**	**N/A**

ORULA   PAGE#

Acediana, Arcediana	Celosia argentea L.	11
Aceitunillo	Beilschmiedia pendula (Sw.) Hemsl.	13
Aguinaldo Morado *	Ipomoea crassicaulis (Benth.) B.L. Rob.	22
Albahaca Menuda	Ocimum minimum L.	37
Almorejo	Pennisetum glaucum (L.) R.Br.	47
Altea	Hibiscus syriacus L.	48
Arabo	Erythroxylum havanense Jacq.	57
Arabo Colorado	Erythroxylum confusum Britton	58
Astronomía	Lagerstroemia indica L.	77
Bastón de San Francisco	Leonotis nepetifolia (L.) R.Br.	92
Bejuco de Fideos	Cuscuta americana L.	105
Coco-**Corteza de Coco de Agua**	Cocos nucifera L.	218
Colonia	Alpinia zerumbet (Pers.) B.L.Burtt & R.M.Sm.	223
Copey	Clusia rosea Jacq.	229
Galán de Noche	Cestrum nocturnum L.	286
Ojo de Profeta	Thunbergia alata Bojer ex Sims	446
Paraíso	Melia azedarach L.	490

CHANGO   PAGE#

Ácana	Manilkara valenzuelana (A.Rich.) T.D.Penn.	9
Aguacatero Blanco *	Persea americana Mill.	19
Álamo,Álamo Melodioso	Ficus religiosa L.	32
Alcanfor	Cinnamomum camphora (L.) J.Presl	41
Algarrobo	Albizia saman (Jacq.) Merr.	42
Almácigo	Bursera simaruba (L.) Sarg.	44
Arabo	Erythroxylum havanense Jacq.	57
Arabo Colorado	Erythroxylum confusum Britton	58
Atipolá (**Morada**) *	Boerhavia diffusa L.	83
Bejuco Carey	Tetracera volubilis L.	99
Bejuco Colorado	Serjania diversifolia (Jacq.) Radlk.	100
Bejuco Tortuga/de Tortuga	**Bauhinia glabra Jacq.**	**N/A**
Bija	Bixa orellana L.	127
Bledo Blanco	Amaranthus viridis L.	129

Cabina	Garcinia aristata (Griseb.) Borhidi	141
Cajuela	**Hieronyma cubana Müll.Arg.**	**N/A**
Calabaza	Cucurbita moschata Duchesne	152
Calalú	Colocasia esculenta (L.) Schott	155
Camagua	Wallenia laurifolia Sw.	156
Candelilla	Tragia volubilis L.	162
Canutillo Morado	Commelina erecta L.	167
Caña Coro/Canna	Canna indica L.	178
Caña de Azúcar	Saccharum officinarum L.	172
Caoba	Swietenia mahagoni (L.) Jacq.	180
Caramboli	Averrhoa carambola L.	183
Cariel	**?????**	**N/A**
Cedro	Cedrela odorata L.	198
Ceiba	Ceiba pentandra (L.) Gaertn.	199
Combustera Cimarrona	**Manettia lygistum (L.) Sw.**	**N/A**
Cordobán	Tradescantia spathacea Sw.	233
Corojo	Acrocomia crispa (Kunth) C.F.Baker ex Becc.	235
Cresta de Gallo	Celosia argentea L.	237
Cupido la Una	Ginoria americana Jacq.	246
Curujey	**VARIOUS**	247
Ensalada del Obispo	Anredera vesicaria (Lam.) C.F.Gaertn.	621
Flor de Pascua	Euphorbia pulcherrima Willd. ex Klotzsch	273
Framboyán	Delonix regia (Hook.) Raf.	276
Frijolillo	Hebestigma cubense (Kunth) Urb.	282
Geranio	Pelargonium odoratissimum (L.) L'Hér.	291
Granada	Punica granatum L.	295
Granadillo	Brya ebenus (L.) DC.	296
Guabari	**????**	**N/A**
Guacamaya Colorada	Caesalpinia pulcherrima (L.) Sw.	303
Guano Blanco	Copernicia glabrescens H.Wendl. ex Becc.	316
Guano Prieto	Acoelorrhaphe wrightii (Griseb. & H.Wendl.) …	317
Guayabillo	Chloroleucon mangense var. lentiscifolium (C.Wright) …	325
Guengueré/Grénguere	Corchorus olitorius L.	297
Higuereta **Morada**	Ricinus communis L.	338
Jagüey	Ficus membranacea C.Wright.	354
Jobo	Spondias mombin L.	363
Jocuma	Sideroxylon foetidissimum Jacq.	365
Júcaro Bravo, Júcaro de Uña	Terminalia molinetii M.Gómez	366
Jurubana, Jurabaina	Hebestigma cubense (Kunth) Urb.	368
Laurel	Ficus benjamina L.	371
Malacara	Plumbago zeylanica L.	391
Malva Té	Corchorus siliquosus L.	398
Mamey de Santo Domingo	Mammea americana L.	401

Ceiba *	Ceiba pentandra (L.) Gaertn.	199
Celosa Cirmarrona	Duranta erecta L.	201
Chirimoya *	Annona reticulata L.	212
Coco	Cocos nucifera L.	218
Cojate, Colonia Cimarrona	Renealmia aromatica (Aubl.) Griseb.	221
Colonia	Alpinia zerumbet (Pers.) B.L.Burtt & R.M.Sm.	223
Copaiba	Copaifera officinalis L.	225
Coralillo Blanco	Poranopsis paniculata (Roxb.) Roberty	230
Corazón de Paloma	Rauvolfia salicifolia Griseb	232
Diamela	Jasminum sambac (L.) Aiton	250
Extraña Rosa	Callistephus chinensis (L.) Nees	269
Flor de Agua	Eichhornia azurea (Sw.) Kunth	270
Flor de Mayo	Laelia anceps Lindl.	272
Fruta del Pan/Árbol del Pan	Artocarpus altilis (Parkinson ex F.A.Zorn) Fosberg	67
Galán de Día	Cestrum diurnum L.	285
Galán de Noche	Cestrum nocturnum L.	286
Granada	Punica granatum L.	295
Guacalote Prieto	Caesalpinia crista L	300
Guanábana	Annona muricata L.	312
Guanabilla/Guanabanilla	Ouratea nitida (Sw.) Engl.	314
Higuereta **Blanca**	Ricinus communis L.	338
Hinojo	Foeniculum vulgare Mill.	342
Humo	Abarema obovalis (A.Rich.) Barneby & J.W.Grimes	245
Jazmín de la Tierra	**Jasminum grandiflorum L.**	**N/A**
Jícama	Calopogonium caeruleum (Benth.) Sauvalle	361
Lirio/**Frangipani**	Plumeria Sp.;	380
Maboa	Cameraria latifolia L.	384
Malva Blanca	Waltheria indica L.	396
Manto de la Virgen	Plectranthus scutellarioides (L.) R.Br.	410
Maravilla **BLANCA**	Mirabilis jalapa L.	414
Ofón	Vitex doniana Sweet	444
Palo Bobo	Annona glabra L.	458
Palo Guitarra	Citharexylum caudatum L.	470
Paraíso	Melia azedarach L.	490
Peonia	Abrus precatorius L.	499
Piña Blanca	Ananas comosus (L.) Merr.	514
Piñón Botija/Piñón de Botija	Jatropha curcas L.	518
Piñón Florido	Gliricidia sepium (Jacq.) Walp.	8
Salvadera	Hura crepitans L.	556
Salvia de Castilla	Salvia officinalis L.	558
Saúco Blanco	Sambucus canadensis L.	566
Seso Vegetal	Blighia sapida K.D.Koenig	569
Siemprevива	Bryophyllum pinnatum (Lam.) Oken	530

Tamarindo	Tamarindus indica L.	575
Tete Lanyé	**?????**	**N/A**
Trébol	Trifolium repens L.	585
Túatúa, Tubatuba	Jatropha gossypiifolia L.	588
Tuna Blanca	Opuntia ficus-indica (L.) Mill.	590
Varía/**Baría**	Cordia gerascanthus L.	91
Varita de San José	Alcea rosea L.	600
Verdolago Blanca	**?????**	**N/A**
Vicaria, Vicaria Blanca/Morada	Catharanthus roseus (L.) G.Don	609
Yagruma	Cecropia peltata L.	614
Yantén/Llantén	Plantago major L.	381
Yerba Lechosa	**Euphorbia hirta L.**	**N/A**

YEMAYA   **PAGE#**

Aguacate-**Las Hojas**	Persea americana Mill.	19
Alacrancillo	Heliotropium indicum L.	30
Albahaca Morada	Ocimum tenuiflorum L.	36
Amor Seco	Desmodium barbatum (L.) Benth.	51
Añil	Indigofera suffruticosa Mill.	55
Bejuco Amargo	Aristolochia trilobata L.	94
Bejuco Lucumí	Smilax havanensis Jacq.	646
Bejuco Tortuga/de Tortuga	**Bauhinia glabra Jacq.**	**N/A**
Bejuco Ubí	Cissus verticillata (L.) Nicolson & C.E.Jarvis	120
Bejuco Ubí de Hoja Ancha	Cissus verticillata (L.) Nicolson & C.E.Jarvis	120
Bejuco Ubí -Macho	Cissus trifoliata (L.) L.	121
Caimitillo (**Morado**)	Chrysophyllum oliviforme L.	148
Caisimón	Piper peltatum L.;	150
Camagüira	Wallenia laurifolia Sw.	157
Canutillo	Commelina erecta L.	165
Caña Coro	Canna indica L.	170
Cañamazo Amargo	Paspalum conjugatum P.J.Bergius	178
Carquesa	Ambrosia hispida Pursh	188
Cayumbo	Juncus effusus L.	195
Chayote	Sechium edule (Jacq.) Sw.	206
Chinchona	Exostema ellipticum Griseb.	211
Ciruelo	Spondias purpurea L.	217
Comecará	Eugenia aeruginea DC.	224
Copalillo de Monte	Thouinia trifoliata Poit.	227
Coralillo/Coralillo Rosado	Antigonon leptopus Hook. & Arn.	231
Cucaracha	Tradescantia zebrina var. zebrina	241
Culantrillo de Pozo	Adiantum tenerum Sw.	243
Culantro	Eryngium foetidum L.	244

Flor de Agua/Lechuguilla	Pistia stratiotes L.	374
Frescura	Pilea microphylla (L.) Liebm.	278
Fruta Bomba	Carica papaya L.	283
Genciana de la Tierra	Voyria aphylla (Jacq.) Pers.	289
Granadillo	Brya ebenus (L.) DC.	296
Guengueré/Grénguere	Corchorus olitorius L.	297
Guairaje	Eugenia foetida Pers.	307
Guamá de Costa	Lonchocarpus heptaphyllus (Poir.) DC.	310
Guamá Hediondo	Lonchocarpus blainii C.Wright	311
Guásima	Guazuma ulmifolia Lam.	321
Guasimilla	Prockia crucis P.Browne ex L.	322
Güira Criolla/Güira	Crescentia cujete L.	327
Incienso de Playa	Tournefortia gnaphalodes (L.) R.Br. ex Roem. & Schult.	349
Jagua	Genipa americana L.	352
Junco Marino	Parkinsonia aculeata L.	367
Junta-Junto	**?????**	**N/A**
Lechuga	Lactuca sativa L.	373
Lino/Limo de Mar	Ulva lactuca Linnaeus	376
Magüey	Furcraea hexapetala (Jacq.) Urb.	386
Majagua	Hibiscus tilliaceus L./Hibiscus elatus Sw.	389
Malanga	Xanthosoma sagittifolium (L.) Schott	392
Malanga Trepadora	**Epipremnum aureum (Linden & André) G.S.Bunting**	**N/A**
Malanguilla	Xanthosoma cubense (Schott) Schott	395
Matanegro	Rourea glabra Kunth	420
Melón de Agua	Citrullus lanatus (Thunb.) Matsum. & Nakai	424
Naranja Agria	Citrus × aurantium L.	439
Palo Jeringa	Moringa oleifera Lam.	473
Papo de la Reina	Bolusafra bituminosa (L.) Kuntze	488
Paragüita	Hydrocotyle umbellata L.	489
Piñón de Pito	Erythrina berteroana Urb.	520
Resedá	Reseda odorata L.	539
Romero	Rosmarinus officinalis L.	544
Sábila	Aloe vera (L.) Burm.f.	533
Sabina	**Juniperus barbadensis var. australis (Endl.) ined.**	**N/A**
Sanguinaria	**Alternanthera sessilis (L.) R.Br. ex DC.**	**N/A**
San Jacinto	**????**	**N/A**
Sargazo	Sargassum bacciferum (Turner) C.Agardh	563
Siguaraya	Trichilia havanensis Jacq.	570
Túa-túa	Jatropha gossypiifolia L.	588
Verbena	Verbena officinalis L.	603
Verdolaga	Portulaca oleracea L.	604
Vinagrillo	Oxalis violacea L./Oxalis corniculata L.	611
Violeta	Viola odorata L.	612

Extraña Rosa	Callistephus chinensis (L.) Nees	269
Flor de Agua, Flor de Rio	Eichhornia azurea (Sw.) Kunth	270
Flor de Agua, Nelumbio,-**RAIZ** *	Nymphaea alba L.	271
Frailecillo de Monte	Jatropha gossypiifolia L.	274
Frescura	Pilea microphylla (L.) Liebm.	278
Girasol	Helianthus annuus L.	292
Grosella	Phyllanthus acidus (L.) Skeels	298
Guacamaya Amarilla	Caesalpinia pulcherrima (L.) Sw.	302
Guacamaya Colorada	Caesalpinia pulcherrima (L.) Sw.	303
Guacamaya Francesa *	Senna alata (L.) Roxb.;	304
Guamá de Costa	Lonchocarpus heptaphyllus (Poir.) DC.	310
Guengueré/Grénguere	Corchorus olitorius L.	297
Helecho de Rio *	Osmunda regalis L.	332
Hoja Menuda	**Albizia berteriana (DC.) Fawc. & Rendle**	**N/A**
Jaboncillo	Sapindus saponaria L.	351
Jía Amarilla *	Casearia guianensis (Aubl.) Urb.	357
Lagaña de Aura	Plumbago zeylanica L.	369
Lechuga	Lactuca sativa L.	373
Limo de Río, Lino de Río	Potamogeton lucens L.	377
Llantén Cimarrón	Echinodorus grisebachii Small	382
Llerén, Yerén	Calathea allouia (Aubl.) Lindl.	383
Malva Té	Corchorus siliquosus L.	398
Malvira	Bauhinia tomentosa L.	399
Mangle	Rhizophora mangle L.	404
Mango Macho	Mangifera indica L.	406
Manzanilla	Chrysanthellum americanum (L.) Vatke	411
Marañón	Anacardium occidentale L.	413
Maravilla **AMARILLA** *	Mirabilis jalapa L.	414
Melón de Castilla	Cucumis melo L.	425
Mije	**Eugenia rhombea (O.Berg) Krug & Urb.**	**N/A**
Mirto, Muralla	Murraya paniculata (L.) Jack	436
Naranja Agria	Citrus × aurantium L.	439
Naranja Dulce	Citrus sinensis (L.) Osbeck	437
No me Olvides *	Duranta erecta L.	201
Orozuz de la Tierra	Phyla scaberrima (Juss. ex Pers.) Moldenke	449
Palo Mulato	Exothea paniculata (Juss.) Radlk.	477
Palu	**?????**	**N/A**
Papo/Papito/Zapatico de la Reina	Bolusafra bituminosa (L.) Kuntze	488
Pata de Gallina	Eleusine indica (L.) Gaertn.	494
Peralejo de Monte	**Byrsonima crassifolia (L.) Kunth**	**N/A**
Peregrina	Jatropha integerrima Jacq.; Jatropha diversifolia A.Rich.	501
Perejil	Petroselinum crispum (Mill.) Fuss	503
Piña de Salón, Piña de Adorno	Ananas ananassoides (Baker) L.B.Sm.	516

Pomarrosa	Syzygium jambos (L.) Alston	527
Pringa Hermosa	Platygyna hexandra (Jacq.) Müll.Arg.	529
Romerillo *	Bidens pilosa L.	543
Romerillo Francés/de Costa	**Viguiera dentata (Cav.) Spreng.**	**N/A**
Rosa	Rosa indica L.	548
Salvia de Castilla	Salvia officinalis L.	558
Sangre de Doncella	Byrsonima lucida (Mill.) DC.	560
Sapote, Zapote	Manilkara zapota (L.) P.Royen	561
Saúco Amarillo *	Tecoma stans (L.) Juss. ex Kunth	565
Soplillo	Lysiloma latisiliquum (L.) Benth.	572
Titonia	Tithonia rotundifolia (Mill.) S.F.Blake	579
Vainilla Amarilla	Encyclia fucata (Lindl.) Schltr.	597
Vainilla Rosada	Psychilis atropurpurea (Willd.) Sauleda	598
Vetiver	Chrysopogon zizanioides (L.) Roberty	607
Yerba Caimán	Persicaria glabra (Willd.) M.Gómez	625
Yerba de la Niña	Phyllanthus niruri L.	629
Yerba Luisa	Aloysia citriodora Palau	639
Yerba Maravedí	Crossopetalum uragoga (Jacq.) Kuntze	640
Yerba Mulata	**Rumex sanguineus L./Malachra urens Poit. ex Ledeb.**	**N/A**
Yerba Rabo de Alacrán/de Ratón	**Setaria parviflora (Poir.) M.Kerguelen**	**N/A**

OYA   PAGE#

Almendro	Terminalia catappa L.	45
Aralia-**TODOS**	Aralia elegans Linden	60
Avericulo/Espanta Muerto	Eclipta prostrata (L.) L.	261
Bejuco Alcanfor	Peperomia subrotundifolia C.DC.	93
Cabo de Hacha, **Isora**	Trichilia hirta L.	142
Caimitillo	Chrysophyllum oliviforme L.	148
Caimito, Caimito **Morado**	Chrysophyllum cainito L.	149
Chirimoya	Annona reticulata L.	212
Croto/s	Codiaeum variegatum (L.) Rumph. ex A.Juss.	238
Curujey	**VARIOUS**	247
Manto de la Virgen-**TODOS**	Plectranthus scutellarioides (L.) R.Br.	410
Marpacífico	Hibiscus rosa-sinensis L.	418
Meloncillo/Pepino Cimarrón	Melothria pendula L.	426
Tamarindo-**MUERTO**	Tamarindus indica L.	575
Verbena-**HOJAS**	Verbena officinalis L.	603
Yedra	Anredera vesicaria (Lam.) C.F.Gaertn.	621

BABALU AYE   PAGE#

Aceitero	Zanthoxylum flavum Vahl	12

Ajonjolí	Sesamum indicum L.	29
Albahaca Morada *	Ocimum tenuiflorum L.	36
Alejo/Ateje Macho	Cordia sulcata A.DC.	82
Almendro	Terminalia catappa L.	45
Apasote	Dysphania ambrosioides (L.) Mosyakin & Clemants	56
Árbol del Sebo	Triadica sebifera (L.) Small	68
Ardacrana *	????	**N/A**
Artemisa	Ambrosia artemisiifolia L.	75
Bejuco Angarilla	Serjania diversifolia (Jacq.) Radlk.	95
Bejuco de Purgación	Boerhavia scandens L.	108
Bejuco Lombriz	Philodendron consanguineum Schott	112
Bejuco Lucumí *	Smilax havanensis Jacq.	646
Caguairán	Hymenaea torrei Leon	146
Caña Brava	Bambusa vulgaris Schrad.	168
Cañamazo Amargo	Paspalum conjugatum P.J.Bergius	178
Cardo Santo	Argemone mexicana L.	185
Cebolleta	Cyperus rotundus L.	197
Cenizo	Abarema obovalis (A.Rich.) Barneby & J.W.Grimes	202
Chirimoya *	Annona reticulata L.	212
Copaiba	Copaifera officinalis L.	225
Escardón *	Euphorbia lactea Haw.	186
Escoba Amarga **Grande/Flores**	Parthenium hysterophorus L.	258
Frijol Carita	Vigna unguiculata (L.) Walp.	279
Frijol Gandul	Cajanus cajan (L.) Millsp.	280
Guaguasí	Zuelania guidonia (Sw.) Britton & Millsp	306
Henequén	Agave fourcroydes Lem.	335
Incienso	Artemisia abrotanum L.	347
Jía Brava	Casearia aculeata Jacq.	359
Maní	Arachis hypogaea L.	408
Millo	Sorghum bicolor (L.) Moench	429
Mirra	Commiphora myrrha (Nees) Engl.	433
Ortiguilla	Laportea cuneata (A.Rich.) Chew	450
Pica-Pica	Mucuna pruriens (L.) DC.	504
Retama	Neurolaena lobata (L.) R.Br. ex Cass.	540
Romero	Rosmarinus officinalis L.	544
Sabicú	**Lysiloma sabicu Benth./Lysiloma latisiliquum (L.) Benth.**	**N/A**
Salvia, Salvia Morada	Pluchea odorata (L.) Cass.	557
Sargazo	Sargassum bacciferum (Turner) C.Agardh	563
Sasafrás	Bursera graveolens (Kunth) Triana & Planch.	564
Yerba de Guinea *	Panicum maximum Jacq.	628
Yerba de la Vieja *	Flaveria trinervia (Spreng.) C.Mohr	631

YEWA   **PAGE#**

EWE that belong to each Orisha to make Omiero; per Libreta de Santería de María Antoñica Finés; Estudios Afro-Cubanos, Vol.3; Lázara Menéndez.

PLANT NAME-CUBA	SCIENTIFIC NAME	PAGE #
ELEGGUA		PAGE #
Abre Camino	Koanophyllon villosum (Sw.) R.M. King & H. Rob.	3
Albahaca de Hoja Ancha	Ocimum basilicum L.	38
Cardo Santo	Argemone mexicana L.	185
Espartillo	Sporobolus indicus (L.) R.Br.	262
Grama de Caballos	Eleusine indica (L.) Gaertn.	494
Guanina	Senna tora (L.) Roxb.	315
Guizazo de Baracoa	Xanthium strumarium L.	331
Helecho Macho	Dryopteris filix-mas (L.) Schott	334
Ítamo Real	Euphorbia tithymaloides L.	350
Lengua de Vaca	Sansevieria hyacinthoides (L.) Druce	375
Mamao/Yamao	Guarea guidonia (L.) Sleumer	616
Meloncillo	Melothria pendula L.	426
Pastillo	Paspalum notatum Flüggé	493
Pata de Gallina	Eleusine indica (L.) Gaertn.	494
Piñón Botija	Jatropha curcas L.	518
Piñón Criollo	Jatropha curcas L.	518
Sabelección	Lepidium virginicum L.	419
Yerba Fina	Cynodon dactylon (L.) Pers.	636
OGGUN, OCHOSI		PAGE #
Alacrancillo	Heliotropium indicum L.	30
Albahaca Mondonguera	Ocimum basilicum L.	40
Albahaca Morada	Ocimum tenuiflorum L.	36
Aralia (**all types**)	Polyscias guilfoylei (W.Bull) L.H.Bailey	60
Caña Santa	Costus spicatus (Jacq.) Sw.	175
Canutillo	Commelina erecta L.	165
Cogollo de Caña	Saccharum officinarum L.	172
Cogollo de Palma	Roystonea regia (Kunth) O.F.Cook	453
Díez del Día	Portulaca pilosa L.	635
Dormidera	Mimosa pudica L.	568
Ébano	Diospyros crassinervis (Krug & Urb.) Standl.	255
Huevo de Gallo	Rauvolfia nitida Jacq.	344
Ítamo Real	Euphorbia tithymaloides L.	350
Jagüey	Ficus membranacea C.Wright.	354

Manajú	Garcinia aristata (Griseb.) Borhidi	403
Paragüita	Hydrocotyle umbellata L.	489
Pata de Gallina	Eleusine indica (L.) Gaertn.	494
Pegojo	Tabernaemontana citrifolia L.	343
Romerillo	Bidens pilosa L.	544
Rompezaragüey	Chromolaena odorata (L.) R.M.King & H.Rob.	547
Salvadera	Hura crepitans L.	557
Siempreviva	Bryophyllum pinnatum (Lam.) Oken	530
Trepadera	**UNKNOWN**	
Yerba de la Sangre	Cordia bullata var. globosa (Jacq.) Govaerts	631
Yerba Mora	Solanum americanum Mill.	642
Zarzaparrilla	Smilax havanensis Jacq.	647

CHANGO, AGAYU   PAGE

Álamo	Ficus religiosa L.	32
Atipolá	Boerhavia diffusa L.	83
Baría	Cordia gerascanthus L.	91
Bledo Punzo	Amaranthus blitum L.	134
Canutillo Morado	Commelina erecta L.	167
Cordobán	Tradescantia spathacea Sw.	233
Ewéréyeye/Peonia	Abrus precatorius L.	499
Guacalote	Entada gigas (L.) Fawc. & Rendle	582
Guanina	Senna tora (L.) Roxb.	315
Jibá	Erythroxylum havanense Jacq.	360
Jobo	Spondias mombin L.	363
Malva Té	Corchorus siliquosus L.	398
Moco de Pavo	Amaranthus cruentus L.	434
Paraíso	Melia azedarach L.	490
Platanillo de Cuba	Piper aduncum L.	524
Ruda Cimarrona	Dalea carthagenensis (Jacq.) J.F.Macbr.	634
Siguaraya	Trichilia havanensis Jacq.	571
Verdolaga	Portulaca oleracea L.	605
Zarzaparrilla	Smilax havanensis Jacq.	647

OBATALA   PAGE

Aguinaldo Blanco	Turbina corymbosa (L.) Raf.	21
Algodón	Gossypium barbadense L.	43
Almendro	Terminalia catappa L.	45
Atipolá	Boerhavia diffusa L.	83

Bayoneta	Yucca gloriosa L.	502
Bledo Blanco	Amaranthus viridis L.	129
Bledo de Clavo	Amaranthus crassipes Schltdl.	132
Campana **Blanca**	Brugmansia arborea (L.) Steud.	160
Canutillo Blanco	Commelina erecta L.	165
Guanábana	Annona muricata L.	312
Higuereta **Blanca**	Ricinus communis L	338
Jagua **Blanca**	Genipa americana L.	352
Maravilla **Blanca**	Mirabilis jalapa L.	414
Piñón Botija	Jatropha curcas L.	518
Prodigiosa	Bryophyllum pinnatum (Lam.) Oken	530

YEMAYA, OCHUN   PAGE

Albahaca Morada	Ocimum tenuiflorum L.	36
Añil	Indigofera suffruticosa Mill.	55
Berro	Nasturtium officinale R.Br.	125
Botón de Oro	Abutilon indicum (L.) Sweet	138
Canela	Cinnamodendron cubense Urb.	163
Canutillo Morado	Commelina erecta L.	167
Carquesa	Ambrosia hispida Pursh	188
Colonia	Alpinia zerumbet (Pers.) B.L.Burtt & R.M.Sm.	223
Corazón de Paloma	Rauvolfia salicifolia Griseb.	232
Culantrillo	Adiantum capillus-veneris L.	243
Filigrana	Chromolaena odorata (L.) R.M.King & H.Rob.	546
Flor de Água	Eichhornia azurea (Sw.) Kunth	270
Grama	Cynodon dactylon (L.) Pers.	635
Guacamaya	Caesalpinia pulcherrima (L.) Sw.	302
Guásima	Guazuma ulmifolia Lam.	321
Helecho de Rio	Osmunda regalis L.	332
Huevo de Gallo	Tabernaemontana citrifolia L.	343
Jaboncillo	Sapindus saponaria L.	351
Lechuga	Lactuca sativa L.	373
Lechuguilla	Pistia stratiotes L.	374
Lino de Río	Potamogeton lucens L.	377
Malanga	Xanthosoma sagittifolium (L.) Schott	392
Maravilla **Amarilla**	Mirabilis jalapa L.	414
Mari-Lope	Turnera ulmifolia L.	416
Mazorquilla	Blechum pyramidatum (Lam.) Urb.	421
Meloncillo	Melothria pendula L.	426
Orozuz	Phyla scaberrima (Juss. ex Pers.) Moldenke	449
Oyouro	Rain Water/**Agua de Lluvia**	

OYA PAGE

BABALU AYE PAGE

Yaya   Oxandra lanceolata (Sw.) Baill.   620

ODDUA   **PAGE #**

EWE that belong to each Orisha; per popular Website from the Internet (with **Corrections**)

NAME	SCIENTIFIC NAME

Hierbas de Azowano

NAME	SCIENTIFIC NAME
Abre camino	Koanophyllon villosum (Sw.) R.M. King & H. Rob.
Acacia - paraíso blanco	Moringa oleifera Lam.
Albahaca cimarrona	Ocimum gratissimum L.
Albahaca mondonguera	Ocimum basilicum L.
Apasote	Chenopodium ambrosioides L.
Caisimón de anís	Piper auritum Kunth
Cardón	Euphorbia lactea Haw.
Chirimoya	Annona cherimola Mill. /**Annona reticulata L.**
Ciruela	Spondias purpurea L.
Colonia	Alpinia zerumbet (Pers.) B.L.Burtt & R.M.Sm.
Cundeamor	Momordica charantia L.
Escoba amarga	Parthenium hysterophorus L.
Estropajo	Luffa cylindrica (L.) M.Roem.
Guanábana	Annona muricata L.
Malanga	Xanthosoma sagittifolium (L.) Schott
Maní	Arachis hypogaea L.
Pendejera	Solanum torvum Sw.
Rompe camisa	**Cordia globosa (Jacq.) Kunth**
Rompezaragüey	Vernonia menthifolia/**Chromolaena odorata (L.) ...**
Salvia	Pluchea odorata (L.) Cass.
Vergonzosa	Mimosa pudica L.

Hierbas de Juramento de Aña

NAME	SCIENTIFIC NAME
Alacrancillo	**Heliotropium indicum L.**
Álamo	Ficus religiosa L.
Albahaca	Ocimum basilicum L.
Algodón	Gossypium barbadense L.
Bledo blanco	Amaranthus viridis L.
Ceiba	Ceiba pentandra (L.) Gaertn.
Cordobán	Tradescantia spathacea Sw.
Curujey	Hohenbergia penduliflora (A.Rich.) Mez
Filigrana	Lantana camara L.
Flor de agua	Nymphaea ampla (Salisb.) DC.
Hierba de pascuas/ **Flor**	**Euphorbia pulcherrima Willd. ex Klotzsch**
Hierba gomosa/ **Uva**	**Cordia alba (Jacq.) Roem. & Schult.**
Malanga	Xanthosoma sagittifolium (L.) Schott
Pata de gallina	**Eleusine indica (L.) Gaertn.**

Peonía	Abrus precatorius L.
Piñón [Piñón botija]	Jatropha curcas L.
Prodigiosa	Bryophyllum pinnatum (Lam.) Oken
Yerba de la niña	Euphorbia hirta L.**/Phyllanthus niruri L.**
Yerba fina	Cynodon dactylon (L.) Pers.

Hierbas de Los Jimaguas

Anón	Annona squamosa L.
Canistel	Pouteria campechiana (Kunth) Baehni
Chirimoya	Annona cherimola Mill. **/Annona reticulata L.**
Guanábana	Annona muricata L.
Guayaba	Psidium guajava L.
Mamey de Santo Domingo	Mammea americana L.
Mamoncillo	Melicoccus bijugatus Jacq.
Mango	Mangifera indica L.
Naranja	Citrus sinensis (L.) Osbeck
Piña	Ananas comosus (L.) Merr.
Platanillo /**de Monte**	Canna indica L.
Rompezaragüey	Vernonia menthifolia/**Chromolaena odorata (L.) ...**
Zapote	Manilkara zapota (L.) P.Royen
Zarzaparrilla	**Smilax havanensis Jacq.**

Hierbas de Obatalá

Acacia - paraíso blanco	Moringa oleifera Lam.
Aguinaldo blanco	Turbina corymbosa (L.) Raf.
Algodón	Gossypium barbadense L.
Almendro	Terminalia catappa L.
Anón	Annona squamosa L.
Atiponla **blanco** [Tostón]	**Boerhavia erecta L.**/Boerhavia coccinea Mill.
Bayoneta	Yucca gloriosa L.
Bejuco ubí	Cissus verticillata (L.) Nicolson & C.E.Jarvis
Belladona	Kalanchoe crenata (Andrews) Haw.
Bledo blanco	Amaranthus viridis L.
Bledo de clavo	**Amaranthus crassipes Schltdl.**
Campana blanca	Brugmansia arborea (L.) Steud.
Caña santa	Costus spicatus (Jacq.) Sw.
Canutillo blanco	Commelina erecta L.
Chirimoya	Annona cherimola Mill. /**Annona reticulata L.**
Don chayo [Chayo]	Cnidoscolus urens (L.) Arthur
Eucalipto	Eucalyptus resinifera Sm.
Flor de agua	**Nymphaea alba L.**

Flor de mármol	Sedum monregalense Balb.
Fosforito	**Phyla nodiflora (L.) Greene**
Frescura	Pilea microphylla (L.) Liebm.
Fruta del pan	Artocarpus altilis (Parkinson ex F.A.Zorn) Fosberg
Galán de noche	Cestrum nocturnum L.
Granada	Punica granatum L.
Guanábana	Annona muricata L.
Hiedra	Ficus pumila L./**Anredera vesicaria (Lam.) C.F.Gaertn.**
Higuereta blanca [Higuereta]	**Ricinus communis L.**
Lengua de las mujeres	Pilea nummulariifolia (Sw.) Wedd.
Llantén	Plantago major L.
Malva blanca	Waltheria indica L.**/Sida cordifolia L.**
Mango macho	Mangifera indica L.
Mejorana	Origanum majorana L.
Millo	Sorghum bicolor (L.) Moench
Paraíso	Melia azedarach L.
Piñón botija	Jatropha curcas L.
Prodigiosa	Bryophyllum pinnatum (Lam.) Oken
Quita maldición de espinas	**Caesalpinia bonduc (L.) Roxb.**
Remolacha	Beta vulgaris L.
Romerillo blanco	Bidens pilosa L.
Saúco blanco	Sambucus canadensis L.
Seso vegetal	Blighia sapida K.D.Koenig
Toronja	Citrus paradisi Macfad.
Vencedor	Zanthoxylum flavum subsp. pistaciifolium (Griseb.) Reynel
Verdolaga Blanca [Verdolaga]	Portulaca oleracea L.
Vinagrillo	**Oxalis corniculata L.**
Yerba fina	Cynodon dactylon (L.) Pers.

Hierbas de Ochún

Abre camino	Koanophyllon villosum (Sw.) R.M. King & H. Rob.
Alacrancillo rosado [Alacrancillo]	Heliotropium indicum L.
Albahaca	Ocimum basilicum L.
Almácigo	Bursera simaruba (L.) Sarg.
Anón	Annona squamosa L.
Ashibata o Lirio de agua	**Nymphaea alba L.**
Berro	Nasturtium officinale R.Br.
Botón de oro	Abutilon indicum (L.) Sweet
Calabaza	Cucurbita moschata Duchesne
Canela	Cinnamomum cassia ... /**Cinnamodendron cubense Urb.**
Canistel	Pouteria campechiana (Kunth) Baehni
Cerraja	Sonchus oleraceus (L.) L.

Culantrillo de pozo	Adiantum tenerum Sw. /**Adiantum capillus-veneris L.**
Cundeamor	Momordica charantia L.
Embeleso	Plumbago auriculata Lam.
Flor de agua	**Eichhornia azurea (Sw.) Kunth**
Flor de muerto	Tagetes erecta L.
Fruta bomba	Carica papaya L.
Girasol	Helianthus annuus L.
Guacamaya francesa	Senna alata (L.) Roxb.
Guamá de costa	Lonchocarpus heptaphyllus (Poir.) DC.
Hino macho [Hino]/**Helecho**	**Dryopteris filix-mas (L.) Schott**
Jaboncillo	Sapindus saponaria L.
Lirio de agua	**Nymphaea ampla (Salisb.) DC.**
Mamey colorado	Pouteria sapota (Jacq.) H.E.Moore & Stearn
Maravilla amarilla	Mirabilis jalapa L.
Marilope	Turnera ulmifolia L.
Mejorana	Origanum majorana L.
No me olvides	Duranta repens L.
Oro azul	**Phyla nodiflora (L.) Greene**
Panetela	Phyllanthus angustifolius (Sw.) Sw.
Parra **Cimarrona**	Vitis tiliifolia Humb. & Bonpl. ex Schult
Platanillo de Cuba	**Piper aduncum L.**
Pomarrosa	Syzygium jambos (L.) Alston
Resedá/francesa/**Reseda**	**Reseda odorata L.**
Romerillo amarillo	**Wedelia rugosa var. tenuis Greenm.**
Romero	Rosmarinus officinalis L.
Saúco **Blanco**	Sambucus canadensis L.
Yerba de la niña	Euphorbia hirta L./**Phyllanthus niruri L.**
Yerba de la vieja	Flaveria trinervia (Spreng.) C.Mohr
Zapote	Manilkara zapota (L.) P.Royen
Zarzaparrilla	**Smilax havanensis Jacq.**

Hierbas de Oddúa

Algodón	Gossypium barbadense L.
Campana blanca	Brugmansia arborea (L.) Steud.
Ceiba	Ceiba pentandra (L.) Gaertn.
Flor de mármol	Sedum monregalense Balb.
Hiedra	Ficus pumila L./**Anredera vesicaria (Lam.) C.F.Gaertn.**
Llantén	Plantago major L.
Prodigiosa	Bryophyllum pinnatum (Lam.) Oken
Salvia	

Hierbas de Oggún

Abrojo amarillo	**Tribulus cistoides L.**
Ácana	Manilkara valenzuelana (A.Rich.) T.D.Penn.
Aguacate	Persea americana Mill.
Ají de china	Solanum havanense Jacq.
Ají guaguao	**Capsicum baccatum L.**
Alacrancillo	**Heliotropium indicum L.**
Álamo	Ficus religiosa L.
Anamú	Petiveria alliacea L.
Añil	Indigofera tinctoria L./**Indigofera suffruticosa Mill.**
Aroma	Acacia farnesiana (L.) Willd.
Ateje [corteza sin masa]	Cordia collococca L.
Bledo carbonero	Phytolacca icosandra L.
Campana morada/**Aguinaldo**	Ipomoea crassicaulis (Benth.) B.L. Rob.
Cardo santo	Argemone mexicana L.
Cordobán	Tradescantia spathacea Sw.
Eucalipto	Eucalyptus resinifera Sm.
Flor de muerto	Tagetes erecta L.
Frescura	Pilea microphylla (L.) Liebm.
Guamá	Lonchocarpus domingensis (Pers.) DC.
Guizazo de Baracoa	Xanthium strumarium L.
Incienso de costa	Tournefortia gnaphalodes (L.) R.Br. ex Roem. & Schult.
Lengua de vaca	Sansevieria hyacinthoides (L.) Druce
Meloncillo	Melothria pendula L.
Naranja agria	Citrus × aurantium L.
Peregún	**Yucca gloriosa L./Dracaena fragrans (L.) Ker Gawl.**
Ponasí	Hamelia patens Jacq.
Rabo de zorra	Digitaria insularis (L.) Mez ex Ekman
Rompezaragüey	Vernonia menthifolia/**Chromolaena odorata (L.) ...**
Tuna [Tuna brava]	Opuntia dillenii (Ker Gawl.) Haw.
Vicaria	Catharanthus roseus (L.) G.Don
Yerba de sapo [Oroazul]	**Phyla nodiflora (L.) Greene**
Yerba fina	Cynodon dactylon (L.) Pers.
Yerba mora	Solanum americanum Mill.

Hierbas de Orisha Oko

Aguacate	Persea americana Mill.
Boniato	Ipomoea batatas (L.) Lam.
Calabaza	Cucurbita moschata Duchesne
Fruta bomba	Carica papaya L.
Guanábana	Annona muricata L.
Maíz [espiga]	Zea mays L.

Malanga   Xanthosoma sagittifolium (L.) Schott
Mango   Mangifera indica L.
Ñame   Dioscorea cayennensis subsp. rotundata (Poir.) J.Miège
Quimbombó   Abelmoschus esculentus (L.) Moench
Yuca   Manihot esculenta Crantz

Hierbas de Orumila

Aceitunillo   Beilschmiedia pendula (Sw.) Hemsl.
Aguinaldo morado   Ipomoea crassicaulis (Benth.) B.L. Rob.
Coquito africano   **Cola acuminata (P.Beauv.) Schott & Endl.**
Cundeamor   Momordica charantia L.
Guanina   Senna tora (L.) Roxb.
Mamey de Santo Domingo   Mammea americana L.
Mano de San Francisco/**Bastón** **Leonotis nepetifolia (L.) R.Br.**
Mano poderosa   **????**
Maravilla   Mirabilis jalapa L.
Palma real   Roystonea regia (Kunth) O.F.Cook
Pata de gallina   **Eleusine indica (L.) Gaertn.**
Piña de ratón   Bromelia pinguin L.
Romerillo amarillo   **Wedelia rugosa var. tenuis Greenm.**
Yerba hedionda   Senna occidentalis (L.) Link

Hierbas de Orun

Caña brava   Bambusa vulgaris Schrad.
Sargazo   **Sargassum bacciferum (Turner) C.Agardh**
Yerba de garro/**Garro Blanco** Spermacoce tenuior L.

Hierbas de Oshosi

Aguinaldo blanco   Turbina corymbosa (L.) Raf.
Alacrancillo   **Heliotropium indicum L.**
Bejuco de canastas   Trichostigma octandrum (L.) H.Walter
Cardo santo   Argemone mexicana L.
Coralillo **Rosado**   Antigonon leptopus Hook. & Arn.
Cuaba amarilla/**Blanca**   Amyris balsamifera L.
Dormidera   Mimosa pudica L.
Embeleso   Plumbago auriculata Lam.
Guamá   Lonchocarpus domingensis (Pers.) DC.
Helecho hembra   **Athyrium filix-femina (L.) Roth**
Incienso de costa   Tournefortia gnaphalodes (L.) R.Br. ex Roem. & Schult.
Prodigiosa   Bryophyllum pinnatum (Lam.) Oken

Rompezaragüey   Vernonia menthifolia/**Chromolaena odorata (L.) ...**
Yerba fina   Cynodon dactylon (L.) Pers.

Hierbas de Osun

Alacrancillo   **Heliotropium indicum L.**
Algodón   Gossypium barbadense L.
Bledo blanco   Amaranthus viridis L.

Hierbas de Oyá

Albahaca morada   Ocimum tenuiflorum L.
Caimitillo   Chrysophyllum oliviforme L.
Caimito morado   Chrysophyllum cainito L.
Carolina   Pachira insignis (Sw.) Savigny
Cordobán   Tradescantia spathacea Sw.
Cucaracha   Tradescantia zebrina var. zebrina
Framboyán   Delonix regia (Hook.) Raf.
Hierba la pascua/**Flor**   **Euphorbia pulcherrima Willd. ex Klotzsch**
Mamey colorado   Pouteria sapota (Jacq.) H.E.Moore & Stearn
Manto   Plectranthus scutellarioides (L.) R.Br.
Quiebra hacha   Guibourtia hymenaeifolia (Moric.) J.Léonard
Tamarindo   Tamarindus indica L.
Uva caleta   Coccoloba uvifera (L.) L.
Yagruma   Cecropia peltata L.
Yerba de garro/ **Garro Morado** **Spermacoce laevis Lam.**

Hierbas de Changó

Aguacate cimarrón   Dendrocereus nudiflorus Britton & Rose
Álamo   Ficus religiosa L.
Algarrobo   Albizia saman (Jacq.) Merr.
Atiponla [Tostón]   **Boerhavia diffusa L.**
Canutillo morado [Canutillo]   Commelina erecta L.
Ceiba   Ceiba pentandra (L.) Gaertn.
Ciruela   Spondias purpurea L.
Coralillo **Rosado**   Antigonon leptopus Hook. & Arn.
Cordobán   Tradescantia spathacea Sw.
Curujey   Hohenbergia penduliflora (A.Rich.) Mez
Filigrana   Lantana camara L.
Geranio [Geranio de rosa]   Pelargonium graveolens L'Her.
Grénguere   Corchorus olitorius L.
Guacalote/**Mate Cayajabo**   Canavalia nitida (Cav.) Piper

Higuereta roja [Higuereta]	**Ricinus communis L.**
Hojas de ero africano/**Erún**	**????**
Hojas de kola	Cola acuminata (P.Beauv.) Schott & Endl.
Jagüey	Ficus membranacea C.Wright.
Jengibre	Zingiber officinale Roscoe
Jobo	Spondias mombin L.
Malva té	Corchorus siliquosus L.
Mamey colorado	Pouteria sapota (Jacq.) H.E.Moore & Stearn
Mangle colorado	Rhizophora mangle L.
Mar pacífico	Hibiscus rosa-sinensis L.
Maravilla punzó	Mirabilis jalapa L.
Mazorquilla	Blechum pyramidatum (Lam.) Urb.
Palma **Real**	Roystonea regia (Kunth) O.F.Cook
Peonía	Abrus precatorius L.
Piñón botija	Jatropha curcas L.
Pitahaya	Hylocereus trigonus (Haw.) Saff.
Ponasí	Hamelia patens Jacq.
Quimbombó	Abelmoschus esculentus (L.) Moench
Sacu sacu	**Cyperus alternifolius L.**
Salvadera	Hura crepitans L.
Siguaraya	**Trichilia havanensis Jacq.**
Tuna [Tuna brava]	Opuntia dillenii (Ker Gawl.) Haw.
Yagruma	Cecropia peltata L.
Yerba buena	Mentha nemorosa Willd.
Yerba hedionda	Senna occidentalis (L.) Link

Hierbas de Yemayá

Aguacate	Persea americana Mill.
Ají dulce	Capsicum frutescens L.
Albahaca	Ocimum basilicum L.
Añil	Indigofera tinctoria L./**Indigofera suffruticosa Mill.**
Artemisa	Ambrosia artemisiifolia L.
Ashibata o Lirio de agua	**Nymphaea alba L.**
Belladona	Kalanchoe crenata (Andrews) Haw.
Caisimón	Piper umbellatum L./**Piper peltatum L.**
Cambia voz	Schaefferia frutescens Jacq.
Canutillo	Commelina erecta L.
Ciruela	Spondias purpurea L.
Cuaba negra [**Cuaba prieta**]	Erithalis fruticosa L.
Cucaracha morada	Tradescantia zebrina var. zebrina
Culantro	Eryngium foetidum L.
Diez del día	Portulaca pilosa L.

Flor de agua azul	Eichhornia azurea (Sw.) Kunth/Eichhornia crassipes (Mart.) …
Guásima	Guazuma ulmifolia Lam.
Incienso de costa	Tournefortia gnaphalodes (L.) R.Br. ex Roem. & Schult.
Ítamo real	Euphorbia tithymaloides L.
Jagua	Genipa americana L.
Jiquí	Pera bumeliifolia Griseb.
Lechuguilla	Pistia stratiotes L.
Malanga	Xanthosoma sagittifolium (L.) Schott
Papito de la reina/**Papo**	Centrosema plumieri … /**Bolusafra bituminosa (L.) Kuntze**
Para mí [Ponasí]	Hamelia patens Jacq.
Paragüita	**Hydrocotyle umbellata L.**
Pega pollo	Priva lappulacea (L.) Pers./**Plumbago zeylanica L.**
Rompezaragüey	Vernonia menthifolia/**Chromolaena odorata (L.) …**
Tuatúa	Jatropha gossypiifolia L.
Uva gomosa	Cordia alba (Jacq.) Roem. & Schult.
Verbena	Verbena officinalis L.
Verdolaga	Portulaca oleracea L.
Yagruma	Cecropia peltata L.
Yamagua o Yamao	Guarea guidonia (L.) Sleumer

Hierbas de Eleggua

Almacigo	Bursera simaruba (L.) Sarg.
Aroma amarilla / Olorosa	Acacia farnesiana (L.) Willd.
Atiponla / Toston	**Boerhavia erecta L./Boerhavia coccinea Mill.**
Bejuco San Pedro	**Stigmaphyllon diversifolium (Kunth) A. Juss.**
Bledo blanco	Amaranthus viridis L.
Caumao	Wallenia laurifolia Sw.
Corazon de paloma	**Rauvolfia salicifolia Griseb.**
Croton	Codiaeum variegatum (L.) Rumph. ex A.Juss.
Dominador / Rascabarriga	Espadaea amoena A.Rich.
Espuela de caballero	Jacquinia aculeata Mez
Gambute	Brachiaria platyphylla (Munro ex C.Wright) Nash
Grama / Hierba fina	Cynodon dactylon (L.) Pers.
Guayaba	Psidium guajava L.
Guira	Crescentia cujete L.
Huevo de gallo	Tabernaemontana citrifolia L./**Rauvolfia nitida Jacq.**
Itamo real	Euphorbia tithymaloides L.
Jobo	Spondias mombin L.
Maiz	Zea mays L.
Mastuerzo / Sabe leccion	Lepidium virginicum L.
Mejorana	Origanum majorana L.
Ñame	Dioscorea alata L./**Dioscorea cayennensis subsp. rotundata …**

Ojo de raton	Rivina humilis L.
Palo moro	Psychotria obovalis A.Rich./Psychotria glabrata Sw.
Palo negro	**Haematoxylum campechianum L./Lunania subcoriacea ...**
Paraiso	Melia azedarach L.
Pata de gallina	Eleusine indica (L.) Gaertn.
Pica pica	Mucuna pruriens (L.) DC.
Piña de raton	Bromelia pinguin L.
Piñon de botija	Jatropha curcas L.
Piñon de pito	Erythrina berteroana Urb.
Platano manzano	Musa × paradisiaca L.
Quitamaldicion **con Espinas**	Caesalpinia bonduc (L.) Roxb.
Rabo de gato	Achyranthes aspera L.
Raspalengua	Casearia hirsuta Sw.
Retama	Neurolaena lobata (L.) R.Br. ex Cass.
San diego	Gomphrena globosa L.
Siguaraya	Trichilia havanensis Jacq.
Tabaco	**Nicotiana tabacum L.**
Tripa de jutia	**Stigmaphyllon sagraeanum A. Juss.**

African Wild Daisy	411	Bloodberry	630
Agave	386	Bloodwood Tree	478
Air Potato	442	Blue Taro	392
Akee	569	Blue Yarey Palm	618
Allspice	505	Brazilian Pepper Tree	507
Almondlike Burrwood	474	Broomstick	471
Aloe Vera	553	Broom-weed	397
Amazon Sword Plant	382	Brown Veined Encyclia	597
American Black Elder	566	Browne's Wild Coffee	476
American Muskwood	616	Bull Thatch Palm	451
Angel Flower	595	Burr Marigold	543
Angelica Tree	462	Butterbough Inkwood	477
Anone	458	Buttercup	416
Antille Calophyllum	443	Butterfly Ginger	417
Arrowroot	555	Buttonweed	627
Bahiagrass	493	Cabbage Bark Tree	613
Balsam Torchwood	465	Cantaloupe	425
Banana	525	Caribbean Pine	513
Barbados Nut	518	Cartagena Prairie Clover	633
Barbary Fig	590	Cashew	413
Bastard Cherry	464	Cassava	643
Bastard Coffee	463	Castorbean	338
Bay Laurel	370	Castor-oil Tree	338
Bell Bauhinia	399	Cathedral Bells	608
Belly Ache Bush	588	Century Plant	386
Benjamin Fig	371	Chandelier Plant	390
Bergamot Mint	582	Chinaberry	490
Bermuda Grass	635	Chinese Pepper	506
Bird Cactus	350	Cimarron Taro	395
Bitter Ash	344	Clove	467
Bitter Ash	457	Clustered Yellowtops	631
Bitterbush	344	Cochineal Nopal Cactus	590
Bitterbush	546	Cockspur	644
Bitterwood	540	Cocoplum	336
Black Fig	356	Common Coleus	410
Black Lancewood	619	Common Lady Fern	333
Black Malanga	392	Common Lime	378
Black Mangrove	405	Common Plantain	381
Black Nightshade	641	Common Vervain	603
Black Pepper	505	Coral Berry	447
Black Taro	394	Coralbean	519
Black-eyed Susan Vine	446	Corn	387
Blackwood	478	Country Mallow	396

Pimenta-de-macaco	508	Sapatinho-de-Judeu	350
Pimenta-de-negro	508	Sapatinho-do-Diabo	350
Pimenta-do-reino	505	Sapodilho	561
Pimenta-preta	505	Sapoti	561
Pimenta-redonda	505	Sapotizeiro	561
Pinhão	518	Sargaços	563
Pinhão-branco	518	Sempre-viva	530
Pinhão-branco	521	Sensitiva	567
Pinhão-bravo	588	Sorgo	429
Pinhão-de-purga	518	Suspiro-roxo	559
Pinhão-de-purga	588	Tabacarana	557
Pinhão-roxo	588	Tabaco	573
Pita	386	Tabaibeira	590
Pitaya-vermelha	523	Taioba	392
Piteira	386	Tamarindo	575
Planta-da-ressurreição	549	Tamarineiro	575
Pó-de-mico	504	Tanchagem	381
Portulaca	604	Tapa-buraco	524
Quebra-pedra	629	Taperebá	363
Quiabo	533	Tapete-de-Oxalá	410
Quibombô	533	Taro	394
Quingombô	533	Tomate	580
Quitoco	557	Tomateiro	580
Rainha-da-noite	523	Transagem	381
Rosa-amarela	548	Trevo-azedo	611
Rosa-branca	548	Tuia-compacta	592
Rosa-de-Jericó	549	Umbaúba	614
Rosa-do-deserto	549	Urtiga-de-folha-grande	450
Rosa-vermelha	548	Urtiga-graúda	450
Rosmaninho	544	Valeriana	599
Sabugueiro	566	Vassourinha-de-relógio	397
Salsa	503	Verbena	603
Salsinha	503	Verbena-sagrada	603
Sálvia	558	Vetiver	607
Sálvia-das-boticas	558	Vinca	609
Sálvia-verdadeira	558	Violeta	612
São-Gonçalinho	480	Violeta-de-cheiro	612
Sapateiro	404		

BIBLIOGRAPHY

Barros, José Flávio Pessoa de, (1993); Ewé Òsányìn – O Sagredo das Folhas; Editora Pallas, Rio de Janeiro, Brasil

Barros, José Flávio Pessoa de; Napoleão, Eduardo, (2003); Ewé òrìsà: Uso litúrgico e terapêutico vegetais nas casas de Candomblé Jêje-Nagô; Bertrand Brasil, Rio de Janeiro, Brasil

Barros, José Flávio Pessoa de, (2010); A Floresta Sagrada de Ossaim: o Sagredo das Folhas; Pallas Editora e Distribuidora Ltda., Rio de Janeiro, Brasil

Bolívar Aróstegui, Natalia, (1990); Los Orishas en Cuba; PM Ediciones, Fundación Pablo Milanés, La Habana, Cuba; 1994

Bolívar Aróstegui, Natalia, (2008); Orishas del Panteón Afrocubano; Quorum Editores, Cádiz, España; 2008

BISSEA-Jardín Botánico Nacional, (2016); Lista Roja de la Flora de Cuba; BISSEA-El Boletín sobre Conservación de Plantas del Jardín Botánico Nacional de Cuba; Vol. 10, Numero Especial 1; Enero 2016

Cabrera, Lydia, (1954); El Monte (Igbo-Finda. Ewé Orisha. Vititi Nfinda); Ediciones Universal, Miami, Florida; Séptima Edición, 1992

Cabrera, Lydia, (1957); Anagó: Vocabulario Lucumí (El Yoruba que se habla en Cuba), Prólogo de Roger Bastide; Ediciones Universal, Miami, Florida; 1986

Cabrera, Lydia (1984); Vocabulario Congo (El Bantú que se habla en Cuba); Printed by Daytona Press, Miami, Florida; 1984

Cabrera, Lydia, (1984); La Medicina Popular de Cuba – Médicos de antaño, curanderos, santeros y paleros de hogaño; Ultra Graphics Corporation, Miami, Florida, USA

Cabrera, Lydia; Castellanos, Isabel (2001); Vocabulario Congo (El Bantú que se habla en Cuba), Edición revisada por Isabel Castellanos; Ediciones Universal, Miami, Florida; 2000

Camargo, Maria Thereza Lemos de Arruda, (1998); Plantas Medicinais e de Rituais Afro-Brasileiros II: Estudo etnofarmacobotânico; Ícone Editora, São Paulo, Brasil

Camargo, Maria Thereza Lemos de Arruda, (2014); As Plantas Medicinais e o Sagrado: A etnofarmacobotânica em uma revisão historiográfica da medicina popular no Brasil; Ícone Editora, São Paulo, Brasil; 1ª ed.

Carlomagno, Anna; Pardini, Andrea; Contino Esquijerosa, Yuvàn, (2015); Medicinal plants in ethnobotanical and religious traditions in Cuba: a first review and updating. Associazione Scienze Agrarie Tropicali

Carvalho Pereira, Maria Izabel de (2014); Linguagem Do Cotidiano Em Tendas, Comunidades, Fraternidades, Centros E Barracões De Candomblé, Umbanda E Outros Cultos De Raiz Afro Brasileiros; Editora: Barlavento

Carney, Judith A (2003); AFRICAN TRADITIONAL PLANT KNOWLEDGE IN THE CIRCUM-CARIBBEAN REGION; Journal of Ethnobiology 23(2): 167-185, Fall/Winter 2003

Castellanos, Jorge; Castellanos, Isabel (1988); Cultura Afrocubana; Volumes 1-4; Ediciones Universal, Miami, Florida

Concordia, Maria (Maria Oggunbemi), (2015); Ritual Use of Plants in Lucumí Tradition; 3rd Edition, LuluPress

Denys Adreman, Ediciones; Palo Mayombe 1823

Díaz, José Carlos, (2018); The Plants of Santería and the Regla de Palo Monte; Ediciones Aurelia, Ciudad de Panamá, Panamá

Díaz Fabelo, Teodoro (1956); Lengua de Santeros (Guiné Góngorí); Editorial Adelante, La Habana, Cuba; 1956

Díaz Fabelo, Simeón Teodoro (1983); Cincuenta y Un Pattakies Afroamericanos; Monte Ávila Editores, C.A.; Caracas, Venezuela

Díaz Fabelo, Teodoro (1998); Diccionario de la Lengua Conga Residual en Cuba; Colección Africanía; Santiago de Cuba: Casa del Caribe; Alcalá de Henares, Madrid, España: Universidad de Alcalá; La Habana: ORCALC/UNESCO; 1ra Edición 2004

Duke, James A. (2008); Duke's Handbook of Medicinal Plants in Latin America; CRC Press, Boca Raton, FL, USA; 2008

Ferrer Castro, Armando; Acosta Alegre, Mayda (2007); Fermina Gómez y la casa olvidada de Olókun; Editorial José Martí, Vedado, Ciudad de La Habana, Cuba.

Fuentes Guerra, Jesús; Schwegler, Armin (2005); Lengua y ritos del Palo Monte Mayombe : dioses cubanos y sus fuentes africanas; Madrid : Iberoamericana, 2005

Gabriele Volpato, Daimy Godínez, Angela Beyra and Adelaida Barreto (18 May 2009); Uses of medicinal plants by Haitian immigrants and their descendants in the Province of Camagüey, Cuba; Journal of Ethnobiology and Ethnomedicine 2009, 5:16

Gonsalves, Paulo Eiró, (1992); Livro dos Alimentos; MG Editores, São Paulo, Brasil; 2da Reimpressão, Outubro 2002

Grandtner, Miroslav M. (2005); Elsevier's Dictionary of Trees: Volume 1: North America; 1st Edition 2005; ELSEVIER B.V., Amsterdam, The Netherlands

Grandtner, M.M.; Cheverette, Julien (2013); Elsevier's Dictionary of Trees: Volume 2: South America; 1st Edition 2013; ELSEVIER B.V., Amsterdam, The Netherlands

Hodge Limonata, Ileana, (2002); El uso de las plantas en la Regla Conga y el Espiritismo Cruzado; Revista Enfoques. IPS. Segunda Quincena, Diciembre, 2002

Irizarry, William J. (2012); Ewé Osaín: 221 Plants, Herbs and Trees Essential to the Lucumi Tradition; 1st Edition 2012, USA

Kim, T.K. (2012); Edible Medicinal and Non-Medicinal Plants, Volumes 1 - 6, Fruits; Springer, Springer Science+Business Media, BV; 2012

Laguerre, Michel S., (1987); Afro-Caribbean folk medicine; Bergin & Garvey Publishers, Inc., Massachusetts, USA

Madan, Marcelo, (2005); Enciclopedia de las Hierbas de Ifá; Ediciones Orunmila c.a., Caracas, Venezuela

Manzini, Yaskara (2001); O coletivo feminino na cosmogonia do Universo. Monografia apresentada ao Curso de Pós-graduação (Lato Sensu) da FPA-Faculdade Paulista de Artes; São Paulo, 2001

Megenney, William W. (2008); Bantu Survival in the Cuban "Lengua de Mayombe"; ISLAS, Year 3, No. 10, Pages 51-63; September 2008; Weston, Florida, USA

Menéndez, Lázara (2009); Estudios Afro-Cubanos, Selección de Lecturas; Volumes 1-4; Facultad de Artes y Letras-Universidad de La Habana; Editorial Félix Varela, Vedado, La Habana, Cuba

Monteiro, Marcelo (Oloye Marcelo Monteiro); Folhas

Monteiro, Marcelo (1999); Oro asa Òsányìn: curso teórico e prático de folhas sagradas.

Newcomb, Peggy Cornett (1985); Popular Annuals of Eastern North America, 1865-1914; Dumbar Oaks (Trustees for Harvard University, Washington DC), 1985

Pereira, Rodrigo (2013); Espaço e Cultura Material em casas de Candomblé no Rio de Janeiro; Universidade Federal do Rio De Janeiro; Dezembro do 2013.

Quattrocchi, Umberto (2000); CRC World Dictionary of Plant Names, Common names, Scientific Names, Eponyms, Synonyms and Etymology, 4 Volume Set; CRC Press LLC, Boca Raton, Florida

Quattrocchi, Umberto (2006); CRC World Dictionary of Grasses: Common Names, Scientific Names, Eponyms, Synonyms, and Etymology - 3 Volume Set; CRC Press LLC, Boca Raton, Florida

Quattrocchi, Umberto (2012); CRC World Dictionary of Medicinal and Poisonous Plants, Common Names, Scientific Names, Eponyms, Synonyms, and Etymology, 5 Volume Set; CRC Press, Taylor & Francis Group; Boca Raton, Florida

Quattrochi, Umberto (2017); CRC World Dictionary of Palms: Common Names, Scientific Names, Eponyms, Synonyms, and Etymology, 2 Volume Set; CRC Press, Taylor & Francis Group; Boca Raton, Florida

Quiros-Moran, Dalia, (2009); Guide to Afro-Cuban Herbalism; AuthorHouse, Bloomington, Indiana, USA

Rodríguez, Andrés; Enríquez Rodríguez, Amalia; Robledo Ortega, Lenia (2012); Las plantas en la Regla Ocha: Su representación en el Jardín Botánico de Matanzas; Universidad de Matanzas "Camilo Cienfuegos", Facultad de Ciencias Sociales y Humanidades; Jardín Botánico de Matanzas, Facultad de Agronomía

Roig, Juan Tomás, (1928); Diccionario Botánico de nombres vulgares cubanos; Editorial Científico-Técnica, La Habana, Cuba; Cuarta Edición, 2014

Roig, Juan Tomás, (1945); Plantas Medicinales, Aromáticas o Venenosas de Cuba; Editorial Científico-Técnica, La Habana, Cuba; Segunda Edición, Primera reimpresión, 1988

Rubio, Juan, (2014); Palo Monte y la verdad esotérica; Publicaciones Miami, Miami, FL, USA; 2014

Taylor, Patrick (Editor); Case, Frederick I. (Editor), (2013); The Encyclopedia of Caribbean Religions; University of Illinois Press; 1st edition (August 30, 2013)

Torres-Avilez, Wendy; Méndez-González, Martha; Durán-García, Rafael; Boulogne, Isabelle; Germosén-Robineau, Lionel, (2015); Medicinal plant knowledge in Caribbean Basin: a comparative study of Afrocaribbean, Amerindian and Mestizo communities; Journal of Ethnobiology and Ethnomedicine (2015) 11:18

van Andel, Tinde (2012); What Makes a Plant Magical? Symbolism and Sacred Herbs in Afro-Surinamese Winti Rituals; African Ethnobotany in the Americas pp 247 -284

van Andel, Tinde; van 't Klooster, Charlotte I.E.A.; Quiroz, Diana; Towns, Alexandra M.; Ruysschaert, Sofie; van den Berg, Margot (2014); Local plant names reveal that enslaved Africans recognized substantial parts of the New World flora; PNAS, Published online December 1, 2014

van 't Klooster, Charlotte I.E.A.; Lindeman, Jan C; Jansen-Jacobs, Marion J. (2003); Index of vernacular plant names of Suriname; NATIONAAL HERBARIUM NEDERLAND, Universiteit Leiden branch; BLUMEA Supplement 15

van 't Klooster, Charlotte I.E.A; Haabo, Vinije; Ruysschaert, Sofie; Vossen, Tessa; van Andel, Tinde (2018); Herbal bathing: an analysis of variation in plant use among Saramaccan and Aucan Maroons in Suriname; Journal of Ethnobiology and Ethnomedicine (2018) 14:20

Verger, Pierre Fatumbi (1981); ORIXÁS (ÒRÌṢÀ); Desenvolvimento-Deuses Iorubás na África e no Novo Mundo-Tradução de Maria Aparecida da Nóbrega; MBJ Desenvolvimento; Editora Corrupio Comércio ; São Paulo, Brasil

Verger, Pierre Fatumbi (1995); Ewé – The Use of Plants in Yoruba Society; São Paulo, Brazil; Odebrecht

Verger, Pierre Fatumbi (1999); Notas sobre o Culto aos Orixás e Voduns na Bahia de Todos os Santos, no Brasil, e na antiga Costa dos Escravos, na África; Editora da Universidade de São Paulo, São Paulo, Brasil

Yronwode, Catherine (2002); Hoodoo Herb and Root Magic: A Materia Magica of African-American Conjure; Lucky Mojo Curio Company, Forestville, California, 2002

http://www.theplantlist.org/1/   **The Plant List**; Royal Botanic Gardens, Kew and Missouri
Botanical Gardens

http://powo.science.kew.org/   **Plants of the World Online**; Kew Gardens

http://floradobrasil.jbrj.gov.br/   **Flora do Brasil 2020.** Jardim Botânico do Rio de Janeiro.

http://www.algaebase.org/   **Algae Data-base**

https://www.gbif.org/   **GBIF - Global Biodiversity Information Facility**

http://www.llifle.com/   **LLIFLE**-Encyclopedias of Living Forms https://www.iucnredlist.org/   The **IUCN RED LIST** of Threatened Species

https://floradelcaribeilustrada.blogspot.com/   **Flora del Caribe Ilustrada**

http://www.cybertruffle.org.uk/vinales/eng/   **Plants of Viñales: A pictorial guide**

https://www.ecured.cu/EcuRed:Enciclopedia_cubana   **EcuRed**: Enciclopedia cubana

https://naturalhistory2.si.edu/botany/WestIndies/   **Smithsonian-Flora of the West Indies**

https://npgsweb.ars-grin.gov/gringlobal/search.aspx?   **U.S. National Plant Germplasm System**

https://adewewemarcio.blogspot.com/   **Èwé Ervas Sagradas - Candomblé**

https://ocandomble.com/ervas/   **Folhas, Ervas - Candomblé**

http://temploluarazul.wixsite.com/temploluarazul   **Ewé Umbanda**

http://www.orula.org/   **ORULA.ORG** - Odun of Ifá

https://nfinda.wordpress.com/category/palos-fuertes/   **NFINDA** - Palos Fuertes

http://zindoki.com/kindoki-herbs-latin/ Latin Names of Plants Used in African and Diaspora Hispanic and Caribbean Medicine and Mysticism

www.santeria.fr ; Plantas usadas en Santería y Palo Mayombe – Oshun Bomiré

Apostilas Mon'a'xí: Folhas Sagradas; https://www.scribd.com/

Ensina o Uso correto das folhas nos Rituais de Candomblé Ketu; (2013); Uploaded by Bruno Gama to SCRIBD January 07, 2013; https://www.scribd.com/doc/119294563/Uso-das-ervas-no-candomble-ketu

http://www.archivocubano.org/bot_yor_02.html   **Botanica degli Yoruba della Nigeria**

http://www.girasdeumbanda.com.br   **Portal Giras de Umbanda**

http://gunfaremim.com   **GUNFAREMIN** - Folhas, Ervas

http://www.tatazaze.com.br/tatazaze/ervas.htm   **Candomblé de Angola- As Ervas e os Inkises**

https://lilamenez.wordpress.com/   **Orixás e entidades da Umbanda e do Candomblé**

https://www.woodworkerssource.com/   Wood Database and Searchable Library

https://herbologiamistica.blogspot.com/   Herbología Mística

http://castelodosonhar.blogspot.com/2011/12/ervas-e-conhecida-importancia-dos.html
Ervas Umbanda

http://www.orishaimage.com/blog/   Orisha Blog

https://cubayoruba.blogspot.com/   Orisha Blog

https://en.wikipedia.org/wiki/Siddha   **Siddha**

https://en.wikipedia.org/wiki/Book_of_Saint_Cyprian   **Book of St. Cyprian**

https://pt.wikipedia.org/wiki/Batuque_(religião)	**Batuque (religião)**
https://pt.wikipedia.org/wiki/Candomblé	**Candomblé**
https://pt.wikipedia.org/wiki/Candomblé_bantu	**Candomblé Bantu**
https://meuorixa.wordpress.com/	**Candomblé, Umbanda, Nkisi, Voduns**
https://pt.wikipedia.org/wiki/Linhas_da_Umbanda	**Linhas da Umbanda**
https://pt.wikipedia.org/wiki/Nkisi	**Nkisi**
https://pt.wikipedia.org/wiki/Omolokô	**Omolokô**
https://pt.wikipedia.org/wiki/Vodum	**Vodum**
https://pt.wikipedia.org/wiki/Águas_sagradas	**Abô**
https://pt.wikipedia.org/wiki/Banho_de_ervas	**Amassi/Amacis**
https://pt.wikipedia.org/wiki/Apanan	**Apanan**
https://pt.wikipedia.org/wiki/Axé	**Axé**
https://pt.wikipedia.org/wiki/Axexê	**Axexê**
https://pt.wikipedia.org/wiki/Axogun	**Axogun**
https://pt.wikipedia.org/wiki/Babalosaim	**Babalosanyin/Olosanyin**
https://pt.wikipedia.org/wiki/Ebori	**Ebori/Borí/Oborí**
https://pt.wikipedia.org/wiki/Erê	**Erê**
https://pt.wikipedia.org/wiki/Fazer_a_cabeça	**Feitura**
https://pt.wikipedia.org/wiki/Feitura_de_santo	**Feitura de santo**
https://pt.wikipedia.org/wiki/Mão_de_Vumbe	**Mão de Vumbe**
https://pt.wikipedia.org/wiki/Otá	**Otá, Okutá**
https://pt.wikipedia.org/wiki/Ajê_Salugá	**Ajê Salugá**
https://pt.wikipedia.org/wiki/Bessem	**Bessem**
https://pt.wikipedia.org/wiki/Boiadeiro_na_Umbanda	**Boiadeiro na Umbanda**
https://pt.wikipedia.org/wiki/Caboclo_de_Umbanda	**Caboclo de Umbanda**
https://pt.wikipedia.org/wiki/Ciganos_na_Umbanda	**Ciganos**
https://pt.wikipedia.org/wiki/Dadá_Ajaká	**Dadá Ajaká**
https://pt.wikipedia.org/wiki/Egungun	**Egúngún**
https://pt.wikipedia.org/wiki/Egunitá	**Egunitá**

https://pt.wikipedia.org/wiki/Exu-Mirim	**Exú Mirim**
https://pt.wikipedia.org/wiki/Yabas	**Iabás**
https://pt.wikipedia.org/wiki/Iemanjá	**Iemanjá**
https://pt.wikipedia.org/wiki/Ipeté_de_Oxum	**Ipeté de Oxum**
https://pt.wikipedia.org/wiki/Iroko_(orixá)	**Iroko**
https://pt.wikipedia.org/wiki/Iyami-Ajé	**Iyami-Ajé**
https://pt.wikipedia.org/wiki/Katendê	**Katendê**
https://pt.wikipedia.org/wiki/Kaviungo	**Kaviungo**
https://pt.wikipedia.org/wiki/Legba	**Legba**
https://pt.wikipedia.org/wiki/Logunedé	**Logunedé**
https://pt.wikipedia.org/wiki/Matamba_(Nkisi)	**Matamba**
https://pt.wikipedia.org/wiki/Nzazi	**Nzazi**
https://pt.wikipedia.org/wiki/Ogum	**Ogum**
https://pt.wikipedia.org/wiki/Oxaguian	**Oxoguiã**
https://pt.wikipedia.org/wiki/Oxum	**Oxum**
https://pt.wikipedia.org/wiki/Oxumarê	**Oxumarê**
https://pt.wikipedia.org/wiki/Oyá_Igbalé	**Oyá Igbalé**
https://setecaminhos.weebly.com/logunanoya-tempo.html	**Oyá Logunã**
https://pt.wikipedia.org/wiki/Pombajira	**Pombajira, Pomba Gira**
https://pt.wikipedia.org/wiki/Pambu_Njila	**Pambu Njila**
https://pt.wikipedia.org/wiki/Sakpata	**Sakpata**
https://www.raizesespirituais.com.br/iroko-orixa-raro/	**Tempo-Iroko**
https://pt.wikipedia.org/wiki/Kindembu	**Tempo/Kindembu**
https://pt.wikipedia.org/wiki/Xangô	**Xangô**
https://pt.wikipedia.org/wiki/Airá	**Xangô Airá**
https://pt.wikipedia.org/wiki/Xapanã	**Xapanã**
https://en.wikipedia.org/wiki/Abakuá	**Abakuá**
https://en.wikipedia.org/wiki/Arará	**Arará**
https://en.wikipedia.org/wiki/Abiku	**Abikú**

https://en.wikipedia.org/wiki/Yewa   **Ẹgbado**, now **Yewa**

https://es.wikipedia.org/wiki/Irunmoles   **Irunmoles**

https://religionysanteria.blogspot.com/2009/11/ituto.html   **Ituto**

https://en.wikipedia.org/wiki/Opon_Ifá   **Opon Ifá**

https://es.wikipedia.org/wiki/Palo_(religión)   **Palo-Religión**

http://readersandrootworkers.org/wiki/Nkisi_Ndoki   **Nkisi-Ndoki**

http://santeriachurch.org/obi-the-coconut-kola-nut-oracle/   **The Story of Obí**

http://eleda.org/blog/2008/11/11/the-lukumi-pantheon-orishas-worshiped-by-the-lukumi-english/
                          The Lukumí Pantheon: Orishas worshiped by the Lukumí

https://es.wikipedia.org/wiki/Abita   **Abita**

https://en.wikipedia.org/wiki/Anima_Sola   **Anima Sola**

https://es.wikipedia.org/wiki/Ayaó   **Ayaó**

https://es.wikipedia.org/wiki/Babalú_Ayé   **Babalú Ayé**

https://es.wikipedia.org/wiki/Inle   **Inle**

http://readersandrootworkers.org/wiki/Kobayende   **Kobayende**

https://es.wikipedia.org/wiki/Nanán_Baruqué#Nana_Buluku_en_el_reino_Dahomey   **Nanà Burukú**

http://readersandrootworkers.org/wiki/Nkuyu   **Nkuyu**

http://readersandrootworkers.org/wiki/Nsasi   **Nsasi**

https://es.wikipedia.org/wiki/Obatalá   **Obatalá**

https://es.wikipedia.org/wiki/Obbá   **Obbá**

https://es.wikipedia.org/wiki/Oshun   **Ochún**

https://es.wikipedia.org/wiki/Oduduwa   **Odùdúwà** (Odudúa, Odúa, Oòduà)

https://es.wikipedia.org/wiki/Oggun   **Oggun**

https://es.wikipedia.org/wiki/Olokun   **Olokun**

https://es.wikipedia.org/wiki/Orun   **Oró/Orun**

https://es.wikipedia.org/wiki/Yemayá   **Yemayá**

https://es.wikipedia.org/wiki/Yewá   **Yewá**

http://www.cubarte.cult.cu/periodico-cubarte/san-fan-kong-del-bambu-a-la-cana-brava/
San Fan Kong, del bambú a la caña brava; GERARDO E. CHÁVEZ SPÍNOLA |CUBARTE| 27 Oct 2016

Made in the USA
Lexington, KY
18 December 2019

58692716R00243